PIMLICO

630

GEORGE CRABBE

Neil Powell is a poet, biographer, editor, and lecturer. His books include five collections of poetry – *At the Edge* (1977), *A Season of Calm Weather* (1982), *True Colours* (1991), *The Stones on Thorpeness Beach* (1994) and *Selected Poems* (1998) – as well as *Carpenters of Light* (1979), *Roy Fuller: Writer and Society* (1995) and *The Language of Jazz* (1997). He lives in Suffolk.

GEORGE CRABBE

An English Life: 1754–1832

———

NEIL POWELL

PIMLICO

Published by Pimlico 2004

2 4 6 8 10 9 7 5 3 1

First published in Great Britain by Pimlico in 2004

Pimlico
Random House, 20 Vauxhall Bridge Road,
London SW1V 2SA

Random House Australia (Pty) Limited
20 Alfred Street, Milsons Point, Sydney,
New South Wales 2061, Australia

Random House New Zealand Limited
18 Poland Road, Glenfield,
Auckland 10, New Zealand

Random House South Africa (Pty) Limited
Endulini, 5A Jubilee Road, Parktown 2193, South Africa

The Random House Group Limited Reg. No. 954009
www.randomhouse.co.uk

A CIP catalogue record for this book is available from the British Library

ISBN 0-7126-8999-0

Papers used by Random House are natural, recyclable products made from wood
grown in sustainable forests; the manufacturing processes conform
to the environmental regulations of the country of origin

Printed and bound in Great Britain by
Clays Ltd, St Ives plc

For Peter Scupham

People speak with raptures of fine prospects, clear skies, lawns, parks and the blended beauties of art and nature, but give me a wild, wide fen, in a foggy day; with quaking boggy ground and trembling hillocks in a putrid soil: shut in by the closeness of the atmosphere, all about is like a new creation and every botanist an Adam who explores and names the creatures he meets with.

George Crabbe, 1 October 1792

I am a very middling, wellish-disposed kind of man . . .
George Crabbe, 21 December 1812

To talk about Crabbe is to talk about England.
E. M. Forster, 1941

CONTENTS

One

The Sea and the River

1754–1768

I

He stares out to sea – this short, grim, disappointed man – from his vantage point on the sporadically busy, now deserted quay. Although the river by which he stands has ten more miles to flow, often a mere hundred yards or so from the shore, before it eventually joins the German Ocean at Shingle Street, he has an uninterrupted view to the south and east of him, across the pathless marshes and the long pebbly finger of Orford Ness. The sea, in moodily shifting patches of lead-grey and clay-brown, has changed its colours for winter, and it is almost always winter here.

Or so it seems to him. An insistent onshore breeze from the east can generally be relied upon to take the edge off any summery weather, but that is not the problem. Times are hard, and they are likely to get harder: he knows the East Anglian coast well enough to understand that its towns and ports are in slow terminal decline. The great medieval city of Dunwich has already been consumed by the sea, reduced to the deserted shell of All Saints' church on the cliff top by a great storm as lately as December 1740: 'The Wind blowing very hard about the North-East with a Continuance for several Days, occasioned great Seas, doing much Damage on the Coast during that Time by Inundations breaking down the Banks, and overflowing many Marshes . . .' All along the coast, the ocean is encroaching; the cliffs are crumbling; the river mouths are silting up; and the towns are dying. How much longer this little port of Slaughden can survive is anybody's guess. Yet that is not quite the problem either. For what most depresses him is less the state of the world in general than the fact that he has come down in it. After all, those of his family who remained inland have apparently managed to prosper in towns and villages around the fertile Waveney valley: his younger cousin John, for instance, is a successful farmer in the south Norfolk village of Seething (where he will eventually die in January 1830, at the great age of eighty-three, and be buried close to the door of its handsome round-towered parish church). What can have induced George to end up on this inhospitable shore, as the salt tax collector on Slaughden Quay?

His name is George Crabbe, but he is not the poet. That will be his eldest son, born on Christmas Eve 1754, baptised on 1 January 1755, and named after this father – who will eventually come to exert a stranger and more pervasive influence over the younger George's literary career than either of them could possibly imagine.

2

Mortality and money shaped the elder George Crabbe's life, as of course they shape everyone's; but in his case their effect was one of cumulative erosion, like the sea's on the shore. His grandfather, William Crabbe, had been a gentleman farmer at Carleton St Peter in Norfolk and a Freeman of the City of Norwich; his grandmother, Jane (*née* Sydnor), was the daughter of a Norwich alderman. These Crabbes had two sons: William, who was destined to inherit the bulk of the family's Norfolk property, and Robert, who in 1720 married a widow, Elizabeth Miller, and set off to find his own fortune in her home town of Aldeburgh, on the Suffolk coast. Within six months of their marriage, Elizabeth had died; but by then Robert had already begun to make his mark on the little borough. He was to become successively a burgess, a junior bailiff, Chamberlain and – the town's highest honour – Bailiff; in 1732, he was appointed Collector of Customs. By this time, he had remarried: his second wife was a local girl, Rachel Syer, and the wedding took place in 1729, at the church of St John Maddermarket in Norwich, a location which seems clearly to reflect the esteem in which he was now held by his family in Norfolk. Their first child, a daughter, lived less than a year; but in 1733, two months after Robert had been elected Bailiff, Rachel was successfully delivered of a son, George. It looked as though Robert Crabbe was doing rather well, after all.

Ten months later, however, he was dead. His civic honours and his responsible job were of no help in feeding his widow and child. George grew up in poverty, snatching an education where he could, but before he had reached his late teens he was trying his hand at schoolmastering in the church porch at Orford – the desperate yet effective strategy of an intellectually undernourished young man learning through teaching. At any rate, he did it well enough to be appointed parish clerk and schoolmaster at Norton Subcourse, a south Norfolk village close to Seething, where his uncle William's family now lived. William Crabbe himself had died in 1749, and his first two sons had died in infancy, so George's five-year-old cousin John was notionally head of the family and heir to its property. It must have looked – mortality and money again – as if this ambitious, impoverished elder cousin were hovering like a sparrowhawk on the edge of the vulnerable family estate. What is certain is that the appointment was relatively short-lived and that when George went back to Aldeburgh he was not yet twenty years old.[2]

We are unlikely ever to know precisely what went wrong – if anything did go wrong – for the elder George Crabbe at Norton; but it is very striking that when he returned to Aldeburgh it was not as a schoolmaster nor even as a clerk but as a warehouseman on Slaughden Quay. In time he was to become Saltmaster, at a salary of £10 a year, as well as parish overseer and churchwarden: in all of this there is a clear sense of George following in his father's footsteps without ever managing quite to fill them. On 2 February 1754 he married Mary Lodwick, a publican's widow eight years older than himself: here again, one can't help recognising (as he surely did) that in terms of social status this wasn't quite the match for which he or his parents might once have hoped. But in every other respect, Mary was probably a better wife than he deserved.

Our impression of Mary Crabbe is inescapably filtered: first through the devoted eyes of her eldest son, the poet George Crabbe, and then through the no less devoted eyes of his eldest son and first biographer.[3] She was 'a woman of the most amiable disposition, mild, patient, affectionate, and deeply religious in her turn of mind';[4] she seems to have possessed genuine humility and simple goodness, in exact contrast to her husband's disappointed ambition and increasingly violent temper. While her son George may have inherited both his obstinacy and his love of literature from his father, his moral balance and his uncomplicated theology were his mother's.

3

No English writer is more firmly associated with a specific town than Crabbe – one twentieth-century biography is actually subtitled 'The Story of George Crabbe, The Aldeburgh Poet'[5] – so it is ironic that his birthplace and his childhood home should be impossible to locate, demolished long ago and almost certainly now beneath the North Sea. There are various sketches and engravings of a low thatched house with rounded eaves which purports to be 'Crabbe's birthplace'; but, according to his son, it is no such thing:

> When my grandfather first settled in Aldeburgh, he lived in an old house in that range of buildings which the sea has now almost demolished. The chambers projected far over the ground-floor; and the windows were small, with diamond panes, almost impervious to light. In this gloomy dwelling the Poet was born. The house, of which Mr Bernard Barton has published a print as 'the birth place of Crabbe', was inhabited by the family during my father's boyhood.[6]

That looks decisive enough. And yet the biographer son is guilty of such startling inaccuracies – for instance, on the same page he gives his grandmother's surname from her first marriage as 'Loddock', not 'Lodwick' – that we may doubt whether Crabbe was born in the town of Aldeburgh itself: it seems much likelier that his father's home was at first near his work on Slaughden Quay; and that the ramshackle collection of dwellings and warehouses there, on the narrow strip of land between river and sea, would indeed have comprised, by the time the son's *Life* appeared in 1834, 'that range of buildings which the sea has now almost demolished'.

The Crabbe family would within a few years outgrow the house at Slaughden and move into Aldeburgh, for young George was soon joined by siblings: his sister Mary was born on 17 October 1756, his brother Robert on 9 July 1758. William, his second brother, born on 5 February 1761, died in infancy (more than one writer on Crabbe says he was 'scarcely a month old', but the Aldeburgh Parish Register gives the date of his burial as 11 June 1762); another brother, also named William, was born on 26 August 1763, and the family was completed with the birth of John on 18 March 1768. Mary was to marry a local builder, Thomas Sparkes: apart from a spell in Ipswich, she would continue to live in Aldeburgh until her death in 1827, eventually becoming Crabbe's only surviving link with his birthplace. His three younger brothers were to develop distinct but notably practical talents. Robert remained in Suffolk, working as a glazier in Southwold. John, after serving in the Royal Navy, became captain of a Liverpool slave ship and married the owner's daughter. However, 'he perished by an insurrection of the slaves' on his very next voyage: 'The negroes, having mastered the crew, set the whole of them adrift in an open boat; and neither Captain Crabbe nor any of his companions were again heard of.'[7] William's career was still more surprising. Like John, he went to sea, but he was captured by the Spanish and deposited in Mexico; there he married and became a successful silversmith, 'until his increasing riches attracted a charge of Protestantism'. He was last seen, by a sailor from Aldeburgh, on the coast of Honduras in 1803, and his story forms the basis of Crabbe's 'The Parting Hour' in *Tales*, 1812.

The boys' father owned a small river craft as well as a share in a sea-going fishing vessel, so the younger brothers had plenty of opportunities to develop their skills early on, in contrast to the eldest, the exasperatingly impractical, bookish George. 'That boy,' the Saltmaster would grumble, 'must be a *fool*. John, and Bob, and Will, are all of some use about a boat; but what will that *thing* ever be good for?'[8] It sounds like a stereotypically hearty father's complaint about his sissy intellectual son, but it is more complex than that: this father was, after all, something of a frustrated and disappointed intellectual himself, and he would in due course try to further his eldest child's education as best he could.

For the time being, although young George's imaginative world might be randomly expanded by the books he devoured and by the poems he would soon begin to salvage from his father's monthly copies of Benjamin Martin's *General Magazine of Arts and Sciences*, his daily existence remained restricted to the town of Aldeburgh and the port of Slaughden, bounded by the sea and the river. And, precisely because he didn't share his younger brothers' straightforward enjoyment of messing about in boats, his engagement with these places was from the beginning of a more thoughtful, introspective sort than theirs. Nowhere is this more evident than in Crabbe's own account of an expedition by boat to Orford, on which he accompanied his father and several other adults one summer's day in 1759 or 1760: the year can only be guessed at, but George must have been thought just old enough to join the party – he would then have been five or six years old – though Robert was still too young. The plan, which to the child would have seemed hugely adventurous, was to sail down the Alde, skirting Havergate Island and almost reaching the estuary at Shingle Street; then they intended either to stop for refreshment in the town of Orford or to picnic on the shingle strip known as Orford Beach before returning home in the afternoon. The river is tidal as far as Snape Bridge, some four miles upstream from Slaughden, so the enterprise needed to be carefully thought out. Perhaps it was; all the same, the unprecedented treat which the child had so eagerly anticipated was to turn into a very different sort of day.

4

Crabbe remembered and described that occasion more than fifty-five years later in his poem 'Infancy – A Fragment', the manuscript of which is dated 16 April 1816; in a 'List of MSS' in Crabbe's hand, dated 8 May 1816, on the front cover of a notebook, the title (evidently of the same poem) is 'Orford Expedition'. We shall discover much later on why he found it possible, or indeed necessary, to revisit his childhood in such uncharacteristically direct autobiographical terms at the age of sixty-one. Despite its comparatively modest length of 126 lines, in its formal characteristics 'Infancy' resembles Crabbe's verse narratives: it is in rhyming couplets, varied by an occasional alexandrine rhyming triplet for additional emphasis; and it is continuous, with indented paragraphs but without stanza breaks. The first 56 lines are essentially a meditation on capitalised abstractions – 'Memory', 'Pleasure', 'Pain'; lines 57–71 recall specific mortalities, especially that of 'an infant sister' (this is so strange an error, for the sibling who died was of course a brother, that one wonders if it were perhaps a fiction invented by his distraught parents as, in eighteenth-century terms, a lesser and more bearable loss); and lines 72–126 recount, as an extended instance of his argument about pleasure and pain, the fateful events of that day's outing to Orford. In combining particular memories of childhood with more general reflections on human experience, 'Infancy' clearly invites comparison with Wordsworth's 'Ode: Intimations of Immortality from Recollections of Early Childhood', which had been collected in *Poems in Two Volumes* (1807) and to which the rather different emphases of Crabbe's poem might almost be seen as a riposte.

The opening section's central proposition – that pain is the natural and abiding human condition, only fitfully alleviated by transitory pleasures – may strike some modern readers as somewhat gloomy; but it is so self-evident to Crabbe that he deals with it in a tone which, if not exactly cheerful, is unsurprised and not at all morose. He is patient and undeceived, as if his view of the matter is little more than a commonplace; and it is certainly a view which recurs in English literature – as it does, for example, with a quite uncanny likeness in the closing words of Hardy's *The Mayor of Casterbridge*, in which we are reminded that Elizabeth-Jane Henchard 'was one whose youth had seemed to teach that happiness was but the occasional episode in a general drama of pain'. Here is Crabbe on the same subject:

> Yes! looking back as early as I can,
> I see the griefs that seize their subject Man,
> That in the weeping Child their early reign began:
> Yes! though Pain softens, and is absent since,
> He still controls me like my lawful prince.
> Joys I remember, like phosphoric light
> Or squibs and crackers on a gala night.
> Joys are like oil; if thrown upon the tide
> Of flowing life, they mix not, nor subside:
> Griefs are like waters on the river thrown,
> They mix entirely, and become its own. [40–50]

This is workmanlike at worst, and the two clusters of similes – the fireworks and the oil and water – are elegantly done; and yet there is something perfunctory about it, as if this statement of guiding principles is really a sort of poetic warming-up before the intensity of recollection to follow. But here Crabbe springs several surprises. He actually gets the first memory wrong, as we have seen; then he briefly alludes, in a notably Wordsworthian phrase, to 'other deaths, that call'd for other tears' (he has his wife's death particularly in mind), before breaking off: 'But here I dwell not – let me, while I can, / Go to the Child, and lose the suffering Man.' And so he turns to the day of the river trip to Orford.

>   Sweet was the morning's breath, the inland tide.
> And our boat gliding, where alone could glide
> Small craft – and oft touch'd on either side.
> It was my first-born joy. I heard them say,
> 'Let the child go; he will enjoy the day.'
> For children ever feel delighted when
> They take their portion, and enjoy with men.
> Give him the pastime that the old partake,
> And he will quickly top and taw forsake.
> The linnet chirp'd upon the furze as well,
> To my young sense, as sings the nightingale.
> Without was paradise – because within
> Was a keen relish, without taint of sin. [72–84]

There is just a hint in the last couplet of the Wordsworthian ideal of childhood in the 'Immortality' ode – the uncorrupted vision which must 'fade into the light of common day' – but otherwise for Crabbe the child essentially *wants* to be a miniature adult: 'For children ever feel delighted when / They take their portion, and enjoy with men.' He is right, of course: that is exactly what children do feel, unless they are unusually privileged or indulged, but such ordinary childhoods were more likely to be observed than experienced by English poets of Crabbe's time: the disadvantaged children in Blake's *Songs* or in Wordsworth's and Coleridge's *Lyrical Ballads* are not retrospective self-portraits; the disadvantaged child in Crabbe is.

However, this short passage is also remarkable in another way: for what it does not contain. We might expect to find a detailed evocation of a treat so eagerly anticipated and so long remembered; yet of the downstream journey to Orford he mentions only the sweetness of the morning as the boat sets sail (lines 71–3) and the fact that the chirping linnet was as pleasing to him as a nightingale (lines 81–2). And that is all. Pleasure – brief and fragile as a firework, as he has already suggested – is obliterated by what immediately follows:

>   A town appear'd – and where an infant went,
> Could they determine, on themselves intent?
> I lost my way, and my companions me,

And all, their comforts and tranquillity.
Mid-day it was, and, as the sun declined,
The good, found early, I no more could find:
The men drank much, to whet the appetite;
And, growing heavy, drank to make them light;
They drank to relish joy, then further to excite.
Their cheerfulness did but a moment last;
Something fell short, or something overpast.
The lads play'd idly with the helm and oar,
And nervous women would be set on shore.
Till 'civil dudgeon' grew, and peace would shine no more.
  Now on the colder water faintly shone
The sloping light – the cheerful day was gone;
Frown'd every cloud, and from the gather'd frown
The thunder burst, and rain came pattering down.
My torpid senses now my fears obey'd,
When the fierce lightning on the eye-balls played.
Now, all the freshness of the morning fled,
My spirits burden'd, and my heart was dead;
The female servants show'd a child their fear,
And men, full wearied, wanted strength to cheer;
And when, at length, the dreaded storm went past,
And there was peace and quietness at last,
'Twas not the morning's quiet – it was not
Pleasure revived, but Misery forgot:
It was not Joy that now commenced her reign,
But mere relief from wretchedness and Pain.
  So many a day, in life's advance, I knew;
So they commenced, and so they ended too.
All Promise they – all Joy as they began!
But Joy grew less, and vanished as they ran!
Errors and evils came in many a form, –
The mind's delusion, and the passions' storm. [85–120]

It would be a ridiculous oversimplification to suggest that this passage supplies us with *the* key to Crabbe; but it certainly provides *a* key. In the first paragraph, those typically eighteenth-century, Augustan checks and balances – which can so often seem to diminish emotional force by overextending it through mechanically self-perpetuating couplets – are used with merciless concision: 'I lost my way, and my companions me, / And all, their comforts and tranquillity.' The astonishing insight – and it is presented, quite plausibly, as the child's insight – is that the adults, in selfishly neglecting him, unconsciously betray their own deficiency of 'comforts and tranquillity': had they been content, they would have been attentive, and *vice versa*. Thus the day starts, both actually and figuratively, to decline; and their vague sense of discontent prompts the adults first to drink and then to drink to excess. Crabbe exactly understands the paradoxes of drunkenness: 'The men drank much, to whet the appetite; / And, growing heavy, drank to make them light; / Then drank to relish joy, then further to excite.' Yet there is nothing pious or sanctimonious about this: the moral point is firmly grounded in the practical observation that drinking too much doesn't necessarily have the results that the drinker expects or wants.

Then comes the storm. The women are frightened, the men exhausted. Eventually calm returns: not 'the morning's quiet', with its delusive innocence, but the state of 'Misery forgot . . . mere relief from wretchedness and Pain' which is the best a sensitive adult can hope for. Days, Crabbe concludes, are often rather like that, beginning in promise and ending in some sort of accommodation with pain. And here, though he still sounds a little like Hardy, he sounds even more like Philip Larkin: not quite for the first time, and certainly not for the last, one is struck by the fact that Crabbe, so far from being an anachronistically old-fashioned writer, is on the contrary a surprisingly modern one who belongs not on the margin but in the centre of English literary history.

5

'Infancy – A Fragment' was not published in Crabbe's lifetime: it was not, after all, a piece which would have readily fitted within his later collections of verse narratives. Yet this increases rather than diminishes our sense of the poem's authenticity and trustworthiness: it was, in Wordsworth's phrase, a 'timely utterance', answering an inner need which had nothing to do with the professional authorship which Crabbe, by 1816, definitely practised. And if the day's outing to Orford affected him as profoundly as the poem suggests – if this was the moment when the child began to sense that pain rather than promise might be the norm in human affairs – then it provides one explanation for his father's surprising decision to send young George, at the age of eight or nine, away to school.

The Saltmaster must have viewed his quietly bookish eldest son with mixed feelings. On the one hand, he showed no sign of turning out to be remotely useful in the practical life of Aldeburgh and Slaughden. On the other, he clearly possessed the intellectual potentialities which the father had felt were so cruelly thwarted in himself. Young George was by all accounts well liked by adults – who found him civil, serious and a bit quaint – though less at ease with the rough and tumble of his fellow children. Furthermore, there was no opportunity for him to obtain any kind of formal education at Aldeburgh. These various considerations must have combined to persuade Crabbe's father, in the somewhat sententious words of the biographer son, 'to give George the advantage of passing some time in a school at Bungay, on the borders of Norfolk, where it was hoped the activity of his mind would be disciplined into orderly diligence'.[9] At this establishment, according to an advertisement in the *Norwich Mercury*, 'Youth are genteelly Boarded, and taught Reading, the English Grammar, Writing in all the several hands in Use, Book-Keeping, in the Italian or any other Method; Together with Any Branch of Mathematics desired, Either Speculative or Practical; by Richard Harvey, in Bungay, Suffolk.'[10]

Yet there was a further 'advantage', either tactfully or innocently unhinted at by the biographer son, which Crabbe's father certainly perceived in this arrangement. Bungay is the market town nearest to the village of Seething, a mere five miles away, which was the home of cousin John and the more prosperous branch of the Crabbe family; as local farmers they would have been regular visitors to the market, a few hundred yards from Mr Harvey's school. It seems inconceivable that the Saltmaster, who of course had his own memories of the area, should not have hoped that his wealthier relations might take an interest in his gifted son. But there was still more to this connection: Richard Harvey, before he opened his school in 1756, had himself come from Seething, while George Harvey had married the widow of William Crabbe – the poet's great-uncle who had stayed in Norfolk when his grandfather left for Aldeburgh – in 1753.[11] Geographical proximity was thus reinforced by a close link between the two families: perhaps some form of adoption or patronage was envisaged; perhaps the Seething Crabbes paid or assisted with Mr Harvey's fees. In any case, George must have seen something of his relatives: their prosperity and his early (for a boy of his background) educational exile would have encouraged him to feel that both material success and intellectual advancement could be attained only through leaving Aldeburgh.

There are two frequently repeated anecdotes, deriving from the biographer son's *Life*, about Crabbe's schooldays in Bungay. One is probably true, though I suspect misinterpreted; the other may well be false. Here is the first:

> The first night he spent at Bungay he retired to bed, he said, 'with a heavy heart, thinking of his fond, indulgent mother'. But the morning brought a new misery. The slender and delicate child had hitherto been dressed by his mother. Seeing the other boys begin to dress themselves, poor George, in great confusion, whispered to his bedfellow, 'Master G—, can you put on your shirt? – for – for I'm afraid I cannot.'[12]

He was young to have been sent away to school and he had been pampered, as far as her limited means permitted, by his doting mother: so much is evident enough. But this disguises a likelihood which the poet's son was too loyal and respectful to acknowledge: that his father, as a child, lacked manual dexterity to an extent which left him in practical matters virtually handicapped. Once that is admitted, much else falls into place: his inability to join with his brothers in the nautical pastimes of the sea and the river; his studious, introspective character; and his subsequent adventures and misadventures in practical affairs. It also provides an especially cogent reason for his father's determination to send him away to school at such an early age.

This is worth bearing in mind when considering the second anecdote. This recounts how George and some of his schoolfellows were punished 'by being put into a large dog-kennel known by the terrible name of the "black hole"'. Crabbe was apparently the first to go in; soon, when the place was full, 'the atmosphere became pestilentially close'.

At last, in despair, he bit the lad next to him violently in the hand. 'Crabbe is dying – Crabbe is dying,' roared the sufferer; and the sentinel at length opened the door, and allowed the boys to rush into the air. My father said, 'A minute more, and I must have died.'[13]

Even as they stand, the story's central elements – the inability to cope with a difficult physical situation, the moment of panic and the retrospective dramatisation – take on a rather different appearance once we suspect that its protagonist suffered from, at the very least, chronic clumsiness; nor was this the last time that Crabbe, who seems to have enjoyed telling a tale or two to his son, would claim to have narrowly escaped death in a youthful escapade. But the anecdote is questionable in any case. Schoolboy allusions to the Black Hole of Calcutta (1756) were commonplace during the 1760s; here, however, the distant image has been conflated with something much more local and potent. For the 'large dog-kennel' known as the 'black hole' sounds suspiciously like a garbled or fanciful invention connected with the legendary Black Dog of Bungay, still to be seen above the town centre in the shape of a weather vane, at the foot of which is this explanatory plaque:

All down the Church in midst of fire
    The hellish monster flew;
And passing onwards to the Quire
    He many people slew.

The Black Dog, or Old Shuck, who is said to have appeared during a thunderstorm in August 1577, is Bungay's chief item of folklore. Mr Harvey's pupils would certainly have heard all about him; so it is more than likely that some shed, or perhaps just a small room, in which miscreants were confined at the school, would have come to be known as the black dog's kennel. If this conjecture is correct – and there is no way of knowing for sure – it tallies both with Crabbe's fondness for embellishing stories and with his biographer son's obliging readiness to believe what he was told.

What – apart from the Black Dog legend and, presumably, how to cope with his shirt – did George learn during his time in Bungay? Like many a bookish child at boarding school, he gained more from his voracious private reading than from the indifferent teaching he received. We know that he read both historical works and fictions as diverse as *Robinson Crusoe* and *The Pilgrim's Progress*; and that, like his father, he enjoyed solving mathematical problems, including one set by a Mr Dilworth in the *Norwich Mercury*. This is important because the date – 16 August 1766 – and the unequivocal attribution of the solution to 'Master George Crabbe, at Mr Harvey's School in Bungay' prove that his stay at the school was lengthier than has been generally supposed, lasting until he was nearly twelve.[14] However, the most significant interest he developed at Bungay, where the natural environment of an inland river valley was so much kinder than that of the windswept coast, was in botany: not only would this become a lifelong preoccupation, especially in those middle years when literary inspiration seemed to desert him; it also ensured that the attention to nature in his poetry would be more rigorous and better informed than that of even his greatest contemporaries. Taken together with the 'Poet's Corner' sections discarded from his father's copies of Martin's monthly *Magazine*, which he habitually saved when at home, these childhood interests already foretell a good deal about Crabbe's adult literary self.

Going away to school had further isolated the boy from his contemporaries in Aldeburgh, but he was the kind of child who would have been isolated anyway. When, back in his inhospitable home town, he was threatened in the street by 'a stout lad, who doubled his fist', his son reports that 'another boy interfered to claim benefit of clergy for the studious George. "You must not meddle with *him*," he said; "let *him* alone, for he ha' got l'arning."'[15] That may be so; yet, more often than not, the schoolboy swot would merely have earned a heftier punch. The successful intercession suggests that there was something a bit more special or strange than mere 'l'arning' about the boy.

Meanwhile his father, for all his faults (and he was well on the way to becoming a vile-tempered, hectoring drunk), continued at least to value George's peculiar talents; and in the autumn of 1766 he contrived to send him to a rather more academic school at Stowmarket. This was run by a well-known mathematician called Richard Haddon – a man highly regarded by the mathematically inclined Saltmaster – whose curriculum included the classics in which Richard Harvey's essentially commercial establishment was conspicuously deficient. That year, Haddon's Stowmarket school was advertised in the *Ipswich Journal* in terms which were clearly intended to emphasise its intellectual superiority over commercial schools such as Harvey's: 'Youth genteelly boarded and expeditiously qualified for business on the following terms: Greek, Latin, French, Geometry, Algebra, Navigation, Merchants-Accounts etc. at 12 guineas per annum and 1 guinea entrance: Reading, Writing and Arithmetic at 11 guineas and 1 guinea entrance.'[16] And it was certainly this school, rather than the one at Bungay, that Crabbe recalled when he wrote to Edmund Burke in June 1781: 'my Father . . . kept me two years at a country boarding school'.[17] (Crabbe's choice of words here is either erroneous, since he had clearly attended two quite separate boarding schools, or else mischievously and pedantically accurate – if it was indeed his wealthier Norfolk relations, rather than his father, who had 'kept' him at the school in Bungay.)

Writing in 1907, René Huchon decided that Crabbe's two years at Stowmarket 'were not the happiest time of his life, to judge by his poems, in which he evidently recalls his impressions';[18] but, unlike 'Infancy – A Fragment', the poems Huchon cites at this point are by no means self-evidently autobiographical. In 1972, Neville Blackburne reported, without citing any supporting documentation, that 'his only regular companion' was Jack Haddon, the schoolmaster's son, according to whom George remained solitary and studious, 'disdainful of a lack of brains, priggish, and often moody and sullen'.[19] Since these are the characteristics of almost every intelligent adolescent, there is every reason to suppose that they would have been shared by Crabbe. On this occasion, the more positive account of the biographer son is also the more instructive: he records that, as well as developing his mathematical skills under Haddon's guidance (so that the solutions to problems set by the Saltmaster now 'came not unfrequently from his son'), Crabbe also 'laid . . . the foundations of a fair classical education'. And he adds: 'Some girls used to come to the school in the evenings, to learn writing; and the tradition is, that Mr Crabbe's first essay in verse was a stanza of doggerel, cautioning one of these little damsels against being too much elevated about a new set of blue ribbons to her straw bonnet.'[20]

6

By the time he left Stowmarket in 1768, it had been decided that George should become a surgeon. If that sounds a comically inappropriate profession for a clumsy boy, it should be remembered, firstly, that the eighteenth-century country surgeon was a rough-and-ready sort of general practitioner who a generation or two earlier would have been indistinguishable from a barber and, secondly, that Crabbe's practical ineptitude had been most evident in comparatively large-scale matters to do with boats and fishing: his elegantly controlled (if decidedly unmedical) mature handwriting is that of a man who, in finely detailed work, would have been meticulous with his hands.[21]

Within a few months, he would find himself apprenticed to a surgeon, further towards the inland south-west corner of Suffolk; those intervening months, meanwhile, had to be spent labouring for his father, shifting boxes and barrels on Slaughden Quay. When they were over, Crabbe must have hoped that the time had come to escape for ever from the uncouth drudgery of the sea and the river; yet, during the fifteen years that followed, he would find himself repeatedly drawn back, in a succession of different guises, to Aldeburgh. In his imagination, he would continue to return for the rest of his life.

Two

The Surgeon's Apprentice
1768–1780

I

The fourteen-year-old boy who set off in 1768 for the village of Wickhambrook, near Bury St Edmunds, travelling by farmer's cart, carried with him an unusually potent mixture of alienation and ambition. The road would have been familiar as far as Stowmarket; after that, George was in uncharted territory, and he had to walk the last ten miles on his own. Following a recent illness, his head had been shaved, so his best hat was perched on top of an ill-fitting wig. When he arrived at his destination, he was greeted with hilarious astonishment by his new master's two daughters. They could scarcely believe their eyes. 'La! Here's our new 'prentice!' cried one of them in mock disbelief. This combination of circumstances, which might have presented challenge enough to a robust and insensitive lad, affected George deeply, though not quite in the way one might at first imagine. Alienation and ambition had done their work: he was prepared to put up with whatever it took to establish himself in a self-sufficient career, for he had already decided to be a poet.

In possessing that kind of determination, in recognising that he and his father had the power to make far-reaching if potentially conflicting decisions about the kind of life he was going to lead, George was participating in a social revolution, 'the eighteenth century's great leap on to the bandwagon of the rising middle class'.[1] The social fluidity of late eighteenth-century English society – in which, for instance, a music master's daughter, Fanny Burney, could achieve the status of a royal courtier before rejecting that to become successively a stateless itinerant in Napoleonic Europe and a grand literary hostess in London society – tended to encourage zigzag personal trajectories of which Crabbe's adolescence and early adulthood provide a series of striking instances. During his lifetime, this fluidity was to be matched by developments in road and rail transport which would create a nation as mobile geographically as it was socially. For the time being, in 1768, the journey across East Anglia was still quite an adventure; the Crabbes, father and son, could only hope that the adventure would prove worthwhile.

Mr Smith of Wickhambrook was, as Crabbe later wrote to Burke, 'poor and had little business but the premium he demanded was small: I continued two years with this man, I read romances and learned to bleed; my master was also a farmer and I became useful to him in that his principal occupation'.[2] His account is typically sardonic and selective. He judiciously omits the fact that he wrote poems at Wickhambrook – a drawerful of them, according to his son, though what that means rather depends on the size of the drawer – and he edges only cautiously towards the crucial point, which of course is that the apprenticeship was useless to him and he might just as well have been a farmer's boy: 'There was indeed no other distinction between the boy at the farm and myself but that he was happy in being an annual servant and I was bound by indentures.' When he rebelled against the conditions of this so-called apprenticeship, it was not because his pride was injured but because his principles were affronted: even though his father had paid for his indentures, George was learning little about surgery and instead spent most of his days as an additional, unpaid farmhand. His only memorable duty involved running lengthy errands, delivering medicines to surrounding villages such as Cheveley, over the county border in Cambridgeshire, where the Duke of Rutland, his future employer's father, owned a residence: the rhapsodic René Huchon and, following him, Neville Blackburne make much of this, inventing a stately home for the awestruck young poet to tour; but the biographer son says the 'house was small, the servants few, and the habits domestic'[3] and, according to Pevsner, the only remaining house of any consequence in the parish is the eighteenth-century rectory. Eventually, in response to Mr Smith's complaints about his 'idleness and disobedience', Crabbe's father 'came and was severe in his correction of them', at first taking the master's side exactly as if his son were in trouble at boarding school. It did no good: George 'became obstinate' – by no means for the last time – and when next his father was summoned he 'put an end to my slavery, he took me home with him, and with me two thirds of the money he had advanced.'[4]

That principled obstinacy, at once awkward and endearing, is among Crabbe's most abiding characteristics. We can glimpse it again, in a slightly different light, in this Wickhambrook anecdote from the son's *Life*:

> One day as he mixed with the herd of lads at the public-house, to see the exhibitions of a conjurer, the magician, having worked many wonders, changed a white ball to black, exclaiming – *'Quique olim albus erat nunc est contrarius albo* – and I suppose none of you can tell me what that means.' 'Yes, I can,' said George. 'The d—l you can,' replied he of the magic wand, eyeing his garb: 'I suppose you picked up *your* Latin in a turnip-field.' Not daunted by the laughter that followed, he gave the interpretation, and received from the seer a condescending compliment.[5]

It's a moment which brings together two differently motivated but, as it happens, perfectly compatible impulses: George's furious resentment at being lumped together with a bunch of ignorant bumpkins and his under-standable readiness to translate a piece of simple schoolroom Latin. After all, he had 'l'arning', an accomplishment which must have seemed even more painfully out of place at Wickhambrook than it had at Aldeburgh.

Indeed, he was himself literally out of place in a sense so gently implicit both in his letter to Burke and in the son's *Life* that it might easily be overlooked. When Crabbe states that 'my master was also a farmer' and complains that there was 'no . . . distinction between the boy at the farm and myself', the barely suppressed disdain which accompanies the words 'farmer' and 'farm' signals the unbridgeable gulf between those who work by the sea and the river, on the coastal strip of Suffolk, and those who work on the land, inland. And when the son records with astonishment that his father 'was made the bedfellow and companion of the ploughboy'[6] and, in a brilliantly placed dismissive metaphor, that he 'mixed with the herd of lads at the public-house', he is making not so much a social distinction (for there is no attempt to disguise the poverty of his father's childhood) as a cultural – one might justly say an *agri*cultural – one. That distinction is powerful and enduring. A much more recent writer, Ronald Blythe, whose imagination was shaped by his inland East Anglian childhood, has described the strange sense of semi-alienation he experienced when for a while he lived on the

Suffolk coast, a sense of being 'both in my own deeply rooted country and on the edge of things'. Blythe notes how, as one reaches the twelve-mile-wide coastal belt called the Sandlings, 'The entire ecology changes long before one even suspects the presence of the Suffolk sea.' And he very interestingly adds that when Benjamin Britten – like Crabbe, a child of the East Anglian coast – 'worked for a brief spell in a cottage sunk in the cornlands of Suffolk, he told me how utterly different the imaginative stimulus was, and I realised that we had shared similar experiences of territorial disorientation within the home area, but from opposite directions'.[7]

That useful phrase of Ronald Blythe's – 'territorial disorientation' – might almost have been coined for George Crabbe: it was this which irked him at Wickhambrook, perhaps even more than the scandalous short-comings of his apprenticeship, and it would repeatedly pull him back towards the Suffolk coast until quite late in his life. It explains, too, why he immediately felt so much more at home when it was arranged that he should spend his remaining five years as a surgeon's apprentice with John Page in Woodbridge – a river port on the Deben, some fifteen miles south-west of Aldeburgh – even though the medical training he received there would still leave much to be desired. 'I was never considered as a regular apprentice,' he told Burke, 'and was principally employed in putting up prescriptions and compounding medicines. I was notwithstanding well treated in every respect, but the principal one, for no pains were taken to give me an idea of the profession I was to live by.'[8] For, of course, he was *not* a 'regular apprentice': since he had served two years elsewhere, the reduced premium paid to Page may have been no more than the sum which Smith had refunded to his father; moreover, there were other – 'regular' – apprentices in Page's large and busy practice, who would have expected and received priority when there were especially interesting cases.

But being in Woodbridge must have made all the difference. Young George already regarded himself as something of a sophisticate: so he was, in comparison with the ignorant agricultural bumpkins of Wickhambrook and, for that matter, with the impoverished and under-educated citizens of Aldeburgh. Yet while education had set him apart intellectually, it had failed to eradicate his intuitive sense of territorial allegiance: Woodbridge, the most thriving town within Suffolk's coastal belt, managed to satisfy both these apparently contradictory aspects of Crabbe's personality. It had prospered during the eighteenth century; by 1770 it would have been as attractive and stimulating a place to live as a young man could hope to find in rural England. George was sixteen years old, ready to discover adult freedoms in this lively, civilised environment. He needed to make friends, to fall in love, to find his muse: while living in Woodbridge he would do all three. No wonder his medical studies came a poor fourth.

2

The years in Woodbridge were the closest Crabbe ever came to enjoying student life – studying half-heartedly, reading avidly, mixing with intelligent people of his own age or, as the biographer son judiciously puts it, 'companions suitable to his mind and habits'. And, like many students away from home, he quickly latched on to a friend who shared something of his own background: William Springall Levett, son of an Aldeburgh surgeon, whom he had known in early childhood before their paths diverged and George found himself despatched successively to Bungay, Stowmarket and Wickhambrook. William Levett was one of several intellectual young men who met socially on a regular basis and who soon invited George to join them: 'I have often heard him speak with pleasure,' says the poet's son, rather coyly, 'of a small society of young men, who met at an inn on certain evenings of the week to converse, over a frugal supper, on the subjects which they were severally studying'.[9] Even if this sounds remarkably like going for a drink with the lads, they were educated and intelligent lads who provided him with exactly the kind of company and conversation he had previously lacked. This process of mutual self-education within the context of an apprenticeship recurs in the lives of later English poets who, like Crabbe, were unable to study at university: for the sixteen-year-old Thomas Hardy and his scholarly fellow apprentice, Henry Bastow, the Dorchester architect's office would prove to be 'an exceptionally literate place for a young man who already had a stock of reading in his head';[10] while Roy Fuller, at the same age, would be swapping literary and philosophical jokes with the other articled clerks at a Blackpool solicitor's. In each case, the writer's distinctive sense of Englishness is grounded in his formative experience of provincial life, turning an apparent deprivation to creative advantage.

If William Levett had done no more than introduce his friend to stimulating intellectual company when he had most need of it, he would have had a profound and lasting effect on Crabbe's development; but his influence was to be far greater than that. Levett was engaged to a young woman named Alethea Brereton, who lived in Framlingham, a handsome market town famous for its twelfth-century (though subsequently altered and rebuilt) castle. She in turn had a close friend called Sarah Elmy, who spent much of her time nearby at Ducking Hall, Parham, the home of her comfortably-off uncle, John Tovell. In common with many other eighteenth-century families – the Crabbes among them – the Elmys and the Tovells had suffered from fluctuating fortunes. Sarah's father, James Elmy of Beccles, a younger son without inheritance but with a respectable business as a tanner, had married Sarah Tovell from Parham: they had four children – a boy, James, and three daughters, Sarah, Mary and Eleanor. During the 1750s, however, James Elmy's business had deteriorated and in November 1759 he was declared bankrupt. Like George Crabbe's younger brother William, he set off to seek his fortune abroad: he ended up in Guadaloupe, 'where he died some time before Mr Crabbe knew the family'.[11]

John Tovell, meanwhile, had done well for himself, inheriting Ducking Hall from his brother and marrying Jane Kemp, the sister of a neighbouring farmer; their daughter, also named Jane, was born in 1763. Their home reflected this marriage of inherited wealth and prudent practicality: on one side, it was an imposing moated mansion; on the other, a working farm. It was a bustling and sociable place, at which the Elmy children were welcome visitors: for young James, a promising painter, his uncle provided substantial financial support, paying his fees at the Royal Academy, where he was studying with Richard Cosway. But it was the eldest girl, Sarah, who spent most time at Ducking Hall. Her friends – including Alethea Brereton and William Levett – were welcome too, and they evidently felt free to extend the Tovells' hospitality still further: 'Why, George,' William casually announced one day in 1772, 'you shall go with me to Parham: there is a young lady there that would just suit you.'[12]

However frivolous William's intention may have been, his judgement was remarkably prescient. Sarah Elmy did indeed 'just suit' George Crabbe, although we may never know quite why: no portraits survive of her when young, and both the poet in his letters and the son in his biography are inhibited by respectful reticence. Born on 12 December 1751, she was twenty, almost exactly three years older than her suitor and eventual husband, when they met. Their son tells us, not very helpfully, that 'Miss Elmy was then remarkably pretty', that she had 'a lively disposition' and that she often received 'more than her share of attention in mixed company'.[13] He also reports that she was musical, which her future husband emphatically was not, and that she tried unsuccessfully to encourage him to play the flute.[14] Of course, there was no question of an early marriage, or even an engagement, between the bankrupt tanner's daughter and the surgeon's penniless apprentice.

But instead of trying to focus on Sarah Elmy – who, at this point, is almost invisible – it might be more profitable to ask what else impressed George Crabbe during his early visits to Ducking Hall. In the opening chapters of E. M. Forster's novel *Howards End*, Helen Schlegel pays a similarly momentous visit, to the country house of the book's title, and there she thinks she falls in love with Paul Wilcox; however, Forster tells us, 'The truth was that she had fallen in love, not with an individual, but with a family.'[15] Crabbe, while indisputably in love with Sarah, had also been captivated by several other things. One, inevitably, was the *idea* of Sarah as a muse: as the dedicatee of poems which would be addressed to 'Mira', a name which neatly combined the final syllables of 'Elmy' and 'Sarah'. Another was the sense – surely for the first time in his life – that this style of living, which was well organised and decently genteel, could be brought within his own reach. And a third must have been the example of Sarah's brother James, the painter who, thanks to the Tovells, had made his escape to London where his tutor, the miniaturist Richard Cosway, was a fashionable and prosperous artist: 'Richard and Maria Cosway,' according to John Brewer, 'filled their quarters in the former Duke of Schomberg's mansion on Pall Mall with three floors of pictures, held large music parties and soirées attended by the Prince of Wales and many foreign ambassadors, and built a garden and greenhouse on the roof.'[16] This world too had suddenly and amazingly become connected to Crabbe's through the Tovells of Ducking Hall, Parham. No wonder he was dazzled.

At the age of eighteen, Crabbe thus acquired a clutch of aspirations which were not merely compatible but interdependent. His writing, including his earliest published poems, was inextricably linked to his love for Sarah, as is abundantly clear from the juvenilia which has survived. The possibility of marriage to Sarah, and of a home which would approach the comforts of Ducking Hall, depended on a dramatic improvement in his worldly prospects. And that in turn could well entail a move to London in search of skills, qualifications, influential friends: George had never been there, but if James Elmy could manage it, so could he. William Levett's casual introduction of him to Ducking Hall had altered Crabbe's life altogether.

3

George Crabbe reacted as dazzled lovestruck adolescents often do: he wrote poems – passionate, but conventional and not especially distinguished ones. 'Crabbe fell in love; his love was returned; and love led to poetry,'[17] as Leslie Stephen said, almost accurately. But he was writing poems already, of course, and during the autumn of 1771 they began to appear in print in two journals, both confusingly called *Lady's Magazine*. John Wheble's *Lady's Magazine* included 'The Prize Poem: Poetical Essay on Hope' and 'To Mira' in the issue of September 1772; a prose piece, 'The Atheist Reclaimed', in November; and 'On Melancholy', 'An Allegorical Fable' and 'The Bee: An Essay, by the Author of "The Atheist Reclaimed"' in December. Meanwhile, 'Solitude' and 'A Song' appeared in Robinson and Roberts' *Lady's Magazine* for September; in October they published 'To Emma', and their November issue contained 'Despair', 'Cupid' and 'Song'. The Robinson and Roberts items have been readily accessible since A. W. Ward printed them in 1905, in the first volume of his *Poems by George Crabbe*; the others, apart from one fragment, are lost, since the relevant issues of Wheble's *Lady's Magazine* (Volume III: 1772) seem not to have survived. This lacuna, irritating in itself, is made all the more tiresome by the fact that Crabbe's son certainly *did* have access to the missing volume: 'As might be supposed,' he writes, 'there is hardly a line in any of these productions which I should be justified in reprinting.'[18] And with that he prints only the final six lines of 'The Prize Poem', subsequently included in Ward's edition, which are all we are likely to have of the Wheble material.

One practical use of these publication dates – whether or not we have the poems before us – is that the appearance of 'To Mira' in September 1772 seems at any rate to prove that Crabbe had met Sarah Elmy by then. But the matter is not at all straightforward. The biographer son tells us that the items now lost, from Wheble's magazine, were signed 'G. C., Woodbridge, Suffolk'; and if that is so, then their authorship can hardly be in doubt. All but one of the Robinson and Roberts poems are, however, signed with the cumbersome quasi-anagram 'G. EBBARE'; that exception is 'To Emma', which in Ward's edition is dated 'Suffolk, Oct. 15, 1772' and signed 'G. EBBAAC'. This presents all sorts of problems. It is hard to see how a poem written on 15 October could have appeared in the same year's October issue of any journal, unless the date of composition is wrong or the publication schedule was running very late. Still more pertinently, it would be extraordinary to find Crabbe writing a poem even to an imaginary 'Emma' when he had just fallen in love with the girl whom he called 'Mira' in a poem published only a month earlier, unless (which is frustratingly possible) he had already hit upon the idealised 'Mira' before he met Sarah Elmy; in that case, the consonance suggested by the names is purely coincidental and the poems are no use whatever in dating that first meeting. Then there is the signature, which is an even poorer shot at an anagram than 'G. EBBARE', though that might very well be a compositor's misreading of the properly anagrammatic 'G. EBBARC'. Perhaps the ludicrous 'G. EBBAAC' of 'To Emma' is a luckless attempt at correction which merely introduced a further error. But the likeliest explanation, and the one which restores the identification of 'Mira' with Sarah, is that 'To Emma' may not be by Crabbe at all but by a mischievous parodist: it is just the sort of trick that one of his cleverer Woodbridge friends, perhaps William Levett himself, would have delighted in playing on the ambitious yet lovesick young poet.

For Crabbe was certainly ambitious and, indeed, exceptionally canny. There is nothing very surprising in a literary teenager's urgent determination to rush into print; but he contrived to make his appearance, deploying a variety of styles and using two easily decipherable signatures, simultaneously in two journals which were widely read in provincial middle-class society. His sustained visibility in both versions of the *Lady's Magazine* throughout the autumn of 1772 amounts to a calculated public announcement that he considered himself to be something other and more than a Suffolk surgeon's apprentice. He knew exactly what he was doing, as he would later tell Burke:

My master occasionally prophesied my ruin, and my father advised me to quit such follies, but the former would sometimes laugh at the things he condemned and my father was a rhymer himself; I therefore paid little attention to these instructions, but was happy to find my signature in the *Lady's Magazine* was known to all the ladies round the place I lived in.[19]

The emphasis, even in the maturer retrospect of 1781, is unambiguous: he wanted a *local* reputation, to be pointed out and spoken about as that bright young George Crabbe whose poems appear in the *Lady's Magazine*. He needed people within his earshot to say how talented he was. Pitching his ambition at this fairly modest level was both understandable, given his age, and shrewd; for the poems would not have withstood the critical attention of a more sophisticated readership.

Their main interest lies in their documentation of the young poet's typical conflict between received influences and developing style; and in Crabbe's case the influences were a random jumble of the doggerel he had enjoyed since childhood and the more thoughtful reading of his Woodbridge years. They also juxtapose conventionally stylised material with glimpses of a recognisably real world. The landscape of 'Solitude', in which the poet purports to live 'in a peaceful valley' near the 'ancient ruins falling / From a worn-out castle's brow', is obviously an off-the-shelf 'poetic' scene, yet it does bear some resemblance to the Alde valley (in which Sarah lived but Crabbe did not) with Framlingham Castle nearby. But the poem's attempted alchemy works in the wrong direction: the actual fails to enliven the conventional, which instead drains the vividness from any hints of local detail. There is nevertheless one phrase in 'Solitude' which is notably prescient in the context of Crabbe's work, and it comes in the teasing form of a parenthesis: 'Giving way to melancholy, / (Joy, when better understood).' Although the enjoyment of melancholy was something of a literary commonplace in the late eighteenth century, it is nevertheless striking to find Crabbe, whose mature view of life would tend towards pleasurable bleakness, finding his own formula for it with such early certainty.

These early poems also provide evidence of Crabbe's wide reading. 'Despair', cast in the form of a dialogue between Tyrsis and Damon, and with an epigraph from Ovid, has its roots in the neo-Ovidian pastorals of Sidney,

Marlowe and Drayton; 'Cupid' owes something to the earlier poems in Fulke Greville's *Caelica*; and the slightly later 'Ye Gentle Gales' (dated 'Woodbridge, 1776') is a lyric pastiche in the manner of Shakespeare or Ben Jonson. Among the Woodbridge juvenilia mentioned by the biographer son are 'The Judgement of the Muse, in the Metre of Spenser' and 'An Address to the Muse, in the Manner of Sir Walter Raleigh'.[20] Such influences strongly suggest that the darkness and sternness of Crabbe's vision spring not only from his East Anglian upbringing but also from an early immersion in Elizabethan and Jacobean literature.

4

William Levett did not marry Alethea Brereton. He died, aged only twenty, in 1774. She subsequently married a Dr Lewis, with whom she emigrated to America; after returning to England around 1790, she published popular novels anonymously and under the pseudonym Eugenia de Acton; and she will eventually reappear, among Crabbe's later correspondents, as Alethea Lewis. Crabbe, meanwhile, memorialised his friend in stately couplets which artfully contrive to praise their own sombre restraint:

> What though no trophies peer above his dust,
> Nor sculptured conquests deck his sober bust;
> What though no earthly thunders sound his name,
> Death gives him conquest, and our sorrows fame:
> One sigh reflection heaves, but shuns excess –
> More should we mourn him, did we love him less.

That closing contention – that profound emotion does not seek extravagant public display – was to become one of his lifelong guiding principles. The death of William Levett, his closest friend during the three most formative years of his personal and literary life, was a devastating loss for him. And it is a loss for us, since had Levett lived he would surely have left some memoir – a portrait of young George as he appeared in his youth to a sharp-eyed contemporary – to help counteract our tendency to see Crabbe always as the respectable clerical figure who dominates his son's biography, as if he had never been young.

5

It is partly the self-defining urgency of his ambition which makes him seem, at this point in his life, older than his years. And the ambition is forked – the paths to literary fame and to financial security diverge irreconcilably – just as his loyalties are divided between Suffolk, which contains Sarah Elmy but also the past he must escape, and the unknown world beyond. In the event, Crabbe's next defining act was a literary one, the publication of his first substantial poem: '*Inebriety*, a Poem in three Parts. Ipswich, printed and sold by C. Punchard, Bookseller, in the Butter-Market, 1775. Price one shilling and sixpence.'

Inebriety is in every respect a piece of apprentice-work. Crabbe has moved on from the Elizabethans, and his model is now Alexander Pope: substantial sections of the poem are pastiches of passages from the *Dunciad* and the *Essay on Man*, and in some places (notably in Part the Third, lines 172–93) Crabbe ingeniously, if rather pointlessly, even takes over many of his line endings from the original. Crabbe himself came to dislike the poem – a note in his hand on the copy eventually owned by Alfred Ainger reads: 'NB. – pray not let this been seen at [Belvoir?] there is very little of it that I'm not heartily ashamed of' – and his readers have had little good, or at all, to say about it. One odd exception is Terence Bareham, who returns quite late in his book to scoop up *Inebriety* in a kindly aside: 'and let it be said, it's a rattling good, vigorous poem for a first serious "go" at writing'.[21] It is that, just about; but the underlying question posed by the poem has been seldom asked. Why on earth is this twenty-year-old apprentice poet, who enjoyed a glass or two, writing a moral satire on drunkenness?

Part of the answer lies in Aldeburgh, at his parents' home, where 'his father's habits had undergone a very unhappy change':

> In 1774 there was a contested election at Aldeburgh, and the Whig candidate, Mr Charles Long, sought and found a very able and zealous agent in Mr Crabbe. From that period his family dated the loss of domestic comfort, a rooted taste for the society of the tavern, and such an increase in the violence of his temper that his meek-spirited wife, now in poor health, dreaded to hear his returning footsteps. If the food prepared for his meal did not please his fancy,

he would fling the dishes around the room, and all was misery and terror.[22]

We need to remind ourselves that this vividly detailed account, from the biographer son's *Life*, of his grandfather's inebriety describes events which took place over a decade before its author was born: it derives, therefore, from his father's recollections of the circumstances in Aldeburgh at exactly the time he was writing *Inebriety*. Although Huchon pointed out that the statement about the election is incorrect – according to *The Public Advertiser*, 18 October 1774, 'On Friday last, Thomas Fonnerau Esq, of Christ Church, and Richard Combe Esq of Earnshill in Somersetshire, were both returned for Aldborough, in Suffolk, without opposition'[23] – the deterioration in the Crabbes' domestic circumstances certainly took place. Mary Crabbe was never fully to recover her health – her apprentice-surgeon son correctly diagnosed her condition as 'dropsical' (i.e. a form of oedema) – and meanwhile she still had to care for a growing family: the youngest boy, John, was only six. To George, who adored his mother, the Saltmaster's intolerable behaviour created a rift between father and eldest son which would eventually become total; and this surely explains the curiously hybrid tone of the poem, in which the satirist's detachment is continually compromised by a sense of angry distress.

Such an imbalance would in itself have been sufficient cause for Crabbe's subsequent dislike of *Inebriety*, but there was a still more pressing reason: because the young poet had as yet no thought of a clerical career, he was free to portray members of the clergy in terms of which his older self could not be seen to approve. The passage in Book the First, where 'The easy chaplain of an atheist Lord / Quaffs the bright juice, with all the gust of sense, / And clouds his brain in torpid elegance', would not have enhanced the standing of the Duke of Rutland's chaplain; while the lines about the drunken vicar in Part the Second would hardly have seemed appropriate or tactful once their author had become a parish priest:

The Vicar at the table's front presides,
Whose presence a monastic life derides;
The reverend Wig, in sideway order plac'd,
The reverend Band, by rubric stains disgrac'd,

The leering Eye, in wayward circles roll'd,
Mark him the Pastor of a jovial Fold,
Whose various texts excite a loud applause,
Favouring the Bottle, and the good old Cause. [49–56]

But when the gay immoral joke goes round,
When Shame and all her blushing train are drown'd,
Rather than hear his God blasphem'd he takes
The last lov'd Glass, and then the board forsakes:
Not that Religion prompts the sober thought,
But slavish Custom has the practice taught.
Besides, this zealous son of warm devotion
Has a true levite Bias for promotion;
Vicars must with discretion go astray,
Whilst Bishops may be d—n'd the nearest way . . . [63–72]

As for the passage in Book the Third about the sexual consequences of drunkenness, 'When Vice in common has one general name, / And male and female Errors be the same', its ribaldry belongs to the departing age of Fielding and Hogarth; Crabbe almost certainly has in mind here another poem by Pope, *An Epistle to Dr Arbuthnot*, which satirises the sexually ambiguous 'Sporus', based on John Hervey (1696–1743). Baron Hervey of Ickworth, mildly described by the *Dictionary of National Biography* (*DNB*) as 'a clever and unprincipled man, of loose morals and sceptical opinions . . . Effeminate in appearance as well as in habits', was not only a famous example of debauchery but also for Crabbe almost a local figure: Ickworth is close to Wickhambrook, the place of his earlier apprenticeship, and he would have passed it whenever his errands took him to Bury St Edmunds, although the present house with its grandiose rotunda was not started until 1795 (it was never finished). Lady Mary Wortley Montagu had famously remarked that 'This world consists of men, women, and Herveys', and Crabbe's youthful proximity to this eccentric family must have coloured his view of the aristocracy; however, it is hard to imagine anything less compatible with his future career than a poem which poked scurrilous fun both at the clergy and at the nobility.

Crabbe provided *Inebriety* with a jaunty Preface, of which the penultimate paragraph, if he reread it later, might also have made the poet-parson blush or at least smile ruefully:

> People nowadays are not to be preach'd into reflection, or they pay *Parsons*, not *Poets* for it, if they were; they listen indeed to a discourse from the Pulpit, for MEN are too wise to give away their money without any consideration; and though they don't mind what is there, 'tis doubtless a great satisfaction to think they might if they choose it; but a MAN reads a *Poem* for quite a different purpose: to be lull'd into ease from reflection, to be lull'd into an inclination for pleasure, and (where I confess it comes nearer the Sermon) to be lull'd – asleep.

6

At the moment Crabbe chose to launch his poetic career, English literary history was being rewritten. The three volumes of Thomas Warton's *History of English Poetry* appeared between 1774 and 1781, while Samuel Johnson's *Lives of the Poets* collected his prefaces to the ten-volume *Works of the English Poets* (1779–81), although some of the lives had been written a good deal earlier. The two enterprises were strikingly different in conception – the one historically exhaustive but uncritical, the other notoriously opinionated – yet both, as John Brewer has shown, were characteristic of the late eighteenth century's desire 'to "order the arts", to give a coherent, critical and historical account of literature, music and painting that placed present-day achievements in a larger context';[24] other books cited by Brewer as part of this ordering include Horace Walpole's *Anecdotes of Painting in England* (1762), Sir Joshua Reynolds's *Discourses* (1769–91), Sir John Hawkins's *A General History of the Science and Practice of Music* (1776) and Charles Burney's *A General History of Music: from the Earliest Ages to the Present Period* (1776–89). These ambitious works, intended for a wide and largely unacademic readership, signal a change in the English cultural climate of which Crabbe would certainly have been aware. By placing the contemporary arts in their historical contexts, they immeasurably increased the pressure on creative practitioners – especially provincial amateurs, who might otherwise have muddled along in a fairly relaxed, uninformed way – to view their own poems, paintings or musical compositions in the demanding light of cultural tradition.

George Crabbe had reached an age at which he must have been acutely
and resentfully aware of his own provincialism. How did he *sound*? The
question is as intriguing as it is unanswerable. His early poetry, almost
invariably written in either respectful or parodic imitation of other writers,
provides very few clues; while later, as the author of East Anglian tales, he
was to avoid the dialect-rich styles of his Suffolk contemporary Robert
Bloomfield and his Cambridgeshire junior John Clare. His voice, as far as we
know it from the poems and from prose fragments such as the Preface to
Inebriety, strives for metropolitan urbanity; and it seems likely that he tried
hard to attain something of the sort in his speech, no doubt intending that
the fashionable society to which he vaguely aspired should not regard him as
a country bumpkin (though in due course that is just what fashionable
society did). But where did this voice come from? Not from Aldeburgh; nor
from his schools at Bungay and Stowmarket which, unlike more prestigious
institutions, would have attracted a relatively local clientele; and certainly not
from his unhappy spell as apprentice-cum-farmhand at Wickhambrook.
Crabbe seems to have tried to create a persona based partly on his reading
and partly on the more intelligent company he kept in Woodbridge: as his
formal apprenticeship drew to a close, in 1775, he was acutely aware of how
ill-suited this newly defined self would be to life in Aldeburgh.

His return to his home town could hardly have been less auspicious. He
had a low opinion of his abilities as a surgeon and felt he had learnt little
from John Page who, as he would drily tell Edward Burke, was 'a man much
esteemed in his profession and I believe he knows something of it, but I had
not the good fortune to find it communicated to me'.[25] Nor was his literary
career looking at all promising: *Inebriety* had not been a success, and the
terms of his agreement with Punchard would certainly have left him out of
pocket. All he seemed to have acquired from his lengthy apprenticeship were
approximate ambitions and pretentious manners, which were sure to
exacerbate the deterioration of his relationship with a father who now had
neither the means nor the inclination to support his clever layabout son.
There was no immediate opening in Aldeburgh for a surgeon or apothecary,
so Crabbe went back to work on Slaughden Quay, 'shouldered about in the
cold by rough fellows and learning the smell of things'.[26]

Though his predicament was very far from unique – he was simply a
version of that ubiquitous figure, the jobless young graduate – it was acutely

painful for one whose strongest motivation had always been to escape from exactly *this*. And it was made all the more galling by his proximity to Woodbridge, as an incident 'which he used to relate, even in his old age, with deep feeling' clearly shows:

> One of his Woodbridge acquaintances, now a smart young surgeon, came over to Aldborough, on purpose to see him; he was directed to the quay at Slaughden, and there discovered George Crabbe, piling up butter casks, in the dress of a common warehouseman. The visitor had the vanity and cruelty to despise the honest industry of his friend, and to say to him, in a stern, authoritative tone – 'Follow me, sir.' George followed him at a respectful distance, until they reached the inn, where he was treated to a long and angry lecture, inculcating pride and rebellion. He heard it in sad silence: his spirit was, indeed, subdued, but he refused to take any decided step in opposition to his parent's will, or rather, the hard necessities of his case. 'My friends,' said my father, in concluding this story, 'had always an ascendancy over me.' I may venture to add, that this was the consequence purely of the gentle warmth of his affections; for he was at heart as grave as affectionate. Never was there a more hopeless task than to rule him by intimidation.[27]

It is another instance of Crabbe's principled obstinacy, and his son – whose *Life* may lack factual accuracy but who had a shrewd understanding of his father's character – is right to recognise it as such. The surgeon was probably a Dr Goodwin, while the inn at Slaughden would have been the Three Mariners, whose sign is still to be seen in the Moot Hall museum at Aldeburgh. Crabbe's position was impossible, of course. Although he hated his work and argued violently with his father – who might otherwise have found him clerical employment more suited to his talents in the Custom House[28] – he was not to be bossed about on his home ground by a smart, successful friend. There is also one crucial sense, though neither man could yet be aware of this, in which the surgeon was wrong: as it turned out, 'learning the smell of things' was better apprenticeship for the kind of poet Crabbe would become than either of them could imagine.

In fact, 'an unlucky opportunity' to escape from Slaughden Quay presented itself within a matter of weeks, when in the summer of 1775 one of the two Aldeburgh apothecaries, James Maskill, was compelled to leave the town. Maskill makes brief and disappointingly sketchy appearances as a pantomime villain in earlier biographies of Crabbe: for Huchon, he is 'an overbearing, brutal man, of scandalous conduct'[29] and, for Blackburne, 'the queer, loose-living James Maskill'.[30] The biographer son says that his father was actually employed as the assistant of this 'stern and powerful man' and records his misfortune in misspelling the name as 'Maskwell', which apparently 'gave great offence'. ' "D—n you, sir," he exclaimed, "do you take me for a proficient in deception? Mask-*ill* – Mask-*ill*; and so you shall find me." '[31] This is so attractive an anecdote that one very much wants to believe it; however, according to Crabbe himself, he only 'meant to serve in a shop': 'The apothecary there was become infamous by his bad conduct, and his enemies invited me to fix there immediately, my father urged it, and my pride assented: I was credited for the shattered furniture of an apothecary's shop, and the drugs that stocked it.'[32] These two accounts are by no means as incompatible as they at first seem: if Crabbe had been engaged to work for Maskill before the latter's mysterious disgrace drove him from Aldeburgh and had then taken over the business, there would have been numerous occasions on which he might have misspelt the name and there would have been every reason for Maskill to feel hostile towards him.

Maskill's was the inferior of the two practices in Aldeburgh; the longer established, more reputable and more expensive surgeon-apothecary was Dr Burham Raymond. On 12 December 1770 at 'a parish meeting pursuant to publick notice' it was agreed 'to pay Burham Raymond twenty shillings a year to attend and supply with all necessaries in the physical, surgery, and midwifery way (fractures excepted) all the parish poor and all such as may become chargeable hereafter'.[33] Finding that the parish had struck all too good a bargain for themselves, Raymond raised his fee first to £4 per year, in 1772, and then much more dramatically to £20 per year in 1775. We may suspect that by this time Raymond had acquired a sufficiency of wealthier patients and no longer cared much for parish work. Consequently, on 17 September 1775, the parish meeting ordered that 'Geo. Crabbe junr. should be employed to cure the boy Howard of the Itch, and that, whenever any of the poor shall have occasion for a surgeon, the overseers shall apply to him for that purpose.' Early in the following year, he was able to submit an invoice for £4 0s. 3d. which was paid on 17 February 1776.

Crabbe would come to regard this whole enterprise as a disastrous false start, and his own gloomy retrospective view would be compounded by the distaste of biographers such as Huchon for the conditions under which he worked and the poverty he encountered. But this is to confuse moral fastidiousness with physical squeamishness – of which Crabbe, with his cheerful habit of dissecting any dead dogs he found washed up on the beach, showed not the least sign – and in any case misses the vital point, which is that in his first three months he had earned more than Raymond's fee (at his 1772 rate) for an entire year. Far from being a hopeless failure, Crabbe had acquired his own practice and a steady if modest source of income within months of ending his apprenticeship: he was doing rather well. A man of easier going temperament might have decided that, since he was preferable to his detested predecessor Maskill and cheaper than his now exorbitant rival Raymond, he should get on with the job, learning as he went. And, for a while, that is what he tried to do. Since he did 'not believe that the knowledge of diseases, and the sciences of anatomy and physiology, were to be acquired by the perusal of Pope's Homer and a Treatise on the Art of Poetry',[14] he devoted himself to medical study: 'I read much, collected extracts and improvement; I studied the Materia Medica, and made some progress in botany; I dissected dogs and fancied myself an anatomist, quitting entirely poetry, novels and books of entertainment.'[35]

Nevertheless, there were drawbacks: his botanical excursions led credulous observers to mutter that Dr Crabbe found his expensive medicines in hedgerows and ditches (in which case, why should they pay for them?); his willingness to attend on the parish poor in the workhouse discouraged more respectable, wealthier clients from seeking his help; and a hitherto unsuspected number of friends and relations of the Crabbe family presented themselves, expecting to receive treatment without payment. Despite this, by the end of 1776, he thought he had sufficient funds to spend some time learning more about his profession in London, 'picking up a little surgical knowledge as cheap as he could'.[36]

7

'I left my little business to the care of a neighbouring surgeon and came to London, where I attended the lectures of Messrs Orme and Lowder on midwifery and occasionally stole round the hospitals to observe those remarkable cases which might indeed, but which probably never would, occur to me again,' Crabbe told Burke.[37] The Scottish male midwives Orme and Lowder were followers of the renowned Edinburgh obstetrician Dr William Smellie, whose work contributed significantly to the reduction of infant mortality – and hence to the growth of the population – during the middle years of the eighteenth century: it was shrewd of Crabbe to have recognised that this was an area in which rural Suffolk was backward and in which his improved skills might therefore benefit both his patients and his practice. But the truly revealing word in the quotation above is the verb 'stole': its suggestion of furtive intrusiveness reminds us that Crabbe, who had never been able to regard himself as a legitimate student of medicine, remained painfully conscious of his status as a bumbling, provincial outsider. He had sailed from Slaughden on a trading sloop and taken lodgings with 'an Aldborough family, humble tradespeople, who resided somewhere in Whitechapel':[38] just over a hundred years later, the area was to become notorious for the 'Whitechapel murders', but the pungent character of the East End was already well established by Crabbe's time. In the mid-seventeenth century, as Peter Ackroyd points out, 'Sir William Petty was lamenting "the fumes, steams, and stinks of the whole Easterly Pyle", and indeed for hundreds of years after that the "Easterly Pyle" became the home of what were known as "the stink industries"; all forms of corruption and noisomeness were fashioned there'.[39] In these circumstances, desperately short of money and surrounded by people almost as impoverished as himself, Crabbe must have felt as far away as ever from the intellectual and cultural hub of London. He worked diligently, but he had no social life, kept no journal and wrote no poems; this continued 'for about eight or ten months, until his small resources were exhausted, when he returned once more to Suffolk, but little, I suspect, the better for the desultory sort of instruction that alone had been within his reach'. There is a real sense in which this first spell in the capital hardly counts.

One might unkindly say that Crabbe was busy proving himself a failure; or, to put it more charitably and more accurately, that he was compelled by his familiar principled obstinacy to pursue his career as a surgeon with as much energy as he could muster, even while he suspected he would never make anything of it. In any case, he had yet to come up with an alternative plan. His son records one incident from these months which is both more and less revealing than it at first appears:

Among other distresses of this time, he had, soon after he reached London, a narrow escape from being carried before the Lord Mayor as a resurrectionist. His landlady, having discovered that he had a dead child in his closet, for the purpose of dissection, took it into her head that it was no other than an infant whom she had had the misfortune to lose the week before. 'Dr Crabbe had dug up William; she was certain he had; and to the Mansionhouse he must go.' Fortunately, the countenance of the child had not yet been touched with the knife. The 'doctor' arrived when the tumult was at its height and, opening the closet door, at once established the innocence of the charge.[40]

Of course, to a modern reader, the most startling aspect of this passage is the entirely matter-of-fact way in which the dead child in the closet is viewed by all concerned: by Crabbe, who intends to enjoy a peaceful night's sleep in the same room; by the landlady, who seems not at all bothered once she has learnt that it is not *her* dead child; and by the biographer son, who finds nothing remarkable about his father's behaviour. In late eighteenth-century London, corpses – some of them dug up from graveyards – were indeed commonly bought and sold for dissection, and there was very little squeamishness about death: infant mortality was commonplace, while until 1783 public hangings at Tyburn provided easily the most popular mass entertainment in the capital. However, not everyone, even in 1776, would have chosen to share their room with an infant corpse before dissecting it. There could scarcely be more dramatic evidence of Crabbe's steely resolve.

All the same, a little scepticism might be justified: we know that he liked to produce grotesque anecdotes for his son's amusement, and the story of the dead child in the closet certainly bears a generic resemblance to that of the child incarcerated in the Bungay 'dog-kennel'. No doubt each had a solid foundation; but each must surely have become improved and embellished in the telling from father to son. Both stories, moreover, chime with a lifelong psychological trait of Crabbe's: a dislike, understandable in one who grew up on the Suffolk coast but bordering on obsessional terror, of being trapped or confined. In the 'dog-kennel' incident, this was self-evident – for the imprisoned child was young George himself – while here it is sublimated or transferred; yet it is very striking that the anecdote, as told by father to son and by son to us, turns on the locked closet door which can be opened only on Crabbe's return. It is a story not so much about death and distress, which hardly figure as noteworthy, as about confinement and release.

If it seems perverse of Crabbe to have wasted so much of his time in the wrong London, we must remind ourselves that he was as yet the wrong George Crabbe. He could not have imagined his later self – the parson-poet whose chief, and somewhat unclerical, urban pleasure was theatre-going – but, had he done so, instead of dutifully attending the justly celebrated lectures of Orme and Lowder, he might instead have witnessed the still more celebrated final performances of David Garrick at Drury Lane. While Crabbe was making his despondent way home to Aldeburgh, out of funds and not much the wiser, in September 1777, Samuel Johnson famously declared: 'When a man is tired of London he is tired of life; for there is in London all that life can afford.' But Crabbe would not have known what Johnson was talking about. He had been in a completely different place.

8

Worse was to follow. Back in Aldeburgh, he found that his locum had cheated him, syphoning off such affluent patients as he had to Burham Raymond and leaving him only the less remunerative parish work; and this was all the more painful since it was his need to acquire skills expected by his more prosperous patients which had taken him to London in the first place. Nor had the Orme and Lowder lectures achieved their desired effect: the second woman he attended at childbirth died within a month. This event was far from uncommon, and the cause may have been ill luck rather than incompetence, but the effect was inevitably to diminish both his slender reputation and his still more precarious self-confidence.

At least he had the loyal support of his fiancée Sarah Elmy, whom he could now see more often at Parham or at Beccles. His parents, 'cordially approving their son's choice, invited Miss Elmy to pass some time beneath their roof at Aldborough', where Crabbe 'had the satisfaction to witness the kindness with which she was treated by both his parents, and the commencement of a strong attachment between her and his sister'; evidently, the Saltmaster could still behave with proper civility when occasion demanded, no doubt nurturing the hope that this sensible young woman might at last make something of his tiresomely unsuccessful eldest son. But during the visit Crabbe himself fell ill of 'a very dangerous fever': we shouldn't discount the possibility that this was a stress-induced condition or a minor nervous breakdown, understandably brought on by a combination of professional and emotional pressures. The biographer son's account certainly implies something of the sort:

> So much was his mind weakened by the violence and pertinacity of this disorder, that, on his dawning convalescence, he actually cried like a child, because he was considerately denied the food which his renovated stomach longed for. I have heard him laugh heartily at the tears he shed, because Sarah and his sister refused him a lobster on which he had set his affections.[41]

No sooner had Crabbe recovered and Sarah returned to Parham than *she* fell ill 'with the same or a kindred disorder, but still more violent and alarming; and none of her friends expected her recovery'. Now it was Crabbe's turn to visit and nurse the patient. He seemed less the skilful doctor than the melancholic poet and botanist, however, as he mournfully tended the little herb garden she had planted at Parham, planning to transplant its contents in Aldeburgh after her death – a strategy which would happily prove to be unnecessary. There is something both touching and comical about this pair of chaste, overwrought young lovers hovering anxiously around each other's illnesses in each other's homes.

Sarah recovered; but on 12 January 1778 the Tovells' only child, their daughter Jane, died of diphtheria. She was fourteen years old. When Crabbe arrived that day at Ducking Hall, he could hardly believe the news which met him in the stable yard, nor the transformation of the hitherto cheerfully robust scene in the parlour:

Mr Tovell was seated in his arm-chair in stern silence; but the tears coursed each other over his manly face. His wife was weeping violently, her head reclining on the table. One or two female friends were there to offer consolation. After a long silence, Mr Tovell observed: 'She is now out of *everybody's* way, poor girl!' One of the females remarked that it was wrong, very wrong, to grieve, because she was gone to a better place. 'How do I know where she is gone?' was the bitter reply; and then there was another long silence.[42]

But Crabbe's own sincere grief was complicated by a consideration which was to have far-reaching consequences for him. Since the Tovells now had no direct descendants, their eldest niece – Sarah Elmy – stood eventually to inherit their property; and since no one seriously doubted that Sarah's engagement would lead eventually to marriage, the inescapable conclusion was that this likeable, penniless young man from Aldeburgh would be the future master of Ducking Hall. Crabbe 'never recollected to have felt any dread equal to that of entering the house on that occasion'; and although in due course the Tovells did their best to make him feel welcome again, the life had gone out of the place and a constraint had entered his relationship with everyone there. The months since his return from London seemed to have comprised a succession of crises and catastrophes; but then a chance event occurred which was to affect his intellectual life as profoundly as his meeting with William Levett in Woodbridge had done at the start of the decade.

During the summer of 1778, members of the Norfolk Militia were quartered at Aldeburgh; in the autumn they were succeeded by a battalion of the Warwickshire Regiment, who remained in the town until early in 1779. The latter employed Crabbe as their doctor, providing him with a valuable supplement to his income and – still more valuably – some new and intelligent company. Their colonel, Viscount Beauchamp, was the eldest son of the Marquis of Hertford, who owned a country seat at Sudbourne Hall, near Orford, a place familiar to Crabbe since his boyhood; but it was with the Viscount's younger brother, Captain Henry Seymour Conway, that he formed a close and influential friendship. Conway, eight years older than Crabbe, had already been Member of Parliament for Coventry and was by now the MP for Midhurst in Hampshire; later, as Lord Henry Seymour Conway, he would move to the Isle of Wight, where he lived at Norris Castle, near Cowes, until his death in 1830. This Conway – as opposed to his identically forenamed uncle, with whom the biographer son unfortunately conflates him – was one of the eighteenth century's benign eccentrics: a philanthropist with a passion for botany, he discovered in Crabbe a companion of exactly compatible views and interests.

The new year of 1779 was ushered in on the east coast by the most violent storms in living memory. Eleven houses were swept away by a single tide, while Crabbe helplessly watched 'the breakers dash over the roofs, curl round the walls and crush all to ruin'. With the floodwaters more than three feet deep in the ground floor of the Crabbes' home, the Saltmaster and his wife had prudently retreated upstairs, taking with them a cask of gin and a tea kettle. Meanwhile, the quixotic Captain Conway was to be seen in a boat on the flooded High Street, fishing out items of furniture with a rake in the hope of saving something for their impoverished owners. When, soon afterwards, the time came for the Warwickshires to leave Aldeburgh, Conway presented Crabbe with a copy of William Hudson's two-volume *Flora Anglica* (1778) which, like almost all scholarly botanical works of the time, was in Latin. Although Crabbe had studied the language at school in Stowmarket, and conspicuously proved his knowledge of it at Wickhambrook, *Flora Anglica* would have presented him with a stiff challenge. The biographer son suggests that labouring over Hudson enabled his father to read Horace and to pass later examinations, and he cites a fragment from one of Crabbe's own notebooks:

When we pluck'd the wild blossoms that blush'd in the grass,
And I taught my dear maid of their species and class;
For Conway, the friend of mankind, had decreed
That Hudson should show us the wealth of the mead.[43]

Though the praise of Conway is unambiguous, these lines fall tactfully short of asserting that his decree was obeyed: to acknowledge that Hudson *should* 'show us the wealth of the mead' is not quite the same as saying that he *did*. In fact, Crabbe, to his subsequent regret, never became fully proficient in Latin.

But Conway's greatest gift to Crabbe was altogether less tangible. It was the revelation that, while in the eyes of the Aldeburgh rabble he would always be the floundering son of a drunken father, intelligent strangers could value and appreciate him. His confidence received an urgently needed boost, and a renewed spirit of independence prompted him to move out of his parents' home (neither it nor his father's temper had been improved by the New Year flood); he took lodgings in the house of Mr Aldrich, a highly respected Justice of the Corporation, where he was joined by his sister Mary. He took to visiting Sarah at her mother's home in Beccles, rather than in the constrained atmosphere of Ducking Hall. Beccles, like Woodbridge, was a town large enough to possess 'a society more adapted to his acquirements'[44] – one, that is, more attuned to the eighteenth century's ideals of politeness than anything in coastal or rural Suffolk – and the Elmy family, despite their reduced circumstances, were counted among its gentry. However, even this was something of a mixed blessing; for, as the biographer son judiciously hints, Crabbe could hardly avoid feeling some unease bordering on jealousy as the 'remarkably pretty' Miss Elmy moved among potential suitors who were more cultivated and eligible than himself.

It was on a visit to Beccles that Crabbe, according to his son, found himself

in the most imminent danger of losing his life. Having, on a sultry summer's day rowed his Sarah to a favourite fishing spot on the River Waveney, he left her busy with the rod and line, and withdrew to a retired place about a quarter of a mile off, to bathe. Not being a swimmer, nor calculating his depth, he plunged at once into danger, for his foot slid on the soft mud towards the centre of the stream. He made a rush for the bank, lost his footing, and the flood boiled over his head; he struggled, but in vain; and his own words paint the situation:

An undefined sensation stopp'd my breath;
Disorder'd views and threat'ning signs of death
Met in one moment, and a terror gave
– I cannot paint it – to the moving grave:
My thoughts were all distressing, hurried, mix'd,
On all things fixing, not a moment fix'd.
Brother, I have not – man has not – the power
To paint the horrors of that life-long hour;
Hour! – but of time I knew not – when I found

Hope, youth, life, love, and all they promised, drown'd.

(Tales of the Hall)

My father could never clearly remember how he was saved. He at last found himself grasping some weeds, and by their aid reached the bank.[45]

Unlike the anecdotes of the suffocating child in the Bungay dog-kennel and the dead one in the Whitechapel closet, this one seems wholly plausible on at least three counts. Firstly, Crabbe's absent-minded ineptitude in water tallies exactly with the Saltmaster's dismal opinion of his eldest son. Secondly, the placid looking River Waveney just east of Beccles is not only broad but, despite its subsequent convolutions on the way to the sea, affected by tides. And thirdly, the description in 'Adventures of Richard' from *Tales of the Hall* – although the biographer son's condensed quotation rather disingenuously obscures the fact that the setting in the poem is a seagoing vessel – has the authentic ring of transmuted autobiography.

The tale of Orlando and Laura, 'The Lover's Journey' (*Tales*, 1812), which also dates from those later years when Crabbe revisited and reshaped so much of his early experience, is very clearly based on his visits to Sarah at Beccles. Orlando's journey begins on 'a barren heath beside the coast'; crosses 'a common pasture wild and wide'; proceeds via a 'sandy road' with 'banks on either side'; and eventually reaches his destination, the inland town in which his lover lives. There he finds she has left him a note which explains that she has gone to visit a friend. Orlando's reaction to this unwelcome news must surely have been Crabbe's on a similar occasion: 'Gone to a friend, she tells me; I commend / Her purpose; means she to a female friend?' He sets off once more, 'by a river's side, / Inland and winding, smooth, and full and wide, and comes to Loddon Hall – a relatively rare occurrence in Crabbe's *Tales* of an actual place-name, for Loddon is indeed to be found between Beccles and Norwich, very close to the home of his farming relatives. Orlando, of course, eventually finds his Laura, his anxieties are quelled, and when he returns home once again to the coast he no longer notices the scenes which had affected him on his outward quest. The poem, in its teasingly encoded way, tells us a good deal about its author's more youthful self; but its crucial point, stated at the very outset, concerns the relationship between natural scenes and the perceiving consciousness:

It is the soul that sees; the outward eyes
Present the object, but the mind descries;
And thence delight, disgust, or cool indiff'rence rise;
When minds are joyful, then we look around,
And what is seen is all on fairy ground;
Again they sicken, and on every view
Cast their own dull and melancholy hue;
Or, if absorb'd by their peculiar cares,
The vacant eye on viewless matter glares,
Our feelings still upon our views attend,
And their own natures to the objects lend;
Sorrow and joy are in their influence sure,
Long as the passion reigns th'effects endure;
But love in minds his various changes makes,
And clothes each object with the change he takes;
His light and shade on every view he throws,
And on each object, what he feels, bestows. [1–17]

Beauty, says Crabbe, is not so much in the eye as in the soul and the mind of the beholder. This distinction, which at first glance may look unimportant, is of huge significance: it is the difference between an aesthetic view of the world and a moral one. The first of these informs several dominant concepts of late eighteenth-century culture, such as the fanciful, the gothic and the picturesque, which share an underlying assumption that the primary function of the observed world – especially in such startling manifestations as ruined castles and abbeys – is to provide aesthetic pleasure. Crabbe is having none of this. For him, man's relationship with the world around him is an altogether more complex transaction, governed less by the innate ability of what is seen to affect the observer than by the observer's inescapable tendency to affect what he sees, depending on his spiritual and psychological state at the time. Consequently, when in his mature work he writes about nature, he is always something other and more than a 'nature poet'.

In 'The Lover's Journey', Crabbe was certainly remembering his younger self of 1779, but in ruminating on the relationship between landscape and man he also had in mind something even more local and specific than his visits to Beccles:

He deliberated often and long – 'resolved and re-resolved' – and again doubted; but, well aware as he was of the hazard he was about to encounter, he at last made up his mind. One gloomy day, towards the close of the year 1779, he had strolled to a bleak and cheerless part of the cliff above Aldborough, called 'The Marsh Hill', brooding, as he went, over the humiliating necessities of his condition, and plucking every now and then, I have no doubt, the hundredth specimen of some common weed. He stopped opposite a shallow, muddy piece of water, as desolate and gloomy as his own mind, called the Leech-pond, and 'it was while I gazed on it' – he said to my brother and me, one happy morning – 'that I determined to go to London and venture all.'[46]

That is one of the most memorable paragraphs in the son's *Life*, and aptly so; all the same, its evocative compactness needs a little unravelling. Firstly, we should place the 'Marsh Hill' with its 'Leech-pond' a mile or two 'above' in the sense of 'north of' Aldeburgh: in winter it remains a bleak and lonely stretch of country, and in Crabbe's time its desolation was unmitigated by the early and late twentieth-century additions of, respectively, the holiday village at Thorpeness and the nuclear power station at Sizewell. If, as he later thought, the bleakness came from within himself, he could hardly have chosen a better spot to complement it.

Secondly, we can hardly fail to notice that this is what in other circumstances we might unhesitatingly describe as a Wordsworthian scene. Had Crabbe been writing the *Lyrical Ballads*, he would readily have found a place for both the hill and the pond; and in one sense it is Wordsworth who curiously makes Crabbe-like use of just such a scene, in 'The Thorn', by turning it into the basis of a narrative. However, this is one of those moments when these two poets, whose lives and works contain so many parallels, stand sharply apart. Wordsworth, like Crabbe, audaciously rejected his chosen career when he committed himself to his literary vocation (ironically, he had been expected to take holy orders); yet Wordsworth was educated at Hawkshead Grammar School and St John's College, Cambridge, where he neglected his studies, whereas Crabbe had attended neither grammar school nor university but had worked as hard as he reasonably could to establish him in the career that had been chosen for him.

Wordsworth had literary friends and influential contacts; Crabbe had none. Wordsworth, though far from well off as a young man, managed to live at least adequately; Crabbe, during 1779, was sometimes too impoverished to buy bread. To point out these differences is not, of course, to belittle Wordsworth but rather to put in context the desperate courage of the step which Crabbe was about to take.

His state of mind is clearly illustrated by two documents – one in verse, the other in prose – which seem to date from the end of 1779. The poem, 'My Birth-Day', actually bears the date 'Aldborough, December 24, 1778', but Huchon very plausibly suggests this is an error:[47] after all, in December 1778 the Warwickshire Militia were in town, Crabbe's fortunes had temporarily improved, and the destructive storm of 1 January 1779 had yet to occur. It is a miserable young man's poem, with a directness and vulnerability which its author would soon leave behind him:

> Through a dull tract of woe, of dread,
> The toiling year has pass'd and fled:
> And, lo! in sad and pensive strain,
> I sing my birth-day date again.
>
> Trembling and poor, I saw the light,
> New waking from unconscious night;
> Trembling and poor, I still remain,
> To meet unconscious night again.
>
> Time in my pathway strews few flowers,
> To cheer or cheat the weary hours;
> And those few strangers, dear indeed,
> Are choked, are check'd, by many a weed.

The most notable aspect of this poem – apart from the subtlety of 'unconscious night', which Crabbe liked so much that he understandably repeated it – is its almost complete lack of *style*: it might have been written by an unhappy young poet at any time during the past five hundred years. And that, of course, is a virtue: he has learnt both from the Elizabethans and from his more recent Augustan predecessors the value of a 'plain style', cutting out unnecessary epithets and relying upon the movement of syntax and metre.

The 'few strangers' of the penultimate line provide fleeting support for the 1778 date; but against that must be set the conclusive evidence of a notebook entry, dated 31 December 1779 and quoted by the son in his *Life*, which exactly replicates the poem's mood:

A thousand years, most adored Creator, are, in thy sight, as one day. So contract, in my sight, my calamities!

The year of sorrow and care, of poverty and disgrace, of disappointment and wrong, is now passing on to join the Eternal. Now, O Lord! let, I beseech thee, my afflictions and prayers be remembered – let my faults and follies be forgotten!

O thou, who are the Fountain of Happiness, give me better submission to thy decrees; better disposition to correct my flattering hopes; better courage to bear up under the state of my oppression.

The year past, O my God! let it not be to me again a torment – the year coming, if it is thy will, be it never such. Nevertheless, not as I will, but as thou wilt. Whether I live or whether I die, whether I be poor or whether I be prosperous, O my Saviour! may I be thine! Amen.[48]

If he had mastered the plain style of versification, he had also mastered the rhetoric of prayer, while concealed within that rhetoric are hints of his determination to 'venture all'.

Having no money, he was in need – not for the last time – of a benefactor: he decided to approach Dudley Long, who lived with his elder brother Charles at Hurts Hall, Saxmundham. It was a shrewd choice: Long (1748–1829) was a cultivated philanthropist who was to become a prominent Whig associate of Charles James Fox. Educated at Bury St Edmunds School and Emmanuel College, Cambridge, he served as MP for half a dozen constituencies between 1780 and 1821; in 1789 he inherited from his aunt the estate of Little Glemham and, in accordance with the terms of her will, assumed the name Dudley North. Crabbe wrote to him, explaining his predicament and asking for a modest loan: ' "and a very extraordinary letter it was," said Mr North to his petitioner some years afterwards: "I did not hesitate for a moment." '49 The sum requested and advanced was five pounds, part of which was needed to settle his debts in Aldeburgh.

So, one winter's day early in 1780, he set off once again from Slaughden Quay for London. As before, he took with him his case of surgical instruments, but this time he intended to sell them. Apart from that, his entire worldly possessions – all of which accompanied him – comprised a box of clothes, three pounds in cash and various papers (among which was the first draft of *The Library*). He sailed on the three-masted lugger *Unity*, owned by the wealthy Aldeburgh sea captain Robinson Groome, living and eating with the crew: whether they regarded this penniless and eccentric young man with amusement or admiration, they must have been fairly sure that they were seeing the last of him.

Three

A Stranger in the City
1780–1782

I

Some seventeen years before George Crabbe reached London aboard the *Unity*, another literary young man in search of a new life made a long journey by road to the capital, arriving on a cold Friday in November 1762. Like Crabbe, he had been to London before, but he too regarded this extended visit as his crucially self-defining experience. 'When we came upon Highgate hill and had a view of London, I was all life and joy,' he wrote. 'I repeated Cato's soliloquy on the immortality of the soul, and my soul bounded forth to a certain prospect of happy futurity.'[1] His name was James Boswell.

Crabbe may not have been quite so jauntily confident – the Saltmaster's son from Aldeburgh could not yet aspire to the social circles which were open to the Judge's son from Edinburgh – but he was optimistic enough. And there were other striking parallels between them. Both were short of money, attempted financial prudence, overspent and experienced real hardship; both were to learn, by trial and error, the necessity of bribing servants to obtain access to influential people; both were to have dealings with the same publisher, the younger of the two Dodsley brothers. We know all this because both of them kept journals. Boswell's *London Journal* – an exuberant, self-regarding and somewhat untrustworthy affair – is, however, very different from Crabbe's, not least in its fondness for laddish pranks and rakish sexual adventures. The differences obviously tell us something about two distinct personalities and two ways of looking at the world; they also imply a good deal about the way in which London social life was changing during the latter part of the eighteenth century; but above all they caution us to remember for whom these journals were originally written. For Boswell sent his in weekly instalments to his Scottish friend and contemporary John

Johnston, whereas Crabbe's was written for the eyes of Sarah Elmy. We should bear in mind the possibility – entirely hypothetical though it may be – that, had William Levett lived and had Crabbe sent his journal in weekly parcels back to *him*, the tone and content might have been very much more like Boswell's. Crabbe was neither a saint nor, so far, even a clergyman. He was a young man of twenty-five on the loose in London, and he is most unlikely to have told everything to his fond and pious fiancée.

Boswell had seen his future spread before him in the fine prospect from Highgate Hill; Crabbe, on the other hand, arrived by river, docking in the decidedly less inspiriting Pool of London. The pungent squalor of this area, with its waterside inns and alleys, was to be memorably described by Dickens in *Our Mutual Friend* (1865); it was no less chaotic and corrupt in the late eighteenth century. But Crabbe, unlike some of his earlier biographers, would not have been unduly shocked or discomfited by this. He had been accustomed from his earliest years to the rough ways of 'a wild amphibious race' and had in any case already made the same journey in 1776; in that sense, it was the aspect of the capital most familiar to him. This time, however, his immediate destination was not Whitechapel but Cornhill, the home of Mr Burcham, a linen-draper who had married a childhood friend of Sarah's. The Burchams were his only immediate contacts in London; that he knew no one else is a poignant indication of the social isolation he had experienced during his earlier visit.

We do not know the exact date on which Crabbe presented himself for the first time on the Burchams' doorstep – where he was received 'with cordial kindness'[2] – but it cannot have been earlier than mid-April. On 21 April he began 'The Poet's Journal': 'I dedicate to you, my dear Mira, this Journal, and I hope it will be some amusement,' he wrote, though we may suspect that its sensible primary purpose was to keep him focused on the business of writing and getting published. Three days later, on 24 April, he

took lodgings at a Mr Vickery's, near the Exchange; rather too expensive, but very convenient – and here I, on reflection, thought it best to publish, if I could do it with advantage, some little piece, before I attempted to introduce my principal work. Accordingly, I set about a poem, which I called 'The Hero, an Epistle to Prince William Henry'.[3]

He would not have wanted to depend on the Burchams' hospitality for more than a day or two, or at most a week or so, and he was glad to find lodgings nearby: in his own third-person autobiographical sketch, he somewhat archly records that he 'resided in lodgings with a family in the city; for reasons he might not himself be able to assign, he was afraid of going to the west end of the town'.[4] That enigmatic form of words – in which he interestingly employs a trio of London colloquialisms in 'city', 'west end' and 'town' – conceals more than it reveals. *Why* was he 'afraid' of the West End and what were these 'reasons he might not himself be able to assign'? The obvious explanation is that the West End was too fashionable and too expensive for him, yet a stronger moral imperative seems to be at work here: is Crabbe coyly hinting that he feared being tempted into a life of Boswellian debauchery? That he was to be haunted by just such a fear is evident from the fifth and sixth stanzas of 'The World of Dreams', a poem written in 1817 (not long after that other searchingly retrospective piece, 'Infancy – A Fragment'). Here he recalls, in Alethea Hayter's words, 'some incident in his early days in London, when he had been inveigled into a brothel, and had seen a bare-breasted prostitute in a filthy room, leering at him':[5]

Where am I now? and what to meet?
    Where I have been entrapt before;
The wicked city's vilest street –
    I know what I must now explore.
The dark-brow'd throng, more near and more,
    With murderous looks are on me thrust;
And lo! they ope the accursed door,
    And I must go – I know I must!

That female fiend! – Why is she there?
    Alas! I know her. – Oh, begone!
Why is that tainted bosom bare?
    What fix'd on me that eye of stone?
Why have they left us thus alone?
    I saw the deed – why then appear?
Thou art not form'd of blood and bone!
    Come not, dread being, come not near!

If Crabbe's terror in 'The World of Dreams' is prompted by a ghostly re-encounter within the dream, his original feelings may have been different or more complicated; there is, however, another way of reading this poem, as we shall discover later on.

As soon as he was installed in his lodgings – his landlord, Mr Vickery, was 'a hair-dresser, then or soon afterwards of great celebrity in his calling'[6] – he set about his heroic poem, but he also found time to explore other ways of earning a living. The very next day, 25 April, he noticed an advertisement in the *Daily Advertiser*: 'Wanted, an amanuensis, of grammatical education, and endued with a genius capable of making improvements in the writings of a gentleman not well versed in the English language.' The paper he was reading was already three days old, but the possible significance of this seems not to have occurred to him. Accordingly, he despatched his reply to Mrs Brooke, Coventry Street, Haymarket, whose address was unmistakably in that terrifying West End: 'A person having the advantage of a grammatical education, and who supposes himself endowed with a genius capable of making emendations to the writings of any gentleman not perfectly acquainted with the English language, would be very happy to act as an amanuensis, where the confinement was not too rigid . . .' A porter verbally informed him 'that the person should call in a day or two'.[7]

When Crabbe did call at Coventry Street, on 27 April, he learnt 'that the gentleman was provided' – an unsurprising enough fact, since prompter applicants would already have been interviewed. He disingenuously grumbled in his journal to Sarah that this had cost him 'twelve long miles walked away, loss of time, and a little disappointment', no doubt assuming that her sense of London distances would be sufficiently vague to permit his transformation of three or four short miles into twelve long ones. Still, he consoled himself with the reflection that his prospective employer might have been hardly better off than he was: 'he might be a sharper, and would not, or an author himself, and consequently could not pay me. He might have employed me seven hours in a day over law or politics, and treated me at night with a Welsh rabbit and porter!' He was so consumed with ridiculous indignation that he almost forgot to mention the day's other event, which he added in a postscript: 'N.B. Sent my poem to Dodsley, and required him to return it to-morrow if not approved, otherwise its author would call upon him.'[8]

2

'Sent my poem to Dodsley': in that matter-of-fact statement Crabbe conceals a quantum leap in his literary ambition. James Dodsley (1724–97) was a partner in the Pall Mall publishing firm of R. & J. Dodsley, which had been founded by his elder brother Robert, a footman turned poet, playwright and bookseller. During the latter part of the eighteenth century, the modern concept of the publishing house – a firm that commissions books, arranges for their printing and distributes them to bookshops – steadily evolved from its more compact predecessor, the bookseller who published and usually printed his books on the premises. Robert Dodsley had established his reputation through the publication of anthology series with titles such as *A Collection of Poems by Several Hands* and periodicals including the *Museum: or, Literary and Historical Register*, which was edited and indeed substantially written by Mark Akenside, the author of *The Pleasures of Imagination*. Like all publishers, Dodsley made some spectacular errors of judgement – in 1759 he turned down an unsolicited manuscript called *Tristram Shandy* by a clergyman from Yorkshire who wanted £50 for the copyright – but the firm he founded and which his younger brother successfully developed, eventually dispensing altogether with its retail side, was by 1780 as reputable a poetry publisher as any in London.

Crabbe's peremptory approach to Dodsley and his confident expectation of a response within twenty-four hours both seem extraordinary by today's standards. Eighteenth-century authors, however, tended to be brusque in their dealings with publishers and Crabbe got his reply the next day:

> Mr Dodsley presents his compliments to the gentleman who favoured him with the enclosed poem, which he has returned, as he apprehends the sale of it would probably not enable him to give any consideration. He does not mean by this to insinuate a want of merit in the poem, but rather a want of attention in the public.[9]

It was, for all its starchy civility, unmistakably a rejection slip. The polite fiction of a public taste incomprehensibly out of tune with a writer's work was an eighteenth-century commonplace: in Francis Hawling's *The Signal:*

or, A Satire against Modesty (1727), the critic disarms the protesting author with the words, 'Sir, I shall careful be of your renown, / But I'm the judge what 'tis will please the town.'[10] Even before Dodsley's rejection reached him, Crabbe had been cautiously preparing for just such a response: 'Judging it best to have two strings to the bow, and fearing Mr Dodsley's will snap', he had ingeniously revised 'that awkwardly-titled piece "The Foes of Mankind"' into a 350-line poem to be called *An Epistle from the Devil*. This he resolved to send to Thomas Becket, also of Pall Mall, but before he could do so a more urgent consideration intervened to claim his attention:

> I find myself under the disagreeable necessity of vending, or pawning, some of my more useless articles: accordingly have put into a paper such as cost about two or three guineas, and, being silver, have not greatly lessened in their value. The conscientious pawnbroker allowed me – he *'thought he might'* – half a guinea for them. I took it very readily, being determined to call for them very soon, and then, if I afterwards wanted, carry them to some less voracious animal of the kind.[11]

He manages to treat this recurring predicament with every appearance of good-humoured amusement. Though he is partly bluffing, his cheerfulness was well-founded: even being broke in London was, for a young poet, a huge improvement on being in debt in Aldeburgh.

On 1 May he thought about 'sending Mr Becket two or three little pieces, large enough for an eighteenpenny pamphlet' (since on the same day he describes himself as 'Still in suspense', he had perhaps already despatched *An Epistle from the Devil*); and on 3 May he sent off *Poetical Epistles, with a Preface by the learned Martinus Scriblerus*, a style of title which, with its allusion to Swift, was all too plainly of the departing literary age. His funds, having been reduced to 5s. 6d., had now somewhat recovered, as he added in a jaunty postscript: 'The purse a little recruited, by twenty-five shillings received for books. Now then, when the spirits are tolerable, we'll pursue our Work, for it's plaguy apt to be clouded.' By 6 May he had not yet heard from Becket who, he thought, 'has had a pretty long time to deliberate upon my "Epistles"' (three days at most), and he began to wonder about writing a novel. His spirits were 'marvellously good, considering I'm in the middle of the great city, and a stranger, too, without money': he could hardly admit to Sarah, or perhaps to himself, that being a stranger in the city was, precisely, the cause of his elation.

On 10 May, a week after he had sent his *Poetical Epistles*, he called on the dilatory publisher: 'Mr Becket,' he reported, 'says just what Mr Dodsley wrote, 'twas a very pretty thing, "but, sir, these little pieces the town does not regard . . ."' However, he was puzzled to find that with each successive setback his spirits, far from being dampened, actually improved:

> I did not, nor could, conceive that, with a very uncertain prospect before me, a very bleak one behind, and a *very* poor one around me, I should be so happy a fellow: I don't think there's a man in London worth but fourpence-halfpenny – for I've this moment sent seven farthings for a pint of porter – who is so resigned to his poverty.[12]

Such precarious happiness was unlikely to last: as the novelty of his situation began to wear off, so did his cheerfulness. On 16 May he glumly noted that he had 'parted with my money, sold my *wardrobe*, pawned my watch, am in debt to my landlord, and finally, at some loss how to eat a week longer'; while two days later his journal contained both a shrewd self-appraisal and a speculative portrait of those around him:

> *May 18.* – A day of bustle – twenty shillings to pay a tailor, when the stock amounted to thirteen and threepence. Well – there were instruments to part with, that fetched no less than eight shillings more; but twenty-one shillings and three-pence would yet be so poor a superfluity, that the Muse would never visit till the purse was recruited; for, say men what they will, she does not love empty pockets nor poor living. Now, you must know, my watch was mortgaged for less than it ought; so I redeemed and repledged it, which has made me – the tailor paid and the day's expenses – at this instant worth (let me count my cash) ten shillings – a rare case, and most bountiful provision of fortune!
>
> Great God! I thank thee for these happy spirits: seldom they come, but coming, make large amends for preceding gloom.
>
> I wonder what these people, my Mira, think of me. Here's

Vickery, his wife, two maids, and a shop full of men: the latter, consequently, neither know nor care whom I am. A little pretty hawk-eyed girl, I've a great notion, thinks me a fool, for neglecting the devoirs a lodger is supposed to pay to an attendant in his house: I know but one way to remove the suspicion, and that in the end might tend to confirm it.

Mrs Vickery is a clear-sighted woman, who appears to me a good wife, mother, and friend. She thinks me a soft-tempered gentleman – I'm a gentleman here – not quite nice enough.

Mr Vickery is an honest fellow, hasty, and not over distinguishing. He looks upon me as a bookish young man, and so respects me – he is bookish himself – as one who is not quite settled in the world, nor has much knowledge of it; and as a careless easy-tempered fellow, who never made an observation, nor is ever likely to do so.

Having thus got my character in the family, my employment remains (I suppose) a secret, and I believe 'tis a debate whether I am copying briefs for an attorney, or songs for 'the lady whose picture was found on the pillow t'other day'.

N.B. We remove to Bishopsgate-street in a day or two. Not an unlucky circumstance; as I shall then, concealing Vickery's name, let my father know only the number of my lodging.[13]

What indeed did the celebrated hairdresser and his wife really make of their strange lodger? The biographer son dutifully reports that Mr Vickery, who was by that time 'a most respectable octogenarian', remembered Crabbe as 'a quiet, amiable, genteel young man: much esteemed by the family for the regularity of all his conduct';[14] but these are the bland pleasantries of an elderly man who had encountered innumerable young heads in his career and had no particular reason to recall this one. The opinions of himself which Crabbe assigns to Mrs Vickery – 'soft-tempered' and 'not quite nice enough' – look much nearer the mark: the Vickerys must have thought him a bit of a mug, for on moving in with them he bought (presumably from Vickery himself) 'a fashionable tie-wig', which he could not afford and which was in any case no longer particularly fashionable, since in London men were giving up wigs and wearing their hair powdered instead. But he had not forgotten his disastrous arrival at Wickhambrook in an ill-fitting wig, and he was sensitive about his receding hair, so the acquisition of a superior and expensive – albeit unfashionable – wig satisfied a long-held ambition.

In two respects, Crabbe's journal entry for 18 May seems artfully ambiguous. In saying that he fails to pay his 'devoirs', is he simply stating that his penury prevented him from tipping the maid? Or is he smugly noting the unreciprocated interest of the 'little pretty hawk-eyed girl', for whose benefit he has left Sarah's picture on his pillow? That might well have had a confusing effect on the maid's 'suspicion', at once explaining Crabbe's indifference towards her and providing her with an object of jealous rivalry: it is a tantalising possibility, which will only seem unlikely if we underestimate Crabbe's ordinary, youthful vanity or forget that, even in old age, he would remain shamelessly a 'ladies' man'. The postscript is equally cryptic: he is evidently not attempting to evade communications from his father, who is to be informed of his new address, but he wants to conceal his landlord's identity from him. The charitable explanation is that his father had been trying to intercede helpfully, paying some of his son's expenses, and that this had offended Crabbe's obstinately independent spirit; but perhaps his father had been interfering in some other meddlesome way. We simply cannot tell for sure. What is striking, however, about both these ambiguities is how subtly nuanced they are, how closely they draw Sarah into his coded confidence, and how firmly they exclude his family in Aldeburgh. John, his youngest brother, was now twelve years old – as good as grown-up by Aldeburgh standards – so any worries George may have had about his siblings would have begun to diminish; equally, his mother no longer had a growing family to deal with (though she still had a difficult husband). In that sense, at least, he had finally left home.

3

Bishopsgate Street, to which the Vickerys and their lodger moved in late May, is just round the corner from Cornhill: had Crabbe lived in the railway age, he would have found himself within a stone's throw of Liverpool Street station and the main line to East Anglia. But even in his own time there is something instinctively apt about this positioning, in the north-eastern corner of the still partially walled city; for here he could cast a wistful eye towards Kingsland Road, which led through the village of Hoxton to open country at least approximately in the direction of Suffolk. He would often walk alone in that now almost unimaginably adjacent countryside with, says the biographer son,

> a small edition of Ovid, or Horace, or Catullus, in his pocket. Two or three of these little volumes remained in his possession in later days, and he set a high value on them; for, said he, 'they were the companions of my adversity'. His favourite haunt was Hornsey-wood, and there he often renewed his old occupation of searching for plants and insects. On one occasion, he had walked farther than usual into the country, and felt himself too much exhausted to return to town. He could not afford to give himself any refreshment at a public-house, much less to pay for a lodging; so he stretched himself on a mow of hay, beguiled the evening with Tibullus, and, when he could read no longer, slept there till the morning.[15]

Although the possibility of ordination had yet to present itself, he already sounds exactly like Parson Adams.

Nor does the resemblance end there. Parson Adams, when he encounters Joseph Andrews on the road in Fielding's wonderful novel of the same name, is on his way to London with the deeply improbable scheme of getting his sermons (which he has in any case left at home) published; Crabbe was having no better luck with poems which, so far, were almost equally out of touch with the fashionable literary taste of the time. And Parson Adams, incorrigibly bookish and hopelessly impractical, would have fully sympathised with the next entry in Crabbe's journal:

> *May 20.* – The cash, by a sad temptation, greatly reduced. An unlucky book-stall presented to the eyes three volumes of Dryden's works, octavo, five shillings. Prudence, however, got the better of the devil, when she whispered to me to bid three shillings and six-pence: after some hesitation, that prevailed with the woman, and I carried reluctantly home, I believe, a fair bargain, but a very ill-judged one.
>
> It's the vilest thing in the world to have but one coat. My only one has happened with a mischance, and how to manage it is some

difficulty. A confounded stove's modish ornament caught its elbow, and rent it halfway. Pinioned to the side it came home, and I ran deploring to my loft. In the dilemma, it occurred to me to turn tailor myself; but how to get materials to work with puzzled me. At last I went running down in a hurry, with three or four sheets of paper in my hand, and begged for a needle, &c., to sew them together. This finished my job, and but that it is somewhat thicker, the elbow is a good one yet.[16]

Despite the apparent spontaneity of the journal form, Crabbe is again being more artful than he cares to admit: there is coy self-congratulation beyond the self-deprecating Dryden anecdote, while the business with the coat, which jumps from an insoluble problem to an ingeniously solved one, seems designed to *look* as if Crabbe has put down his pen, mended the elbow, then taken up the pen once more; but it wears too smug an air of literary artifice. The question again arises of the journal's supposed 'reader', for in this very entry Crabbe finds it necessary to insist: 'I always think I am writing to you for the evening's post; and, according to custom then, shall bid my dear Sally goodnight, and ask her prayers.' But the fact that this is an artificial habit rather than an actuality – we can only assume that he posted off his journal in weekly instalments, like Boswell – admits the possibility of other readers over his shoulder: curious posterity, for which he had already formed an adequate regard, or the no less inquisitive Vickerys. The following paragraph, still from the same day's entry, certainly seems designed not so much for Sarah as for the snooping eyes of the 'clear-sighted' Mrs Vickery:

I am happy in the best family you could conceive me to have been led to; people of real good character and good nature: whose circumstances are affluent above their station, and their manners affable beyond their circumstances. Had I taken lodgings at a different kind of house, I must have been greatly distressed; but now I shall, at all events, not be so before 'tis determined, one way or other, what I am to expect.

This is an unexpectedly sunny account of people who began by swindling him into buying an out-of-date wig and who would end by bringing him within an inch of the debtors' prison. Perhaps Crabbe was simply making the best of things, though in a dangerously self-deluding way. The following day, 21 May, he provided, allegedly for Sarah's edification, a lengthy paraphrase of the sermon preached that morning by the Reverend Thomas Winstanley at St Dunstan-in-the-East – a surprising item for one lover to send to another, even given the exemplary piety of them both. One way and another, Crabbe's journal is turning into a somewhat eccentric document.

What has probably happened is that the account which he at first intended to be a straightforward, day-to-day record of his London life has modulated into something slightly different: it might now be more accurately described as a 'writer's notebook'. He gathers into it all sorts of material which he senses might be useful at some later date – a bookish anecdote, a striking sermon – and tries out literary stances and strategies; so a loss in accuracy is balanced by a steady increase in Crabbe's seriousness *as a writer*. That he viewed his journal critically, as a document which later eyes might read, is implied by his drastic form of editing: after the entries for 23 May and 8 June, the biographer laconically notes: 'Some pages are here torn out.'[17] It is tempting to think that they described adventures of which Sarah would have disapproved; but it is just as likely that, either at the time or later on, Crabbe thought them silly or self-indulgent or poorly expressed.

By now, despite the often stoical cheerfulness of the journal, he and his mended coat were in increasingly desperate circumstances. Consciously or not, he was treading precisely the same path as the greatest literary figures of the day had trodden before him, as John Brewer shows:

> Shabbily genteel people did not wish to risk the humiliation of being turned away at the door. Poor hacks like the young Samuel Johnson and Oliver Goldsmith would wait to go out on what Johnson called 'clean shirt days'; a satire of the 1720s depicted hacks and poets '*cogging* their Stockings and *darning* their Shirt Collars in order . . . to borrow half a Crown and beg a Dinner'.[18]

Francis Hawling, in the satirical poem of 1727 already quoted, provides a memorable image of the relationship between literary life and daily necessity when his penniless author visits 'Old Mother Puff', whose shabby pie stall displays 'Raised paste round blighted fruit and offal meat':

'Goody!', quoth I, 'do you waste paper buy?'
'Sir – pray, a little louder – price? – which pie?'
Inclining of my head and she her ear:
'I've this, I say, to sell.' – 'Um! yes, I hear;
You ask, if I mistake not, what I'll give.
Ah! master, it is very hard to live!'
Then drew her purse: 'Here's what I can afford,
If you'll be pleased to take 't.' I'm at a word:
'And is this all? – is that the most, my dame?'
'Indeed it is.' – 'And what's this pie?' – 'The same.'
Ware then for ware I took, my last appeal,
And ate out twelve months' labour at a meal.[19]

Faced with an early eighteenth-century problem, Crabbe characteristically opted for an early eighteenth-century solution. He would find himself a patron. That times might have changed, or that the turbulent politics of the moment might obstruct his plans, seems not to have occurred to him.

4

Crabbe remembered that his father had 'some years since attended at the House of Commons, on some election business . . . I recollected to have heard him speak with some pleasure of Lord North's condescension and affability.'[20] On the basis of this slender connection, he hoped he might find 'employment in any department that I should be thought qualified for'; accordingly, on 22 May, he called at Lord North's residence in Downing Street to deliver 'a long and laboured account of my motives for this application', together with 'a volume of verses'. A few days later, admitted to Lord North in person, he found himself 'treated with more attention than I should now expect, though with none of the affability I had been led to hope for'. Though chilly, North seemed at least to take him seriously, asking for references and setting a date for a further meeting. But when Crabbe presented himself once more, he was rebuffed by a servant and could get no further: this was to happen repeatedly, with 'only a variation in the mode of answer as the porter was more or less inclined to be civil'. Boswell had experienced the same frustration in gaining admittance to the Duke of Queensberry, until he was informed 'that Old Quant the porter would do nothing without the silver key'.[21] In Crabbe's case the 'silver key' took the substantial form of half a crown, whereupon 'the difficulty vanished: his lordship's porter was now civil and his lordship surly; he dismissed me instantly and with some severity'. According to Crabbe, this futile business took three months; but he is likely to have exaggerated his London months, as he had his London miles.

The fullest account of this episode is not to be found in Crabbe's journal but in his remarkable letter to Edmund Burke of 26 June 1781 – often called the 'Bunbury Letter' – from which the above quotations come; and it is striking that even then, a year after the event, he remained 'astonished at this unnecessary and cruel civility' without showing the faintest understanding of why Lord North might have been other than even-tempered and devotedly interested in his case. Yet this was the period during which, in the words of J. H. Plumb, 'the ministry of Lord North began to crumble under the weight of its own incompetence':[22] he certainly had more troublesome and urgent matters to deal with than an impecunious young poet from Aldeburgh. The war in America was going disastrously: it would soon culminate in independence for the American colonies and North's removal from office. Meanwhile, at home, the passing of the Catholic Relief Act, which provided a modest degree of Catholic emancipation, precipitated the Gordon Riots: these, the most serious civil disturbances in London's post-medieval history, occurred while Crabbe was repeatedly trying to gain admittance to Lord North. He seems initially to have noticed the riots because they got in his way:

> *June 8.* – Yesterday, my own business being decided, I was at Westminster at about three o'clock in the afternoon, and saw the members go to the House. The mob stopped many persons, but let all whom I saw pass, excepting Lord Sandwich, whom they treated roughly, broke his coach windows, cut his face, and turned him back. A guard of horse and foot were immediately sent for, who did no particular service, the mob increasing and defeating them.
>
> I left Westminster when all the members, that were permitted, had entered the House and came home. In my way I met a resolute band of vile-looking fellows, ragged, dirty, and insolent, armed with clubs, going to join their companions. I since learned that there were eight or ten of these bodies in different parts of the City.[23]

The rioting had begun in earnest on the morning of Friday 2 June – when, despite a noisy and violent demonstration orchestrated by Lord George Gordon, Parliament refused to consider his petition for the reinstatement of the repealed anti-Catholic laws – and the 'yesterday' Crabbe cites seems in fact to have been Tuesday 6 June. The phrase 'my own business being decided' is tantalisingly ambiguous: 'decided' suggests a conclusion, which would mean that his 'business' with Lord North took very much less than the three months claimed in his letter to Burke; however, by early June, Crabbe had typically decided to hedge his bets and apply for patronage to Lord Shelburne, and 'decided' possibly means simply that he had delivered this application. In either case, these 'vile-looking fellows' were a tiresome obstacle, though they were sufficiently interesting for Crabbe to return – twice – that same evening for another look. He thus became, rather improbably, one of four important poets who observed the Gordon Riots at their height – Peter Ackroyd points out that Johnson, Cowper and Blake were also present[24] – and he left a vivid account, in prose, of what he saw on that Tuesday evening.

At seven o'clock, he set off again for Westminster. He records, with a distinct hint of disappointment, that there 'the mob were few, and those quiet, and decent in appearance'. After crossing Westminster Bridge, he walked through St George's Fields, one of the scenes of the previous Friday's disturbances, 'which were empty'; then he recrossed the Thames via Blackfriars Bridge and, passing the Old Bailey, 'saw the first scene of terror and riot ever presented to me'.

> The new prison was a very large, strong, and beautiful building, having two wings, of which you can suppose the extent, when you consider their use; besides these, were the keeper's (Mr Akerman's) house, a strong intermediate work, and likewise other parts, of which I can give you no description. Akerman had in his custody four prisoners, taken in the riot; these the mob went to his house and demanded. He begged he might send to the sheriff, but this was not permitted. How he escaped, or where he is gone, I know not; but just at the time I speak of they set fire to his house, broke in, and threw every piece of furniture they could find into the street, firing them also in an instant. The engines came, but were only suffered to preserve the private houses near the prison.

As I was standing near the spot, there approached another body of men, I suppose 500, and Lord George Gordon in a coach, drawn by the mob towards Alderman Bull's, bowing as he passed along. He is a lively-looking young man in appearance, and nothing more, though just now the reigning hero.

By eight o'clock, Akerman's house was in flames. I went close to it, and never saw any thing so dreadful. The prison was, as I said, a remarkably strong building; but, determined to force it, they broke the gates with crows and other instruments, and climbed up the outside of the cell part, which joins the two great wings of the building, where the felons were confined; and I stood where I plainly saw their operations. They broke the roof, tore away the rafters, and having got ladders they descended. Not Orpheus himself had more courage or better luck; flames all around them, and a body of soldiers expected, they defied and laughed at all opposition.

The prisoners escaped. I stood and saw about twelve women and eight men ascend from their confinement to the open air, and they were conducted through the street in their chains. Three of these were to be hanged on Friday. You have no conception of the phrensy of the multitude. This being done, and Akerman's house now a mere shell of brickwork, they kept a store of flame there for other purposes. It became red-hot, and the doors and windows appeared like the entrance to so many volcanoes. With some difficulty they then fired the debtor's prison – broke the doors – and they, too, all made their escape.

Tired of the scene, I went home, and returned again at eleven o'clock at night. I met large bodies of horse and foot soldiers coming to guard the Bank, and some houses of Roman Catholics near it. Newgate was at this time open to all; any one might get in, and, what was never the case before, any one might get out. I did both; for the people were now chiefly lookers on. The mischief was done, and the doers of it gone to another part of the town.

But I must not omit what struck me most. About ten or twelve of the mob getting to the top of the debtors' prison, whilst it was burning, to halloo, they appeared rolled in black smoke mixed with sudden bursts of fire – like Milton's infernals, who were as familiar with flame as with each other. On comparing notes with my neighbours, I find I saw but a small part of the mischief. They say Lord Mansfield's house is now in flames.[25]

Readers of the biographer son's *Life*, in which the surviving pages of Crabbe's journal appear, invariably feel that this is an extraordinary passage: in its eager observation and wry humour – as when he gets into and gets out of Newgate – it is an outstanding instance of a major writer witnessing by chance an event of historical significance. Although the Gordon Riots may have had their origin in the passions of a wayward and arguably deranged aristocrat, they rapidly took on the character of indiscriminate, unfocused revolutionary protest: for instance, the element which began as the storming of Newgate to liberate imprisoned rioters quickly modulated, in three swift stages and within the twenty-four hours of what Horace Walpole called 'Black Wednesday', firstly to the liberation of all the inmates in Newgate and secondly to the attempted release of every prisoner in every London gaol. 'On Wednesday,' wrote Johnson, 'they broke open the Fleet, and the King's-Bench, and the Marshalsea, and Wood-street Compter, and Clerkenwell Bridewell, and released all the prisoners. At night they set fire to the Fleet, and to the King's-Bench, and I know not how many other places; and one might see the glare of conflagration fill the sky from many parts.'[26]

Elsewhere, the damage displayed that malevolent hatred of cultural objects which is so often a characteristic of civil war: when the Sardinian Ambassador offered the mob a thousand guineas to spare the magnificent organ in his chapel, with a further five hundred to save the painting of Christ, both organ and painting were at once destroyed. Observers thought the English had gone mad: Ignatius Sancho, the former slave, servant to the Duke of Montagu, and prolific letter-writer, attempted on Tuesday 6 June 'to give you a very imperfect sketch of the maddest people that the maddest times were ever plagued with . . . at least a hundred thousand poor, miserable, ragged rabble, from twelve to sixty years of age, with blue cockades in their hats, besides half as many women and children, all parading the streets, the Bridge, the Park, ready for any and every mischief'.[27] Dickens, in *Barnaby Rudge*, was to focus an entire novel on the extraordinary events of these few days, yet apart from his journal entry

Crabbe makes nothing more of them: there is no poem called 'The Gordon Riots' or 'Newgate in Flames'. And this is not because he felt low life to be an unsuitable subject for poetry: he had already begun *The Village*, and his later tales would reaffirm his concern with the poor and the deprived. He seems quite simply to have felt that Londoners were beyond his experience, even while he was living in the midst of them, which indicates either a kind of determined obtuseness or an unusually clear sense of where his imaginative world must lie.

5

He *was* obtuse. His appeal to Lord Shelburne, apparently composed over the weekend during which the Gordon Riots were smouldering and delivered just when they re-ignited, is a sustained exercise in hitting the wrong note at the wrong time. It opens with a flowery verse address: 'Ah! SHELBURNE, blest with all that's good or great, / T'adorn a rich, or save a sinking state . . .' It continues in a prose which contrives to be both pompous and self-pitying: 'My Lord, I now turn to your Lordship, and entreat to be heard. I am ignorant what to ask, but feel forcibly my wants – Patronage and Bread.' Crabbe also enclosed a selection of 'poetical pieces', one of which, 'An Epistle to a Friend', concludes: 'Round the reviving bays new sweets shall spring, / And SHELBURNE's fame through laughing valleys ring.'[28] Shelburne's private response was no doubt very similar to Hippolyta's when she is confronted with the mechanicals' play in *A Midsummer Night's Dream*: 'This is the silliest stuff that ever I heard.' His reply to Crabbe, if he bothered to send one, is not recorded. An approach to Lord Thurlow was no more fruitful: with his instinctive sense of East Anglian rootedness, Crabbe would have been encouraged by the fact that the Lord Chancellor's father had been rector of parishes in Suffolk and Norfolk, while Thurlow himself had taken the title Baron Thurlow of Ashfield, Suffolk – the village near Stowmarket where he had been born, adjacent to his father's first parish of Badwell Ash or Little Ashfield, and an area familiar to Crabbe from his schooldays. But Thurlow replied that 'his avocations did not leave him leisure to read verse':[29] a terse response, though one which says more about the rapidly changing nature of late eighteenth-century English political life than it does about Crabbe's poetry.

Even publication itself brought no better luck. Some time during the summer – probably in July and certainly not 'early in 1780' as the biographer son has it – *The Candidate* was printed by John Nichols and published 'by H. Payne, opposite Marlborough House, Pall Mall'. This verse letter 'addressed to the Authors of the Monthly Review' is a further instance of Crabbe's tendency to misjudge tone and occasion, and it may have been just as well that Payne's indolence and subsequent bankruptcy confined most of the 250 copies to his warehouse. The unsigned notice in the *Monthly Review* for September – in fact written by Edmund Cartwright, whom Crabbe later came to know well when they were both Leicestershire clergymen – was critical though far from unfriendly. After drawing attention to the poem's 'petty blemishes', Cartwright concluded:

And we would then also recommend to [the author] to consider, whether his poem, which bears evident marks of haste, might not admit of improvement in other respects; particularly one in which it is materially defective   the want of a subject to make a proper and forcible impression on the mind: where this is wanting, the best verses will lose their effect.[30]

The *Critical Review*, also in September, was much more savage in its attack. It suggested that the anonymous poet was suffering from a serious, though not incurable, illness: 'Temperance in this, as in almost every other case, is the grand specific, we shall confine our prescription, therefore, in a very few words; viz. *Abstinè à plumâ et atramento*; a safe, easy, and we will venture to add, an infallible remedy.' But the effect of the *Critical Review*'s severity was somewhat blunted by the reviewer's inability to understand what Crabbe was saying. Of the inelegant though perfectly intelligible couplet 'The vivid dew hung trembling on the thorn, / And mists, like creeping rocks, arose to meet the morn', he wrote: 'How *mists* can be like *rocks*, and what is meant by *creeping* ones, in particular, we cannot comprehend.' Unlike Crabbe, he had presumably never seen mist rolling in off the North Sea. The *Critical Review* ended with the joke which the poem's title seemed to invite: 'if this *Candidate* (which we suppose is his intention) sets up for the borough of Parnassus, he will most probably lose his election, as he does not seem to be possessed of a foot of land in that county'.[31] The October *Gentleman's Magazine* made a similar point: 'If the authors addressed agree with us in their opinion of this candidate, they will not give him much encouragement to stand a poll at Parnassus . . .'[32]

This was probably about as much as *The Candidate*, a self-advertisement by a paradoxically anonymous poet, deserved. At its heart is a dialogue between the young writer and a wise old man, who is introduced with the direly unpromising couplet, 'There was a night, when wintry winds did rage. / Hard by a ruin'd pile I met a sage . . .' The sage advises his protégé to 'watch the lucky Moment of Success', but this is plainly not it. The best that can be said of the poem is that, in its less preposterous passages, Crabbe handles with competence the form he will later refine into something more flexible and subtle:

> We write enraptured, and we write in haste,
> Dream idle dreams, and call them things of taste;
> Improvement trace in every paltry line,
> And see, transported, every dull design;
> Are seldom cautious, all advice detest,
> And ever think our own opinions best;
> Nor shows my Muse a muse-like spirit here,
> Who bids me pause, before I persevere. [57–64]

These are unexciting but tolerable lines, at any rate until the bathetic final couplet; and even that conceivably has its degree of naïve charm.

After his unsuccessful appeals to North, Shelburne and Thurlow, and the botched publication of *The Candidate*, Crabbe goes underground: his journal ends, so we can only guess at how he spent the remaining months of 1780. We know, from his subsequent letters to Burke, that he received some financial help from the Elmy family in Beccles (though none, it seems, from the Crabbe family in Aldeburgh) and that he sought the patronage of the Tovells' near neighbour, Lord Rochford, who was to have been the dedicatee of a 'poetical miscellany' which he intended to publish by subscription: although a very creditable two hundred or so subscribers were signed up, mostly by the Elmys, this volume never appeared (it was to be superseded by *The Library*). We know too that when his funds permitted, which must have been seldom, he enjoyed the company of three equally impoverished friends, the astronomer Isaac Dalby and the mathematicians John Bonnycastle and Reuben Burrow – intelligent scientific men, reminiscent of his student companions in Woodbridge: Bonnycastle will make a splendid reappearance in Crabbe's life, while Dalby may be familiar to readers of late eighteenth-century memoirs as one of the long-suffering travelling companions of John Byng's *Rides Round Britain*. But it is harder to tell exactly how Crabbe occupied his days, since no one – not even a penurious, ambitious young poet – can spend his entire life reading and writing. The question is worth asking in view of what he seems *not* to have done. For instance, there is no evidence that after his first few days in London he made any further attempt to obtain the kind of secretarial work for which he had applied to Mrs Brooke of Coventry Street; nor is there the slightest sign that he tried to find employment in the field of medicine (one would have thought a young writer with Crabbe's qualifications might quite readily have found a job as an apothecary's assistant, for instance, to ease his financial pressures). One possibility, to which I shall return to in due course, is that some sharp deterioration in his physical or psychological health made him unemployable. But it is also likely that Crabbe, having decided that he would sooner starve than return to such work, actually meant it; and his perversity or principled obstinacy was about to take him to the brink.

6

His first, undated letter to Edmund Burke must have been written in February 1781. 'I am one of those outcasts on the world who are without a friend, without employment and without bread,' he says; he then provides a brief account of his education and of his arrival in London, before turning to his present circumstances:

> The people with whom I live perceive my situation; and find me to be indigent and without friends. About ten days since, I was compelled to give a note for £7 to avoid an arrest for about double that sum, which I owe; I wrote to every friend I had, but my friends are poor likewise; the time of payment approached and I ventured to represent my case to Lord Rochford; I begged to be credited for this sum till I received it of my subscribers, which I believe will be

within one month; to this letter I have had no reply and I have probably offended by my importunity. Having used every honest means in vain, I yesterday confessed my inability and obtained with much entreaty and as the greatest favour a week's forbearance, when I am positively told that I must pay the money or prepare for a prison. You will guess the purpose of so long an introduction . . .[33]

Poverty had certainly improved Crabbe's prose: the wearisome flummery of his earlier appeals has been replaced by a far more effective directness. Whether the Vickerys had finally lost patience with him or whether (as seems more charitable and more likely) they were simply under intolerable pressure from *their* creditors, it is clear that his underfunded London life had arrived at its ultimate crisis. Burke, who as Member of Parliament for Bristol vividly recalled the suicide of his constituent Thomas Chatterton in 1770, would have been especially moved by Crabbe's closing words:

I will call upon you sir tomorrow, and if I have not the happiness to obtain credit with you, I will submit to my fate: my existence is a pain to me, and every one near and dear to me are distressed in my distresses; my connections, once the source of happiness, now embitter the reverse of my fortune; and I have only to hope a speedy end to a life so unpromisingly begun: in which (though it ought not to be boasted of) I can reap some consolation from looking to the end of it.

After delivering his letter to Burke's house in Charles Street, St James's, Crabbe (or so he later claimed) spent the entire night pacing back and forth over Westminster Bridge, a pleasingly Romantic gesture for so devotedly Augustan a poet to make.

Burke's response was swift and sympathetic: indeed, he seems with hindsight to have been so obviously the right person for Crabbe to approach that the only puzzle is why he should have delayed for almost a year before doing so. It is important to recognise that Burke's reaction was not merely a charitable one: Crabbe enclosed with his letter a selection of poems, from which Burke chose an early version of *The Library* as the most promising. In fact, he seems to have been as delighted with his new protégé as Crabbe was with his new patron. After the sluggishness of the preceding months, events now moved with dizzying speed: it seems clear from Crabbe's next two letters to Burke (the second of which is dated 27 March 1781) that by the end of March he had revised *The Library* for publication, given serious consideration to the possibility of ordination and, coincidentally, been presented to his future employer, the Duke of Rutland. He had a firm – though, as it turned out, not wholly accurate – idea of what his preparations for the priesthood should entail, for he promised to 'apply myself diligently to the study of the Greek and Latin languages'; he could depend upon the support of 'a friend in Suffolk', where he might stay 'at any time when it would be expensive and not necessary to me to be elsewhere'; and there was also 'a family in Oxford, who in this way would be of service to me, should my good fortune ever lead me there'.[34] That is the first and last we hear of these Oxonians, who must have been a rather tenuous or perhaps imaginary connection, but their introduction neatly enables Crabbe to signal his readiness to study for a university degree. The haphazard nature of his learning would always trouble him; and he had not yet guessed that university graduates were in general less intellectually organised than he was, nor that there might be easier ways of obtaining a degree.

A little over two years earlier – though the stormy Suffolk winter of 1778–9 must have seemed to him a whole lifetime ago – Crabbe's self-confidence had been temporarily boosted by his friendship with Captain Conway: Burke now fulfilled a similar function, only in an incomparably more sustained and powerful way. The financial assistance which Crabbe received from him was essential for his survival – 'you have saved me from sinking and supported me on shore' – but what mattered even more in the long run was that he once again felt valued. It was on Burke's advice that *The Library* was thoroughly revised by its author and, on 24 July 1781, published by none other than James Dodsley. This wary publisher, reaching for the trusted formula, had observed that 'The taste of the town was exceedingly capricious and uncertain'; consequently, although he 'paid the greatest respect to Mr Burke's opinion that the verses were good', he 'declined the hazard of publication', so any loss would have been borne by the poet or his patron. However, Dodsley made a compensatory gesture of unusual generosity: 'though by no means insensible of the value of money, he gave to the author his profits as a publisher and vendor of the pamphlet'.[35] In the meantime, between April and June, Crabbe gratefully returned to Beccles, where he drummed up more subscribers for *The Library* and, no doubt, applied himself to the study of Greek and Latin.

But Burke's valuing of Crabbe, for all its outward forms, had a more inward and more subtly rewarding aspect. It is clear that, from the start, the two men simply got on; the great statesman felt no awkwardness in introducing the unknown poet to his family circle and to his eminent friends. When the parliamentary session ended in July, he invited Crabbe to his country home – Gregories, at Beaconsfield – where he was 'placed in a convenient apartment, supplied with books for his information and amusement, and made a member of a family whom it was honour as well as pleasure to become in any degree associated with': that is Crabbe himself, in the somewhat orotund mode of his much later 'Autobiographical Sketch', but the point is a crucial one. Always good at thinking or talking while walking, Crabbe accompanied Burke on lengthy conversational rambles around Beaconsfield, continually surprising his patron with the variety if not perhaps with the depth of his knowledge: 'Mr Crabbe,' said Burke to Sir Joshua Reynolds, 'appears to know something of everything.' This praise is less faint than it may seem for, as the biographer son points out, Burke 'often remarked, that there was no profession in which diversity of information was more useful, and, indeed, necessary, than that of a clergyman'.[36] And Burke's straightforward, unfeigned regard for Crabbe was evidently shared by his wife, though not by his servants:

> As a trivial specimen of the conduct of the lady of the house, I may mention, that, one day, some company of rank that had been expected to dinner did not arrive, and the servants, in consequence, reserved for next day some costly dish that had been ordered. Mrs Burke happened to ask for it; and the butler saying, 'It had been kept back, as the company did not come' – she answered, 'What! is not Mr Crabbe here? let it be brought up immediately.'[37]

The biographer son sees this, justly enough, as evidence of Mrs Burke's generosity; he chooses not to remark that it is also, and more pertinently, evidence of his father's continually ambiguous social status, and that exactly this predicament was to recur later on at Belvoir Castle. There too it would be the servants who chiefly resented the manner in which Crabbe had risen above his (and their) station.

7

'The reader will perceive it is the production of no common pen,' wrote Edmund Cartwright of *The Library* in the *Monthly Review* for December 1781.[38] The poem (like Cartwright's notice of it) was anonymous; nevertheless, 'the opinion of Burke had its effect . . . the poet received commendatory *critiques* from the very gentlemen who had hitherto treated him with contemptuous coldness; and though his name was not in the title-page, it was universally known'.[39] Such was still the power of cultural patronage, though it was waning. In fact, the notices were polite rather than at all enthusiastic: 'A vein of good sense and philosophical reflection runs through this little performance, which distinguishes it from most modern poems, though the subject is not sufficiently interesting to recommend it to general attention,' said the *Critical Review* (August 1781),[40] and that was the best of them. 'The rhymes are correct, and the versification smooth and harmonious,' it grudgingly conceded. Nevertheless, *The Library* pleased the town's 'capricious and uncertain' taste sufficiently for the edition to sell out and for a reprint to be needed in 1783.

This 'little performance' of 692 lines owes something to a longer and highly influential work, Mark Akenside's *The Pleasures of Imagination*, first published in 1744; it was reissued in 1772, shortly after its author's death, together with an incomplete revised and expanded version. Just as Akenside deals in turn with the diverse aspects of the imagination, so Crabbe more modestly works his way through the various categories of books to be found in a library, commenting in a more or less witty style on each. It sounds, and it is, something of a practice piece, yet the anonymous lightness provides an effective mask for its more personal and deeply felt aspects. To contemporary reviewers and casual readers, these introductory lines would have seemed nothing more than an extended conceit:

No storm-toss'd sailor sighs for slumbering seas –
He dreads the tempest, but invokes the breeze;
On the smooth mirror of the deep resides
Reflected wo, and o'er unruffled tides

> The ghost of every former danger glides.
> Thus, in the calms of life, we only see
> A steadier image of our misery;
> But lively gales and gently-clouded skies
> Disperse the sad reflections as they rise;
> And busy thoughts and little cares avail
> To ease the mind, when rest and reason fail. [13–23]

After this, Crabbe soon turns to the consolations of reading and thus to his main theme; but, taken in isolation, the passage makes a very different impression. Not only is it very clearly and carefully written out of Crabbe's actual experience of coastal life; in its central perception that calms are far more melancholic than storms ('Thus, in the calms of life, we only see / A steadier image of our misery'), it exactly prefigures his most famous poem, 'Peter Grimes', which was not to appear until almost thirty years later. The way in which it does this – through a sustained, intimate comparison between marine weather and mental health – is strikingly characteristic of Crabbe's more mature writing, a fact which has important implications for our reading of *The Library* and, no less, of 'Peter Grimes'.

That is the first surprising feature of *The Library*, but it is by no means the last. A substantial opening section (down to line 127) is mainly devoted to generalised praise of reading: books, says Crabbe, have a clear moral purpose –

> they give
> New views on life, and teach us how to live;
> They soothe the grieved, the stubborn they chastise;
> Fools they admonish, and confirm the wise. [41–4]

– but his more insistent emphasis is subtly different. Again and again, he returns to the idea, which is perhaps slightly troubling in so young a writer, of books as a consolatory refuge *from* life. They supply the 'magic' which 'can dispose / The troubled mind to change its native woes', a point relentlessly pursued in the following curious passage:

> Come, Child of Care! to make thy soul serene,
> Approach the treasures of this tranquil scene;

Survey the dome, and, as the doors unfold,
The soul's best cure in all her cares behold!
Where mental wealth the poor in thought may find,
And mental physic the diseased in mind.
See here the balms that passion's wounds assuage;
See coolers here, that damp the fire of rage;
Here alt'ratives by slow degrees control
The chronic habits of the sickly soul;
And round the heart, and o'er the aching head,
Mild opiates here their sober influence shed. [51–62]

Perhaps we shouldn't make too much of this; for it is, among other things, an extended conceit of a fairly conventional sort. But two aspects of the passage demand further attention. No reader of Crabbe – certainly no one who has read quite recently discovered poems such as *The Voluntary Insane* – will need to be told that mental illness, in various forms, is one of his major preoccupations. This has usually been attributed, reasonably enough, to his experiences as a parish priest and to his wife's deteriorating mental health in the later years of their marriage. Yet these insistent lines on the subject from *The Library* pre-date his ordination by months and his marriage by years. Moreover, they conclude by comparing books to 'Mild opiates' for 'the heart' and 'the aching head'. We know that, after fainting in an Ipswich street almost a decade later, Crabbe took opium for the rest of his life, and of course it may well be that the exactness of the prescription here derives purely from his expertise as a physician; but it is impossible not to suspect that he may have already experienced 'Mild opiates' as a patient. Although this is a heavy burden for twelve lines to bear, the suggestion offered here is that during the second half of 1780 – in those silent months between the end of his journal and his appeal to Burke – Crabbe almost certainly suffered a mental breakdown and very probably had recourse to quite substantial doses of opium; and, if that is the case, the 'suicidal' final paragraph of his first letter to Burke, quoted above, finds him even closer to the psychological brink than we might previously have supposed.

This hypothesis has at least a tangential bearing on a passage later in the poem. When, in his subject by subject tour of the library, Crabbe arrives at the books on medicine, he has scarcely a good word to say of them; nor is this very surprising, given that it was the profession at which he had conspicuously failed. Nevertheless, the virulence with which he insists that *it* had let *him* down, rather than the other way round, is unmistakable:

> Ye frigid tribe, on whom I wasted long
> The tedious hours, and ne'er indulged in song;
> Ye first seducers of my easy heart,
> Who promised knowledge ye could not impart;
> Ye dull deluders, truth's destructive foes;
> Ye sons of fiction, clad in stupid prose;
> Ye treacherous leaders, who, yourselves in doubt,
> Light up false fires, and send us far about –
> Still may yon spider round your pages spin,
> Subtile and slow, her emblematic gin!
> Buried in dust and lost in silence, dwell;
> Most potent, grave, and reverend friends – farewell! [407–18]

Not only is this pungent stuff in a poem which began with such comprehensive praise of books; it also implies that medicine has failed Crabbe personally – as if, beyond his professional disaster, it provided no help to him when most he needed it. The disappointed physician here sounds very like an embittered patient.

When Crabbe revised *The Library* for inclusion in his *Poems* of 1807, he indulged in a certain amount of decorous re-ordering, notably improving the status of theology, but he left these vulnerable sections unaltered except for a word or two: he was always a poet who liked to reveal himself by hints. In other respects, the poem is indeed conventional, though not without a winsome awkwardness, as when he makes his own sly bid for immortality –

> Delightful prospect! when we leave behind
> A worthy offspring of the fruitful mind,
> Which, born and nursed through many an anxious day,
> Shall all our labour, all our care repay. [87–90]

– or when, in his closing lines, he inserts a peculiar tribute to his future patron: 'Some breast that glows with virtues all divine; / Some noble RUTLAND, Misery's friend and thine'. These lines and a tortuous sentence in Crabbe's letter to

Burke of 27 March 1781 – 'If the line wherein the Duke of Rutland is indirectly
mentioned be such as would offend his Grace, or if you disapprove it, it is
almost unnecessary I hope to say, it shall be immediately altered' – make it clear
that he had been presented to the Duke soon after his first meeting with Burke,
though whether he identified himself as the errand boy who had once delivered
medicines to the ducal residence at Cheveley is unfortunately not recorded.

Among all those 'gentlemen who had hitherto treated him with such
contemptuous coldness', one in particular now made a handsome
restitution. Soon after the publication of *The Library*, Crabbe found himself
invited, almost certainly at Burke's urging, to breakfast by the hitherto
dismissive Lord Chancellor Thurlow. 'The first poem you sent me, Sir, I
ought to have noticed – and I heartily forgive the second,' said Thurlow.
When they parted, he placed in Crabbe's hand 'a sealed paper', adding:
'Accept this trifle, Sir, in the meantime, and rely on my embracing an early
opportunity to serve you more substantially when I hear that you are in
orders.'[41] Crabbe, he would discover, was a man to take him at his word.
Meanwhile, the 'trifle' in the sealed paper proved to be a banknote for £100.

8

Although *The Library* had successfully launched Crabbe's literary career, there
remained the vexatious question of how he was actually to get himself 'in
orders'. The possibility of the priesthood, which had emerged so early in his
conversations with Burke, resurfaced with greater urgency during his summer
stay at Beaconsfield. 'It is most fortunate,' said his sponsor, 'that your father
exerted himself to send you to that second school; without a little Latin we
should have made nothing of you: now, I think we shall succeed.'[42] And indeed
the notion of an impoverished author being shoe-horned into the clergy was
not new: Boswell records in his *London Journal* (17 December 1762) a
conversation with Sheridan, who 'said Lord Holdernesse with the greatest
difficulty got Mr Mason, the author of *Elfrida*, a living of £200 a year'.[43] What
Lord Holdernesse had done with difficulty for Mason, Burke could surely do
for Crabbe with comparative ease. But Crabbe, though admirably suited in
both moral and intellectual terms, had the disadvantages of a scattered
education and an extremely patchy subsequent career: reduced to the bare
bones of a curriculum vitae, he would not have looked at all promising.

By accident or design – probably the latter, remembering that he had earlier thought 'it best to have two strings to the bow' when seeking a publisher – he embarked, supported by Burke's recommendations, on two parallel routes to ordination. One led via the Suffolk MP Sir Charles Bunbury to Dr John Warren, the Bishop of St David's; the other, via Dudley Long, to Dr Philip Yonge, the Bishop of Norwich. On 24 August, he reported to Burke that he had 'lately visited the Mr Longs at Saxmundham, and was received by both with more than civility. Mr Dudley Long spoke to me concerning the Bishop of Norwich, and the probability of his consent to my ordination.'[44] He was now embarrassed by the possibility that both applications would succeed, so that he would end up by offending either Dudley Long or Sir Charles Bunbury (not to mention their respective bishops) when he turned one of them down. 'I shall certainly prefer the diocese of Norwich,' he added, doubtless reflecting that Wales was rather a long way from Beccles.

This was just as well. Dr Warren evidently had reservations about Crabbe's character, which he frankly expressed to Bunbury, proposing a year's probation, or 'quarantine'; in turn, Bunbury passed this information on to Burke, whose reply to his friend (4 October 1781) is both steadfast in its defence of Crabbe and perceptive in identifying one characteristic weakness:

> On what ground does he [Dr Warren] suspect or seem to suspect Crabbe's moral character? Dudley Long says he has the best that is possible, among all those he has always lived with. He had even when I saw him some smattering of Greek, and I dare say what would do on the common examination for orders. He has been studying it since I saw him. It is a disadvantage to him that he always puts the worst face on his own qualifications. This year's quarantine would be far more necessary for nine tenths of those who are put into orders without all this rigour, and who have not other qualifications to compensate their wants.[45]

Dr Yonge, however, seems to have been favourably impressed. But here Crabbe found himself in a further pickle, for the curacy which the Longs were able to procure for him turned out to be at Aldeburgh. On 9 October, he wrote a candid and distressed letter to Burke:

It happens a little unfortunately that the place my friends here chose for me is Aldbro' and in this interval of suspense I consider it more than a little so: but there it is most convenient on account of two neighbouring half curacies to which Mr Long and his friends will procure me a title; – I cannot say to them that I have no peace there: that I was very miserable and miserably treated and *cannot* esteem a great part of the inhabitants who must be conscious that they did not use me well . . . On this subject I may farther say (though perhaps it is not a proper place for it) that my affection and my duty to my father leads me to avoid him. – It is only to you, sir, that I can say these things – my father and I are in perfect agreement; we parted with every appearance of it and I am persuaded there was deceit in none: but if I live in the same place, I know that it is impossible to please him and others or myself: to separate our interests without making him angry or unite them without making myself miserable: his employments, his inclinations, his connections and mode of living are so different from my own that there is no way to preserve that harmony there is and should be betwixt us but by our separation: I know that I give you pain in speaking thus, but I beg that you would not have too low an idea of my filial duty: I love my father, but I have other duties and stronger affection and cannot give up these though I could many things, to his pleasure – This and every other consideration make me wish to avoid a place, where however if I be situated I will endeavour to be satisfied and to give satisfaction; but these things will I hope be my excuse to my friends there, for my readiness to depart whenever an opportunity offers . . .[46]

This is an extraordinary formulation of a quite common human predicament – that of the son who loves and honours but simply cannot get on with his father – and it is also extremely canny: even before he gets there, Crabbe is carefully preparing the ground for his departure from Aldeburgh and by implication soliciting Burke's help in 'finding an opportunity' elsewhere.

He spent much of the summer and early autumn of 1781 with the Elmys in Beccles. From there, on 6 August, he wrote intriguingly to the printer John Nichols, 'on the subject of your bills', asking for 'an account of the quantity of paper used' and for the return of *The Village* 'separated from the other pieces'.[47]

This demonstrates beyond doubt, firstly, that the production of the proposed 'miscellany' had been well advanced before it was cancelled and replace by *The Library* and, secondly, that *The Village* already existed in a publishable state (consisting of the first book and possibly part of the second). When in the autumn he returned to London it was not to the Vickerys but to lodgings closer to Burke's home in Charles Street: he dined there regularly and continued to be introduced to Burke's influential friends, some of whom he had already met at Beaconsfield. It was, however, at the table of Sir Joshua Reynolds 'that he first had the honour of meeting Dr Johnson'. This encounter, according to the biographer son, was not a success; and his account of it, though distant, provides a characteristic instance of Crabbe's blundering manners:

> at this first interview, he was particularly unfortunate: making some trite remark, or hazarding some injudicious question, he brought on himself a specimen of that castigation which the great literary bashaw was commonly so ready to administer. He remembered with half comic terror the Doctor's *growl*; but this did not diminish Mr Crabbe's respect and veneration for the Doctor, nor did his *mal-à-propos*, on the other hand, prevent Johnson from giving him a most courteous reception, when, at Burke's suggestion, he some days afterwards called on him at Bolt Court.[48]

He still lacked both finesse and funds: despite the generosity of his patrons and his friends in Beccles, the expenses of living in the hitherto avoided West End and of dressing appropriately for the company he now kept were daunting for a young man without regular income.

On 21 December 1781, 'at a general ordination held at Park Street Chapel, near Grosvenor Square', Crabbe was admitted 'into the Holy Order of Deacons' by the Bishop of Norwich. It was a substantial triumph for the Saltmaster's son; but to say that 'Thus the first part of his life ended in a complete victory'[49] or to describe 1781 as Crabbe's '*annus mirabilis*'[50] is to oversimplify the matter. He was still poor; he had yet to prove himself in his new career; above all, he had yet to return to Aldeburgh – and he had a very fair idea of the difficulties he would find there.

Four
The Duke's Chaplain
1782–1789

I

The late eighteenth-century curate was typically a university-educated younger son who had been admitted to deacon's orders after taking his degree at Oxford or Cambridge. Although he could preach, he could not officiate at communion. Nor, as Terence Bareham points out in his useful account of 'Crabbe's Church', was he guaranteed either pulpit or stipend: 'He had to look either to his college for a fellowship, to a patron to find him a place, or to his own initiative and fortune to offer himself as curate to an absentee vicar'; alternatively, he might take 'a sideways path into the household of some wealthy family, as chaplain'.[1] Curates might be pitifully poor, but they thus had at least the appearance of being learned; and Crabbe, with his outsider's reverence for university degrees, was acutely aware of his own apparent deficiency. He had no idea of the opportunities for intellectual idleness which were provided by eighteenth-century Oxbridge; indeed, later in the 1780s, William Wordsworth would be thought by his family to be destined for a career in the church precisely *because* he had wasted his time at St John's College, Cambridge, and failed to obtain an honours degree. Crabbe's problem was that he did not feel or even sound like a university man; and this, apart from the availability of the curacy and the advantage of working with a vicar (the Reverend James Benet of Aldeburgh) who was likely to report favourably on him in due course, must have provided a persuasive reason for his friends, with what they thought was tact, to send him back to the Suffolk coast for his first clerical appointment.

Crabbe, on the contrary, had well-founded apprehensions about the scheme, as he had so frankly confessed to Burke. The one great moderating influence on the chilly relationship between him and his father had vanished with his mother's death in July 1780; that the father now professed a boozy, sentimental admiration for his eldest son's work, copying out *The Library* by hand to prove it, only made matters worse. He was no company for the curate; yet a curate, of all people, could hardly show less than a proper regard for his father. Nor were the sour and sceptical parishioners of Aldeburgh at all impressed by the latest manifestation of young Crabbe. They all too clearly remembered young Crabbe, the Saltmaster's bookish son; young Crabbe, the unsuccessful surgeon who had poked about in ditches; and even young Crabbe who in his darkest days had taken to drowning his sorrows in a most unclerical manner – as if in this at least he might follow in his father's footsteps. Some of them must have humorously wondered in what guise he would turn up next and found the reality to exceed their wildest satirical imaginings. The two daughters of Robinson Groome – the owner of the *Unity*, on which Crabbe had sailed to London two years earlier – spoke for the town when, 'smoothing their black mittens', they remarked: 'We never thought much of Mr Crabbe.'[2]

Nevertheless, there were more attractions for Crabbe in returning to Aldeburgh than he cared to admit. He was once more within easy visiting distance of Beccles and Parham. His sister Mary kept house for him, so he lived in a more suitable style than would have been possible beneath his father's roof: 'it was their invariable practice to read a portion of the Scriptures together every evening', the biographer son approvingly notes.[3] Every Monday he travelled to the White Hart at Blythburgh, where he would meet his brother Robert, now a glazier in Southwold, to 'exchange the news of the week' over 'tea and a glass of punch'.[4] No doubt he missed the more distinguished and stimulating company he had eventually kept in London; but he remained at heart a countryman, and in this sense he had regained his natural habitat. He was never to spend so long in a big city again.

Thus the pros and cons of Crabbe's situation in the first part of 1782 stack up rather more evenly than we might at first have supposed. The balance could have been tipped either way by his success or failure in his role as curate, and here he found himself hampered not merely by local memory of his past selves but by a persistent rumour that while in London he had acquired Methodist sympathies. This misinformation derived from an unlucky coincidence of a sort which begins to seem characteristic, as the biographer son wryly explains: 'an Aldborough sailor, happening one day to enter Mr Wesley's chapel at Moorfields, had perceived my father, who had gone thither, like himself, from pure curiosity, standing on the steps of the pulpit; the place being so crowded that he could find no more convenient situation'. The pulpit steps provide the clinching detail, of course, and to an observer Crabbe must indeed have appeared to be among Wesley's most devoted followers; it is the sort of thing which might have happened to Parson Adams. Added to an equal if not altogether compatible suspicion that he had been spoilt by his fancy London friends, it did him no good at all. 'I had been unkindly received in the place,' he said later, recalling the occasion of his first sermon. 'I saw unfriendly countenances about me, and, I am sorry to say, I had too much indignation, though mingled, I hope, with better feelings, to care what they thought of me or my sermon.'[5] This does not sound like a recipe for success.

Rumour had got it wrong, but had nevertheless hit on an awkward and interesting point; for although Crabbe was no Methodist, he was certainly an admirer of Wesley – and he would remain so, as we shall see later on. His openness of mind on such matters sets him apart from many of his more inward-looking contemporaries: in a period of controversy and schism within the Anglican church, he subscribed to no faction, partly because he had never had the opportunity of joining one. His faith, which had initially been formed by his mother's teaching, was sustained by his remarkably devout fiancée; but it had also, most unusually, been shaped and tested against his experiences of both rural and urban poverty. This mixture, which in a modern country parson would be found unsurprising and mildly commendable, was not at all the typical background for an eighteenth-century curate: it made Crabbe a most uncommon clergyman, and his uncommonness made him the subject of suspicious gossip.

How candid was the relationship between Crabbe and James Benet, his immediate superior? The question is in an obvious sense unanswerable, but it is perhaps guessable. Benet had been the incumbent at Aldeburgh since the 1760s; and we know that, rather engagingly, Crabbe's father was among those of his congregation who decided on 8 November 1761 that the parish should buy their vicar an umbrella – an article which may have proved to be of limited use on the windy Suffolk coast.[6] The Reverend Benet had therefore known young George Crabbe, as the saying has it, man and boy; moreover, he had known Crabbe's father both in his respectable days and during his subsequent decline. In these circumstances, it seems impossible that the relationship between the curate and his vicar should have been other than unusually frank. Crabbe must have made no secret of his unhappiness and his desire to move on as rapidly as possible, while Benet seems to have done his best to facilitate this wish. J. H. Evans, himself a clergyman, remarked in 1933 that Benet 'had been the parish rector for over twenty years, and should, therefore, know how to write the most important testimonial in the student's favour, required then, as now, by the Bishop of the Diocese'.[7] In fact, Benet reported both favourably and swiftly, for on 4 August 1782 Crabbe was ordained priest by Philip Yonge, Bishop of Norwich, 'in the Chapel belonging to the Palace in the city of Norwich'.

In the meantime, despite the additional responsibilities he had acquired on his appointment as Paymaster of the Forces in Rockingham's administration on 27 March, Burke had remembered Crabbe's heartfelt plea for an early escape route from Aldeburgh. He had learnt from the Duke of Rutland that his chaplain was about to retire and that he would happily appoint Crabbe to that position as soon as a substitute could be found for his curacies in Suffolk. Though the cross-party friendship between Burke and the Duke is not at all odd, it is a little surprising that the Whiggish, provincial Crabbe should have been thought so strong a candidate for the post of domestic chaplain in a Tory, aristocratic household. The Suffolk connection probably appealed to the Duke, especially if Crabbe had indeed owned up to his errand-boy past, as did the fact that the two men were almost exactly the same age. Furthermore, there is just a hint that Burke may have been becoming fed up with his protégé: certainly, whenever Crabbe made an influential connection he tended to work at it somewhat insistently. A sense of awkwardness and strain is apparent in his letter of 16 April to Burke, which begins with a decidedly oily paragraph of congratulation on his recent appointment:

> I have long delayed, though I much wished to write to you, not being willing to take up any part of your time with the impertinence of congratulation; but I now feel that I had rather be thought an intruder on your patience than not to be a partaker of the general joy. Most heartily indeed do I rejoice, being well assured that if the credit and happiness of the Kingdom can be restored, the wisdom and virtues of my most honourable friend and his friends will bring

forward so desirable an event, and if not, it will be some satisfaction
to find such men lost to the confidence of the people who have so
long demonstrated their incapacity to make a proper use of it.

Even bearing in mind the formality of the occasion, this is ridiculously
stilted. Typically, Crabbe only regains his natural diction when he turns to
his own affairs in the second paragraph: 'Having procured a successor to my
curacies, I expect to be in town within a few days, and for a few . . .'

On 15 May, he wrote to Burke in his most stately style, from Belvoir
Castle: 'It is my duty to inform you that His Grace appointed me his
domestic Chaplain on Sunday last [12 May], and to thank you for this as every
other advantage I have obtained since I had the happiness to know you. I
hope so to conduct myself that you may never repent your recommendation.'
His pride is understandable: it was only two years since, in debt even after
pawning his possessions, he had been 'at some loss how to eat a week
longer'. Nevertheless, he must have at once discovered that the domestic
chaplaincy on its own would be less remunerative than he might have hoped,
for on 14 May – even before he wrote to thank his friend and sponsor – he
had written to Thurlow, remembering the latter's hope to have 'an early
opportunity to serve you more substantially'. But this opportunity was
evidently too early, and the tone of Thurlow's reply a fortnight later clearly
suggests that he too had had enough of Crabbe for the time being:

> I have thought of writing to you frequently in answer to your last
> letter of 14th May, but have stopped for want of imagining of how to
> shape my answer, and this is only to tell you that when you think it
> fit to take full orders, as you must come to town on that account, I
> shall be glad to see you and enter more fully into the affairs you
> allude to . . . I wish you well, and if you make yourself capable of
> preferment, I shall try to find an early opportunity of serving you.[8]

Despite this setback, Crabbe now had, for the first time, the prospect of
suitable employment and modest financial security which would enable him
at last to marry Sarah. It was hardly the moment for him to worry too much
about his ability to fit in with a milieu which would be very unlike either
Suffolk or London.

2

Charles Manners, fourth Duke of Rutland, was born on 15 March 1754. Educated at Eton and Trinity College, Cambridge, he was returned as MP for the University of Cambridge in October 1774; just over a year later, he married Lady Mary Isabella Somerset, the youngest daughter of the Duke of Beaufort and 'the most celebrated beauty in England'.[9] In May 1779, he succeeded to the title and in July became Lord-Lieutenant of Leicestershire; he was invested a Knight of the Garter in October 1782, soon after Crabbe had joined his household. Although he was to serve briefly in Shelburne's cabinet as Lord Steward of the Household, significant political preferment would come later with his appointment in Pitt's administration as Lord Privy Seal (December 1783) and Lord-Lieutenant of Ireland (February 1784).

Pitt's benevolence towards the not spectacularly able Rutland – characterised by G. F. R. Barker in the *DNB* as 'an amiable and extravagant peer, without any particular talent, except for conviviality' – was essentially a favour repaid. Rutland had first supported Pitt's unsuccessful candidacy for his own former seat, the University of Cambridge, in 1780; he then turned to his friend Sir James Lowther, who ensconced him in the seat of Appleby, Westmoreland, enabling him to enter Parliament at the age of twenty-one in January 1781. Lowther occupies a special place in the rogues' gallery of eighteenth-century electoral politics. He had begun his own political career as a Whig but had opportunistically altered his allegiance, following his marriage in 1762 to Lady Mary Stuart, daughter of the Earl of Bute, at the time of her father's brief tenure as First Lord of the Treasury. During the 1760s he was involved in protracted and acrimonious disputes concerning his Lake District estates, and when he was re-elected as MP for Cumberland in 1768 he was subsequently unseated after a petition was presented against his return. In 1769 he was elected for Cockermouth and in 1774 for Cumberland and Westmoreland; he chose to sit for Cumberland until the dissolution of 1784, after which he was created Earl of Lonsdale and took his seat in the Lords. One of Lowther's agents, who seems knowingly and readily to have carried out many of his employer's highly duplicitous schemes, was John Wordsworth; the house in which his son William was born belonged to Lowther. Like Rutland, he has the benefit of a memorably brisk *DNB* summary from Barker: 'Lowther, who was known throughout Cumberland and Westmoreland as the "bad earl", was a man of unenviable character and enormous wealth.' A contemporary cartoon by James Gillray portrays him as 'Satan in All His Glory'.

The significance of Lowther in this context – apart from the curiosity of the Wordsworth connection – is that at Belvoir Crabbe was to find himself mixing with powerful and sometimes (to him) distasteful members of the Tory hierarchy. And the nature of that 'mixing' was itself problematical. Crabbe, as we have seen, had been treated by Burke as a social equal and introduced by him to some of the greatest Englishmen of the age; now, however, he was to be the employee of a wealthier but in all other respects much inferior patron. Moreover, the social status of a domestic chaplain was not at all clearly defined. Crabbe's son tactfully points out that 'such situations' were 'commonly filled either by relations of the noble family itself, or by college acquaintances, or dependants recommended by political service and local attachment':[10] any of these circumstances would have provided a bridge of shared interests or friendships to ease the chaplain's way into the conversational life of the household. But Crabbe lacked these social advantages and possessed only the shakiest sense of appropriate formal behaviour. In fact, the very qualities which endeared him to the Duke – his youth, his unconventional East Anglian background, his growing literary reputation – were precisely those likely to make his role more rather than less difficult.

He was on his own. His marriage to Sarah was still more than a year away and, although he spent much of the summer after his ordination at Beccles, where he suffered from a mysterious illness of which the chief symptom was perpetual giddiness, he was no longer within visiting distance once he was permanently installed at Belvoir Castle. To add to his sense of isolation, on 5 June 1782 his father remarried: the Saltmaster's second wife was Mary Revett, a widow from Monewden, near Wickham Market, with a young family of her own. Almost exactly two years had passed since the death of Mary Crabbe – a relatively, though not scandalously, brief interval – but it was an act which George, devoted as he was to his mother's memory, could not countenance. He never communicated with his father again. Of his brothers, Robert was in Southwold, William was at sea and John, now fourteen, was about to join the Royal Navy. When, later in 1782, his sister

Mary moved from Aldeburgh to Ipswich to work as a milliner, he must have thought that his ties with his home town had finally been severed.

In his early months at Belvoir, Crabbe suffered a degree of culture shock (though he would have been happily innocent of that expression) unequalled in his previous experience: 'the situation he filled at Belvoir,' says his son, 'was attended with many painful circumstances, and productive in his mind of some of the acutest sensations of wounded pride that have ever been traced by any pen'.[11] The worst days of his poverty in London had been unpleasant but hardly unfamiliar; he had lodged with people of his own class and acquainted himself with intelligent if impecunious friends. Now, having worked hard to earn his place in cultivated society, he faced the shattering recognition that the wealthy can be at least as stupid and ill-mannered as the poor. He had no feeling for their recreations – Leicestershire is hunting country, whereas coastal Suffolk is not – and no sympathy for their politics. He found one improbable kindred spirit among the Duke's friends, a reckless young man called Robert Thoroton, who shared Crabbe's imperviousness to physical danger. And the Duke himself did his best: he appreciated the arts, admired learning and, according to the biographer son's over-respectful account, 'would frequently dismiss a splendid party from his gates, and himself ride, accompanied only by Mr Crabbe, to some sequestered part of his domain, to converse on literary topics, quote verses and criticise plays'.[12] If this is so – and it is hard to guess quite what is meant by 'frequently' – then the crucial implication is not that the Duke was profoundly interested in literature but that he was acutely aware of Crabbe's extreme discomfort in the household.

The discomfort came with the job, the inherent contradictions of which would have tried even a man of more malleable temperament. One very telling instance of his father's frustration was known to Crabbe's son, though he tactfully excluded it from his biography: 'I have heard my father mention but few occurrences in this period of his life; and if I had, the privacy of a family is not to be invaded because of its public station.'[13] Nevertheless, he told his friend Edward Fitzgerald of an occasion on which the Duchess had brought one of her children to Crabbe to be scolded for swearing. In his copy of the *Life*, Fitzgerald noted against the laconic sentence 'The Graces' children were still in the nursery':[14] '*She* came in one day with one of them by the hand to be reproved by the chaplain for *swearing* some oath picked up from the then common conversation of dukes royal and other.'[15] Such situations called for a degree of diplomacy and a capacity for moral fudging which Crabbe neither possessed nor had the slightest intention of acquiring.

When he next met the mercurial Lord Chancellor, in March 1783, Thurlow's alternating moods towards him had swung once more in his favour, even though the favour was accompanied by a distinct hint of whimsy. Thurlow presented him with the livings of Evershot and Frome St Quintin in Dorset: there was no suggestion that Crabbe would want to live there, of course, but he would have to visit them, and the choice of such decidedly westerly places for so easterly an incumbent seems more than mildly perverse. The 'rough old Chancellor' was evidently amused by Crabbe who, he said, 'was as like Parson Adams as twelve to a dozen',[16] although this had become something of a commonplace to describe any supposedly unworldly cleric: the Reverend John Coleridge, for example, was considered by his youngest son, Samuel Taylor Coleridge, to be 'a perfect Parson Adams'.[17] And there is a sense in which Thurlow's judgement was no longer really accurate: the young man who had curled up in the Hornsey hay with only a volume of Latin poetry for company had certainly been Adams-like, but Crabbe had developed depths and complexities which were beyond the range of his loveable fictional counterpart.

3

Crabbe's response to his uncomfortable predicament at Belvoir was an act of defiant self-definition: he decided at last to publish *The Village*. The poem had been a long time in the writing and revising. Alfred Ainger went so far as to place its origins 'during those early years when George's father read aloud to his family the pastorals of the so-called Augustan age of English poetry'; then, 'the boy was first struck with the unreality and consequent worthlessness of the conventional pictures of rural life'.[18] That may well be the case, though we are hardly to suppose that the budding poet began composing his riposte there and then. However, he had certainly begun it before he left Aldeburgh for London in 1780; then he put it aside while he tried, with limited success, to address a more sophisticated metropolitan audience. Early in 1781, he showed a version to Burke, who tactfully preferred *The Library* as the poem likeliest to win friends for his new protégé; later that year, he had included it in the abortive 'miscellany' which was to have been printed by John Nichols; and he perhaps returned to it – or simply found his earlier view of village life confirmed – while he was curate at Aldeburgh. The closing encomium to the Duke of Rutland and his late brother, Robert Manners, must have been added after his arrival at Belvoir: writing to Burke in August 1782 from Beccles, he enclosed the 'verses on [the Duke's] brother's death', which were to be incorporated in Book II of *The Village*, for 'your kind correction'.[19] Some time during that autumn, he nervously sought Sarah's advice about its possible publication: her opinion, firm beneath its show of deference, was that, like *The Library*, it should be entrusted to James Dodsley. In December 1782, he sent it with a typically self-deprecating letter once again to Burke, who replied: 'I have got the poem, but I have not yet opened it. I don't like the unhappy language you use about these matters. You do not easily please such a judgement as your own – that is natural; but where you are difficult every one else will be charmed.'[20]

The Village had thus been thoroughly mulled over and tinkered with even before Sir Joshua Reynolds passed a copy of the manuscript to Dr Johnson, early in 1783. Any young poet would have been gratified to have had the seventy-four-year-old Johnson's approval, but of all Crabbe's early poems *The Village* might have seemed the one least likely to appeal to someone with so slight an interest in rural life: 'Sir,' said Johnson to Boswell, shortly afterwards, 'it is in the intellectual world as in the physical world: we are told by natural philosophers that a body is at rest in the place that is fit for it; they who are content to live in the country, are *fit* for the country.'[21] In fact, Crabbe's deflation of the pastoral ideal pleased the thoroughly urban Johnson, though for exactly the wrong reason: where Crabbe had intended to attack the idealisation of village life by those who had never experienced it, Johnson found ample confirmation of his belief that country people were uncouth and disagreeable. However, there was a subtler motive, in which we may detect the unseen but politically shrewd hand of Burke, in submitting the poem to Johnson: for nothing could have been better calculated to deflect criticism of the Whiggish young chaplain and his decidedly radical poem than a blessing from the greatest living literary Tory.

When Reynolds forwarded Johnson's comments on *The Village* to Crabbe, he enclosed his own somewhat cautionary note: 'I have returned your poem with Dr Johnson's letter to me; if you knew how sparing Dr Johnson deals out his praises, you would be very well content with what he says. I feel myself in some measure flattered in the success of my prognostication.'[22] He saw more clearly than Crabbe – whose pleasure in Johnson's endorsement remained undiminished when he quoted it in the Preface to his *Poems* of 1807 – that Johnson's praise, while generous, is not quite unqualified:

> Sir, – I have sent you back Mr Crabbe's poem, which I read with great delight. It is original, vigorous, and elegant. The alterations which I have made, I do not require him to adopt; for my lines are, perhaps, not often better than his own: but he may take mine and his own together, and, perhaps, between them, produce something better than either. He is not to think his copy wantonly defaced: a wet sponge will wash all the red lines away, and leave the pages clean. His dedication will be least liked: it were better to contract it into a short sprightly address. I do not doubt of Mr Crabbe's success. I am, sir, your most humble servant, Samuel Johnson

This is enthusiastic, certainly, but it is also careful. Johnson scrupulously avoids engaging with the content of the poem and his one substantial emendation (of lines 15–20, accepted by Crabbe) refines a classically allusive passage which is not at all characteristic of the poem as a whole; Boswell, understandably, makes much of this insignificant change. Apart from the fact that he knew nothing about rural life – which would not necessarily have inhibited him from commenting on it – there was a good reason for Johnson's reticence. For *The Village* is a poem aimed both at general urban ignorance about the country and at a specific literary target: Oliver Goldsmith's *The Deserted Village*, which had appeared in 1770.

Johnson had praised Goldsmith's poem as 'a very fine performance' when he first read it, but during the following decade his feelings about the man and his work became more complicated. Boswell, quoting their mutual friend Bennet Langton, records Johnson's contemptuous reaction in 1780 to Goldsmith's idea of an expedition to Aleppo, 'to acquire a knowledge . . . of any arts peculiar to the East':

> When this was talked of in Dr Johnson's company, he said, 'Of all men Goldsmith is the most unfit to go out upon such an inquiry; for

he is utterly ignorant of such arts as we already possess, and consequently could not know what would be accessions to our present stock of mechanical knowledge. Sir, he would bring home a grinding-barrow, which you see in every street in London, and think that he had furnished a wonderful improvement.' . . . Of Dr Goldsmith he said, 'No man was more foolish when he had not a pen in his hand, or more wise when he had.'[23]

Identifying Goldsmith's ignorance of practical matters, or 'real life', Johnson inadvertently shows what is wrong with *The Deserted Village* and right with *The Village*; but this was something he could hardly say when he came to read Crabbe's poem without contradicting his earlier favourable judgement of Goldsmith's. Moreover, Goldsmith was one of Johnson's London social circle – both men were founder members of The Literary Club – whereas Crabbe was not. And of course *The Deserted Village* has its virtues: the mournful account of decay and dereliction is effective and, on its own terms, shocking. But the idyllic past with which this is contrasted – 'I see the rural virtues leave the land' – is a sentimental fantasy, and Goldsmith's smoothly conventional descriptions entirely lack the tang of first-hand experience in Crabbe.

Crabbe's decision to publish *The Village* was a more courageous one than its modern readers usually appreciate: had he prepared his ground less carefully, he might easily have upset both the Belvoir grandees and the London literary set. Unlike *The Library*, it is a poem which proclaims that he is a countryman who knows what he is talking about; and for many of Rutland's friends and guests, it must have provided clinching evidence that the ducal chaplain was a very odd fish indeed. It opens with a cursory dismissal of the pastoral tradition, tactfully couched in terms which suggest that his target is Virgil rather than Goldsmith. Yet within forty lines he has entered the poem as an impatiently disputatious first person: 'I grant indeed that fields and flocks have charms / For him that grazes or for him that farms . . .' Such privileged persons are mentioned only to be briskly despatched in favour of 'The poor laborious natives of the place' and a frankly autobiographical assertion of his own competence to deal with such a subject:

No; cast by Fortune on a frowning coast,
Which neither groves nor happy valleys boast;

> Where other cares than those the Muse relates,
> And other shepherds dwell with other mates;
> By such examples taught, I paint the Cot,
> As Truth will paint it, and as Bards will not . . . [49–54]

As a manifesto, this looks modest enough, as well as a little wobbly in its syntax. In fact, it is startlingly original on two counts. One is Crabbe's explicit insistence, in sharp contrast to his more decorous eighteenth-century predecessors, that he is the kind of poet he is *because* he is the Saltmaster's son from Aldeburgh, not in spite of it. And the other is his rejection, almost twenty years before Wordsworth was to make a similar point in the Preface to the *Lyrical Ballads*, of the conventional late Augustan approach to rural description.

In this respect, at least, Crabbe is unusual though not unique. There had been attempts at pungent rural realism earlier in the century, such as George Farewell's *The Country Man* (1733); and Cowper, in 'Hope' (1782), similarly recognises how unlike the actual lives of the rural poor were to their conventional poetic representations:

> The poor, inur'd to drudg'ry and distress,
> Act without aim, think little, and feel less,
> And no where, but in feign'd Arcadian scenes,
> Taste happiness, or know what pleasure means.

It might almost be Crabbe himself; but the distance in that 'almost' is immense. For Cowper, the poor are *they*; for Crabbe, the poor are his young self, his family, his neighbours. It is the inwardness of Crabbe's identification with his subject which singles him out, coupled with the equally astonishing fact that this author is no peasant-poet but the Duke of Rutland's chaplain.

The Village is, at least to start with, an angry and exact poem. Though this is not the place for a full commentary, a lengthier than usual quotation will help to illustrate its peculiarities of tone and method as Crabbe, still quite near the beginning of the poem, homes in on the subjects he knows best:

> Lo! where the heath, with withering brake grown o'er,
> Lends the light turf that warms the neighbouring poor;
> From thence a length of burning sand appears,

Where the thin harvest waves its wither'd ears;
Rank weeds, that every art and care defy,
Reign o'er the land, and rob the blighted rye:
There thistles stretch their prickly arms afar,
And to the ragged infant threaten war;
There poppies, nodding, mock the hope of toil;
There the blue bugloss paints the sterile soil;
Hardy and high, above the slender sheaf,
The slimy mallow waves her silky leaf;
O'er the young shoot the charlock throws a shade,
And clasping tares cling round the sickly blade;
With mingled tints the rocky coasts abound,
And a sad splendour vainly shines around.
So looks the nymph whom wretched arts adorn,
Betray'd by man, then left for man to scorn;
Whose cheek in vain assumes the mimic rose,
While her sad eyes the troubled breast disclose;
Whose outward splendour is but folly's dress.
Exposing most, when most it gilds distress.
    Here joyless roam a wild amphibious race,
With sullen wo display'd in every face;
Who far from civil arts and social fly,
And scowl at strangers with suspicious eye.
    Here too the lawless merchant of the main
Draws from his plough th'intoxicated swain;
Want only claim'd the labour of the day,
But vice now steals his nightly rest away.
    Where are the swains, who, daily labour done,
With rural games play'd down the setting sun;
Who struck with matchless force the bounding ball,
Or made the pond'rous quoit obliquely fall;
While some huge Ajax, terrible and strong,
Engaged some artful stripling of the throng,
And fell beneath him, foil'd, while far around
Hoarse triumph rose, and rocks return'd the sound?
Where now are these? – Beneath yon cliff they stand,

To show the freighted pinnace where to land;
To load the ready steed with guilty haste;
To fly in terror o'er the pathless waste;
Or, when detected in their straggling course,
To foil their foes by cunning or by force;
Or, yielding part (which equal knaves demand),
To gain a lawless passport through the land. [63–108]

In many respects – though not, perhaps, in suppleness of versification –
these lines clearly prefigure the kind of poet Crabbe was to be for the rest of
his life. Their lack of descriptive richness is more than outweighed by their
uncompromising authenticity. Crabbe demands that we know what bugloss
and charlock are – as Cyril Connolly evidently did when, in *Enemies of
Promise*, he took 'The Charlock's Shade' as overall title for the book's second
part and compounded his homage by entitling chapters within it 'The
Blighted Rye', 'The Blue Bugloss', 'The Thistles', 'The Poppies', 'The
Charlock's Shade' and 'The Slimy Mallows'. Connolly was able to discover
'convenient symbols' on Crabbe's heath (which in the Penguin edition of
1961 charmingly becomes Crabbe's 'health') precisely because he recognised
that these tenacious weeds were at once symbolically apt and botanically
precise: their strange resonance comes not from literary artifice but from
intimate knowledge. The poem's simplest statements are impregnated with
the complexity of lived experience: 'With mingled tints the rocky coasts
abound, / And a sad splendour vainly shines around.' To an urban eye this
might look like sloppy writing; yet East Anglian coastal scenes are
mysteriously lit in just this way, when the source of light seems to come not
from the sky but from 'mingled tints'. And then, 'a sad splendour vainly
shines around' – a clause in which every word qualifies and refines the
image: 'sad splendour' embodies the concession which Crabbe will in truth
have to make often enough, that this bleak coast has its own magnificence;
'vainly' has a fine ambiguity – here it primarily means 'futilely', but four
lines later the echoing 'in vain' reinforces the secondary notion of foolish
pride; while even 'shines around' is surprisingly exact in portraying the
directionless light of a cloudy or foggy coast.

This couplet perfectly evokes a coastal landscape; yet there is still more to
it. Not for the first or the last time, Crabbe has embedded precise local

information in apparently artless lines. The remembered scene here is the long shingle spit south of Aldeburgh, between the sea and the river, which becomes Orford Ness: it is the area which most haunted him, as we know from 'Infancy – A Fragment', and which was also to haunt his most celebrated creation, Peter Grimes. After a disastrous storm in October 1627, during which thirty-two ships were wrecked off Orford Ness, the first lighthouse was built there; this, like several of its successors, was to be destroyed by storms and coastal erosion, but the lighthouse built in 1732 – one of the first to use oil instead of candles – would have been among the memorable landmarks of Crabbe's childhood. Though 'a sad splendour vainly shines around' well describes foggy coastal light, it is even more precisely right for the lighthouse. Crabbe knew how 'vainly' it shone: shipwrecks remained common occurrences, and the tower itself would be destroyed by a storm in October 1789. Its replacement, built in 1792, still stands.

The characterisation, too, is authentic. Until quite recently, when some Suffolk coastal villages began to resemble (in John Seymour's notable phrase) 'a kind of seaside Hampstead Garden Suburb',[24] the scowling and suspicious 'wild amphibious race' was much in evidence: these were Crabbe's people, about whom he had no illusions. Like Goldsmith, he contrasts the present with a better past, but his is a rough-and-ready version of arcadia in which the 'swains' played convincing rustic games. Just as the 'nymphs' have turned to prostitution, so the 'swains' have become smugglers, whom it was Crabbe's father's business to intercept: everything about this poem is stamped with the author's first-hand knowledge. Now, as if to reassert this intimacy with his subject, he re-enters his poem: 'Here, wand'ring long amid these frowning fields, / I sought the simple life that Nature yields . . .' (Is there a tantalisingly distant echo here of Marvell's search for 'Quiet' and 'Innocence' in 'The Garden': 'Mistaken long, I sought you then / In busy companies of men'?) A little later, he records that, like the swallows on the beach awaiting a favouring wind, 'So waited I the favouring hour, and fled . . .' (line 122); he was better informed about the migratory habits of swallows than Dr Johnson, who thought that they hibernated under water, and frank about his own compulsion to escape from this impoverished existence. There was, of course, nothing extraordinary about the literary depiction of low life: the eighteenth-century novel is full of it. What is remarkable is that a ducal chaplain should so unambiguously insist that this had been *his* world.

Crabbe repeatedly summons up his past selves, as if picking at the scabs of wounds which will not heal. One such self appears when, among 'this tribe', he sees 'the youth of slender frame / Contend with weakness, weariness, and shame'. Two others are more obliquely conjured up when we reach the parish poorhouse, where a dying man is visited first by a surgeon and then by a priest – the roles successively filled by Crabbe himself in Aldeburgh. They are not self-portraits but caricatures of former acquaintances. The 'potent quack', 'All pride and business, bustle and conceit', is plainly based on Burham Raymond, the Aldeburgh surgeon who became too grand for parish work. The priest turns out to be an idle curate, 'A jovial youth, who thinks his Sunday's task / As much as God or man can fairly ask': this is not Crabbe as the young curate he was but as he might have been; perhaps, as with the surgeon, he is modelled on an Aldeburgh predecessor. What of the parish priest himself? 'And doth not he, the pious man, appear, / He, "passing rich with forty pounds a year"?' He doth not: probably he is an absentee pluralist, a condition which Crabbe himself was about to embrace without obvious qualms. Though he remains off-stage, no contemporary reader could have failed to recognise the phrase 'passing rich with forty pounds a year'. It is from the description of the parish priest in Goldsmith's *The Deserted Village*.

The second book of *The Village* is shorter, more generalised and less abrasive than the first: Crabbe is qualifying his position and moving, rather awkwardly, towards the fulsome praise of his noble patron and his patron's late brother which will end the piece. In effect, it has turned into a different sort of poem, because it now belongs to a different sort of occasion: the boors who spill out of the inn and riot on the village green may look like survivors from the world of Book I, but the 'grave justice' at 'yonder Hall' is not a subject for satirical comment nor even for proper characterisation; his favouritism is gently mocked, and that is all. The angry young man who begins the poem necessarily gives way to the cautious, respectful chaplain who concludes it. And so, despite its many qualities, *The Village* fails to make much sense as a coherent entity, as Crabbe's most perceptive early critic, Edmund Cartwright, pointed out in his unsigned review:

> Considered as a whole, its most strenuous advocates must acknow-
> ledge it to be defective. The first part asserts as a general proposition

what can only be affirmed of individuals; and the second part contradicts the assertion of the first. The chain of argument is illogical, and it is carried on, for the most part, without any apparently determinate object.[25]

Or rather, the 'determinate object' shifts during the course of the poem from social and literary satire to conventional praise of the author's patron. If the reader finds that an awkward transition, then so did Crabbe.

4

The unseasonable summer of 1783 seems to have been as peculiar as that of 1594, with its 'contagious fogs' and 'hoary-headed frosts':

> The spring, the summer,
> The chiding autumn, angry winter change
> Their wonted liveries, and the mazèd world
> By their increase now knows not which is which.

Titania's famous description in Act II of *A Midsummer Night's Dream* finds its echo in Cowper's account of the later strange season in Book II of *The Task*:

> When were the winds
> Let slip with such a warrant to destroy?
> When did the waves so haughtily o'erleap
> Their ancient barriers, deluging the dry?
> Fires from beneath, and meteors from above,
> Portentous, unexampled, unexplain'd,
> Have kindled beacons in the skies; and th'old
> And crazy earth has had her shaking fits
> More frequent, and foregone her usual rest.
> Is it a time to wrangle, when the props
> And pillars of our planet seem to fail,
> And Nature with a dim and sickly eye
> To wait the close of all? [53–65]

According to Cowper's own notes, the meteors appeared on 18 August while, he explained, the last lines quoted allude 'to the fog that covered both Europe and Asia during the summer of 1783'.[26] In a letter to William Unwin of 29 September, he added:

> We are rational; but we are animal too, and therefore subject to the influences of the weather. The cattle in the fields show evident symptoms of lassitude and disgust in an unpleasant season; and we, their lords and masters, are constrained to sympathise with them: the only difference between us is, that they know not the cause of their dejection, and we do, – but, for our humiliation, are equally at a loss to cure it.[27]

On the momentous evening of 18 August 1783, Crabbe and his fiancée, Sarah Elmy, were riding across open country near Beccles; the chaplain was on leave of absence, following the end of the parliamentary session in July. What happened next is memorably described by the biographer son:

> It was late, dull, and cloudy: in an instant the dark mass opened just in front of them. The clouds were rolled back like a scroll; and the glorious phenomenon burst forth as large as the moon, but infinitely more brilliant; majestically sailed across the heavens, varying its form every instant, and, as it were, unfolding its sub-stance in successive sheaths of fire, and scattering lesser meteors, as it moved along. My mother, who happened to be riding behind, said that, even at that awful moment (for she concluded that the end of all things was at hand), she was irresistibly struck with my father's attitude. He had raised himself from his horse, lifted his arm, and spread his hand towards the object of admiration and terror, and appeared transfixed with astonishment.[28]

This is so persuasive an account – and so much more vivid than the dull paraphrases of Crabbe's subsequent biographers – that it may seem perverse to concentrate on the one questionable aspect of the son's interpretation. No doubt he is right to record his mother's belief that the end of the world had come; but what are we to make of his father's 'admiration and terror'? That is a coupling deeply rooted in literary history: in, for example, Horatio's 'What is it you would see? / If aught of woe or wonder, cease your search.' Wonder or admiration – *ad mirare*, to wonder at – Crabbe would certainly have experienced; terror, on the other hand, was a state almost unknown to him. Indeed, personal recklessness – as when he nipped in and out of burning Newgate, almost drowned himself in the Waveney or, later on, refused to get out of bed when told that the French were about to invade Suffolk – is one of his recurring characteristics. And so what his frightened fiancée and his respectful son both took for terror is perhaps something else: amazement or delight or even revelation. For that outstretched hand is a gesture which we might otherwise associate with another transformed and astonished traveller: on the road to Damascus, Saul becoming Paul.

5

It is pleasant to imagine that on the meteoric evening of 18 August 1783, George Crabbe and his future wife may have settled the date of their forthcoming marriage, which was to take place later that year. Certainly, the cosmic disturbance presaged – in appropriately Shakespearian fashion – an epoch of unexpected upheavals at the very moment when Crabbe's life seemed to be moving towards stability. Before this, however, there was an autumn season to be divided as usual between Belvoir, Cheveley and, when Parliament resumed on 11 November, London. Although Crabbe was seldom entirely at ease in the city, where his inability to cut a fashionable figure made him a conspicuous oddity in the Duke's circle, he had developed a somewhat unclerical passion for the theatre: he was, says his son, a particular admirer of Mrs Siddons, Mrs Abingdon and Mrs Jordan. At Drury Lane that November, Kemble was playing Richard III and Mrs Siddons Isabella in *Measure for Measure* as well as Mrs Beverley in Edward Moore's *The Gamester*. When, on one of these occasions, Robert Thoroton introduced him into the box of the Prince of Wales's equerries, 'his royal highness inquired, with some displeasure, who he was that had so intruded there; but hearing that it was the poetical chaplain of his friend the Duke of Rutland, he expressed himself satisfied, and a short time after, Mr Crabbe was presented to his royal highness by his noble patron'.[29] That phrase, 'the poetical chaplain of the Duke of Rutland', exactly captures Crabbe's ambivalent status: in one light, he is a distinguished literary man; in another, an eccentric domestic pet. He was fully aware of both implications.

From London, Crabbe travelled to Beccles, where he had an appointment of some importance to keep: 'George Crabbe, Clerk, of this parish, single-man, and Sarah Elmy, of the same, single-woman, were married in this church by licence from the Chancellor this fifteenth day of December 1783 by me P. Routh, Curate.'[30] Two aspects of this may strike us as odd: the humbly unspecific description of Crabbe as a 'Clerk', though this of course is perfectly accurate in its proper sense of 'clergyman', and his designation as 'of this parish' – a sharp reminder that Beccles had indeed been his only constant point of anchorage since his departure from Aldeburgh for London almost four years earlier. An extended honeymoon would have suited neither the circumstances nor the temperaments of the couple, and after a brief wedding trip within East Anglia they were back in Beccles on 19 December, ready to set off for Belvoir. It was a prospect which Sarah viewed with both excitement and apprehension: she knew of her husband's difficulties at the castle – if he told no one else, he certainly confided in her – and she naturally wondered whether she would get on any better. She had never mixed in aristocratic society nor yet visited London; and she came from a troubled, impoverished family in whose history both bankruptcy and insanity figured. On the other hand, she had used her limited resources well, keeping the most cultivated company available to her: she was now a mature, accomplished woman of thirty-two and – for the time being, at least – emotionally steadier than her sometimes impetuous and hot-tempered husband. As for Crabbe himself, the relief of at last having the constant support and companionship of the woman he loved must have been incalculable.

Yet, even before they reached Belvoir, a political development had occurred which would completely change the course of their future life. On 17 December 1783, the Fox–North coalition ministry collapsed; and, with the subsequent accession of his friend William Pitt the Younger as Prime Minister, the Duke of Rutland could once more look forward to high office. In the event, the post offered to him was Lord-Lieutenant of Ireland. For the Crabbes, it was a perverse twist of fate: had Rutland been given any domestic portfolio, they might have looked forward to meeting the greatest political and cultural figures of the time, both at Belvoir and in London, where there would also have been plenty of evenings at Drury Lane for George to enjoy.

Now, however, they were presented with alternative courses, neither of them obviously attractive. One was to accompany the Duke to Ireland, which would take them far from eastern England and their respective families; the other was to remain at a dukeless Belvoir, where their role would be uncertain and their relationships with the remaining servants uncomfortable. They chose, if they had a choice, the latter option. It seems likely that the Duke, who was fond of Crabbe, sensibly doubted whether his poetical chaplain would be happy in Ireland. Allowing him to remain at Belvoir was an act of conspicuous generosity: most patrons would have insisted that their chaplain either accompany them as part of the household or be dismissed.

When the Duke left for Ireland in February 1784, taking Robert Thoroton with him as his private secretary, Crabbe – no doubt feeling that there was nothing much for him to do at Belvoir – set off with Sarah to visit the livings in Dorset, Evershot (St Osmund) and Frome St Quintin, which he had received from Thurlow almost a year earlier and where he seems to have had a capable and uncomplaining curate in the Reverend Nathaniel Bartlett. On 25 March, Crabbe preached at Evershot on 'the duties of the ministers of the Christian religion';[31] Mr Bartlett and his parishioners may have permitted themselves wry smiles and the reflection that one such duty might be to visit the parish more than once a year. These two small villages lie only three miles apart, almost midway between Dorchester and Yeovil; both St Osmund and St Quintin are attractive churches, and Pevsner also admires the Old Rectory at Evershot, though whether it is sufficiently old to have been the rectory in 1784 he doesn't say. But the point is worth mentioning, since the Crabbes stayed in Dorset from February until early June, far longer than a courtesy visit could have demanded: they evidently investigated the possibility of moving there permanently. Crabbe, despite his imaginative affinity with the bleak east coast, took a liking to the softer landscape of the south-west and, if a suitably remunerative additional living could have been found nearby, he would have been tempted to settle there; he was to return thirty years later. His wife, however, had stronger, less compromised family allegiances in Suffolk, from which she was unwilling to be quite so distant.

At the end of their visit, the Crabbes travelled back to Belvoir via London. There, on 6 June, they dined with the Burkes at Charles Street: on this, the first occasion on which Crabbe had been able to present his wife to the man who had rescued him from ruin and starvation, 'he and she experienced the kindest reception'.[32] Among the other guests were Richard Shackleton, a Quaker friend whom Burke had known since his schooldays, and his daughter Mary who, as Mary Leadbeater, later became one of Crabbe's most prolific correspondents. Shackleton, who had read and admired *The Village*, amiably assured its author that 'Goldsmith's village would henceforth be really the *deserted* village'.[33] It was the kind of praise which Crabbe affected to shrug off but which he appreciated and needed: mixing with Burke and his friends invariably provided a boost for his literary self-esteem.

On returning to Belvoir, Crabbe was soon able to find a convenient source of additional employment and income. He accepted the vacant curacy at Stathern, a mere three miles away, within sight and walking distance of Belvoir Castle; the incumbent, Dr Thomas Parke, Archdeacon of Stamford, unsurprisingly chose to live in the more prosperous and prestigious town rather than in the modest village parsonage. The Crabbes had no immediate need to move there either, for the chaplain retained his nominal duties and his comfortable quarters at the castle. There were, as the biographer son observes, 'many obvious advantages to a couple of narrow income in this position', but 'although the noble owner of the seat had given the most strict orders that their convenience should be consulted in every possible manner by his servants, it was soon found to be a disagreeable thing to inhabit the house, and be attended by the servants, of an absent family'.[34] It was the old problem: Crabbe had no difficulty in earning the respect and admiration of his social superiors, but his inferiors found the transmogrified Saltmaster's son a ludicrous figure. In the concise words of a more recent Belvoir chaplain, the Reverend F. W. Knox: 'They teased him.'[35] This domestic awkwardness was compounded later in 1784 by a more intimate unhappiness: the Crabbes' first son, born at Belvoir and immediately christened with his father's name, died within a few hours. It was to be by no means the last such loss which Sarah would have to endure.

6

Crabbe's readers commonly express astonishment that, in his next poem *The Newspaper* (published by Dodsley on 15 March 1785), he should have so entirely failed to build on the strengths of *The Village*, returning instead to the bookishly satirical mode of *The Library*. But this astonishment is ill-founded: the pungent first book of *The Village*, as we have already seen, had been in Crabbe's mind for a very long time. It certainly pre-dated *The Library* in his creative chronology: that *The Newspaper* should have more in common with *The Library* than with *The Village* is therefore only to be expected. Moreover, the notion that *The Newspaper* was an inferior work which had been consigned to a bottom drawer and was now brought out to earn a little extra money – the assumption behind Ainger's assertion that it 'was probably "old stock" '[36] is manifestly false. Writing from Belvoir Castle a week before the poem's publication, Crabbe apologised to Burke for failing to seek his advice while the work was still in manuscript, 'as I had very prevailing reasons for a hasty publication, of which I fear my poem will bear many tokens'.[37] If it had been as old as Ainger implies, Burke would certainly have seen it long ago; so the faults of *The Newspaper* must be attributable to rushed composition and topical haste.

This alters, but fails to solve, the problem; for it is not altogether easy to see what about *The Newspaper* seemed so urgently topical to Crabbe. The poem is a gently satirical account of newspapers and their failings – some of them familiar enough more than two hundred years later – interspersed with typically rueful coded references to his own life. At best, he displays an engaging lightness of touch:

> I sing of NEWS, and all those vapid sheets
> The rattling hawker vends through gaping streets;
> Whate'er their name, whate'er the time they fly,
> Damp from the press, to charm the reader's eye:
> For, soon as morning dawns with roseate hue,
> The Herald of the morn arises too;
> Post after Post succeeds, and, all day long,
> Gazettes and Ledgers swarm, a noisy throng.
> When evening comes, she comes with all her train
> Of Ledgers, Chronicles, and Posts again –
> Like bats, appearing, when the sun goes down,
> From holes obscure and corners of the town. [49–60]

The jauntily arranged list of names anticipates the inn signs of *The Borough*, and there is jauntiness of another sort when Crabbe turns to the Sunday paper, 'the sainted Monitor': 'So Moral Essays on his front appear, / But all is carnal business in the rear.' That surprising innuendo is perhaps unintentional; though equally possibly it is not, especially if we recall the remarkable words which Jane Austen puts into Mary Crawford's mouth in the sixth chapter of *Mansfield Park*: 'Certainly, my home at my uncle's brought me acquainted with a circle of admirals. Of *Rears*, and *Vices*, I saw enough. Now, do not be suspecting me of a pun, I entreat.'

In *The Newspaper*, as in *The Library*, Crabbe comments on his own immediate concerns within what at first appears to be a generalised satirical context. One notable instance comes in the paragraph beginning at line 169, where he turns his attention to the rural scene. Even in the village, he says, newspapers spread their dull-brained party allegiances, often in a topsy-turvy way, to 'the Whig-farmer and the Tory-swain': 'Hither, with all a patriot's care, comes he / Who owns the little hut that makes him free.' But this freedom-enhancing hut at once recalls a very different poem, the wryly melancholic little piece of doggerel which the biographer son quotes as exemplifying his father's disenchantment with Belvoir:

> Oh! had I but a little hut,
>   That I might hide my head in;
> Where never guest might dare molest
>   Unwelcome or unbidden.
> I'd take the jokes of other folks,
>   And mine should then succeed 'em,
> Nor would I chide a little pride,
>   Or heed a little freedom.[38]

On the other hand, preserving a balance both politic and scrupulous, he scolds his freeholder who, 'with a muddled mind', joins in the vulgar cry 'That all the courtly race / Are venal candidates for power and place'.

In the latter part of the poem, Crabbe gently mocks three aspects of his own past, beginning with his relatively recent enthusiasm for the theatre. The stage is not to be confused with reality, nor is it (for the concept had not become clearly defined in eighteenth-century taste) 'high art':

> Thither from real life the many run,
> With Siddons weep, or laugh with Abingdon;

Pleased, in fictitious joy or grief, to see
The mimic passion with their own agree;
To steal a few enchanted hours away
From care, and drop the curtain on the day. [339–44]

The modern vernacular 'real life' is momentarily startling; evidently, Crabbe's genuine enjoyment of the theatre was, perhaps disconcertingly for his later readers, very like that of the businessman who goes to a play after a busy day at the office. No sooner has he done with the stage than he turns to 'PUFFS and all the puffing race', taking as his example a character well known to him:

The simple barber, once an honest name –
Cervantes founded, Fielding raised his fame –
Barber no more, a gay perfumer comes,
On whose soft cheek his own cosmetic blooms;
Here he appears, each simple mind to move,
And advertises beauty, grace, and love. [361–6]

Here, and in the florid speech by the barber, full of extravagant claims on behalf of his art's transforming powers, which follows, Crabbe plainly recollects his London landlord, Mr Vickery; perhaps this is his delayed revenge on the man who sold him that unaffordable and unfashionable wig. Finally, he settles an even older score:

Last in these ranks and least, their art's disgrace,
Neglected stand the Muse's meanest race:
Scribblers who court contempt, whose verse the eye
Disdainful views, and glances swiftly by:
This Poet's Corner is the place they choose,
A fatal nursery for an infant Muse;
Unlike that corner where true poets lie,
These cannot live, and they shall never die;
Hapless the lad whose mind such dreams invade,
And win to verse the talents due to trade. [431–40]

Crabbe himself had been just such a hapless lad in his own earliest publications; moreover, his literary ambitions had originally been formed by the indifferent verse which his father had read to him from the 'Poet's Corner' in his magazines and which Crabbe as a child had cut out to keep.

Contemporary reviews of *The Newspaper* damned it with faint or at any rate qualified praise. The *Critical Review* of April 1785, in the bafflingly self-contradictory manner of the time, thought it 'a work of genius' and 'in the first class of modern productions', but it was not 'so highly finished as *The Village*' and 'we do not perceive that force and spirit in the present poem which is in general deemed essential to compositions of this kind'.[39] In his unsigned notice for the *Monthly Review* of November 1785, Charles Burney also had reservations but more astutely, or more kindly, ended by comparing *The Newspaper* to *The Library* rather than to *The Village*: 'But still the poem has uncommon merit, and sufficiently evinces, if it were possible to doubt it, after reading *The Library*, that the Author is possessed of genius, taste, and imagination.'[40] Although *The Newspaper* is no masterpiece, it is a more interesting and engaging poem than most of its readers admit.

7

In the summer of 1785, armed with the Duke's generous insistence that they must return to Belvoir Castle if their new home should prove at all unhealthy, George and Sarah Crabbe moved to the house adjacent to the parish church of St Guthlac at Stathern: the son rather disparagingly describes it as 'this obscure parsonage', but Evans, who lived nearby and provided a photograph as irrefutable evidence, calls it 'the large and lofty double-fronted Rectory'.[41] The four years they were to spend there would be, Crabbe told his son, 'on the whole, the very happiest in his life'.[42] It is not hard to see why. This homeliest of men, whose attachment to his domestic life approached that of Jane Austen's Mr Woodhouse, had for the first time a home he could properly call his own and – what was hardly less satisfying – a garden he could cultivate. In November 1785 his son and future biographer, George, was born, followed in October 1787 by John and in January 1789 by Sarah Susannah; both the boys would grow up to become clergymen. Meanwhile, Crabbe found himself, as he would throughout his years in rural parishes, frequently called upon to practise his abandoned vocation, attending sick-beds in the mildly paradoxical capacity of physician and priest: his parishioner-patients must have reflected with grim humour that, if the medical Mr Crabbe were to prove ineffective, the spiritual Mr Crabbe might usefully take over.

Although he liked to make the most of his influential connections, Crabbe never acquired the black art of courting general popularity. The Reverend J. W. Taylor, who became Rector of Stathern in 1866, told Canon Ainger that Crabbe was remembered in the village for speaking 'through his nose' (presumably with a residual Suffolk accent, though that isn't especially nasal) and for being 'peppery of temper': 'an exceedingly youthful couple having presented themselves for holy matrimony, Crabbe drove them with scorn from the altar with the remark that he had come there to marry "men and women, and not lads and lasses".'[43] That tale has probably improved in the telling, though it is true enough to his character: his robust common sense was seldom mitigated by tact, and straightforward people usually appreciated his straightforwardness. His son notes that 'in accordance with the usual habits of the clergy then resident in the vale of Belvoir', he reluctantly donned a velveteen jacket and made a further unsuccessful attempt at hunting; and, 'as to coursing, the cry of the first hare he saw killed, struck him as so like the wail of an infant, that he turned heart-sick from the spot'.[44] His steadily deepening interest in the country was to be that not of the sportsman but of the naturalist.

On 3 June 1786, Crabbe's father died at Aldeburgh. If there was anything to inherit, it went to his second wife and the numerous children she had brought with her to his modest house. Crabbe, who had refused to have anything to do with him since his remarriage, put on a passable show of indifference; yet that complex and troubled relationship was not to be so easily discarded. Later in the same year, on 2 October 1786, his sister Mary, the Ipswich milliner, married Thomas Sparkes, the Aldeburgh builder. With his parents dead, his sister married, one brother settled in Southwold, the other two at sea, he had every reason to feel grateful for his home, his wife, his children. There is no reason to doubt the essential accuracy of his son's earliest memories:

> My first recollection of him is of his carrying me up to his private room for prayers, in the summer evenings, about sunset, and rewarding my silence and attention afterwards with a view of the

flower-garden through his prism. Then I recall the delight it was to me to be permitted to sleep with him during a confinement of my mother's; how I longed for the morning, because he would be sure to tell me some fairy tale, of his own invention, all sparkling with gold and diamonds, magic fountains and enchanted princesses. In the eye of memory I can still see him as he was sat that period of his life, his fatherly countenance, unmixed with any of the less loveable expressions that, in too many faces, obscure that character – but pre-eminently *fatherly*; conveying the ideas of kindness, intellect, and purity; his manner grave, manly, and cheerful, in unison with his high and open forehead: his very attitudes, whether as he sat absorbed in the arrangement of his minerals, shells, and insects – or as he laboured in his garden until his naturally pale complexion acquired a tinge of fresh healthy red; or as, coming lightly towards us with some unexpected present, his smile of indescribable benevolence spoke exultation in the foretaste of our raptures.[45]

Obviously, this is a conflation of memories, not all of which need refer to Stathern; but if they are indeed his 'first' recollections, then most of them surely do – his mother's confinement is presumably that which preceded the birth of his sister, Sarah Susannah, in young George's fourth year.

Yet, while it may look as if Crabbe had simply exchanged the role of ducal chaplain for that of parish priest (and devoted family man), this was by no means the case: Belvoir Castle and the Manners family were to remain more pressing concerns during these years than he could possibly have foreseen. First of all, there was the continuing matter of the Duke's late brother, Lord Robert Manners: apart from the elegy in the second book of *The Village*, Crabbe had also written an obituary article on 'Lord Robert Manners, late Commander of his Majesty's Ship the Resolution, of 74 Guns' for Dodsley's *Annual Register*. It is clear from Crabbe's letter of 29 September 1785 that the Duke wished to add his own recollections but was frustrated by the fact that 'the pages . . . were all laid out, though so long before publishing, in such a manner that [Dodsley] finds it impossible to alter them or to make any addition'. There might be room in a future number, Crabbe hopefully adds, before assuring the Duke that 'I shall think myself happy if I can be instrumental in setting forth such an example and portraying such a character as that of Lord Robert Manners'.[46] One way in which he made himself 'instrumental' was in taking charge of the inscriptions for Lord Robert Manners' tomb at the family burial place, the parish church of St Mary the Virgin, Bottesford. Given the necessity of consulting the Duke in Dublin about every detail, this turned out to be a surprisingly lengthy and tiresome task.

But there was a far more devastating blow in store for the Manners family. On 24 October 1787, after returning to Dublin from a tour round Ireland, the Duke became ill with a sudden fever and died almost immediately: he was thirty-three years old and had lived – it seems generally agreed – not wisely but too well. For Crabbe, it was the loss not merely of a valued and necessary patron but of a friend and contemporary: a kind of shock he had experienced on only one previous occasion, when William Levett died in 1774. The Duke was buried at Bottesford on 25 November 1787, after which the mourners returned to the chapel at Belvoir Castle to hear Crabbe preach a restrained, dignified memorial sermon, for which he took as his text a verse from St Paul's second epistle to the Corinthians: 'But we had the sentence of death in ourselves, that we should not trust in ourselves, but in God which raiseth the dead' (2 Corinthians, 1: 9). Even allowing for the mortality rate of the late eighteenth century, the Manners family had been exceptionally unlucky. 'It is most remarkable,' said Crabbe,

> that one family should afford three individuals so eminently distin-
> guished in so short a period, and those a father and his two sons, a
> father venerated and almost adored for his humanity and courage,
> and celebrated through Europe for his honour and military achieve-
> ments . . . Of his sons, one endowed with every amiable virtue, talent,
> and accomplishment fell at an early period in the moment of an
> important victory which gave life and peace to his nation, death and
> glory to him. His noble brother a few years survived him, arriving at
> the highest honours which a subject can enjoy in one kingdom, and
> being sovereign in another, where he filled the most exalted station in
> the most critical period with firmness and dignity; and after raising
> expectation by his virtues and exceeding hope in his success, he died
> at an age when even mong the eminent of mankind talents only begin
> their promise and our applause, awaiting the decision of time . . .

The Duchess, greatly moved by this address, asked Crabbe to arrange for its publication: 'I am desired by the Duchess of Rutland to print a discourse which I read at Belvoir Chapel at the funeral of the late Duke,' he told Dodsley on 17 January 1788. However, Dodsley was in the process of withdrawing from business, and Crabbe was in some confusion about how to proceed:

> The sermon I am now to print is very short: about 100 copies will be wanted for the Duchess, partly in town and part to be sent to Belvoir Castle directed to me: how many more ought to be printed for sale, together with the manner of their being printed (for I could wish it to be the best, with respect to paper and types) I am at a loss, not having you for my director: but if you will write and inform me what you think a proper number and who I am to apply to, with what other advice may occur to you on the occasion, I will consider it as a particular obligation.[47]

This is a frankly panicky letter. Crabbe was evidently one of those authors whose understanding of printing and publishing is minimal; in the circumstances, it may seem odd that he, rather than a private secretary, should have been entrusted with such practicalities, but the Duchess must have thought that, given his previous dealings with Dodsley, he would be the very man. It is also worth noting that the letter is addressed from Belvoir Castle, where he clearly retained an office, as is the dedicatory epistle (dated 31 January 1788) to *A Discourse on II Corinthians, 1.9., read in the chapel at Belvoir Castle after the funeral of the Duke of Rutland*, which Dodsley, making the best of Crabbe's muddled instructions, duly published.

Crabbe's Stathern curacy was, of course, a stop-gap: his principal livings remained in Dorset, and he had been relying on the Duke's influence to persuade Thurlow to exchange them for something more lucrative and more conveniently situated. In his letter of 29 September 1785, he had complained, as vigorously as he decently could, that

> Lord Thurlow keeps me yet in suspense, neither giving me the living I applied for in exchange to any other, nor giving me any reason to hope for it . . . he will certainly consent, whenever it

becomes absolutely necessary, to my exchanging with some person in your Grace's neighbourhood. Should you, my Lord, hear from the Chancellor on this subject, I will be much indebted to you for the information, as this suspense, besides the pain of it, is a real hindrance to me . . .

The Duke's death might have put an end to this source of influence; however, the Duchess, who remained keen to do her best for Crabbe, provided him with a letter to present to the Lord Chancellor, in which she supported the proposed exchange of livings. But in Thurlow, Crabbe (as he might already have surmised) had met his match for hot-tempered obstinacy:

'No,' he growled; 'by G—d, I will not do this for any man in England.' But he did it, nevertheless, for a woman in England. The good Duchess, on arriving in town, waited on him personally, to renew her request; and he yielded. My father, having passed the necessary examination at Lambeth, received a dispensation from the Archbishop, and became rector of Muston, in Leicestershire, and the neighbourhood parish of Allington, in Lincolnshire.[48]

The 'dispensation from the Archbishop' and the 'examination at Lambeth' may need some explanation. Crabbe's unconventional education, and in particular his lack of a university degree, remained a bar to his preferment. One attempt had already been made to overcome this: in March 1783, when he was granted his Dorset livings, 'the Bishop of Llandaff (Dr Watson) very kindly entered his name on the boards of Trinity College, Cambridge, that he might have the privilege of a degree, after a certain number of terms, and without residence'.[49] The trouble was that the 'certain number of terms' added up to ten years.

On 9 January 1789 Crabbe was presented with the livings of Muston and West Allington, which with a combined income of about £270 per year were worth £80 more than Evershot and Frome St Quintin. He had then to receive a dispensation from the Archbishop of Canterbury, enabling him to hold both livings at the same time; but for this he needed in turn to possess the university degree which he was not due to obtain for another four years – formalities which had hitherto been overlooked, either because the Dorset livings had seemed distant and insignificant or because he was not actually going to reside there, whereas a resident incumbent could hardly get away with lacking the proper credentials. The Church of England's wonderfully pragmatic solution to this sort of clerical quandary was called a 'Lambeth Degree': it merely required the candidate to turn up and sit a single examination, held at Lambeth Palace, for the ecclesiastical degree of MA or LLB. Crabbe presented himself for this mildly absurd procedure the very next day. Even Huchon, who is not easily amused, seems tickled by it:

> At the appointed day and hour Crabbe complied with the summons of the Archbishop's chaplain, was waited on by a servant, who brought him pens, ink, and paper, as well as a dictionary, and was invited to discuss in his best Latin a subject of the following kind: *Aevum quo advenit Jesus, unde constet esse commodissimum*. Two hours were allowed him for the composition of his thesis. When it was finished, the chaplain reappeared, declared himself satisfied, and on January 10th 1789, the author of *The Village* was granted the ecclesiastical degree of Bachelor of Laws.[50]

This comical little ritual was made all the more ludicrous by the fact that Crabbe, as we shall see later, remained far from proficient in Latin. But that was hardly the point of the exercise.

And so, at the age of thirty-four, George Crabbe at last became a graduate and a rector in his own parish. He would, of course, continue to be connected with Belvoir Castle, but his earlier intimacy there was over. Not only was the fourth Duke, his patron Charles Manners, dead; his friend Robert Thoroton, who had accompanied the Duke to Ireland, burdened by financial troubles and ill health, committed suicide. Crabbe's friendship with the dowager Duchess, Lady Mary Isabella, remained undiminished; but her influence at Belvoir inevitably began to decline as her eldest son grew up, and most of her later life was to be divided between Cheveley and Sackville Street, London, where she died in 1831. As for the son – John Henry Manners, who in 1787 would succeed to the title as the fifth Duke of Rutland – he at this time was an eleven-year-old boy whom the chaplain had once had to scold for swearing. His relationship with Crabbe was never to be an easy one.

Five

The Botanical Gardener
1789–1796

I

'It was on the 25th of February, 1789,' says the biographer son, 'that Mr Crabbe left Stathern, and brought his family to the parsonage at Muston.'[1] The move, though complicated by the presence of two young sons and a month-old daughter, was by no means a distant one. It simply involved the partial circumnavigation of the Belvoir estate, from a south-westerly point to a northerly one: the Crabbes remained, in a perfectly literal sense, very much within its orbit. At Muston, a Gothic archway cut in the thick hedge of the rectory garden framed a view of the castle. And so, in that revolutionary year, Crabbe seems to be burrowing ever more deeply into rural England, paying little attention to what was happening in France or even in London. It looks like an evasion, but in truth he was making the best of the hand he had been dealt: if the late Duke's career had turned out differently, Crabbe might have found himself not in a Leicestershire parsonage but close to the heart of English politics.

Accounts of Crabbe's life often tend to accelerate briskly at this point, as if his middle years – at least until he began to publish poetry again in 1807 – were of no particular interest. But they are, on the contrary, remarkable and complicated years; their intertwined strands shaped the rest of his life and profoundly affected the poetry and prose which he continued to write, and sometimes to destroy, during them. One of the most significant of these strands had begun in an encounter which took place while he was still at Belvoir and which would prove, in its quieter way, as momentous for Crabbe as his meetings with Edmund Burke or Charles Manners. It was with Edmund Cartwright, the Rector of Goadby Marwood, a parish adjacent to Stathern.

Cartwright was eleven years older than Crabbe. Born in April 1743, he was educated at Wakefield Grammar School and University College, Oxford, where he gained his BA in 1764 – becoming in the same year a Fellow of Magdalen – and his MA in 1766. He published *Armine and Elvira*, 'a legendary poem', in 1772 and continued at intervals to produce poetry of no very great distinction. He was appointed Rector of Goadby Marwood in 1779 and there became both a farming parson, conducting agricultural experiments on his glebe land, and a literary one, contributing to the *Monthly Review*. In 1786, he was made Prebendary of Lincoln, a position which he held for the rest of his life. But Cartwright's main claim to historical importance, though it is a disputed one, lies elsewhere.

In 1784, while on holiday at Matlock, he became interested in Richard Arkwright's cotton-spinning mills at nearby Cromford. On his return to Goadby Marwood, he constructed a prototype of the power loom, which he patented on 4 April 1785; later the same year, with apparently reckless confidence, he established a factory in Doncaster, where he could put his invention into practice on an industrial scale. Some four years after this, the factory was converted to steam power – a development which, together with his wool-combing machine of 1790, provoked violent opposition. Cartwright seems not to have profited financially from his innovations, but in 1809 Parliament awarded him £10,000 and he retired to a farm in the Weald of Kent. He remained a farmer – and an inventor – until his death in 1823.

The coincidental proximity of these two literary-scientific clergyman is pleasing though not especially remarkable. What is astonishing is that Cartwright had already been Crabbe's most perceptive early critic at a time when neither man could possibly have heard of the other. Cartwright's *Monthly Review* notices of *The Candidate* in September 1780 and of *The Library* in December 1781 both comfortably pre-date the time when there was any thought of Crabbe becoming a ducal chaplain; by the time his notice of *The Village* appeared (*Monthly Review*, November 1783), Crabbe was well established at Belvoir, although it may well have been written before the two men met. It seems likely that Cartwright initiated a meeting some time during 1783: as a local incumbent, though not always a resident one, he would have known the name of the Duke's new chaplain before the chaplain had found his way round the neighbouring parishes. Evidently, the two men were well acquainted with each other by the time Crabbe preached at Goadby Marwood in January 1785.

René Huchon remarks on the 'peculiar interest of seeing the poet of "rural England" thus coming into casual contact with one of the initiators of that "industrial revolution" which, although Crabbe could not foresee it, was soon to transform the aspect of the country and give the towns a preponderance over the rural districts'.[2] Huchon is perfectly correct, though it is equally noteworthy – and so improbable that some have found it hard to credit – that the power loom should have been invented by a parson in his rural rectory. Crabbe, however, is a more than decently level-headed witness: we know that he and his wife visited Cartwright's Doncaster premises in the summer of 1787, and that when Mrs Crabbe 'entered the vast building, full of engines thundering with resistless power, yet under the apparent management of children, the bare idea of the inevitable hazard attendant on such stupendous undertakings, quite overcame her feelings, and she burst into tears'.[3] Her husband, we may safely assume, looked on with his usual calm, fearless interest. This little incident points both backwards and forwards: it recalls their respective reactions to the meteors of August 1783, and it anticipates the world of emotional extremes which Sarah would subsequently inhabit.

The friendship between the two men was a relaxed and convivial one. In August 1789, Crabbe asked either Cartwright or his son to find him 'a greyhound fit for coursing this season, one of moderate abilities, which will occasionally kill a hare at Muston':[4] he had clearly decided to have another stab at pretending to be a sporting parson. Two months later, Cartwright unexpectedly provided him with a dog called Torrent. 'Your letter and your dog surprised me much when I returned from Allington on Sunday last,' wrote Crabbe. 'I have heard of those who have parted with their horses and hounds before and we have known those who will lend their money, but a favourite greyhound, I thought, never was consigned to any man upon any conditions: poor Torrent!'[5] Towards the end of the letter, however, he reported that poor Torrent was becoming 'reconciled to his situation'; Crabbe had found the dog a hare, which he promptly lost, to his new master's evident relief. 'I believe I shall not be a true courser,' he added, unnecessarily. He had, however, decided 'to ruin myself by farming. I have bought beasts and sheep and seed corn: I have gotten thirty or forty ton of hay, a barn of oats and a stack of beans.' His easy, amused and self-deprecating tone is almost as striking as the enterprise itself.

Cartwright's son, born in 1774 and also named Edmund, was at Balliol College, Oxford, when Crabbe wrote to him on 29 February 1790 with a gracious and charming request:

> I congratulate you on both your studies and friendships at Oxford and only beg that the latter may not totally expel your former partialities for us in Leicestershire, though we admit we must give place.
>
> When Mr Cartwright called, Mrs Crabbe was indisposed: she is now recovered and joins with me in requesting that you would do our little boy the honour of being his godfather. We have named him Edmund and will defer the remaining part of the ceremony till it may suit you to be present; but should even that be inconvenient, we will get a proxy for you. At any rate we must engage you.[6]

Besides being godfather to Edmund Crabbe – who had been baptised on 25 January 1790 and who was actually named, though Crabbe tactfully omitted to mention it, after Edmund Burke – the younger Edmund Cartwright was a keen botanist. Botany had, of course, been one of Crabbe's earliest and most enduring passions: an interest, formed on the coastal heaths and developed in the river valleys of Suffolk, which he had already utilised to impressive effect in *The Village*. During the years that followed, a highly detailed correspondence would take place, conducted on Crabbe's part in a spirit of delightfully respectful equality, between the botanical parson and his young friend, an exchange not only of letters but of seeds and plants.

Meanwhile, Crabbe had also been pursuing his related interests in local and natural history. The printer and publisher John Nichols was keen to have his assistance in producing *The History and Antiquities of Leicestershire*, an enormous undertaking which was to be published by subscription between 1795 and 1815: on 22 August 1789 Crabbe offered Nichols 'the best local history I can' for the parishes of Knipton, Granby, Harby, Stathern, Croxton, Brandiston, Easton, Eastwell, Goadby Marwood and Waltham on the Wolds, and requested 'a clue of what I should enquire and search after relative to Belvoir Castle'.[7] In fact, his essay on 'The Natural History of the Vale of Belvoir' first appeared in *Bibliotheca Topographica Britannica*, published by Nichols as early as 1790; his account of the castle itself was to take a little longer. With his growing family, his two parishes, his farming, his botany and his natural history, Crabbe must at last have seemed to be putting down the sturdiest of roots in the Vale of Belvoir.

2

One fine summer day in 1787, Crabbe was seized 'with so intense a longing to see the sea, from which he had never before been so long absent, that he mounted his horse, rode alone to the coast of Lincolnshire, sixty miles from his house, dipped in the waves that washed the beach of Aldborough, and returned to Stathern'.[8] That is an engaging and wholly authentic-sounding picture. It is also the portrait of a man who was homesick.

Following his father's death in June 1786 and his sister's return to Aldeburgh that October, Crabbe knew that he could once again revisit his home town: the coast was clear. During the next three years, he made several brief trips to Suffolk, but his first extended return visit – and the first on which he was accompanied by his wife and eldest child – was from mid-September until early November 1790. He wrote to John Nichols on 7 September, expecting to be away for 'about five weeks', during which time he could be reached 'at Aldborough, near Saxmundham, Suffolk', the home of his sister, Mrs Sparkes: it is interesting – a mark of tactful caution or nostalgic habit – that he should have given Aldeburgh as his contact address instead of Parham, which was to be the Crabbes' primary destination and their main base during their stay. For young George, who would be five years old in November, it was his first memorable adventure, and it is the subject of those wonderful pages in the *Life* where biography begins to mesh with autobiography:

Never can I forget my first excursion into Suffolk, in company with my parents. It was in the month of September, 1790 . . . that, dressed in my first suit of boy's clothes (and that scarlet), in the height of a delicious season, I was mounted beside them in their huge old gig, and visited the scenes and persons familiar to me, from my earliest nursery days, in their conversation and anecdotes. Sometimes, as we proceeded, my father read aloud; sometimes he left us for a while to botanise among the hedgerows, and returned with some unsightly weed or bunch of moss, to him precious. Then, in the evening, when we had reached our inn, the happy child, instead of being sent early as usual to bed, was permitted to stretch himself on the carpet, while the reading was resumed, blending with sounds which, from novelty, appeared delightful – the buzzing of the bar, the rattling of wheels, the horn of the mail-coach, the gay glamour of the streets – everything to excite and astonish, in the midst of safety and repose. My father's countenance at such moments is still before me; with what gentle sympathy did he seem to enjoy the happiness of childhood![9]

When he wrote the *Life* – and he began it before his father's death – the younger George Crabbe was a middle-aged clergyman as well as a properly respectful son: we expect both forms of piety to colour his account, as often they do. Consequently, his candour and humour here are all the more admirable. The glimpse of the botanist with his unsightly but precious weed is as delightfully convincing as that of the indefatigable reader-aloud. Yet the euphoria of this carefully written passage is subtly qualified by one word, 'seem', with its unobtrusive acknowledgement that Crabbe was more emotionally complicated than he allowed himself to appear to his children.

The biographer son's description of life at Ducking Hall, Parham, as he found it in the autumn of 1790, is doubly interesting: it is the essential prelude to his father's later troubled relationship with the place and it is also an authoritative account of a style of rural existence which was then already in decline. As such, it has often been quoted; but, since the *Life* is (at the time of writing) not in print, it may be worth including some fairly extensive quotation here. The first point to notice is that the admirable Mr Tovell, who combines an inadequate commercial education with hearty good manners, proves to be a closer spiritual kinsman for Crabbe than one might have supposed:

On the third day we reached Parham, and I was introduced to a set of manners and customs, of which there remains, perhaps, no counterpart in the present day. My great-uncle's establishment was that of the first-rate yeoman of the period – the Yeoman that already began to be styled by courtesy an Esquire. Mr Tovell might possess an estate of some eight hundred pounds per annum, a portion of which he himself cultivated. Educated at a mercantile school, he often said of himself, 'Jack will never make a gentleman'; yet he had a native dignity of mind and of manners, which might have enabled him to pass muster in that character with any but very fastidious critics. His house was large, and the surrounding moat, the rookery, the ancient dovecot, and the well-stored fishponds, were such as might have suited a gentleman's seat of some consequence; but one side of the house immediately overlooked a farm-yard, full of all sorts of domestic animals, and the scene of constant bustle and noise. On entering the house, there was nothing at first sight to remind one of the farm: a spacious hall, paved with black and white marble – at one extremity, a very handsome drawing-room, and at the other a fine old staircase of black oak, polished till it was as slippery as ice, and having a chime-clock and a barrel-organ on its landing-places. But this drawing-room, a corresponding dining parlour, and a handsome sleeping apartment up stairs, were all *tabooed* ground, and made use of on great and solemn occasions only – such as rent days, and an occasional visit with which Mr Tovell was honoured by a neighbouring peer. At all other times the family and their visiters lived entirely in the old-fashioned kitchen along with the servants. My great-uncle occupied an arm-chair, or, in attacks of gout, a couch on one side of a large open chimney. Mrs Tovell sat at a small table, on which, in the evening, stood one small candle, in an iron candlestick, plying her needle by the feeble glimmer, surrounded by her maids, all busy at the same employment; but in winter a noble block of wood, sometimes the whole circumference of a pollard, threw its comfortable warmth and cheerful blaze over the apartment.

At a very early hour in the morning, the alarum called the maids, and their mistress also; and if the former were tardy, a louder alarum, and more formidable, was heard chiding the delay – not that scolding was peculiar to any occasion, it regularly ran on through all the day, like bells on harness, in spiriting the work, whether it were done ill or well. After the important business of the dairy, and a hasty breakfast, their respective employments were again resumed; that which the mistress took for her especial privilege being the scrubbing of the floors of the state apartments.

A new servant, ignorant of her presumption, was found one morning on her knees, hard at work on the floor of one of these preserves, and was thus addressed by her mistress: '*You* wash such floors as these? Give me the brush this instant, and troop to the scullery and wash that, madam! . . . As true as G—d's in heaven, here comes Lord Rochford, to call on Mr Tovell. – Here, take my mantle (a blue woollen apron), and I'll go to the door!'

If the sacred apartments had not been opened, the family dined on this wise: the heads seated in the kitchen at an old table; the farm-men standing in the adjoining scullery, door open – the female servants at a side table, called a *bouter*; with the principals, at the table, perchance some travelling rat-catcher, or tinker, or farrier, or an occasional gardener in his shirt-sleeves, his face probably streaming with perspiration.[10]

The biographer son permits himself a good deal of amusement at these domestic arrangements, which might have belonged to a relative of Fielding's Squire Western. He is particularly tickled by the picture of a mistress of the house who scrubs the floors of her own best rooms and is outraged by the impudence of a housemaid who dares to undertake the task. He finds this and much else quaintly anachronistic, not because he is wealthier than the Tovells (he is not), but partly because he is better educated and partly because times and tastes have changed. This is worth emphasising because he is at this point out of sympathy with his father. For even though this was a style of life which Crabbe, with his hard-won and sometimes rather frigid dignity, could never emulate, its egalitarian rough-and-tumble was a quality he had known and understood since his youth and could still intermittently envy; and that feeling for human warmth was to surface, more often than is usually acknowledged, in his later poems.

The after-dinner scene at Ducking Hall was, from the son's retrospective point of view, still more comical:

On ordinary days, when the dinner was over, the fire replenished, the kitchen sanded and lightly swept over in waves, mistress and maids, taking off their shoes, retired to their chambers for a nap of one hour to the minute. The dogs and cats commenced their siesta by the fire. Mr Tovell dozed in his chair, and no noise was heard, except the melancholy and monotonous cooing of a turtle-dove, varied, however, by the shrill treble of a canary. After the hour had expired, the active part of the family were on the alert, the bottles (Mr Tovell's tea equipage) placed on the table; and as if by instinct, some old acquaintance would glide in for the evening's carousal, and then another, and another. If four or five arrived, the punch-bowl was taken down, and emptied and filled again. But, whoever came, it was comparatively a dull evening, unless two especial Knights Companions were of the party – one was a jolly old farmer, with much of the person and humour of Falstaff, a face as rosy as brandy could make it, and an eye teeming with subdued merriment; for he had that prime quality of a joker, superficial gravity – the other was a relative of the family, a wealthy yeoman, middle-aged, thin, and muscular. He was a bachelor, and famed for his indis-criminate attachment to all who bore the name of woman – young or aged, clean or dirty, a lady or a gipsy. He had peopled the village green; and it was remarked that, whoever was the mother, the children might be recognised in an instant to belong to him. Such was the strength of his constitution, that, though he seldom went to bed sober, he retained a clear eye and stentorian voice to his eightieth year, and coursed when he was ninety. He sometimes rendered the colloquies over the bowl peculiarly piquant; and so soon as his voice began to be elevated, one or two of the inmates, my father and mother for example, withdrew with Mrs Tovell into her own *sanctum sanctorum*; but I, not being supposed capable of understanding much of what might be said, was allowed to linger on the skirts of the festive circle; and the servants, being considered much in the same point of view as the animals dozing on the hearth, remained, to have full benefit of their wit, neither producing the slightest restraint, nor feeling it themselves.[II]

That this is a splendid description, vigorous and good-humoured, goes without saying; yet it is not, as it were, good-humoured all the way through. The note of disapproval, though subdued, is acidic: in the paragraph which follows, as he takes his leave of Parham, the son will describe its inhabitants as 'this primitive set'. Unlike his father – and despite his father's delicately withdrawing with Mrs Crabbe as soon as the company threatened to become bawdy – the biographer son is actually a bit of a prig; and that is less a criticism of him than another instance of a way in which, by the time he came to write the *Life*, times had changed.

The Crabbes spent several weeks at Ducking Hall before moving on to visit Thomas and Mary Sparkes at Aldeburgh. Young George, who had never previously been to the coast, was to remember 'my father watching the effect of the first view of the sea on my countenance, the tempered joyfulness of his manner when he carried me in his arms to the verge of the rippling waves, and the nameless delight with which I first inhaled the odours of the beach'.[12] The wary reader will once again note the qualification of Crabbe's pleasure, in 'tempered joyfulness'; the son quite reasonably adds that his father's happiness would have been 'unmingled . . . had his mother survived to see him as a husband and a father', but there are plenty of other reasons – his unhappy experiences there as child, warehouseman, surgeon, curate – for his feelings about his home town to have remained deeply ambivalent.

Next, they went on to Mrs Elmy at Beccles – which 'seemed a paradise, as we visited from house to house with our kind relations' – and thence to Normanston, where before her marriage Sarah had spent much time in the company of (as Crabbe called them) 'the ladies of the lake':

Here four or five spinsters of independent fortune had formed a sort of Protestant nunnery, the abbess being Miss Blacknell, who after-wards deserted it to become the wife of the late Admiral Sir Thomas Graves, a lady of distinguished elegance in her tastes and manners. Another of the sisterhood was Miss Waldron, late of Tamworth – dear, good-humoured, hearty, masculine Miss Waldron, who could sing a jovial song like a fox-hunter, and like him, I almost said, toss a glass; and yet there was such an air of high *ton*, and such intellect mingled with these manners, that the perfect lady was not veiled for a moment – no, not when, with a face rosy red, and an eye beaming with mirth, she would seize a cup and sing 'Toby Fillpot', glorifying as it were in her own jollity. When we took our morning rides, she generally drove my father in her phaeton, and interested him exceedingly by her strong understanding and conversational powers.[13]

Miss Waldron certainly seems to have been a vivid example of a recognisable type: today she might have presented a television series on cookery or country life. She had already exerted a considerable influence on Sarah and, through her, on George: their second surviving son, who was now three years old, had been named John Waldron Crabbe in her honour. Nor was she the only remarkable character the Crabbes encountered during their sojourn at Normanston, for on one of several visits to nearby Lowestoft they entered the Methodist chapel to hear John Wesley preach: he was eighty-seven years old and had, unsurprisingly, to be 'attended, almost supported in the pulpit, by a young minister on each side'. Crabbe, whose later quarrel with Methodism was to be on characteristically pragmatic rather than on theological grounds, had always admired Wesley; at Lowestoft, he was 'much struck by his reverent appearance and his cheerful air . . . and, after the service, introduced himself to the patriarch, who received him with benevolent politeness'.[14] Unlike his wife and son, he could fully relish the ironic satisfaction of this moment: having been seen listening to Wesley in London had done real harm to his reputation as curate at Aldeburgh. The very fact that he could now chat with Wesley and shake him by the hand was a quietly triumphant assertion of the confidence he had subsequently acquired.

During their East Anglian autumn of 1790, George and Sarah must surely have considered the possibility of settling once more in Suffolk if the opportunity should arise. For Sarah, especially, such a move may have already begun to seem a compelling need; and the fact that little George was delighted with everything he saw would have been another persuasive factor. However, little George, in his grown-up embodiment as the biographer son, does not at this point record (though he glancingly mentions it later) one very specific event which took place during their stay in Suffolk. He was not actually present, he may have thought it unimportant, or he may have found its importance difficult to deal with. But it was to change his father's life.

3

The main facts are straightforward; or at least they seem to be. One day in the autumn of 1790 Crabbe, who had for many years suffered from attacks of vertigo, staggered and collapsed while walking along a street in Ipswich. He may have left his wife at a nearby inn, as his son suggests, though it seems just as likely that both wife and son had remained at Parham. As he was helped to his feet, one of the passers-by, supposing him to be drunk, said: 'Let the gentleman alone, he will be better by and by.' However, he was taken to the inn which may have contained his wife (although at this point she vanishes from the son's account), where a physician, Dr Clubbe, was sent for. This Dr Clubbe's verdict was unambiguous: 'There is nothing the matter with your head, nor any apoplectic tendency; let the digestive organs bear the whole blame: you must take opiates.' So, for the rest of his days, Crabbe took opium and, says his son, 'to a constant but slightly increasing dose of it may be attributed his long and generally healthy life'.[15] Thanks to the drug, in the years that followed, his personal appearance improved, his countenance acquired 'a new charm' and his 'rather thin and weakly' figure became 'muscular and almost athletic'. It seems not to occur to the son that gardening and long botanical walks may have had something to do with his father's improving condition.

The biographer son's account and interpretation are questionable for two main reasons. One, to which I shall return shortly, is that opium simply did not have the innocently beneficial effect he describes on his father: its impact was to be on the inner rather than the outer man, on his creative work and, possibly, on his family. The other is that this was by no means the first time he had used opium – which was, in itself or its derivative forms such as laudanum, the commonplace tranquilliser and painkiller of the day. William Harrison's 'In Praise of Laudanum' (published in Richard Steele's *Poetical Miscellanies* of 1714) succinctly states the eighteenth century's view of the matter and contains a nominal coincidence which, if he knew the poem, can hardly have failed to impress Crabbe:

I feel, O Laudanum, thy power divine,
And fall with pleasure at thy slumb'ring shrine:
Lulled by thy charms I 'scape each anxious thought,
And everything but Mira is forgot.[16]

One might concoct a heady hypothesis on the basis of these four lines. Perhaps Crabbe's interest in laudanum went back as far as his Woodbridge days – the surgeon's apprentice would certainly have had access to the drug – and chancing on this little poem, which so charmingly vindicated his own use of it, also provided him with the perfect literary name for Sarah Elmy.

This is by no means impossible, especially as the young Crabbe was a voracious reader of earlier poets, from whom he was happy to borrow and to learn; moreover, Steele's influential role in early eighteenth-century English culture had ensured a wide and continuing audience for his *Poetical Miscellanies*, which was just the sort of anthology for an aspiring poet to pick up. But, in any case, it has already been suggested that Crabbe's experience of 'mild opiates', as evidenced by *The Library,* dates back at least to the dreadful London autumn of 1780, exactly ten years before the Ipswich incident. What cannot, of course, be known for certain is whether he continued to use the drug at all regularly during the following decade. My guess – which has the modest merit of fitting the known facts – is that he did so, but that he attempted to give it up, probably at Sarah's urging, either around the time of his marriage to her or on moving to Muston. The dizzying illness from which he had suffered while staying with the Elmys at Beccles in the summer of 1783 and the subsequent attacks of vertigo, which so alarmed his wife that she thought, after his first sermon at Muston in 1789, that 'he would preach very few more', sound remarkably like withdrawal symptoms at times when he might have been unable to obtain opium; and the astute Dr Clubbe either deduced this or was informed of it by Crabbe himself. No wonder his prescription was so confident. Or – outrageously but, again, not impossibly – was this Dr Clubbe, whose ludicrous name so uncannily mirrors his stumbling patient's, a fictional *alter ego* dreamed up by the tale-telling Crabbe to explain his self-prescription? Ipswich, after all, as the county town for both Woodbridge and Aldeburgh, was the very place in which he might have been best remembered as a medical man himself.

In her book *Opium and the Romantic Imagination* (1968), Alethea Hayter accepts that Crabbe's first use of opium was in 1790 and consequently fails to spot the earlier reference to 'opiates' in *The Library* ; she is also necessarily unaware of a then-undiscovered poem, *The Voluntary Insane*, which would (as we shall see later on) have crucially affected her argument. But in every other respect, her treatment of Crabbe's opium addiction is exemplary. Quite early in her book, while describing in fairly general terms different kinds of addiction, she mentions

one class of addicts, not a large one, who when they have discovered the dosage which preserves them from the wretchedness of withdrawal symptoms, will restrict themselves to that amount and continue for many years, perhaps for all the rest of their lives, taking only so much opium and no more. Opium now gives them nothing positive, nothing they would not have had if they had never taken it at all; it simply saves them from the pains of giving it up. They are like diabetics dependent on their regular injections of insulin to keep them in normal health. Addicts of this type can lead conventional responsible lives, and their addiction may not be detected even by their family and friends.[17]

She cites as instances of this sort of addiction William Wilberforce and George Crabbe, and adds that they must possess 'strong and well-balanced characters' in order to maintain so strictly controlled a regime. The puzzle is that strong and well-balanced characters do not become addicted to drugs in the first place.

This is a contradiction which rather hangs in the air until Hayter reaches her chapter on Crabbe; and even then it is not fully resolved, for the contradiction is at the heart of the man. On the one hand, he was gifted with the most robust, frank self-confidence; he was straightforward in manner and speech, and entirely without physical fear in dangerous circumstances. On the other, he was perpetually aware of his social and educational disadvantages, tormented by violent and terrifying dreams and obsessed with insanity. Alethea Hayter concludes that Crabbe, for all his outward appearance of well-balanced strength, 'had two of the predisposing characteristics of the potential addict – curiosity about abnormal states of mind and a certain inadequacy in human relationships'.[18] That interest in mental abnormality will be amply demonstrated in his later writings, but the 'certain inadequacy in human relationships' is of more pressing concern.

It is clear that by this time Crabbe had become a man whom some people – among them, Burke, the late Duke of Rutland and, of course, Mrs Crabbe – liked and admired extravagantly, while others, including many of his parishioners, found him chilly and withdrawn: although he was 'thoughtful, sincere, merciful and brave', as Hayter says, 'he was not always able to have easy relationships with other human beings'.[19] The teasingly ambiguous point about this lack of sympathetic or emotionally engaged interest in other people is that, while it may indeed have been among the

predisposing *causes* of Crabbe's opium addiction, it would certainly also have
been among its *effects*. For opium blunts the feelings at the same time as it
appears to sharpen the perception: the user feels himself to be a highly
sensitive observer but a disengaged one. And if, as seems to be the case,
Crabbe had struck even his Aldeburgh patients and parishioners as
somewhat semi-detached, this may be another sign that he had acquired the
habit either in London or earlier still.

The immediate effect of his commencement or, more likely, resumption
of opium-taking in 1790 on his writing may not have been significant.
Hayter is surely right to insist that the absence of any publication until his
1807 collection cannot be attributed to the drug. We know, in any case, that
'although he for so many years made no fresh appeal to the public voice, he
was all that time busily engaged in composition'.[20] However, even if his
'constant but slightly increasing dose' did not prevent him from writing –
nor from enjoying a busy and energetic life – it was to have a perceptible
effect on what he wrote and what he did with it. Dreams and extreme states
of mind would figure increasingly in his subject-matter; and the great
bonfires of manuscripts, which so entertained his sons during their
childhood, may have resulted in part from another of opium's known effects,
a tendency to lose confidence in one's own work (and in one's ability to form
reliable judgements of it). But those bonfires also had more ordinary causes,
as we shall see.

Finally, at least for the time being, there is the entirely speculative matter
of opium's effect on Crabbe's family. We have, of course, the eloquent and (on
this matter) trustworthy testimony of his son to prove that Crabbe was a
responsible, devoted and tirelessly considerate father and husband. It is
possible that his was one of those rare families, cited by Hayter, in which the
wife and children were unaware of the father's addiction; but it is just as
possible that it was not. It seems to have gone generally unnoticed that, judged
by the medical criteria of the day, the member of the family most likely to be
prescribed opium was not Crabbe himself but his increasingly ill wife; indeed,
the extreme manic-depressive mood swings of her later years might have been
caused rather than cured by the drug. There is, moreover, the question of the
Crabbes' children, only two of whom were to survive into adulthood. Hayter
reminds us that children were routinely dosed with opium derivatives as a cure
for common ailments, and that these medicines had supposedly comforting

names such as Godfrey's Cordial, Dalby's Carminative, McMunn's Elixir, Batley's Sedative Solution and Mother Bailey's Quieting Syrup;[21] she also notes that overdosing children with these 'remedies' frequently had fatal results. We shall never know for certain whether Sarah Crabbe took opium, whether she gave opium-based medicines to her children, or whether the drug contributed to her or their deaths. But the probability – given its widespread use and its steady availability in Crabbe's household – must be that opium played its part.

4

On his return to Muston in November 1790, Crabbe found plenty to occupy him in the interlocking fields of local history, natural history and botany. He had some catching-up to do. Having delivered his essay on 'The Natural History of the Vale of Belvoir', he had in September promised John Nichols 'to do everything in my power towards the Natural History of your intended large work': he was now casting his net more widely and had resolved that he 'ought to go round it [the county of Leicestershire], that is to Ashby de la Zouch and from thence on the Warwickshire side towards Atherstone, then to [Market] Harborough and especially Gumly, where the curious Mr Hanbury planted, and so on to the Rutlandshire border homeward'.[22] Instead of doing any of this, he had taken himself off to Suffolk for two months. Now, he needed to get back to work; and evidently he did so, for he was able to send 'The Present State of Belvoir Castle' off to Nichols on 21 January 1791, together with an assortment of other material. His local research was methodical, well-informed and unimaginative: indeed, it provided him with a welcome refuge from his increasingly turbulent imagination.

This 'curious Mr Hanbury' whom Crabbe mentions – he was William Hanbury (1725–78), the late Rector of Church Langton – was curious in the extent rather than in the nature of his interests. He managed large plantations in his own parish and nearby at Gumly, devoting the profits to charitable work; in 1767 he published *The History of the Rise and Progress of the Charitable Foundations at Church Langton* and in 1773 followed this with the wonderfully titled *Complete Body of Planting and Gardening; containing the Natural History, Culture, and Management of Deciduous and Evergreen Forest Trees, with Practical Directions for Raising and Improving Woods, Nurseries, Seminaries, and Plantations.* Hanbury was plainly a clergyman-naturalist on an unusually grand scale: although his concern was with trees and plants, his enterprise had developed, like Edmund Cartwright's, to a degree which might justly be called 'industrial'. Nearer home and still usefully alive, a more modest version of the clergyman-naturalist was William Mounsey, the curate of Bottesford, who assisted Crabbe in his Vale of Belvoir researches as well as occasionally officiating for him at Muston (the Crabbes, who didn't particularly like him, called him 'Mousey').

These naturalising and botanising Leicestershire clergymen reflect those aspects of the late eighteenth-century intellectual climate which were appropriate to their skills and their situation. In William Hanbury's passion for 'improving' his woodlands, there is an arboreal echo of the landscaping 'improvements' favoured by Lancelot 'Capability' Brown (1715–83) and his successor, Humphrey Repton (1752–1818): this was not a fashion universally admired – Jane Austen was to make it the preoccupation of the vacuous, tastless Mr Rushworth in *Mansfield Park* – and it had no appeal for Crabbe. His sympathies were with the admirable Squire Asgill in *The Borough* – 'He never planted nor inclosed – his trees / Grew like himself, untroubled and at ease' (XVI. 80–81) – and his own more specifically botanical interests mirror those of another eccentric contemporary, Erasmus Darwin (1731–1802). Darwin, though not a clergyman, was like Crabbe a physician; and, though long resident in Samuel Johnson's home town of Lichfield, he had been born a few miles north of Belvoir, at Elston: so on both counts he has some claim to be viewed as a detached cousin of this botanical brotherhood. In *The Botanical Garden*, which was published at exactly this time in two reversed parts (the second, 'The Loves of the Plants', appeared in 1789, and the first, 'The Economy of Vegetation', in 1791), Darwin makes fanciful use of the system devised by Linnaeus. *The Botanical Garden* is a long poem on Crabbe's consuming interest, in his favourite form of heroic couplets, and it appeared near the start of his poetically silent years: it is perfectly possible that he would have written a poem along similar lines, though no doubt with greater literary distinction, in the early 1790s if Darwin had not published his first. Yet that possibility, though it seems superficially attractive, fails to ring true. Crabbe was simply not that sort of poet. In fact, he found Darwin's quaintly anthropomorphic vegetables mildly amusing: he was to include a brief but effective parody of *The Botanical Garden* in the first book of *The Parish Register*. Here we encounter Peter Pratt, who gives his children botanical names, baffles his rustic friends by calling onions and leeks 'Allium', and fully shares Darwin's sense of the emotional life of plants:

> Not Darwin's self had more delight to sing
> Of floral courtship, in th'awaken'd Spring,
> Than Peter Pratt, who, simpering, loves to tell
> How rise the Stamens, as the Pistils swell;
> How bend and curl the moist-top to the spouse,
> And give and take the vegetable vows;
> How those esteem'd of old but tips and chives,
> Are tender husbands and obedient wives;
> Who live and love within the sacred bower –
> That bridal bed the vulgar term a flower. [1. 633–42]

Such amiable digressions apart, Crabbe's poetic interest was increasingly focused on human narrative and the human psyche; meanwhile, he would create a botanical garden of his own and write about it in prose.

Though he now set about this project in earnest, it was not until the summer of 1792 that Crabbe's botanical garden really began to take shape, as his letters to the younger Edmund Cartwright written in an excited, spontaneous style which contrasts markedly with his often ponderous formal prose – indicate. On 5 September, he wrote to Edmund, who was spending the month near Boston in Lincolnshire at the home of his uncle, Major John Cartwright, with some ticklish problems:

> I am much in your debt for the plant you have favoured me with: if it had been unaccompanied with any account, I should have called it, after some hesitation, *Bupleurum tenuissimum*; the specific name 'minimum' I do not find in Linnaeus except among the Synomma. – That it is of the class and order *Pentandria Digynia* is evident, from the fructification and the twin seed and styles. The stamina are withered but no variation in their number could alter the natural situation of the plant, which though not strictly umbellated (any more than the *Caucalis nodosa*) is like that to be placed among the Umbellata. – I was in hope that the seed of this specimen might vegetate but on examination this morning I find it improbable: you

will oblige me therefore by either procuring me a few ripe seed (for the plant is annual I think) or a root that will grow and produce them this year. The *Atriplex pedunculata* I should also be glad to receive: I find the atriplices grow very well in my garden, but are not easily propagated from seed: there is a conveyance from Boston to Grantham by which (if you will not think me too troublesome) I shall be thankful for a root or two of both these plants (particularly the *Bupleurum*) but as I am ignorant what are the days the cart goes from Boston or arrives at Grantham, may I trouble your servant to enquire? And then before the plants are sent off, I will thank you for a line informing me when and at *what inn* they will be left. This is really taking too much of your time, but a new inhabitant for a botanical garden is too great a prize to be sacrificed: you will therefore pardon me. If you be with or near Mr J. Cartwright I will further trouble you for a small root or a few fresh seeds of woad.[23]

Though the excellent young man seems to have been unable instantly to conjure up all Crabbe's requirements, he resolved to do the next best thing, for he added a memorandum to himself on the letter: 'Mem: to send Mr Crabbe the following seeds: *Panicum dactylon, Stipa pennata, Ligusticum cornubisense.*' He made a brave attempt to identify the *Atriplex pendunculata* by sketching it, but Crabbe was not at all convinced by this: 'Your figure,' he wrote, 'I believe is that of some other plant: this Atriplex however has whole leaves obtuse and fasciculate, but I imagine larger than your figure.'[24] He went on to suggest other plants which he would be 'well pleased to have', including '*Statice reticulata*, matted thrift, and the *Artemisia campestris* or *caerulescens*'. But, most of all, he still wanted his Bupleurum.

By 1 October, he had it. He wrote to Cartwright in the most grateful terms: 'I shall try the Bupleurum immediately, having observed that many take in the autumn (the natural time of semination) which fail in the summer following.' And that was not all: 'I am more indebted to you for these and your obliging promises of the Stipa, Ligusticum and Panic Grass than I can express. They are treasures which money cannot purchase, nor diligence acquire: certainly you make me greatly in your debt by favouring me with those seeds and the seeds of any others which our gardeners and the London shops cannot furnish us with.'[25] By now, the botanical garden had become Crabbe's consuming interest, although he found time for a typically affectionate and good-humoured reference to Cartwright's godson: 'Edmund is, I think, of all rude rogues, the rudest.'

Yet perhaps the most interesting and revealing passage in this letter concerns neither his garden nor his family. It reaffirms Crabbe's true roots in the marshland around the River Alde; it is an eloquent riposte to all 'improvers' of the landscape, such as Brown and Repton; and it is as passionately felt as any paragraph in the whole of his writing:

> I envied your wet journey to the boggy ground of Friskney and will remember it, as one of the places I purpose to visit. People speak with raptures of fine prospects, clear skies, lawns, parks and the blended beauties of art and nature, but give me a wild, wide fen, in a foggy day; with quaking boggy ground and trembling hillocks in a putrid soil: shut in by the closeness of the atmosphere, all about is like a new creation and every botanist an Adam who explores and names the creatures he meets with.

5

While Crabbe contentedly sowed his seeds of Bupleurum at Muston, John Tovell lay mortally ill at Ducking Hall, Parham; and, on 6 October 1792, he died. Crabbe, who 'was enclosing a new garden for botanic specimens, and had just completed the walls',[26] hastened to Suffolk for the funeral on 12 October and to carry out out his duties as co-executor with William Shuldham of Tovell's will. This document, though not particularly unusual, might have been expressly designed to create disharmony. John Tovell's widow Jenny was left an annuity of £100 a year and the use of the house, which was inherited jointly by his married sister, Mrs Elmy, and his unmarried sister, Elizabeth; since the Tovells' only child, their daughter Jane, had died in 1778, the title in the property would pass to his niece Sarah and her husband George – who, as joint executor, found himself in the advantageous if invidious position of being both administrator and bene-ficiary. In due course, the property was to be inherited by the biographer son: according to White's *History, Gazetteer, and Directory of Suffolk*, published in 1844, a dozen years after Crabbe's death, 'Parham Lodge [as Ducking Hall had by then become], a neat modern mansion, belongs to the Rev. G. Crabbe, and was the seat of the late Mr Crabbe.'[27] By then, the house had been greatly altered, and in 1851–2 it was again completely rebuilt.

Crabbe was, of course, a man of strong instincts and enormous obstinacy. From the moment he heard of John Tovell's death, it would have been plain to him that he must install himself as master of Ducking Hall. The widow could not be expected to manage the place and the unmarried sister had a cottage of her own nearby, so his decision might have been plausibly rationalised. But it was not a rational decision. It was an intuitive, emotional one, and it went back to that day in 1772 when William Levett had said to him: 'Why, George, you shall go with me to Parham: there is a young lady there that would just suit you.' He had gone to Parham. He had met the young lady, he had seen the house and he had fallen in love with both. After that, he had waited nearly twelve years before he could marry Sarah; now another eight years had passed, and it was high time he had the house as well.

There is no certainty that Crabbe formulated the matter with such brutal frankness (though one suspects that he did, regarding any evasion as humbug). Within days of the funeral, he had written to Sarah, proposing that the family should move to Ducking Hall as soon as possible. On 22 October, she replied with understandable astonishment: 'You talk, my dearest Mr Crabbe, about living at Parham, but *can* we live there? For even the rent of the house is part of it my aunt's, furniture the same, and she will part with her teeth, if she had any, as soon as her rent.'[28] She had known Miss Elizabeth Tovell a long time and she had a shrewder sense of her aunt's probable disposition than her husband, but she knew his intransigence well enough to accept his decision, merely adding, '*Frugality* must still be *our* motto.' Her question, nevertheless, was a pertinent one: how on earth did her husband imagine they were to live at Ducking Hall? The precariousness of their claim and the certain animosity of her relatives would have been obstacles enough to deter most people. Then there would be the problem of finding a curate for Muston and Allington, the livings which Crabbe had been granted on the clear understanding that he would reside there and where he had been for less than four years; conversely, he would need to acquire for himself some appropriate clerical employment within reach of Parham. What was to happen to the farm at Muston ('another ewe is dead,'

Sarah wrote, as if that scale of practicality might bring her husband to his senses)? And what would become of the botanical garden? The scheme was a ridiculous one.

In forcing it through, Crabbe displayed one of his best qualities and one of his worst: determination and insensitivity. The determination was made up of several tightly knotted strands. There was that powerful instinctive belief that Parham was where he and Sarah ought to end up; there was his gentler feeling that returning to Suffolk would be good for his wife and children; and there was his nagging sense of disappointment with life in Leicestershire – his patron was dead, his relationship with Belvoir Castle was increasingly distant and he had no great fondness for his parishioners at Muston. These factors must have been persuasive advocates for a wrong decision. Taking it, however, demanded a staggering degree of insensitivity in a man who should have been well acquainted, both professionally and per-sonally, with bereavement and its aftermath. As a clergyman, he dealt with it regularly; while as a son he had been so outraged by his father's remarriage, two years after his mother's death, that he broke off all contact with him. Yet here he was, proposing to buy up the furniture and move his family into the bereaved widow's home, within weeks of Tovell's death. There were those at Parham who had thought young Crabbe a gold-digger twenty years ago, but even they were shocked by this ruthless and indecent haste.

On 25 November 1792, the Crabbes, preceded by their furniture, set off from Muston for the new home which they intuitively regarded as their old and allotted home. As they were leaving, 'a stranger, though one who knew my father's circumstances, called out in an impressive tone, "You are wrong, you are wrong." The sound, he said, found an echo in his own conscience, and during the whole journey seemed to ring in his ears like a supernatural voice.'[29] It is a nice touch, though precisely the kind of thing which Crabbe might have made up. And, on its own terms, the mournful prophecy would prove to be accurate enough. But there is an important sense in which wrong decisions may be more use to a poet than right ones: they may provide him both with material and with emotional insights of which uncomplicated happiness must remain innocent. In returning to his roots, leaving his parish and his botanical garden in the hands of a succession of curates, Crabbe was actually daring to re-engage with his past and his ghosts.

6

Besides turning its back on the sea at Slaughden and electing to run parallel to the coast for another dozen miles, the River Alde has at least two further peculiarities. One is that, as it passes Orford on its seaward journey, it takes on the name of that town and calls itself the Ore: etymologically, indeed, this is the more plausible of its two names, since while 'Orford' means either 'sea-crossing' or 'crossing on the Ore', 'Aldeburgh' or 'old fort' has nothing at all to do with a river. The other is that, further upstream near Blaxhall, the river divides and reassumes its two names. The Ore, rising near Saxstead, flows through Framlingham and then past the villages of Parham, Hacheston and Marlesford on a wide, fertile agricultural plain. The Alde has its source further north, near Badingham; it proceeds far more secretively along a winding and sometimes wooded valley, through Bruisyard, Rendham and Swefling, and forms the boundary between the villages of Farnham and Stratford St Andrew – which motorists on the A12 today are likely to perceive as an irritating double bend with two churches and a bridge. The different characters of these river valleys form the background to the next part of Crabbe's life.

When the family reached Ducking Hall on 28 November, only Sarah had an accurate idea of the welcome they were to receive; and she must have kept tactfully quiet about it, for the biographer son was to remember 'jumping for very joy' as he got out of the chaise, shouting, 'Here we are – here we are, little Willy and all!'[30] Little Willy, the Crabbes' last child, was barely two months old, and this most recent evidence of their determination to inherit the earth, or at any rate Parham, can have done nothing at all to improve the dispositions of the grieving widow and her dragonish sister-in-law. 'Our arrival in Suffolk was by no means palatable to all my mother's relations,' says the son, with masterly understatement, while sharply observing that the altered feelings between the adults were the product of that peculiarly intense grief which occurs 'when death has caused a transfer of property'. The two ladies of Parham were evidently determined to make the most of the occasion: 'Mrs Tovell and her sister-in-law, sitting by the fireside weeping, did not even rise up to welcome my parents, but uttered a few chilling words, and wept again.' They can hardly have been weeping since the beginning of October, so they were clearly putting on a performance. Miss Tovell, very well aware of her skills in this department, liked to boast that she could 'screw Crabbe up and down like a fiddle'; and she was fond of lamenting any insignificant change – such as a picture being moved from one room to another – as a vast and unthinkable catastrophe, which would cause her late brother, poor 'Jacky', to turn in his grave. She stalked around Ducking Hall, grumbling and scolding, carrying an ivory-tipped walking-cane a least a foot taller than she was.

What had possessed Crabbe to bring his family to this frosty, inhospitable place? Even by the following summer, things were no better. He wrote to young Edmund Cartwright, inviting him to visit but simultaneously advising him to stay well away:

> I am in this place, my dear sir, neither as a tenant, an heir nor an executor, but in some measure, as all these. I am neither master of the house, nor guest. Mrs Crabbe neither commands nor obeys: the servants are neither ours nor any other person's. Mrs Tovell (the widow of our uncle, who is most likely remembered by Mr Cartwright) is in some degree mistress and house-keeper. – In short, this is nobody's house and nobody governs, nobody obeys; nobody is satisfied, but everybody agrees that it is a miserable place and joins in hope that it will be better – better I think it soon will be and in the meantime, should your hard fortune lead you into such quarters do not wholly despair: I have a decent bottle of port; I can make interest for a beef steak or a mutton chop and peradventure Mrs Crabbe will find you a tolerable bed; so be not apprehensive of inhospitality with us; but comforts, conveniences and pleasures we promise none.
>
> My little boys wonder what strange place they are arrived at: they are not accustomed to many things beyond mere decent accommodations at Muston, but they had at least tolerable attendance and saw something like a habit of government and regularity in their house. – Here everything and everybody are huddled together. A confused equality blends us all and even the days of the week (as if Sunday were a usurper) pass without distinction. We dethrone order, but let not our anarchy fright you (if you be near) from approaching us. . .[31]

This is funny and engaging but also cunningly disingenuous: for, while Crabbe justly complains that his hybrid role 'neither as a tenant, an heir nor an executor, but in some measure, as all these' is intolerable, he omits to mention that this is exactly the position he had contrived for himself, against his wife's better judgement. Even if the domestic arrangements had been more satisfactory, if the termagant aunt had vanished from the face of the earth (as she would ten years later, dutifully attended to the end by Crabbe), he would still have felt out of place. He lacked both the temperament and the experience to be a 'squarson': the straitened circumstances of his early life and the cautionary example of his father, his bookish and botanical interests, his absorption in his family and his wife's delicate health had all prevented him from developing any taste for noisy and rumbustious sociability.

Ducking Hall was no longer the jovial, welcoming place it had been in Tovell's day, and to that extent Crabbe's local detractors had a point:

> He invited none of the old compotators, and if they came received them but coolly; and it was soon said that 'Parham had passed away, and the glory thereof.' When the paper of parish rates came round, he perceived that he was placed on a much higher scale of payment than his wealthy predecessor had ever been for the very same occupation; and when he complained of this, he was told very plainly: 'Why, sir, Mr Tovell was a good neighbour: we all miss him sadly; and so, I suppose, do you, sir; and – and –' 'I understand you,' said my father, 'perfectly; now, sir, I refuse this rate: take your remedy.' He resisted the charge; and the consequences may be guessed.[32]

This is interesting – and not only for the insight it provides into the way parish rates were calculated in the 1790s. Crabbe appears to have been incapable of moving into any house without entangling himself in an acrimonious financial argument. On his first arrival in Muston, he had sought the professional advice of Richard Burke at Lincoln's Inn – the barrister brother of his first patron – to determine whether he had any entitlement to arrears of tithes: Burke's opinion was that he had not, but the reasoning was to prove useful to him later on. His eventual return to Muston would prove troublesome in other ways, while his final move to Trowbridge was to be accompanied by complex disputes concerning tithes, the state of the rectory and other matters. Some readers deduce from this that Crabbe was a difficult and highly litigious man (as was Shakespeare), but one suspects that the humbler truth is that in financial matters he was desperately unsure of himself, continually nervous about being taken for a ride. The slightest suggestion that his unconventional, largely self-educated background made him easy to dupe – as he knew he had been in his youth – invariably provoked a fierce reponse from him.

His insecurity and his courage (compatible rather than contradictory qualities, since the one necessitated the other) were very closely linked, as the son's next anecdote neatly implies:

> Having detected the bailiff in some connection with smugglers, he charged him with the fact. The man flew into a violent passion, grasped a knife, and exclaimed with an inflamed countenance, 'No man shall call me a rogue!' My father smiled at his rage, and said, in a quiet tone, – 'Now, Robert, you are too much for me: put down your knife, and then we can talk on equal terms.' The man hesitated: my father added, lifting his voice, 'Get out of the house, you scoundrel!' and he was obeyed. On all occasions, indeed, he appeared to have a perfect insensibility to physical danger.

Although the point about physical danger is, as we have already seen, a perfectly accurate one, Crabbe's psychological state is perhaps more equivocal than the son admits. His successive stances – the temporising smile, the artificially friendly tone and the abrupt change to the raised voice of authority – happily proved effective, but they are at least as likely to have stemmed from panicky improvisation as from calm strategy. The Saltmaster's son, of course, had an ingrained reason to be sensitive about smuggling; whereas old John Tovell, one suspects, might have taken a rather more relaxed attitude towards the whole affair. That Crabbe was not John Tovell was a fact that Parham from almost every point of view found hard to accept.

7

He did the inevitable, which was luckily also the creditable, thing. He behaved like himself and made no attempt to emulate his jovial predecessor. He spent several months in the early part of 1793 at Aldeburgh, staying with his sister and brother-in-law, and placing his two eldest sons, George and John, 'under the tuition of one of the good old dames who had taught himself his letters'. In one sense, he was able to see the place clearly for the first time, unencumbered by the unhappiness of his childhood, the disagreeable presence of his father or the burden of his own professional failures there; in late April, he preached twice at the church where he had previously been so 'unkindly' received. On his return to Parham, he accepted the curacies of Swefling – Richard Turner, the rector, lived at Great Yarmouth, where he was 'perpetual curate', in exactly the same way as the Rector of Stathern had lived at Stamford – and of Great Glemham: 'henceforth,' says the biographer son, 'his occupations and habits were very much what they used to be at Muston'.[33]

He was fortunate in his friendship with Turner, a polymathic intellectual clergyman somewhat in the mould of Edmund Cartwright. Even more than most writers, Crabbe needed to bounce his ideas off an intelligent friend; but Turner proved to be much more than a judicious reader of work in progress. In the preface to his *Poems* of 1807, Crabbe would describe him as 'the kind of critic for whom every poet should devoutly wish, and the friend whom every man would be happy to acquire'. He was, says the son, 'one of the chief sources of comfort all through my father's residence in Suffolk', not least because he seemed to be able to muster a genuine interest in almost any subject: 'With my father he would converse on natural history, as if this had been his whole study; with my mother, on mechanical contrivances and new inventions, for use or ornament, as if that were an exclusive taste; while he would amuse us young folks with well-told anecdotes, and to walk or ride with him was considered our happiest privilege.'[34] Turner's visits to Parham and, later, to Great Glemham and Rendham were valued by the entire family, but he was not Crabbe's only intellectual lifeline.

In 1789 Dudley Long – formerly of Hurts Hall, Saxmundham, and Crabbe's first benefactor – had inherited the estate of Little Glemham and taken the name Dudley North. Little Glemham Hall is no Belvoir Castle, but it is a fine early eighteenth-century mansion with an exceptionally handsome early Georgian interior; North, moreover, was a Whig whose distinguished friends were much more to Crabbe's taste than the Duke of Rutland's predominantly Tory circle. North now resumed his benevolent role, providing the Crabbes with a 'profusion' of 'game, fruit, and other produce of his domain' – the son makes Little Glemham sound like a reincarnation of Ben Jonson's Penshurst – as well as a comprehensively stocked medicine chest for the parson-physician. During a fortnight-long shooting party in the autumn of 1794, Crabbe 'had the honour of meeting at Mr North's, a large party of some of the most eminent men in the kingdom – the Honourable Charles (now Earl) Grey, the Earl of Lauderdale, Mr Fox, Mr Roger Wilbraham, Dr Parr, Mr St John, and several other public characters'. In reporting this, Crabbe's son seems more star-struck than his father would have been, for this was precisely the sort of company he had been accustomed to keep with Burke: Fox, for example, was an old acquaintance who amiably scolded the poet for his creative silence and offered to read and to revise any future work of his before publication. Although Crabbe was to reject (on Turner's advice) many of the poems he wrote at this time, he was already assembling material which would appear in *The Parish Register*, and quite possibly in later poems too: this kind of practical encouragement from a distinguished friend had always been the most effective way of spurring him on. One day, as the guests proceeded to dinner, 'Mr Fox playfully pushed my father first, saying, "If he had had his deserts, he would have walked before us all." If this was an unmerited compliment, it was assuredly a very good-humoured one.'[35]

Meanwhile, life at Parham had also begun to resemble life at Muston in a more melancholy way. The Crabbes' youngest son William, who had been so joyfully introduced on their arrival, died in September 1793; nor was this to be the last of their bereavements. By the following July, however, a degree of domestic harmony had been achieved at Ducking Hall and Crabbe could report to young Cartwright that 'peace has been for some time established and Mrs Crabbe enjoys that freedom and authority which were her due long before she had them'.[36] And, as a consequence, he could once more enjoy the freedom of some serious botanising.

8

Although Parham is in the agricultural river valley of the upper Ore, the Suffolk Sandlings are within easy riding or, for a fit countryman like Crabbe, walking distance. Nowhere, as he ruefully admitted to young Edmund Cartwright, was closer to his botanising heart or – he might have added – to his emotional one:

A more flat, uniform and tame district can scarcely be imagined than that part of the Suffolk shore opposite to my present habitation. A light sand constitutes the surface, and you are obliged to look minutely before you be able to discover any vegetable clothing in many parts of it. It was to this coast I alluded in some verses I formerly wrote wherein I spoke of the poppy, mallow, darnel and bugloss as the few ornaments (and those ornaments of sterility) which the soil could boast of. It is however my fortune in some measure to sing (at least to say) a recantation; for this despised place has afforded me much amusement and not that only, but has empowered me (so far as I know at present) to introduce to the botanical world a new species of British plant, or rather a new species speaking more generally . . .[37]

Crabbe's discovery was *Trifolium suffocatum*, or suffocated clover. The apparent punning reference to his home county is a fortuitous one, more recently put to use by John Fuller in a rather unkind line from 'The Shires': 'To live in Suffolk is to suffocate.'[38] *Trifolium suffocatum* is certainly not a common plant, though it may still be found on the coast around Aldeburgh, and W. Keble Martin provides the following concise description of it: 'Stems short, nearly buried in sand; leaf petioles long; flower heads sessile, often confluent; calyx teeth recurved. In sand on S. and E. coasts, local and rare. Flowers July–August.'[39] Unfortunately for Crabbe, a Mr Lillywigg had collected a specimen of *Trifolium suffocatum* at Great Yarmouth a year earlier; it was exhibited at a meeting of the Linnean Society on 7 May 1793. This Crabbe would have in due course learnt from Sir Joseph Banks, the President of the Royal Society, to whom Cartwright had forwarded on his behalf a detailed description of the plant together with a not wholly satisfactory specimen: 'I had laid by three or four specimens to transmit to you and Sir Joseph,' wrote Crabbe, 'but unluckily your Godson, or some little mischievous creature like him, has ruined the plants and I have only one left and that discoloured and ill preserved; yet as it is the whole plant I believe Sir Joseph will readily by that, and by an accompanying description of the flowering and fructification, be able to pronounce on its claim to a discovery . . .'

Trifolium suffocatum was decidedly Crabbe's sort of plant. He had an affinity with tenaciously surviving species which, like himself, were doing surprisingly well despite their initially unpropitious circumstances. As his son very judiciously puts it, 'I should be inclined to say, that those usually considered as the least inviting had the highest attractions for him. In botany, grasses, the most useful, but the least ornamental, were his favourites; in minerals, the earths and sands; in entomology, the minuter insects.' In the garden, he adds, 'the usual showy foreigners gave place to the most scarce flowers, and especially to the rarer weeds, of Britain; and these were scattered here and there only for preservation'.[40] He was, in fact, less a typical eighteenth-century gardener than what we would now call a conservationist or an ecologist; and his priorities, which the landscape 'improvers' of his time would have found laughable, were almost exactly those of green campaigners two hundred years later. The biographer son duly admires these traits of his father's, but he also recognises – in one of the severest passages in the *Life* – that they are closely allied to 'his remarkable indifference to almost all the proper objects of taste. He had no real love for painting, or music, or architecture, or for what a painter's eye considers as the beauties of landscape.'[41] To a striking degree, Crabbe turns this deficiency to his advantage: in his finest work his gaze is so often attentively and generously fixed exactly where the eye of 'taste' would be averted. But a deficiency it remains, nevertheless, and it is not to be explained simply by his humble origins: during his London years, we never hear of him going to a concert or to the opera, despite the richness of late eighteenth-century musical life, while such interest in painting as he possessed seems to have been entirely focused on his acquaintance with the useful and influential Reynolds.

Culturally, Crabbe could still seem to be an outsider: although many doors had by now opened to him, others continued to slam firmly in his face. Early in 1795, though disappointed by the news about his *Trifolium*, he told young Cartwright that he had several 'bookish affairs in my hands';[42] among these was a botanical treatise in English, of which he had already proposed publication to Dodsley. As was so often his deferential habit, he consulted an eminent friend – in this case, John Davies, the Vice-Master of Trinity College, Cambridge – for an expert opinion; and Davies's view, academically proper though already well on the way to being archaic, was that he 'could not stomach the notion of degrading such a science by treating it in a modern language'.[43] Remembering Captain Conway's gift of Hudson's *Flora Anglica*, which he had supposedly read, and the Lambeth examination in Latin, which he had supposedly passed, we must assume that Crabbe's knowledge of Latin had either grown rusty or, more likely, had never been up to much; he enjoyed reading Latin poetry, but that was a long way from writing scientific prose in the language. The English botanical treatise ended up on the bonfire at Parham, in one of the 'grand incremations' so enjoyed by his children. He seems, curiously, to have had no instinct to publish and be damned nor even to keep the work for his own interest and reference.

Early in 1796, the Crabbes' youngest surviving son, Edmund, 'was suddenly taken from us by a severe and (to me) unknown disease';[44] he was buried at Parham on 11 March. Crabbe's bafflement is noteworthy: in his dual roles of parson and physician, he would have been familiar with all common childhood illnesses – including, or especially, the life-threatening ones. Four other children of theirs had died in or near infancy, and the fact that Edmund had grown to vigorous and (as we know from asides in Crabbe's letters) mischievous six year old made the loss all the more terrible. For Sarah, who already suffered from 'those nervous disorders which render life so grievous to be borne' and who had 'long added the aid of medicine to the endeavours of her naturally good spirits' (which looks very like a reference to opium), it was too much to bear. Her son says that 'it caused a nervous disorder, from which she never entirely recovered',[45] although it seems more probable that it greatly exacerbated an already existing condition. There was, of course, a history of mental illness in her family: her brother James had died 'in a fit of hypochondria' as recently as 1788, while according to Fitzgerald her sister Eleanor 'turned crazy' and 'was for years mad under the charge of her sister Mary'.[46] Sarah clearly suffered from acute manic depression, of which her son's description is exact and unmistakable:

> . . . during the hotter months of almost every year, she was oppressed by the deepest dejection of spirits I have ever witnessed in any one, and this circumstance alone was sufficient to undermine the happiness of so feeling a mind as my father's. Fortunately for both, there were long intervals, in which, if her spirits were a little too high, the relief to herself and others was great indeed. Then she would sing over her old tunes again – and be the frank, cordial, charming woman of earlier days.[47]

Her condition may have been intermittently controlled but it is most unlikely to have been improved by 'the aid of medicine' to which she had recourse.

The modern reader may understandably feel not only sorry for Mrs Crabbe, who had borne seven children and lost five of them, but angry with her husband for putting her through this ordeal: no one, after all, was fonder of preaching about sexual restraint, in his sermons and his poetry, than the Reverend George Crabbe, and in any case methods of contraception existed. But this would be to miss two points. Firstly, while conventional Christian teaching demanded sexual abstinence outside marriage, it was no less axiomatic that the married couple's duty was to have as many children as was possible or prudent. Secondly, the Crabbes' predicament was far from uncommon, as T. H. White pointed out in *The Age of Scandal*: 'Five of Crabbe's seven children died; Gibbon was the sole survivor of seven siblings; four of Sterne's six brothers died; Gray was the only one who lived, from a family of twelve.'[48] Among the anonymous poor, the mortality rate was often still higher. Indeed, statistically speaking, Crabbe was comparatively lucky in having two sons who survived into successful adulthood and a wife who, despite her failing health, lived to the age of sixty-two.

Every time the Crabbes seemed about to transcend the residual gloom of Ducking Hall, a new misfortune occurred to re immerse them in it. Respite now came once more in the benevolent shape of Dudley North, who offered them at much reduced rent a property of his which had become vacant: Great Glemham Hall. The house at Parham would eventually be theirs, of course, but in the meantime Mrs Tovell and her sister-in-law could do what they liked with it. Crabbe was unashamedly relieved to get away from Miss Tovell: 'I will hope for a little repose,' he wrote, 'and with so much more prospect of success as it increases the distance between us and some malignant spirit which has taken the form of a woman indeed, but no other disguise whatever.'[49] This time, his hope was to be fulfilled. On 17 October 1796, 'the *lares* were removed from Parham, where they had always been unpropitious, to this beautiful residence, where my parents remained for four or five years, to their entire satisfaction'.[50]

Six

Telling Tales
1796–1809

I

When did Crabbe start to tell tales? He invented glittering fairy stories for his young children; he made several attempts at novel writing during these Suffolk years; and in his poetry there is a notable difference – an alteration in impulse as well as in method – between the earlier discursive works and the later narrative ones. During the 1790s, at Parham and especially at Great Glemham, storytelling increasingly became Crabbe's way of managing his imaginative and intellectual life.

Like so many of Crabbe's homes, Great Glemham Hall no longer exists: it was replaced in 1814 by the present Glemham House and the grounds were remodelled by Humphrey Repton. The dovecote and stables remain from Crabbe's time, and the place retains its strongly literary character as the home of the Gathorne-Hardy family. For the biographer son, 'Glemham itself is, and ever will be, the Alhambra of my imagination'.[1] It is a curious image for so rural and tranquil a place, but standing in the churchyard, where George Crabbe junior's words are carved on the gate, one can readily see why he and his father loved it. Although village life has, of course, altered immeasurably over the past two hundred years, the physical outline of Great Glemham has changed hardly at all:

A small well-wooded park occupied the whole mouth of the glen, whence, doubtless, the name of the village was derived. In the lower ground stood the commodious mansion; the approach wound down through a plantation on the eminence in front. The opposite hill rose at the back of it, rich and varied with trees and shrubs scattered irregularly; under this southern hill ran a brook, and on the banks

above it were spots of great natural beauty, crowned by whitethorn
and oak. Here the purple scented violet perfumed the air, and in one
place coloured the ground. On the left of the front, in the narrower
portion of the glen, was the village; on the right, a confined view of
richly wooded fields. In fact, the whole parish and neighbourhood
resemble a combination of groves, interspersed with fields
cultivated like gardens, and intersected with those green dry lanes
which tempt the walker in all weathers, especially in the evenings,
when in the short grass of the dry sandy banks lies, every few yards,
a glowworm, and the nightingales are pouring forth their melody in
every direction . . .

    The summer evenings especially, at this place, dwell in my
memory like a delightful dream. When we had finished our lessons,
if we did not adjourn with my father to the garden to work in our
own plats, we generally took a family walk through the green lanes
around Glemham; where, at every turn, stands a cottage or a farm,
and not collected into a street, as in some parts of the kingdom,
leaving the land naked and forlorn.[2]

The son is remembering, and inevitably idealising, the most enjoyable phase
of his own growing up: after his elementary education in Aldeburgh, he had
been sent to a school in Ipswich run by 'the late excellent Mr King', on whose
retirement in 1798 it had been decided that young George would be tutored
by his father until he went up to Cambridge. Although Crabbe had by this
time amassed an eclectic range of scholarship, on subjects from mathematics
to classics, which would have put most university-educated schoolmasters to
shame, his son cheerfully recalls that 'to my infinite satisfaction, this new
academy had much more of vacation than term-time: contrasted with
Ipswich, it seemed little else than one glorious holiday'.

    Holiday or not, his learning continued, and it was augmented in notably
un-school-like ways. On those summer evening walks, his father would read
aloud from a novel: 'he seldom passed a day without reading part of some
such work, and was never very select in the choice of them'. He sounds exactly
like a man addicted to stories. In winter, 'the reading was carried out more
systematically, and we had generally books of a superior description; for a
friend lent us every Christmas a large box of the most reputable works

recently published, especially of travels'. So the seasons of novels alternated with seasons of non-fictional narratives, read aloud 'in that natural and easy manner' which Crabbe also took with him to the pulpit. There, his style was at once down-to-earth and mildly eccentric, a combination well enough suited to his Suffolk congregations: 'Once or twice, finding it grow dark, he abruptly shut his sermon, saying, "Upon my word I cannot see; I must give you the rest when we meet again." Or he would walk into a pew near a window, and stand on the seat and finish his sermon, with the most admirable indifference to the remarks of his congregation.'[3] When tithes were due, he would simply say, as he left the pulpit: 'I must have some money, gentlemen.'

It was during the winter evenings at Great Glemham that Crabbe began to write his three novels. He seems, reasonably enough, to have been unsure whether he should write his fictional narratives in prose, as was by then usual, or in his own preferred medium of verse; and it is clear from his son's recollection of the novels that their subjects were very close to those of the narrative poems published later on. One was called *The Widow Grey*, of which the son remembered nothing 'except that the principal character was a benevolent humourist, a Dr Allison'. The second, much more enticingly, was *Reginald Glanshaw, or the Man who Commanded Success*: this was 'a portrait of an assuming, overbearing, ambitious mind, rendered interesting by some generous virtues, and gradually wearing down into idiotism. I cannot help thinking that this Glanshaw was drawn with very extraordinary power; but the story was not well managed in the detail.'[4] The biographer son had forgotten the title of the third novel; but he knew 'that it opened with a description of a wretched room, similar to some that are presented in his poetry, and that, on my mother's telling him frankly that she thought the effect very inferior to that of the corresponding pieces in verse, he paused in his reading, and, after some reflection, said, "Your remark is just."' Sarah was almost certainly right, although we must regret the practical consequence of her judgement: for, after carefully rereading his three novels, Crabbe consigned them to another of his grand bonfires. This is so decisive an event that it would be easy to overlook the hugely significant implication of Mrs Crabbe's remark, which is that 'the corresponding pieces in verse' were already in existence by 1800 or so: one such correspondence, even given the limited information available to us, would clearly have been between *Reginald Glanshaw* and 'Sir Eustace Grey', which Crabbe included in his *Poems* of 1807; and the prior existence of this poem in some form may help to explain the otherwise unlikely assertion by the son that its fifty-five stanzas were all composed at a single sitting, 'during a great snow-storm'[5] in 1804. The winter of 1798–9, a particularly severe one, may well have provided the initial catalytic snowstorm.

Of course, since we cannot retrieve the raw materials of Crabbe's bonfire, we shall never know for certain what these novels were like. Some readers, noting other affinities between the two writers, have imagined them as the work of a sort of clerical Jane Austen; but Crabbe's prose had none of Austen's musical suppleness nor had he, despite his wry sense of humour, her ironic poise. On the other hand, it shouldn't be assumed that, because Crabbe's prose is frequently cumbersome, the novels must therefore have been terrible: he could be stiff and pompous on formal occasions, but the style of his informal letters is agreeably relaxed (though usually in need of an editor). Perhaps his fiction was more obviously influenced by his reading of popular and gothic novels – those books about which 'he was never very select' – than seemed proper, especially to Mrs Crabbe; for instance, one wonders whether he had read, aloud or not, Matthew Lewis's scandalous *The Monk*, published in 1796. Given his interest in the extreme and the grotesque, this is by no means impossible: here again, the intriguing *Reginald Glanshaw* is the missing novel which might have held the key.

The important point, however, is that Crabbe wrote novels at all; for it reminds us that he differed in kind from the more clearly focused poets of his time. He was not simply a poet: he was a writer. He contributed a substantial botanical appendix to Richard Loder's *The History of Framlingham*, published in 1798: drawing on his lifelong study of Suffolk flora, this was precisely the kind of methodical, pedestrian work he needed as a counterbalance to his darkening imagination. And, distant as he was from Muston, another of his writerly tasks continued to make claims on his attention: 'The Natural History of the Vale of Belvoir' for John Nichols's *History and Antiquities of Leicestershire*. He had been neglecting this, with good reason, 'the health of a part of my family and particularly of Mrs Crabbe being in a precarious state';[6] but in the summer of 1798 – with his reduced family happily settled at Glemham and the Framlingham appendix out of the way – he once again confronted this problematical task. The main trouble, as he told Nichols, was that 'several years are past during which I have had very little opportunity of increasing my knowledge of the n[atural] history of

Leicestershire'; he hoped that Nichols would be able to direct him to suitable sources of information on local ornithology, on coal pits and slate quarries, and on 'the quantities of rain'. He was, moreover, not at all certain how long the natural historical section of this work should be: he had seen a review of Richard Polwhele's *The History of Devonshire* (published between 1793 and 1806) and was dismayed to learn that it contained 'over 135 folio pages' on the natural history of the county. 'I am sure,' grumbled Crabbe, 'he must be very diffuse or take in objects the most common – this I see is the case with the N[atural] H[istory] of Staffordshire, where the most common articles are included.' Beyond this criticism lurks the old insecurity about his scholarly capabilities, the worry that he might not be up to so extensive and detailed an account. However, he pressed on through the following winter, delayed and interrupted by 'floods and frost',[7] but receiving some assistance both from Richard Loder in Woodbridge and from his old friend William Mounsey.

By now Crabbe was in his mid-forties, a popular country clergyman with two sons in their early teens and no prospect of further children: at last, the circumstances seemed right for a revival of that poetic career which he had left in such strange abeyance almost fifteen years earlier. His former publisher, James Dodsley, had died in 1797, so Crabbe very sensibly approached a young bookseller and publisher in Piccadilly, John Hatchard, who was delighted with the prospect of re-establishing this distinguished but dormant literary reputation. Accordingly, Crabbe began to assemble 'a series of poems, sufficient to fill a volume – among others, one on the Scriptural story of Naaman; another, strange contrast! entitled "Gipsy Will"; and a third founded on the legend of the Pedlar of Swaffham'.[8] At this point, says the son, not wholly without irony, 'he judiciously paused to consult the well-known taste of the Reverend Richard Turner, already mentioned as rector of Sweffling'. Turner recommended 'further revision', and this – just as was the case with John Davies's rejection of the botanical treatise and Sarah Crabbe's mild criticism of the novels – seems to have been sufficient to condemn the manuscripts to the bonfire. Crabbe had no regrets and in his Preface of 1807 would warmly thank Turner for his 'friendly attentions', although his later readers may understandably rank this readiness to destroy literary evidence among his more irritating characteristics. Whether we regard it as indicating a pathetic lack of self-confidence or an admirable lack of self-importance probably says more about our state of mind than about his.

2

The Great Glemham idyll could not last, for two reasons. In July 1800, the Bishop of Lincoln, Dr George Pretyman, informed his clergy – among whom Crabbe, as Rector of Muston and Allington, was one – that he required 'from every incumbent in his diocese who did not reside upon his benefice, the reasons of his non-residence in writing'.9 Crabbe, of course, had excellent reasons for wishing to remain in Suffolk, but they were to do with his wife, his sons and his own temperament, and they had no bearing whatsoever on his efficacy as a clergyman. Moreover, he knew perfectly well that the bishop was right: the words of his Muston parishioner – 'You are wrong, you are wrong' – had returned to haunt him. On the other hand, Crabbe could be an extremely obstinate man and he had no great liking for Pretyman, who owed much of his immense influence to the fact that he had been Pitt's tutor at Cambridge. He was also Dean of St Paul's, a circumstance which seems not to have affected his readiness to scold others for pluralism and absenteeism. In 1803, Pretyman was to inherit the estate of Marmaduke Tomline in Riby, Lincolnshire, assuming his benefactor's surname; and in 1820 he became Bishop of Winchester, in which role, by a strangely apposite coincidence, he earns an unflattering mention in Thomas Hardy's *The Return of the Native*, where the 'mediocrity' of his spiritual guidance is equated with 'the poetry of [Samuel] Rogers' and 'the paintings of [Benjamin] West'.10 The ever-benevolent Dudley North approached Pretyman on Crabbe's behalf, going out of his way to praise 'his kindness and attention to his present parishioners';11 however, this surprisingly naïve tactic seems to have misfired, convincing the bishop instead that his absentee rector was far too valuable a commodity to waste on Suffolk, when it was the people of Muston and Allington who should be benefiting from his admirable qualities. The best North could do was to obtain an extension of four years to Crabbe's leave of absence. As a final bid to keep his friend and protégé in Suffolk, North offered him the living of Great Glemham, when it became vacant; but this, says the son, was 'too small to be held singly', and so the Crabbes prepared for an eventual move back to Leicestershire.

Still, they had a respite of four years – long enough for Crabbe to complete young George's home education and see him safely installed at Cambridge –

to which they could look forward. Unfortunately for them, in 1801 Dudley North and his brother, the joint owners of Glemham Hall, decided to sell the property and divide the assets; and in October the Crabbes moved once again, to a house known as Lady Whincup's in the nearby village of Rendham. This charming, stuccoed Georgian building, lying in the Alde valley at the foot of a gentle hillside meadow, is the only one of Crabbe's homes in Suffolk which remains standing: John Mitford, the poetical rector of nearby Benhall who became editor of the *Gentleman's Magazine*, disparagingly described it in 1834 as 'a house at the bottom of the hill, just opposite the new parsonage, which is now inhabited by a farrier' (that 'new parsonage' is now, inevitably, The Old Rectory). By the relatively grand standards of Ducking Hall or Glemham Hall, Lady Whincup's is certainly, in Huchon's words, 'a much more unpretending house',[12] a consideration which probably troubled the two boys more than it did their parents; for neither Crabbe nor his wife would ever acquire the knack of managing a large establishment.

Lady Whincup's tenant between 1801 and 1805 enters one of his elusive phases. This is unsurprising: his concerns at this time were private and familial. In his literary life, he was experiencing one of those secretive, subterranean creative patches, familiar to all writers, which seem alternately to promise everything and nothing. One or more of the novels may well have been written at Rendham: it is sometimes assumed that he began them only after Richard Turner had dissuaded him from publishing his proposed collection of poems in 1799, but he is more likely to have been stimulated positively by his reading than negatively by his friend's discouragement. Trying to date two-hundred-year-old bonfires is in any case a pointless task. What we can say with some certainty is that he was already working on material which would appear in *The Parish Register* and *The Borough*, and on several shorter poems which were very different in form and character. Yet here, too, any attempts at establishing an exact chronology are likely to be frustrated. A notable instance is the poem 'Hester', an apparently uncharacteristic piece in the form of a Wordsworthian lyrical ballad. The central character, who is introduced as 'An humble vagrant', and the bleak, craggy landscape may indeed owe something to the Lake Poets, whom Crabbe only mildly admired: the son rather condescendingly notes that although his father 'smiled at the exceeding simplicity of the language' he nevertheless 'found something in it peculiarly attractive'.[13] Or perhaps he was responding to his reading of gothic novels; for although Suffolk boasts a surprising number of castles, it is entirely deficient in mountains, and this poem has both. 'Hester' has not been much admired: for Peter New, 'its only merit lies in the description of the misery of prostitution to the prostitute',[14] while Neville Blackburne rashly remarks that 'the dead level flatness of its lines displays the rustiness of his talent';[15] but Crabbe was writing variously and prolifically at this time, so if there is a problem here it can hardly have been caused by rustiness. Evidently, he was attempting something he regarded as experimental and, since he did not publish the poem, unsuccessful. What on earth was he up to?

Two chronological clues present themselves, and both prove to be mirages. The text that we have of 'Hester' comes from one of the John Murray notebooks: it is dated 'Glemham 1804'. As Arthur Pollard notes in his Introduction to *New Poems by George Crabbe*, this must be 'a fair draft, into which a few changes have been introduced', almost certainly of the poem which Sarah Hoare described as 'an unpublished tale of the poet's called "Esther"'.[16] The date, therefore, may refer to the original composition or to its transcription and revision into this notebook: we have no way of knowing which. But, whatever it may mean, the date itself is suspect: Crabbe had left Glemham in 1801, so either the place or the year is incorrect. The likelihood, then, is that this is a very much later transcription, in which these details have been incorrectly remembered or inaccurately copied. Nor is the second chronological clue any more helpful. The biographer son, resorting to his customary formula of 'about this time' (and the time in his previous paragraph is specifically the autumn of 1803), tells us of his father 'casually stepping into a bookshop in Ipswich' and there discovering Sir Walter Scott's *The Lay of the Last Minstrel*: 'A few words only riveted his attention, and he read it nearly through while standing at the counter, observing, "a new and great poet has appeared!"'[17] It would certainly be attractive and plausible to imagine him, so strongly impressed, going home and attempting a quite new sort of poem, using shorter lines and setting it in an imaginary, Scott-like landscape. But *The Lay of the Last Minstrel* was not published until 1805. Although Crabbe may have found a copy in Ipswich before he returned to Muston, he could not have written a poem influenced by it either in 1804 or in Great Glemham.

Does any of this matter? In itself, the case of 'Hester' neatly illustrates the slipperiness of determining exactly when and where Crabbe wrote what. However, it is more important than that because, as Professor Pollard implies in his far more judicious comments on the poem,[18] Blackburne's and New's evaluations of 'Hester' are startlingly wide of the mark. Sarah Hoare was right to call it a 'tale', and it is arguably the first of Crabbe's works to which this description unequivocally applies: it is almost entirely told by its subject, a simple country girl who, though engaged to a virtuous shepherd, finds herself seduced and ultimately destroyed by the 'youthful peer' who is the heir to a 'frowning' castle. Quite early in the poem, Crabbe seems almost tempted to introduce a tale within a tale, lingering over the word as if he has just discovered the key to his creative future:

> 'There was a lad who loved me well,
>   A shepherd down the dale,
> Who with the tale that shepherds tell
>   Told yet another tale.'

This second 'tale' is, of course, the declaration of his love for Hester. And there is one further sense in which this crucial little word reverberates in the poem, as the following quatrain may suggest:

> 'My Lord was youthful, handsome, tall,
>   In dress a very King,
> And when he clasped my waist so small,
>   How jocund would he sing . . .'

The hints of archaic diction here – 'my waist so small', 'jocund' – are of a very specific sort: they are Chaucerian. And, indeed, the construction of 'Hester', in which a character is briefly introduced before narrating a personal story and drawing a moral from it, is precisely that of a Canterbury tale.

These factors would be more than sufficient to establish the importance of 'Hester' in Crabbe's work, but it is also a poem of surprisingly subtle nuances. There is Hester's father, a gentle gamekeeper who helplessly observes his daughter's progress:

> 'My father's duty was to chase
>   The poacher from his prey.
> The robber's timid step to trace,
>   And watch him on his way;

Both kind and just, he took his time
   All cruelty to shun,
He rather would prevent a crime
   Than punish it when done.'

If we were to restore Crabbe's capitalisation for 'Father' and 'He', the point
would be clearer still: he is an emblem of the 'kind and just' God, whose
ambiguous gift is free will. There is the patient, neglected shepherd whose
name, William, enables the melancholic pun with which Hester first
acknowledges her temptation: 'I wept, and said: " 'Tis not my Will." / And yet
it was my shame.' And, above all, there is Hester herself who is at first
repulsed by, and then irresistibly drawn into, the corrupt ways of the castle.
For this wearing down of Hester's resistance, Crabbe boldly chooses an
image drawn from his own childhood. In one sense, it is absurdly
inappropriate, since it is so remote from the narrator's own experience, but
that very incongruity makes it all the more striking:

'Thus was I like the tender boy,
   Compelled at school to stay,
Where all his fellows' noisy joy
   Increases his dismay;
He never dreams the time will come
   When he will join their play,
Forget his dear, his pleasant home,
   And be as loud as they.

'But rather counts with anxious mind
   The days of his distress,
And wonders, as he counts, to find
   His sorrows growing less;
He then begins to hide his tears,
   His bolder friends reprove,
While pleasures, suited to his years,
   His yielding spirit move;
Till like his fellows he appears,
   And shares the sports they love.'

This comes close to a naïvely Rousseauesque equation of education and corruption, but Crabbe's perceptions are gentler and more persuasive: all establishments and institutions assimilate newcomers in much the same way; the unhappy child at school learns to be happy, or to pretend to be happy, and to the external world it hardly matters which. As usual, Crabbe reveals his deepest emotions under cover of a hefty disguise; and there are pungent hints of his later self, too, in Hester's initial reaction to aristocratic life. The women are 'A vain, a forward race'; the men, though 'trim and smart, / And civil in their way', are 'insolently gay'; while the 'manners of the servants' hall' are 'profligate and base'. Where could her creator have formed such opinions but at Belvoir? He even manages neat barbs at his own professions. Once she is established as the peer's mistress, Hester discovers that

> 'His friends were happy to obey
>   A nymph so fair and kind,
> Except the priest, who came to pray,
>   And he was growing blind.'

While, as for the literary life:

> 'There was a poet, and his fame
>   Was at the castle known,
> He surely ought to share my shame,
>   Who never felt his own . . .'

In the end, Hester is condemned to the same fate as the Ancient Mariner, to tell and retell her tale: 'Compassion,' she says, 'Gave me to live in peace to tell / The evils I have known.'

In describing an arching curve of fortune, 'Hester' has much in common with its better-known near-contemporary 'Sir Eustace Grey'. Why, then, did Crabbe not publish it? Though we should hesitate before casting the long-suffering Mrs Crabbe in the role of a killjoy, it is certainly possible that she disliked the sexual frankness of the poem, just as she had disliked something about his novels. For us, though, both 'Hester' and 'Sir Eustace Grey' are fascinating transitional pieces, both of which find Crabbe telling tales of a kind he may also have tried in prose fiction, without so far having hit on the simple formal solution which he would find in *The Parish Register*.

3

Apart from the state of his wife's health – which seemed to improve following the death of her mother, Mrs Elmy, in 1802 and her aunt, Miss Tovell, in 1803, doubtless because of the long-term financial stability which the provisions of their respective wills, including the outright inheritance of Ducking Hall, assured – Crabbe's principal concern at this time was the education of his two sons. Over the next few years, the cost of keeping them both at Cambridge proved to be a major headache; for the time being he had to make sure that they would actually get there. His own self-education had, as we have seen, given him an exaggerated regard for university degrees; but, more to the point, he knew very well the practical difficulties of beginning a clerical career without one. He had consequently resolved long ago that both his sons must be educated at Cambridge: when he so humbly deferred to the judgement of his friend John Davies, the Vice-Master of Trinity College, over the publication of his botanical treatise, he had more than his own reputation in mind.

Visiting Muston in July 1802, for the last time before his permanent return there, Crabbe carefully arranged that he and his seventeen-year-old elder son should pass through Cambridge during Commencement week. While he obviously wanted George to enjoy the pomp and circumstance of the occasion, and no doubt to be encouraged by the thought that in a few years' time he would be participating in it, Crabbe had other motives too. For instance, the Vice-Master of Trinity introduced him to the young Duke of Rutland, whom he had not seen since his Belvoir days: he had rather tactlessly declined an invitation to attend the Duke's twenty-first birthday celebrations in 1799, and meeting him on such a formal public occasion must have seemed a convenient way to patch up their always uneasy relationship. Among the many other public figures present, with whom Crabbe took the opportunity to exchange an uncharacteristically diplomatic word, was Bishop Pretyman of Lincoln. His son was suitably impressed by it all, as he 'saw from the gallery of the Senate House the academical ceremonies in all their imposing effect, and viewed them, with the more interest because I was soon after to be admitted to Trinity'.[19] Indeed, on their return journey through Cambridge from Muston, he 'was examined, and entered' – he makes it sound as cursory an affair as Crabbe's Lambeth examination, which probably it was – and, in October 1803, he duly went up to Trinity. Keeping the Vice-Master sweet can have done no harm at all.

Crabbe had adopted Cambridge as his own surrogate university, and luckily it seems to have taken to him. He would habitually visit the Botanic Garden, where the curator, James Donn – who, says the son, 'read my father's character at once' – seems to have allowed the benign and eccentric botanical clergyman the freedom to take 'such duplicates of plants as could well be spared from the garden'.[20] When, a few years later, both his sons were in residence (George studying for his MA at Trinity, John an undergraduate at Gonville and Caius), Crabbe enjoyed several extended visits, 'dining in [Caius] or Trinity every day, and passing his mornings chiefly in the botanic garden'.[21] If, botanising in boggy fenlands apart, there was an earthly paradise for him, then this was surely it. On one of these occasions, his younger son – more relaxed and outgoing than his elder brother in such matters – drove him out to the races at Newmarket: he 'booked no bets' but 'enjoyed his ride quite as much as many of the lads by whom he was surrounded' and viewed 'such juvenilities' with an 'enlarged and benignant eye'. The biographer son, in regarding the expedition as a somewhat outlandish novelty for his father, seems to have forgotten that the Rutland household, its chaplain included, would decamp for the very purpose of the Newmarket racing season to Cheveley, where earlier still the apothecary's apprentice had delivered medicines.

Returning to Suffolk after his first term at Cambridge, for the vacation of Christmas 1803, young George found his parents staying in Aldeburgh 'for the winter': Crabbe's two curacies were certainly, weather permitting, within riding distance, but it sounds nevertheless as if he may have been adopting a rather casual, demob-happy attitude to his parishioners as the end of his Suffolk years drew closer. He was relaxed in other ways, too. One night, when the family had retired to bed, the biographer son was awoken in the early hours by gunfire at sea, which was in turn answered by the great cannon at the fort (now Fort Green) to the south of the town. Napoleon was reportedly preparing to invade Britain: Aldeburgh was reckoned to be a likely landing place throughout the early years of the nineteenth century, and the largest of the Martello towers was to be built at Slaughden in 1810–12.[22] George naturally thought that the fateful moment had arrived and, with some difficulty, woke his father to tell him that the French were landing: 'I then mentioned that the alarm gun had been fired, that horsemen had been despatched for the troops at Ipswich, and that the drum on the quay was then beating to arms.'[23] Crabbe replied: 'Well, my old fellow, you and I can do no good, or we would be among them; we must wait the event.' When the son returned three quarters of an hour later, to report a false alarm, he found his father fast asleep again.

Though this story is fully consistent with Crabbe's fearlessness on other extraordinary occasions, it also raises more troublesome questions: what are we to make of his political quietism and his astonishing indifference to the great issues of his day? There is no particular reason why a country clergyman at this time should have had strong views on these matters: most probably did not. But Crabbe was more than simply a country clergyman: he was a literary man with wide intellectual interests, and such people are expected to *think*. However, the life he had led since leaving Belvoir had become in many ways increasingly withdrawn; Edmund Burke, his political and intellectual mentor, had died in 1797; and his faith, though well adapted to questions of individual morality, was not of a sort to embrace grand ideological gestures. He had no firm sense of political commitment: in elections he invariably gave his support to the candidate who seemed to him worthiest, irrespective of party allegiance. Like Wordsworth, he had at first been well-disposed towards the French Revolution, though subsequently disillusioned; and his residual feeling about a possible invasion might almost have been that, as long as they behaved decently, there was no great harm in it – a view which, steeped as it is in English pragmatism, is not nearly as anachronistic and unpatriotic as it may sound.

Nevertheless, there is no avoiding the fact that Crabbe's lack of interest in political ideas and events is – like his peculiar lack of appreciation for music and painting – an aspect of his character which restricts his range as a writer. There are whole areas of cultural and intellectual experience, close to the heart of most literary lives, which we must not look for in Crabbe; and, while it would be pointless to regret their absence, it would be equally foolish to deny it.

4

The Crabbes returned to Muston towards the end of August 1805. They had spent several weeks at Aldeburgh where Sarah, badly affected by the prospect of leaving Suffolk, was 'extremely and (as she supposes) even dangerously ill, and though I am in hope of a more favourable termination, yet I cannot look to a day when I can leave her'.[24] In one of his last sermons at Swefling, preached on 14 July, Crabbe had assured his congregation that 'the comforts of a pious mind greatly overbalance the restraints our duties lay upon us',[25] and he must very much have hoped that this would prove to be true. By the time he preached once again in his own church on 1 September, he may have begun to have his doubts: his flock had indeed 'strayed from thy ways like lost sheep', and he cannot have avoided the recognition that this was substantially his own fault. During his absence, a succession of curates – Richardson Balderston, John Scott, Thomas Norris, James Henry Pugh, James Salisbury, Montague Welby and George Kendrick – had come and gone under clouds of various shapes and sizes: some had been troublesome or incompetent, but the alarmingly rapid turnover suggests that most of them cared even less for Muston than Crabbe did. Into this spiritual vacuum a Wesleyan minister had stepped and 'formed a thriving establishment'; worse still, though on a much smaller scale, 'a disciple of Huntington' had succeeded 'in spreading in the same neighbourhood the pernicious fanaticism of his half-crazy master'.[26] This was not, as the biographer son makes painfully clear, simply a matter of theological disagreement but one of personal embarrassment and wounded pride, for among the converts were two of his own long-standing household servants: 'The man, a conceited ploughman, set up for a Huntingtonian preacher himself; and the woman, whose moral character had been sadly deteriorated since her adoption of the new lights, was at last obliged to be dismissed, in consequence of intolerable insolence.'[27] It was exactly the kind of situation – simultaneously an affront to his standing as rector and as employer – to reawake all Crabbe's old insecurities, and he reacted predictably: that is to say, he overreacted. His son ruefully notes that 'the warmth with which he began to preach against dissent only irritated himself and others, without bringing back disciples to the fold'.

The Huntingtonians, or Calvinistic Methodists, followers of William Huntington, 'The Coal-Heaver', are not to be confused with the Huntingdonians or The Countess of Huntingdon's Connection, a far less extreme Calvinistic Methodist denomination founded by George Whitefield and Selina, Countess of Huntingdon. Huntington's doctrine – at the heart of which was the convenient notion that the 'elect', being assured of salvation in the next life, could do whatever they pleased in this one – was a transitory and opportunistic one from which Crabbe had little to fear. But for him to take on the Wesleyan or Arminian Methodists, as he now did with almost fanatical fury, was both unproductive and absurd. Had he not admiringly listened to Wesley in London and later, in Lowestoft, even introduced himself to the great man? Wesley himself was now dead, but of all theological gulfs that between Crabbe's undemonstrative Anglicanism and Wesley's Methodism should have remained the narrowest: his repeated attempts to widen it, both in his sermons and his poetry, had nothing to do with theological sense and everything to do with his own guilty insecurity. The fuse was a slow-burning one: in his teasingly contradictory Preface to *The Borough* (1810), he attacks Huntington at ferocious and wasteful length, though he tries to hedge his bets over the Arminians. On one page, he writes loftily: 'I must entreat that I may not be considered as one who takes upon him to censure the religious opinions of any society or individual.' On the next, he describes Methodism as 'this spiritual influenza', which sounds very like 'censure'. And, of course, in Letter IV of *The Borough*, 'Sects and Professions in Religion', despite the protestations of his Preface, he denounces with varying severity almost every non-Anglican denomination known to him. What is worth noticing at this point is the way in which Crabbe, once forced on to the defensive, becomes a typical, even a somewhat reactionary country parson of his time. The generation gap between him and his son, who is able to take a far more relaxed attitude towards the whole business, is nowhere more evident than here.

Crabbe had another reason to feel disputatious. Miss Elizabeth Tovell's will had not provided him with the financial breathing space for which he had hoped, and he was engaged in a long, acrimonious correspondence with James Wenn, the Ipswich lawyer acting for the executors, as he tried to release some funds to pay for his two expensive sons' years at Cambridge. In 1804 he had estimated that he would need about £80 per year to pay George's bills at Trinity,[28] and after John went up to Caius in 1807 his costs escalated: 'keeping two young men at an university in these times is, I find, beyond my ability,' he told Wenn early in 1808. 'The young men being one in his 23rd, and the other in his 21st year, and their mother earnestly and anxiously joining in our request, I am disposed to think that we shall not meet with difficulty in our wishes to dispose of so much of the funded property left to Mrs Crabbe and her children by her aunt as will reach £200,' he added.[29] This request to have £200 released, against the value of Miss Tovell's estate, for the education of its ultimate beneficiaries sounds eminently reasonable, but Wenn turned it down. Relations between the two men deteriorated sharply, ending with a bill and a threatening letter from the lawyer and a proudly indignant response from Crabbe, who had by now found another way to improve his finances: his difficulties, he said, 'were removed by means more pleasant and honourable than by an application to gentlemen in your profession'.[30] Although it seems natural to side with Crabbe, Wenn's reluctance may not have been wholly unjustified: the potential conflict of interests he perceived was precisely the difficulty which Crabbe had been storing up for himself from the moment he allowed himself to become both an executor and a beneficiary of John Tovell's will. Miss Tovell's ability to 'screw Crabbe up and down like a fiddle' had miraculously outlived her. She would have been pleased.

5

'I have been hard at work, and have had a good morning,' Crabbe liked to report, after a session spent either at his writing desk or 'walking and versifying'; he was 'fond of considering poetical composition as a species of task and labour'.[31] And so it is, especially for a writer engaged on a project such as *The Borough* or *Tales* or even *The Parish Register*: had not Cowper's great long poem actually been entitled *The Task*? Nevertheless, one can see why the son – whose notion of 'poetical composition' is perhaps closer to the second-generation Romanticism of Keats's poetry coming 'as naturally as leaves to a tree' – finds his father's method quaint; while, for us, it may more immediately resemble the working habits of a novelist such as Graham Greene, who famously wrote an exact number of words each morning. This does not turn Crabbe into a novelist, but it does make him a professional writer – and that was the 'means more pleasant and honourable' than further recourse to Wenn and his kind by which he had resolved to put right his finances.

At Little Glemham in 1794, Charles James Fox had urged him to break his creative silence and offered to 'peruse any work I might send to him previous to its publication'. As we have seen, Crabbe acted on the first part of this advice almost immediately; for, contrary to the apparent pattern of his publications, he hardly stopped writing during his 'silent' years. When, having been once deterred by Richard Turner, he at last came to assemble his next collection, he

> found my Right Honourable Friend engaged by the affairs of a great empire, and struggling with the inveteracy of a fatal disease; at such time, upon such mind, ever disposed as that mind was, I could not obtrude the petty business of criticising verses: but he remembered the promise he had kindly given, and repeated an offer, which, though I had not presumed to expect, I was happy to receive. A copy of the poems, now first published, was immediately sent to him, and (as I have the information from Lord Holland, and his Lordship's permission to inform my readers) the poem which I have named *The Parish Register* was heard by Mr Fox, and it excited interest enough, by some of its parts, to gain for me the benefit of his judgement upon the whole. Whatever he approved, the reader will readily believe, I have carefully retained: the parts he disliked are totally expunged, and others are substituted, which I hope resemble those, more comfortable to the taste of so admirable a judge. Nor can I deny myself the melancholy satisfaction of adding, that this poem (and more especially the story of Phoebe Dawson, with some parts of the second book) were the last compositions of their kind, that engaged and amused the capacious, the candid, the benevolent mind of this great man.

One might have supposed that, by the age of fifty, Crabbe would have outgrown the need to revise his work according to the superior taste of a public figure: this was, indeed, the last occasion on which he would do so (though he was seldom a man to deny himself 'melancholy satisfaction' if an opportunity presented itself). Fox died in September 1806: *Poems* of 1807 is dedicated, in Crabbe's most fulsome and fawning style, to his nephew, Henry Richard Vassall Fox, Lord Holland.

With its confidently minimalist title, *Poems by the Rev. George Crabbe, Ll.B.* would prove to be one of the most spectacularly successful relaunches in the history of English literature: although that anachronistically modern term 'relaunch' would, of course, have been unfamiliar to its author, it was exactly what he intended. As late as May 1807, we find him writing to his publisher, John Hatchard, about the book's running order in terms which show a shrewd appreciation of the literary marketplace: 'I should have preferred the longer poem of *The Parish Register* to have preceded the rest . . . as the new matter is far the larger portion it might look better to have that first placed, so as not to have the air of a republication.'[32] However, as he guessed, it was too late to make changes. The book, when it was published in October, was in fact even more artfully arranged, with *The Village* preceding *The Parish Register*, as logically and thematically it must; the two less characteristic longer poems, *The Library* and *The Newspaper*, came next, with the more recent shorter pieces – 'The Birth of Flattery', 'Reflections upon the Subject . . .', 'Sir Eustace Grey', 'The Hall of Justice' and 'Woman!' – at the end. The effect was to foreground Crabbe's developing reputation as the narrative poet of rural England, while cushioning the poems which now looked rather old-fashioned between more recent work. It was a skilful piece of publishing.

Poems officially appeared on 29 October 1807; Crabbe had presentation copies to send out three weeks earlier. One went to Sir Charles Bunbury, accompanied by a brisk and eloquent explanation of the author's long silence which could hardly be bettered:

> I ought to have acknowledged your obliging attention to me at an earlier period and I have ever thought of doing so; having purposed many years since, a republication of my poems with the addition of more compositions; but the loss of my former society, the death of the late Duke of Rutland, the small cares of a clergyman and his family not wholly unmixed with greater cares all tended to procrastinate my purpose . . . [33]

Another copy went with a more formal (but less elegant) letter to Lord Holland, who replied in suitably delighted terms; however, in a postscript, he advised Crabbe 'to be very careful in correcting the press as the printer has committed some very unfortunate and discernable blunders – in one instance he has printed *more* instead of *now* at the end of a line and left the couplet without a rhyme'.[34] Crabbe took this advice to heart. When the second edition of the book was published in August 1808, he not only corrected the error but made numerous other minor changes: 'the Author has endeavoured to avail himself of such remarks as have been communicated to him since the publication of his work; and, so far as the time allowed, he has sought to make the improvements suggested.' He had already written to John Nichols, who had reviewed *Poems* anonymously in the *Gentleman's Magazine* of November 1807, where he had inadvertently included the offending couplet in a lengthy quotation:

> Whenever you may find room for the remaining part of my little volume (I mean your examination of it etc.) will you have the goodness to correct an error of the press, which being in my book your compositor has copied: it stands in page 1037 in the middle of the first column, where *more* is made to rhyme to *how*: the second line should be 'And where he wonder'd *then*, to cavil *now*'. This will be of use to me, even more than I should find in any other way, for your magazine in all probability will be seen by *all* my readers and they may then correct it for themselves.[35]

Crabbe makes some interesting assumptions here. The first, of course, is that Nichols himself wrote the review in the magazine of which he was publisher and editor; the second is that Nichols would be happy to correct an error not of his making in a subsequent article on the book; and the third is that Crabbe's readers – *all* his readers – would devotedly compare their texts with that in the *Gentleman's Magazine* and make the necessary correction. Though that looks like *folie de grandeur*, it is something slightly different: the recognition on Crabbe's part that he had written a poem which would last, so he had better get it right. Indeed, in the second edition, he not only corrected the word but rewrote the line as 'And where they once agreed, to cavil now'. Having done with this business in his letter to Nichols, Crabbe switches hats with typical abruptness and turns to the 'plates of Leicestershire fossils' for *The History and Antiquities of Leicestershire*, a subject which seldom failed to quicken the enthusiasm of both men.

The other reviews of Crabbe's *Poems* were almost unanimously favourable. The writer in the *Oxford Review* went so far as to describe his 'revisal of these poems' as 'the most agreeable task that we have had to perform, since we commenced our critical labours'; his conclusion – 'These poems will go down to posterity, and be often found upon the same shelf with those of

Dryden, Pope, Goldsmith, and Churchill'[36] – is more perceptive than it appears, in ranking Crabbe with the major poets of the preceding century rather than either lesser or newer writers. This was a point more virulently taken up by Francis Jeffrey, whose notice in the *Edinburgh Review* of April 1808 marked the critical turning point in Crabbe's career: 'within two days after the appearance of Mr Jeffrey's admirable and generous article,' says the son, 'Mr Hatchard sold off the whole of the first edition of these poems'.[37] Jeffrey at last made explicit the hitherto implicit fault line which divided Crabbe from his somewhat younger Romantic contemporaries, 'all that misguided fraternity', and in particular Wordsworth. The distinction which Jeffrey draws between the two poets is a fascinating (if arguably obtuse) one; for, without actually mentioning the Preface to the *Lyrical Ballads*, he manages to suggest that it is Crabbe rather than Wordsworth himself who fulfils the promises of that great literary manifesto:

> Mr Crabbe exhibits the common people of England pretty much as they are, and as they must appear to every one who will take the trouble of examining into their condition; at the same time that he renders his sketches in a very high degree interesting and beautiful, – by selecting what is most fit for description, – by grouping them into such forms as must catch the attention or awake the memory, – and by scattering over the whole, such traits of moral sensibility, of sarcasm, and of useful reflection, as every one must feel to be natural, and own to be powerful. The gentlemen of the new school, on the other hand, scarcely ever condescend to take their subjects from any description of persons that are at all known to the common inhabitants of the world; but invent for themselves certain whimsical and unheard of beings, to whom they impute some fantastical combination of feelings, and labour to excite our sympathy for them, either by placing them in incredible situations, or by some strained and exaggerated moralisation of a vague and tragical description. Mr Crabbe, in short, shows us something which we have all seen, or may see, in real life; and draws from it such feelings and such reflections as every human being must acknowledge that it is calculated to excite. He delights us by the truth, and vivid and picturesque beauty of his representations, and by the force and pathos of the sensations with

which we feel that they ought to be connected. Mr Wordsworth and his associates show us something that mere observation never yet suggested to any one. They introduce us to beings whose existence was not previously suspected by the acutest observers of nature, and excite an interest for them, more by an eloquent and refined analysis of their own capricious feelings, than by any obvious or very intelligible ground of sympathy in their situation. The common sympathies of our nature, and our general knowledge of human character, do not enable us either to understand, or to enter into the feelings of their characters. They are unique specimens and varieties of our kind, and must be studied under a separate classification.[38]

Jeffrey goes on to cite some specific Wordsworthian characters (of Martha Ray, he says that we learn 'nothing whatever . . . but that her name is Martha Ray; and that she goes up to the top of a hill, in a red cloak, and cries "Oh misery!"') before 'we turn with pleasure to the manly sense and correct picturing of Mr Crabbe'. The underlying point is, of course, a moral as well as a comical one: for Jeffrey has discovered that Wordsworth, despite the fine words of his Preface, is not terribly interested in ordinary people. Precisely the same discovery was to be made by Lewis Carroll, when he mercilessly converted the leech-gatherer of Wordsworth's 'Resolution and Independence' into the aged man of the White Knight's tale. But there is a difficulty here, and within it lies the reason why Wordsworth remains more widely admired as a poet than Crabbe.

Though brilliant as far as it goes, Jeffrey's argument fails to take account of two crucial factors. One is that we may be less interested in the ostensible subject of a poem than in its authorial perspective; the other is that we may remember a poem not primarily for its content but for its expression. On both counts, Crabbe can seem to be at a disadvantage: he is often thought to be an uninteresting man (which he is not) or a monotonous writer (which he sometimes is). At its worst, the danger with Jeffrey's line of advocacy is this: we might find ourselves persuaded that Crabbe was extraordinarily good at something that wasn't worth doing.

But it was worth doing. In *The Parish Register*, Crabbe 'must be considered as having first assumed that station among British poets which the world has now settled to be peculiarly his own'. He had, the son continues, essentially created a new kind of poem:

In the former works, a few minute descriptions had been introduced – but here was nothing but a succession of such descriptions; in them there had been no tale – this was a chain of stories; they were didactic – here no moral inference is directly inculcated: finally, they were regularly constructed poems – this boldly defies any but the very slightest and most transparently artificial connections. Thus differing from his former self, his utter dissimilarity to any other author then enjoying public favour was still more striking; the manner of expression was as entirely his own as the singular minuteness of his delineation, and the strictness of his adherence to the literal truth of nature; and it was now universally admitted, that, with lesser peculiarities, he mingled the conscious strength, and, occasionally, the profound pathos, of a great original poet.[39]

Though neither an impartial nor an expert critic, the biographer son surprisingly makes a stronger case than Jeffrey by choosing to compare *The Parish Register* with his father's earlier work rather than with Wordsworth's; above all, he valuably reminds us that, despite the mildly old-fashioned look of its heroic couplets, this is a radical, innovatory poem.

6

Although Crabbe begins *The Parish Register* with a sturdy and purposeful couplet – 'The year revolves, and I again explore / The simple annals of my parish poor' – the introductory section which follows is the weakest part of the poem. Instead of launching, as he seems to promise, straight into the substance of the piece, he proceeds via a deferential nod to the mock-epic ('No Muse I ask, before my view to bring / The humble actions of the swains I sing') to generalised sketches of assorted village locations. Clearly, his intention is to provide a descriptive context for readers who are unfamiliar with village life; but this tempts him towards the kind of moral simplification – the admirably neat cottage of an 'industrious swain' set against the irredeemably squalid public house – which the poem will otherwise largely avoid. Even so, his lightness of touch promises well, as in this summary of the virtuous peasant's reading matter:

> On shelf of deal, beside the cuckoo-clock,
> Of cottage-reading rests the chosen stock;
> Learning we lack, not books, but have a kind
> For all our wants, a meat for every mind:
> The tale for wonder and the joke for whim,
> The half-sung sermon and the half-groan'd hymn. [I. 70–75]

Tone is vitally important in Crabbe – when he misjudges it, the consequences can be disastrous – and the voice of his parson-narrator, virtually indistinguishable from his own, is continually authenticated by its inwardness: unlike a clergyman from a more prosperous background, he can affectionately satirise the lives of the parish poor because he has been one of them (moreover, when he pokes gentle fun at the clerical profession, as he does in the last line quoted, it is usually a good sign). In this case he goes on to comment on the individual books in a benign spirit far removed from *The Library*, though he is necessarily severe about Bunyan. Even when he deals with the unspeakable public house, he provides telling details which prove that he knows exactly what he is talking about: 'Here are no wheels for either wool or flax, / But packs of cards – made up of sundry packs.' The rhyme is jauntily outrageous, the repetition typical of Crabbe when he is enjoying himself; but it is that tiny detail – the knowledge that the pub's much-used, well-thumbed packs of cards are cannibalised from assorted incomplete packs – which shows him to be an insider.

Crabbe's confident good humour in *The Parish Register* springs from this intimate knowledge of his subject-matter. When he turns to individual baptisms, the first is the illegitimate child of the miller's daughter, swept off her feet by a handsome sailor who subsequently goes back to sea and is killed. In an obvious sense, it is a grim little tale; but it is lightened by the sailor's wonderfully extravagant argument for his acceptance as a suitor by his prospective father-in-law:

> 'Cheer up, my lass! I'll to thy father go –
> The Miller cannot be the Sailor's foe;
> Both live by Heaven's free gale, that plays aloud
> In the stretch'd canvas and the piping shroud;
> The rush of winds, the flapping sails above,

And rattling planks within, are sounds *we* love;
Calms are our dread; when tempests plough the deep,
We take a reef, and to the rocking sleep.' [I. 321–8]

This is both ingenious, unfolding as it does from a deft pun on 'sails', and funny; it is also an early instance of the way in which Crabbe's characters in *The Parish Register* come to self-generating life. The individuals in Wordsworth are by comparison static and emblematic (which is perhaps why he takes only intermittent notice of them). In E. M. Forster's terms, Wordsworthian characters tend to be flat, whereas Crabbe's are round; and that well-known distinction from *Aspects of the Novel* will also suggest why those who seem capable of surprising themselves (and us), such as the whimsically delusive sailor or the delightful Peter Pratt with his horticulturally named children, are rounder than those whose stories are aimed at simpler moral targets. Richard Monday, the foundling bleakly named after the day of his discovery and given the one forename unshared with any man in the village, is memorable as an anecdote but not as a character. After his mean parish upbringing, he prospers – 'Now Richard's talents for the world were fit, / He'd no small cunning, and had some small wit' – and Crabbe is sternly unforgiving about this: unlike Dickens, who was to learn much from him, he has no sense of Monday's steely unscrupulousness as a direct and even pitiable consequence of the way in which he was treated as a child. Richard Monday eventually dies at Monday Place, leaving his vast wealth to 'reforming charities', 'the blind and dumb', 'missions' and the provision of bibles:

But, to his native place severely just,
He left a pittance bound in rigid trust –
Two paltry pounds, on every quarter's day,
(At church produced) for forty loaves should pay:
A stinted gift, that to the parish shows
He kept in mind their bounty and their blows! [I. 761–6]

Rather than being at all astonishing, this is precisely what the parish deserves and we should expect: the tale commands our assent, but the character remains indistinct.

The voice of Part II, 'Marriages', is distinctly that of the Crabbe who at

Stathern had protested against marrying 'lads and lasses'. He begins by quoting Ovid – 'Disposed to wed, e'en while you hasten, stay; / There's great advantage in a small delay' – although, no longer young himself, he adds some counterbalancing advice: 'Yet not too long in cold debate remain: / Till age, refrain not – but if old, refrain.' One who fails to heed this advice is Gaffer Kirk, cheated out of his life-savings by 'an artful jade'; he is followed in the register by Donald, who has 'left the lasses on the banks of Tay' to travel south and win the hand of Mistress Dobson (readers alert to the correlations between Crabbe and Hardy will want to see in him a humbler precursor of Donald Farfrae in *The Mayor of Casterbridge*). Among the other memorable characters in this part of the poem are Lucy Collins, who falls for the superficial graces of an elegant footman before returning to her worthy but humble suitor Stephen Hill ('He mourns a flame revived, and she a love of lace'), and Fanny Price, who is courted by 'an amorous knight', Sir Edward Archer: 'Come then, my mistress, and my wife; for she / Who trusts my honour is the wife for me.'

> To this the damsel, meekly firm, replied:
> 'My mother loved, was married, toil'd, and died;
> With joys, she'd griefs, had troubles in her course,
> But not one grief was pointed by remorse;
> My mind is fix'd, to Heaven I resign,
> And be her love, her life, her comforts mine.' (II. 558–63]

Both the 'meekly firm' character and the essential shape of her story – rejecting the chance to marry above herself, Fanny settles for a more equal and more modest match – will be replicated in Fanny Price's namesake, the heroine of *Mansfield Park*. Jane Austen, who was one of Crabbe's most devoted readers, certainly intended this allusive homage. *Her* Fanny Price, of course, marries a clergyman.

At the heart of 'Marriages', however, Crabbe reverts to his opening proposition with the tale of Phoebe Dawson, which so impressed the terminally ill Fox. Of course, Fox's singling out of this episode may have been no more than a polite gesture; yet one can readily see why it should have caught his attention, for the story is clearly distinguished from those around it. Crabbe does something emphatic and odd here. He prefaces the tale with a moralising couplet ('Ah! fly temptation, youth, refrain! refrain! / I preach for ever; but I preach in vain!'); he repeats a version of this at the story's climax ('Ah! fly temptation, youth; refrain! refrain, / Each yielding maid and each presuming swain!'); and he concludes with a third version of the same idea ('Then fly temptation, youth; resist, refrain! / Nor let me preach for ever and in vain!'). These rhetorical interventions of a voice so very like the author's own may suggest that Phoebe Dawson and her husband are drawn closely from life, but we need to be cautious about making that kind of deduction: a notable weakness of some earlier biographers is their tendency to assume that the subjects of Crabbe's tales can be readily translated back into his life, whereas this author's assumption is that the majority are properly 'fictional' composites of actual and imaginary material. On the other hand, we have already seen that Crabbe is a poet who likes to reveal himself through coded hints, and in the mature narrative poems he does this in a variety of surprising ways: this is perhaps one of them. If we take into account the fairly limited topographical data Crabbe provides, we might tentatively identify the likeliest location as Parham, in which case the errant husband – 'By trade a tailor, though, in scorn of trade, / He served the Squire, and brush'd the coat he made' – would have been one of his own servants at Ducking Hall; and that would certainly account for his unusually forceful indignation at Phoebe's fate.

We may reasonably assume that Crabbe's time spent in Parham, Glemham and Rendham – and his simultaneous experience as curate of Great Glemham and Swefling – provides the raw material for *The Parish Register* (the actual parish registers of Swefling for these years confirm the general pattern though they do not provide exact correspondences). Two passages in particular seem to confirm this. One is the description in Part II of the farmers, 'coarsely kind and comfortably gay', whose wives can now boast such refinements as carpets 'form'd in Wilton's loom' and 'prints along the paper'd wall': these are the cultural contradictions he uneasily discovered at Ducking Hall. (During the Napoleonic Wars, grain and commodity prices rose, and farmers prospered accordingly, as Huchon points out; in one of his more helpful digressions, he adds that despite the harsher economic conditions of twenty years later, William Cobbett still found Suffolk farmers to be remarkably well-off.) The other passage is, famously, the description of the Widow Goe in Part III, 'Burials': she was 'an active dame', 'admired, if not approved; / Prais'd, if not honour'd; fear'd, if not beloved'. She is evidently a portrait of Mrs Tovell, who has perhaps been given – as if she needed it – a supplementary injection of her sister-in-law's acidity:

> 'Come,' if she said, they came; if 'go,' were gone;
> And if 'do this,' – that instant it was done.
> Her maidens told she was all eye and ear,
> In darkness saw and could at distance hear; –
> No parish-business in the place could stir,
> Without direction or assent from her . . . [III. 135–40]

In Crabbe's description of the Widow Goe there is an unmistakable sense, which will recur in some of his later tales, of the author closing in on a known subject with exact and teasing detail. All the same, he remains a wily fictionaliser. When Andrew Collett of the Crown Inn dies, one might be tempted to note that an inn of this name stood (and stands) within a few hundred yards of Great Glemham Hall; but that is, of course, an excellent reason for supposing that Crabbe has quite another inn in mind, and the White Horse at Swefling looks a likelier candidate. When he uses a local name, he is inclined to move it sideways. Isaac Ashford, 'a noble Peasant' based on the former parish clerk at Great Glemham, is the subject of the most delicatedly restrained elegiac lines in the poem:

> I feel his absence in the hours of prayer,
> And view the seat and sigh for Isaac there:
> I see no more those white locks thinly spread
> Round the bald polish of that honour'd head . . . [III. 490–93]

There is an Ashford House not in any of Crabbe's village parishes but in the nearby town of Saxmundham. In fact, the predominant relationship between the author and his material in *The Parish Register* is that which we might ordinarily expect to find in a novel.

Nowhere is this more strikingly evident than in the overall construction of the poem. In one sense, it is absolutely consistent with Crabbe's earlier work: after all, in *The Library* he had devised a form which enabled him to move from topic to topic in an easy, apparently random way. The huge advance in *The Parish Register* is that those topics are replaced by individuals, each with their own tale, who appear in the purportedly 'found' sequence of the register itself. Although as a narrative method this obviously owes something to the eighteenth-century picaresque novel, it is also an intensely modern idea, with its swift transitions and apparently random juxtapositions. Eliot or Joyce or Virginia Woolf would have understood perfectly what Crabbe was up to; René Huchon, writing in the pre-modernist year of 1907, plainly did not. In his reading of *The Parish Register*, he transforms the introductory section into an imaginary tour of the village conducted by the clergyman and then reorganises the characters into a descending order of social classes, thus seeming to make an orderly, discursive argument out of the poem. Having rearranged an unconventional work as an entirely conventional one, Huchon is able to proclaim, with breathtaking complacency, that *The Parish Register* lacks 'boldness' and 'does not contribute any new idea to literature'.[40] His complete incomprehension is in its way the most remarkable testimony to Crabbe's originality.

Equally misguided, though much more peculiar, is J. H. Evans's account of the poem, published in 1933. Evans would have had no chronological excuse for failing to apply the terms of modernism to Crabbe's work, if he had been in the slightest degree literary; he was, however, the vicar of Croxton Kerrial and Rector of Branston-by-Belvoir, and he was as devoted to the Vale of Belvoir as the centre of his universe as, in *Pride and Prejudice*, Jane Austen's Mr Collins was to Rosings (one chapter of his book on Crabbe is headed 'Croxton Kerrial's Charming Situation'). Accordingly, he is anxious to discover the models for *The Parish Register* not in Suffolk but in and around the parish of Muston, to which Crabbe had only recently returned. For the most part this is a ludicrous enterprise, unassisted by Evans's idiosyncratic and often ungrammatical prose, and yet in one respect it is both interesting and plausible. Evans states unequivocally that Dibble, the last character in *The Parish Register*, is 'Muston's parish clerk'. And so, coming as he does at the end of the poem, he might well be: after all, Crabbe had already tacked on a Leicestershire conclusion to a Suffolk poem in *The Village*. Dibble tells, in his own departed voice, a tale within a tale, of the five former rectors he had served: 'Good master Addle', 'Parson Peele', 'Dr Grandspear', 'the Author-Rector' and 'a youth from Cambridge'. Evans convincingly identifies 'Addle' as the Parson Trulliber-like Samuel North, who came to Muston in

January 1738 and was buried there in March 1758, while 'Peele' is Francis
Bacon, who was succeeded by his son, Francis Bacon DD ('Dr Grandspear')
in April 1768; the 'Author-Rector' who follows him is obviously Crabbe
himself. This makes perfect sense, and the sideways disguise of 'Peele' for
Bacon – one Elizabethan writer for another – is absolutely typical of Crabbe.
But Evans wants *The Parish Register* to correspond too literally with his local
history, so he has to conclude with the 'Author-Rector' and to omit his
successor, the 'youth from Cambridge' who, like Crabbe himself though in
an altogether more impressionable state, has evidently heard the evangelical
Charles Simeon preach at Little St Mary's; the university and the vocation are
all this youth has in common with the biographer son. Evans also has to
ignore the fact that the 'Author-Rector' in the poem is dead. Killing himself
off, of course, is one of Crabbe's more drastic fictionalising strategies, for
this is clearly meant at least in part as a self-deprecating self-portrait:

>   'Then came the Author-Rector: his delight
> Was all in books; to read them, or to write:
> Women and men he strove alike to shun,
> And hurried homeward when his tasks were done.
> Courteous enough, but careless what he said,
> For points of learning he reserved his head;
> And, when addressing either poor or rich,
> He knew no better than his cassock which.
> He, like an osier, was of pliant kind,
> Erect by nature, but to bend inclined;
> Not like a creeper falling to the ground,
> Or meanly catching on the neighbours round. –
> Careless was he of surplice, hood, and band –
> And kindly took them as they came to hand;
> Nor, like the doctor, wore a world of hat,
> As if he sought for dignity in that.
> He talk'd, he gave, but not with cautious rules,
> Nor turn'd from gipsies, vagabonds, or fools;
> It was his nature, but they thought it whim,
> And so our beaux and beauties turn'd from him . . .' [III. 865–84]

If with the gluttonous 'Addle' we were in the world of Fielding, with 'Dr Grandspear' who, in that marvellous phrase, 'wore a world of hat' we approach the world – and surely meet the prototype – of Trollope's archdeacon, Dr Grantly.

Crabbe ends *The Parish Register* with a personal, autumnal coda: 'Like flowers we wither, and like leaves we fall.' He was in his fifties, with two grown-up (but still educationally expensive) sons and an ailing wife, in a place for which he had no great affection; he can have had little doubt that he would end up, like his fictionalised counterpart, buried at Muston. Autumn, however, had always been his most productive season for writing, and his creative life had hardly begun.

7

Crabbe lost no time in sending copies of *Poems* not only to his patrons and sponsors, such as Lord Holland and Sir Charles Bunbury, but also to both old and new friends. One recipient who must have been more surprised than most was John Bonnycastle, now a teacher of mathematics at Woolwich Academy, who had last seen Crabbe in his impoverished London days:

> The pleasure of hearing from you [wrote Bonnycastle in reply], after a silence of more than twenty-eight years, made me little solicitous to inquire how it has happened that two persons, who have always mutually esteemed each other, should have no intercourse whatever for so long a period. It is sufficient that you are well and happy, and that you have not forgot your old friend; who, you may be assured, has never ceased to cherish the same friendly remembrance of you. – You are as well known in my family as you are pleased to say I am in yours; and whenever you may find it convenient to come to this part of the world, both you and yours may depend upon the most sincere and cordial reception.[41]

Bonnycastle goes on to tell Crabbe about his own children: there is a grown-up daughter as well as a son 'upon the point of becoming an officer in the engineers and two younger boys, who at this moment are deeply engaged in your poems, and highly desirous of seeing the author, of whom they have so often heard me speak'. He renews his invitation, gently indicating in passing that he too keeps distinguished company: 'Life, as my friend Fuseli constantly repeats, is very short, therefore do not delay coming to see us any longer than you can possibly help.' It is a splendid letter, combining proper formality with real affection and a sly hint of mutual reproach at the two old friends' failure to keep in touch over the intervening years. They would indeed meet again, though not next at Woolwich.

Another recipient whose response seems nicely judged was Jane Burke. She too wrote with both warmth and politeness, but the heart of her letter is a just tribute to her late husband's perceptive generosity in supporting Crabbe: '*Your friend* never lost sight of worth and abilities. He found them in you, and was most happy in having it in his power to bring them forward.'[42] The son understandably prints these, together with other, less sharply focused replies to his father: thank-you letters to authors are not always easy to write, especially if the book remains unread. William Mansel, the Master of Trinity who the following year became Bishop of Bristol, 'found it to be almost the only book of late times which I could read through without making it a sort of duty to do so';[43] but he cannot have read it through very carefully, for his praise of 'delightful poems' and 'charming scenes' seems far enough from the relatively abrasive *Poems* to have provoked a wry smile in the rectory at Muston. Other letters of thanks and congratulation duly arrived from George Canning, Lord Grey and Roger Wilbraham.

While Crabbe's venture with Hatchard prospered – a second and a third edition of *Poems* were both called for in 1808 – his other London publisher suffered a disastrous misfortune. On 8 February 1808, John Nichols's premises in Red Lion Passage, off Fleet Street, burnt down and his entire stock was destroyed: his 'losses in excess of insurance were nearly £10,000'.[44] Curiously, Crabbe waited for almost a year before commiserating with his friend, and his explanation for the delay is curious too: 'I did not (nor indeed did I consider it as an act of friendship) write on the occasion.'[45] There is a glimpse in that simple sentence of his abiding reticence and shyness, his uncertainty about the appropriate way to respond to a difficult occasion. And this is confirmed by his next sentence, in which he sounds – as he very seldom does in his letters to literary friends – exactly like the parson he is: 'I trust in God your mind is not to be overborne by the pressure of outward circumstances only, melancholy and trying as they truly are.' Only when he returns to the practicalities of their mutual interest, *The History and Antiquities of Leicestershire*, does his style relax: 'For many years I have ceased to fossilise and have not much attended to natural history . . .' He promises to 'set about the vale-fossils' and to send on the plates and references 'with my and Mr Mounsey's account of them'.

There was, however, a further reason why Crabbe might have been reluctant to write to Nichols in 1808. He refers in his letter to a debt 'so long remembered that, as Dr Young observes, it was forgotten'; and this seems, almost incredibly, to have been the unpaid bill for Nichols's work on the abortive 'poetical miscellany' of 1781. Crabbe, as we have already seen, was extremely short of money in 1808, with both sons still at Cambridge and with no financial help forthcoming from the recalcitrant Wenn. But by the beginning of 1809, the success of *Poems* meant that he had funds on account with John Hatchard, and accordingly he hoped that Hatchard would be able to discharge on his behalf the ancient debt with Nichols. He remained cautious, having by the end of his letter fully metamorphosed from moralising clergyman into sceptical professional author: 'If Mr Hatchard's account corresponds with the good opinion of the public I shall consider the attempt as fortunate, but I am afraid we authors are looked upon as a kind of creatures who ought to be satisfied with very moderate return for our labours. I shall see.'

By March, Hatchard had indeed settled the debt, and Crabbe was able without regret to 'conclude the printed verses were long since destroyed, or if not, that they perished with so many better things in an event which every literary, indeed every feeling person will not cease to lament'.[46] It is a decent sentiment, though it may not be altogether true. Since a considerable part of Nichols's stock must have consisted of material as obsolete and unsaleable as Crabbe's abandoned miscellany – and this was insured, even if at less than its notional retail value – the publisher might not have been sorry to see the back of it. Certainly, the progress of the Leicestershire history seems to have been encumbered more by its authors' sluggishness than by its publisher's misfortune; but now that he had found a way to clear his debt and his conscience, Crabbe was able to press on and finish his task. He insisted that his collaborator, who 'had all the trouble and difficulty of arrangement', should receive due credit (as he did) and that his own name should appear 'where your kindness may find room for it': the appropriate section is headed 'The Natural History of the Vale of Belvoir. By the Rev. George Crabbe, B.D.

Rector of Muston.' Not only had his financial pressures eased; he was also able to report to Nichols that 'Mrs Crabbe is in rather better than usual health'. Moreover, he was shortly to deliver to Hatchard a book-length collection of linked narrative poems, precisely designed to build on the success of *The Parish Register*. He had certainly – as he quaintly put it to Nichols – 'ceased to fossilise'.

Seven

In Search of Peter Grimes

1810

I

Crabbe's son tells us that his father had started writing *The Borough* 'while he lived at Rendham', to which we need merely add: 'if not before'. Its author insisted on referring to it as 'the Poem' but it is, of course, more accurately an ambitious and disparate sequence of narrative poems which encompasses material from his entire life. It seems certain that some of this was sketched at Parham and Glemham, while other sections – such as the notorious Letter IV on 'Sects and Professions in Religion' – all too clearly reflect the bees in Crabbe's bonnet after he returned to Muston. The crucial point to recognise at the outset is that *The Borough* is a complicated and not altogether satisfactory hybrid, rather than the unified fiction which Crabbe seems to promise, with a typical mixture of blathering apologia and strategic cunning, in his Preface. It is worth attending to that Preface, if only to discover the ways in which the author would like to mislead us.

He begins by declaring that he has been 'encouraged by some proofs of public favour' to publish *The Borough*; indeed, once he had formed an opinion of 'the ensuing Letters' and 'began to conceive that they might not be unacceptable to the public, I felt myself prompted by duty, as well as interest, to put them to the press'. He is comically insistent that he is now at last relying upon his own judgement rather than on the critical opinions of his friends: 'I am willing to confess that I have lost some portion of the timidity once so painful, and that I am encouraged to take upon myself the decision of various points, which heretofore I entreated my friends to decide.' The friends who were once his 'council, whose opinion I was implicitly to follow' have now been demoted to 'advisers, whose ideas I am at liberty to reject'. This conjures up a vision of the poet surrounded by a kind of deferential literary cabinet, but the distinction is in any case ridiculous, since Crabbe had always possessed this 'liberty', even if he had previously chosen not to use it. In fact, when Crabbe and his family visited Aldeburgh in 1809, he took the draft manuscript of *The Borough* with him and once again sought the opinion of his old friend Richard Turner at Great Yarmouth. Turner, no doubt remembering the dramatic consequences of his comments on Crabbe's earlier work, was cautious: his reaction, according to the biographer son, was 'highly favourable', although he hinted 'that there were portions of the new work which might be liable to rough treatment from the critics'.[1]

After this, Crabbe's Preface becomes more subtly disingenuous. 'When the reader enters into the Poem,' he writes, 'he will find the author retired from view, and an imaginary personage brought forward to describe his Borough for him.' What he perhaps sought, but lacked the means to achieve, was that mysterious ambiguity of the Proustian narrator who both is and is not the author; as an alternative strategy, he might have concealed his first person within a mask of absurdity, as Sterne had done in *Tristram Shandy*, if only he had possessed that sort of comic invention (or intention). As it is, however, Crabbe swiftly undermines the autonomy of his 'imaginary personage', not only later in the Preface but flagrantly in *The Borough* itself, where the opening 'General Description' is immediately followed by the very three subjects – 'The Church', 'The Vicar – The Curate' and 'Sects and Professions in Religion' – on which it would have been least possible for him to sustain a plausible distance between author and narrator. Like the novelists of the earlier eighteenth century (his admired Fielding in particular) rather than his more sophisticated contemporaries, he is blithely forgetful of fictional convention whenever it suits him.

Yet there is one sense in which *The Borough* is properly fictionalised, and ironically it is a point on which casual readers often ignore Crabbe's clear intention. In his Preface he excuses the absence of 'a more historical account of so considerable a Borough' on the curious grounds of 'the utter repugnancy which subsists between the studies and objects of topography and poetry'. Since he does – as he immediately states – include 'the sea, and the country in the immediate vicinity; the dwellings, and the inhabitants', he is evidently using 'topography' in a sense which we may find unusual; for by the ordinary dictionary definition of the word as 'the detailed study, description, or features of a limited area', as Chambers has it, *The Borough* is plainly a topographical poem. What it is not, despite the predisposition of readers to see it as such, is a poem about Aldeburgh. The clue is there in the phrase 'so considerable a Borough' as well as in the 'General Description': late eighteenth-century Aldeburgh was not 'considerable' – its earlier prosperity had been eroded by tide and storm, while its reinvention as a nineteenth-century resort still lay in the future – and it could not have contained the number or variety of streets, buildings and other features described in Crabbe's poem. For example, his Letter XI, 'Inns', mentions some twenty inns and ale-houses, whereas the Aldeburgh listing in White's directory of 1844 – by which time the population had almost doubled from 804 in 1801 to 1,557 in 1841 – has only ten. Crabbe has combined recollections of his home town (such as the unmistakable description of the street which now bears his name in Letter XVIII, 'The Poor and Their Dwellings', lines 242–73) with elements drawn from Woodbridge, Beccles and his imagination to create a seaport on a distinctly larger scale; Aldeburgh, he later explained, was simply 'a Suffolk Borough which helped me to my scenery and some of the characters in the poem which I have called by that name'.[2] And this is important because it succeeds where his narrative self-denial fails: it is the fictionalised setting, rather than the fictionalised speaker, which prevents *The Borough* from veering back towards simple autobiography. Although it deals glancingly with 'the growth of a poet's mind', it is not *The Prelude*, even in disguise.

Despite its geographical unity and its formal consistency, *The Borough* contains three very different sorts of poem. In the first group, the local description is subservient to more general, polemical points about religion and politics; in the second, Crabbe deals with various professions and trades but, with partial exceptions such as the lawyer Swallow in Letter VI, he does not examine a single character at anything like a full poem's length. The transition to the third group comes at Letter XIII, 'The Alms-House and Trustees', among whom is Sir Denys Brand, 'the proud ostentatious man in the Borough, who disguised a little mind by doing great things' and who is 'the nearest to real life'[3] in Crabbe's work. After this, the major character studies appear, and the vast improvement in these later poems confirms what Crabbe's readers must have already suspected, that his sustained and sympathetic interest is in the poor of the borough – and in telling tales. This progression sounds perfectly reasonable, but it is not quite as logical as it looks. If Crabbe had written the poems of *The Borough* in the sequence in which they appear in print, the steady movement towards his most successful writing would make sense; however, we have already seen that this cannot be the case, since the anti-Methodist Letter IV must have been among the last to be completed. Like many poets, he was not a particularly good judge of his own work: perhaps his earlier dependence on his friends' judgement was not so foolish after all.

2

The seven 'letters' devoted to single characters in the second half of *The Borough* – 'Blaney', 'Clelia', 'Benbow', 'The Parish-Clerk', 'Ellen Orford', 'Abel Keene' and 'Peter Grimes' – represent an extraordinary progression: it is as if Crabbe begins by demonstrating the conventional limitations of his chosen form, the moral tale in mock-heroic couplets, and then makes a series of adjustments to his mixture before arriving finally at a poem which triumphantly surpasses anything which this recipe might have been expected to produce. The inherent difficulty with the moral tale is its tendency to lock together cause and effect so rigidly that the reader's capacity for interested surprise is eliminated: that was the trouble with, for instance, Richard Monday in *The Parish Register*. And it remains the trouble with the three inhabitants of the almshouse here. Blaney repeatedly squanders his wealth; Clelia is flighty and frivolous; Benbow drinks to excess. Each is rewarded with a morally appropriate fate, which makes for a less gripping tale than a morally inappropriate fate might have done.

There is a little more than that to it, obviously. Clelia, for instance, is given some fragments of her creator's past, notably his fondness for the theatre:

> She with the London stage familiar grew,
> And every actor's name and merit knew;
> She told how this or that their part mistook,
> And of the rival Romeos gave the look;
> Of either house 'twas hers the strength to see,
> Then judge with candour – 'Drury-Lane for me.'

What made this knowledge, what this skill complete?
A fortnight's visit in Whitechapel-street. [XV. 23–30]

There is a wonderfully sly irony in locating Clelia's London visit in Whitechapel, where Crabbe himself had stayed in 1777 during his first, conspicuously non-theatrical, stay in the capital. In Benbow, too, there are moments at which the tang of lived experience seems unmistakable. All too familiar with the effects of alcohol on his father, Crabbe as usual treats drunkenness with an inward understanding which mitigates his severity:

With wine inflated, man is all upblown,
And feels a power which he believes his own;
With fancy soaring to the skies, he thinks
His all the virtues all the while he drinks;
But when the gas from the balloon is gone,
When sober thoughts and serious cares come on,
Where then the worth that in himself he found? –
Vanish'd – and he sank grov'ling on the ground. [XVI. 44–51]

The last line, with its bathetic reduction of an extended conceit to a mere physical collapse, is overemphatic, but the account of the drunk's self-delusions is shrewd and not unsympathetic.

The first real surprise in this group of poems comes with Letter XIX, 'The Parish-Clerk'. At the very start of the poem we learn that the clerk, Jachin, has no sense of humour: he 'was the gravest man on ground, / And heard his master's jokes with look profound'; however, he nurses a secret, unfulfilled longing for worldly wealth. This in itself is fair warning that Crabbe, whose bone-dry humour should never be underestimated, is about to have some fun with him; and so it quickly proves, as we discover Jachin's absurdly vigilant defence of himself against the temptations of Satan. He will not drink, nor return women's smiles, nor tolerate music except in church:

No wonder Satan took the thing amiss,
To be opposed by such a man as this –
A man so grave, important, cautious, wise,
Who dared not trust his feeling or his eyes;

No wonder he should lurk and lie in wait,
Should fit his hooks and ponder on his bait;
Should on his movements keep a watchful eye;
For he pursued a fish who led the fry. [XIX. 45–52]

This bitterly sarcastic passage not only hints at Jachin's ultimate undoing; it reminds us strikingly of Crabbe's own full-blooded humanity. What is truly unforgivable about Jachin is that he 'dared not trust his feelings or his eyes': his specious morality is a cover for his refusal to engage with life, and this Crabbe will not tolerate. The simpler moral equations of the earlier poems give way to the much more interesting and complex spectacle of a man driven by the wrong sort of morality. (Crabbe blames John Bunyan, naturally.) Jachin's downfall thus impresses us as different in kind from the fates of those who merely spent too much, drank too much or enjoyed too many unstable relationships: his destiny is not merely pathetic but tragic.

Crabbe achieves this transformation with some skill. Jachin begins as a laughing-stock, taunted by his – or Satan's – friends, who do their best to get him drunk and to set him up with 'an artful lass'; but the author does not share their laughter. His point of view is subtly distanced: his acidic amusement is as much at the expense of these brainless 'friends' as of the self-deluding clerk himself. Perhaps he had in mind the taunting of Malvolio by Sir Andrew and Sir Toby: certainly, Jachin's frigid dignity becomes, like Malvolio's, more troubling than funny and this allows darker elements to disrupt the comedy, just as they do in *Twelfth Night*. When the transition comes, it is with an ominously creaking scene change: 'Thus far the playful Muse has lent her aid, / But now departs, of graver theme afraid'. Crabbe's task now is the tragedian's one of simultaneously destroying his central character and rebuilding the reader's sympathy for him. The 'worthy clerk' is aggrieved, and not without cause: though 'arrived at fame', he remains poor and is galled by the respect accorded to the 'weakest burgess'. Moreover, 'The year was bad, the christening-fees were small, / The weddings few, the parties paupers all.' In these unpropitious circumstances, it seems to him that some of the church collection for the parish poor might justifiably go into his pocket – since he is, after all, both of the parish and poor. It is the kind of only mildly skewed logic which underpins Shakespearian tragedy, as when (for example) Macbeth reasons that since it has been decreed that he shall be king, he may as well help things along by murdering Duncan. On one level, Jachin's actions, like Macbeth's, make perfect sense.

The first of Jachin's thefts from the wealthier worshippers in their box pews is described in beautifully paced detail:

> The morning came: the common service done –
> Shut every door – the solemn rite begun;
> And, as the priest the sacred sayings read,
> The clerk went forward, trembling as he tread;
> O'er the tall pew, he held the box, and heard
> The offer'd piece, rejoicing as he fear'd.
> Just by the pillar, as he cautious tripp'd,
> And turn'd the aile, he then a portion slipp'd
> From the full store, and to the pocket sent,
> But held a moment – and then down it went. [XIX. 189–98]

There is a teasing ambiguity here – and in the following paragraph, when a gold coin clinks noisily in the pocket which Jachin, in his nervous haste, has forgotten to fill with bran – which stems from the fact that we don't quite want him to be caught out. What Jachin is doing, though obviously wrong, is not wholly unsympathetic. When his theft is discovered and he is publicly disgraced, we feel with him (as we do with the hero in Act V of a tragedy) rather than with his self-satisfied accuser. And in his disgrace, Jachin bears a marked resemblance to Crabbe's more famous tragic figure, Peter Grimes:

> In each lone place, dejected and dismay'd,
> Shrinking from view, his wasting form he laid;
> Or to the restless sea and roaring wind
> Gave the strong yearnings of a ruin'd mind.
> On the broad beach, the silent summer-day,
> Stretch'd on some wreck, he wore his life away;
> Or where the river mingles with the sea,
> Or on the mud-bank by the elder-tree,
> Or by the bounding marsh-dyke, there was he;
> And when unable to forsake the town,
> In the blind courts he sate desponding down –

Always alone; then feebly he would crawl
The church-way walk, and lean upon the wall. [XIX. 270–82]

This is one of those resonant passages in which Crabbe taps into his deepest imaginative source, the landscape and seascape of childhood which would provide the scene for 'Infancy – A Fragment': this is his most distinctive tone, in which Augustan discipline is perfectly fused with the emotional charge of Romanticism.

We meet it again not, surprisingly, in Letter XX, 'Ellen Orford', despite the local significance of her name, but in Letter XXI, 'Abel Keene'. Abel's story reprises some familiar elements – a drab, gullible youth, he finds work as a clerk, is teased into folly by friends including his employer's son who, when his father dies, promptly sacks Abel – before he too finds himself in that bleak, ostracised solitude which so engages Crabbe's imagination:

And now we saw him on the beach reclined,
Or causeless walking in the wint'ry wind;
And, when it raised a loud and angry sea,
He stood and gazed, in wretched reverie;
He heeded not the front, the rain, the snow;
Close by the sea he walk'd alone and slow.
Sometimes his frame through many an hour he spread
Upon a tombstone, moveless as the dead;
And, was there found a sad and silent place,
There would he creep with slow and measured pace.
There would he wander by the river's side,
And fix his eyes upon the falling tide;
The deep dry ditch, the rushes in the fen,
And mossy crag-pits were his lodgings then:
There, to his discontented thoughts a prey,
The melancholy mortal pined away. [XXI. 191–206]

This is so similar in mood and tone to the description of Jachin's equally 'wretched reverie' that a casual reader might accuse Crabbe of repetition. But it is something more profound than that: there is something obsessional nagging away in this combination of a melancholy outcast and the landscape of his childhood. In 'The Parish-Clerk' and 'Abel Keene', Crabbe seems to be exploring and refining this powerful formula. It was about to produce his most remarkable poem.

3

Peter Grimes, the central figure in Crabbe's great poem, has three character-istics in common with Hamlet, the central figure in Shakespeare's great tragedy. It was C. S. Lewis who once said that he wouldn't cross the street to meet Hamlet, because Hamlet was always with him. Something of the sort is true of Peter Grimes. This doesn't mean, of course, that each of us carries within himself a bewildered prince whose mother has just married his regicidal uncle or a deranged fisherman given to fatally ill-treating his apprentices. It means, however, that Hamlet and Grimes, in their very different ways, engage their readers at an unusually deep and complex level: as a consequence, the works in which they appear can withstand endless interpretation and reinterpretation, a process greatly encouraged by the fact that each of their respective authors is writing at his best. That is the first and most important similarity between them. The second follows from it: Grimes, like rather few figures in nineteenth-century English literature (though Michael Henchard in *The Mayor of Casterbridge* springs to mind as another), is a tragic figure of truly Shakespearian dimensions, despite the relative brevity of the poem to which he gives his name. The third similarity can, for the time being, wait.

Most of us who have come to 'Peter Grimes' in the late twentieth century, or for that matter the early twenty-first, have done so by a peculiar route which its author could not have envisaged. There is nothing wrong with the route – this is, after all, a poem which invites and demands inter-pretation – but, since it involves nothing less than the transmutation of 'Grimes' through two of the age's greatest creative minds, it is bound to have had a significant impact on our view of the poem itself. The first of these minds is E. M. Forster's. In 1941, he wrote and delivered a talk for the BBC Overseas Service called 'George Crabbe: The Poet and the Man', which was subsequently printed in *The Listener*;[4] just over seven years later, in June 1948, he gave a lecture at the first Aldeburgh Festival on 'George Crabbe and *Peter Grimes*'.[5] One occasion was the direct result of the other, for the second creative mind was Benjamin Britten's: 'it was in California in the unhappy summer of 1941,' Britten would later recall, 'that, coming across a copy of the Poetical Works of George Crabbe in a Los Angeles bookshop, I first read his poem, *Peter Grimes*; and, at the same time, reading a most perceptive and revealing article about it by E. M. Forster, I suddenly realised where I belonged and what I lacked'.[6] Crabbe, with his unquenchable bittersweet homesickness for the Suffolk coast, would have utterly understood Britten's 'where I belonged and what I lacked'. In speaking through his *Listener* article to an unhappy expatriate, Forster had become the catalyst both for an operatic masterpiece and for a major music festival.

'To talk about Crabbe is to talk about England,' he began. And he swiftly moved on – writing in a slightly quaint, simple style which proves surprisingly evocative – to describe Aldeburgh for his Overseas Service listeners:

> It is a bleak little place: not beautiful. It huddles round a flint-towered church and sprawls down to the North Sea – and what a wallop the sea makes as it pounds at the shingle! Near by is a quay, at the side of an estuary, and here the scenery becomes melancholy and flat; expanses of mud, saltish commons, the marsh-birds crying. Crabbe heard that sound and saw that melancholy, and they got into his verse . . .
>
> He escaped from Aldeburgh as soon as he could . . . Yet he never escaped from Aldeburgh in the spirit, and it was the making of him as a poet. Even when he is writing of other things, there steals again and again into his verse the sea, the estuary, the flat Suffolk coast, and local meanness, and an odour of brine and dirt – tempered occasionally with the scent of flowers. So remember Aldeburgh when you read this rather odd poet, for he belongs to the grim little place, and through it to England.[7]

By the time Britten had read this far, the seeds of his *Peter Grimes* and his Aldeburgh Festival had probably been sown. Of Grimes himself, Forster says: 'he was a savage fisherman who murdered his apprentices and was haunted by their ghosts'. And of Crabbe the poet: 'I like him and read him again and again: and his tartness, his acid humour, his honesty, his feeling for certain English types and certain kinds of English scenery, do appeal to me very much.'[8]

It may seem a small matter, but transmutation has already taken place: 'a savage fisherman who murdered his apprentices and was haunted by their ghosts' sounds very like a character in a Britten opera and, though it is true to the facts, not quite like a character in a Crabbe poem. Britten, of course, had just read the poem itself for the first time and he would also have been struck – as Forster must have been – by its apparently inescapable sexual sub-text: the story of a man who acquires from London a series of young apprentices, whom he subsequently assaults and murders, carries overtones which two twentieth-century homosexuals couldn't conceivably ignore. It is well enough known that Britten was both attracted to adolescents and obsessed by the violent corruption of innocent youth: four of his operas – *Peter Grimes, Billy Budd, The Turn of the Screw* and *Death in Venice* – are centrally concerned with aspects of this theme. However, it is important to insist that, in Bernard Levin's elegant words, 'his private life was a model of devotion and integrity – it is not at all an exaggeration to say that the example set by Britten and Pears went far to instil throughout this country a sympathetic understanding, so long and brutally denied, of homosexual love'.[9] In fact, the obsession and the devotion are equal partners in the greatness of his *Peter Grimes.*

'Sadler's Wells! Any more for Peter Grimes, the sadistic fisherman!'[10] was the memorable cry of a London bus conductor whose vehicle stopped outside the theatre during the opera's triumphant first production in the summer of 1945. What would Crabbe have made of that? For the most part unshocked by the peculiarities of human behaviour, he might have managed a wry smile. He would also, no doubt, have wanted to point out that Britten's librettist, Montague Slater, had ruined a perfectly good poem; but that is what librettists do. Certainly, this *Peter Grimes,* though on its own terms a masterpiece, is no longer Crabbe's. And so, since 1945, the title *Peter Grimes* is most likely to conjure up Hobson's opening cry of 'Peter Grimes!', Grimes's anguished question 'What harbour shelters peace?', his haunting soliloquy 'Now the Great Bear and Pleiades . . .', or the magical scene-painting of the sea interludes. These are marvellous things, but they stand in the way of Crabbe's poem, to which we must now try to find a more direct route.

4

For directness or intimacy or immediacy are the sort of qualities which readers invariably find distinguish 'Peter Grimes' from almost all of

Crabbe's other narrative poems: its emotional commitment seems
unusually intense, its psychological penetration especially deep. One very
obvious explanation is that, although Crabbe's *Borough* is a fictional and
composite place, this poem is plainly set in the childhood landscape and
seascape, briefly invoked in 'The Parish-Clerk' and 'Abel Keene', which
would subsequently reappear in the powerfully autobiographical 'Infancy
– A Fragment'. But although this accounts for the detailed authenticity of
the descriptive passages, it does not necessarily bring us any nearer to
Grimes himself. To do this, we might perhaps turn to the son's annotation
of 1834:

> The original of Peter Grimes was an old fisherman of Aldborough
> while Mr Crabbe was practising there as surgeon. He had a
> succession of apprentices from London, and a certain sum from
> each. As the boys disappeared under circumstances of strong
> suspicion, the man was warned by some of the principal
> inhabitants, that if another followed in like manner he should
> certainly be charged with murder.

He subsequently added a manuscript note identifying the fisherman by
name as Tom Brown. Moreover, as Frank Whitehead points out, the events
in the poem appear to conflate Brown's story with another actual case
history, that of 'John Bennett, a fisherman living at Hammersmith, who was
indicted for the murder of his apprentice, George Main': the boy was said to
have fallen from the mast (as is the case with Grimes's second apprentice)
and it was also 'stated that Bennett had returned to Hammersmith with the
corpse of the boy *and* with a load of fish' (which is very like the fate of
Grimes's third apprentice). Whitehead further suggests that the appropriate
surname 'may have been suggested by the young man Grimes in Chapter 7
of Godwin's *Caleb Williams*, a novel that we know the poet to have possessed
in his library at Trowbridge'.[11] All this – though we shall return to the name
– seems convincing enough. The only trouble is that the weight of
background information is likelier to turn the main character into an
external figure than to bring him into such sharp, internalised psychological
focus.

It may be worth (as it often is) turning to Crabbe's own Preface:

The character of Grimes, his obduracy and apparent want of feeling, his gloomy misanthropy, the progress of his madness, and the horrors of his imagination, I must leave to the judgement and observation of my readers. The mind here exhibited, is one untouched by pity, unstung by remorse, and uncorrected by shame: yet is this hardihood of temper and spirit broken by want, disease, solitude and disappointment, and he becomes the victim of a distempered and horror-stricken fancy. It is evident, therefore, that no feeble vision, no half-visible ghost, not the momentary glance of an unbodied being, nor the half-audible voice of an invisible one, would be created by the continual workings of distress on a mind so depraved and flinty. The ruffian of Mr Scott [Marmion] has a mind of this nature: he has no shame or remorse: but the corrosion of hopeless want, the wasting of unabating disease, and the gloom of unvaried solitude, will have their effect on every nature; and the harder that nature is, and the longer time required to work upon it, so much the more strong and indelible is the impression. This is all the reason I am able to give, why a man of feeling so dull should yet become insane, and why the visions of his distempered brain should be of so horrible a nature.

This is subtle almost to the point of disingenuousness, and we certainly shouldn't be taken in by the apparently baffled shoulder-shrugging in the final sentence. Here, if we dare to disentangle them, are the reasons why Grimes seems so alarmingly close to his author – and to us. Crabbe knew about the 'progress' of 'madness' because he saw it every day in his wife; he knew about the 'horrors' of 'imagination' because he experienced them every night in dreams. There are moments in the poem – the descriptive paragraph beginning 'When tides are neap . . .' is an obvious instance – when it is Crabbe himself who has stepped into Grimes's shoes. But at the heart of Crabbe's prefatory remarks (and of the poem) is the portrait of a man 'untouched by pity, unstung by remorse, and uncorrected by shame' whose 'hardihood of temper and spirit' has been 'broken by want, disease, solitude and disappointment'. And that is a portrait of Crabbe's father.

5

He provides clues. At the start of the poem, Peter Grimes is compared with his identically named father (the third similarity with Hamlet), of whom he proves to be an unhappier and less successful version, precisely as had been the case with Crabbe's father and grandfather. This grandfather was, as we have seen, named Robert, although various writers – including the bio-grapher son and, following him, Forster in his BBC broadcast – have insisted that he was called George, making (since the poet's grandson would bear the same name) five generations of George Crabbes. Whitehead's explanation of 'Grimes' is perfectly plausible, but there is no reason why Crabbe, who so enjoyed codes and ciphers, should not also have indulged a fancy of the sort which certainly pleased him. Writing to the sculptor Sir Francis Chantrey in 1822, he confessed: 'I cannot account for the vanity of that one of my ancestors who first (being dissatisfied with the four letters which composed the name of "Crab", the sour fruit, or "Crab", the crusty fish) added his *be* by way of disguise'.[12] Similarly, 'by way of disguise', Crabbe might very well have extended the four letters of 'grim' to create the name 'Grimes'. Moreover, the everyday sense of 'grime' was precisely what Crabbe had encountered while working for his father on Slaughden Quay; and in Edward Moor's 1823 dictionary of *Suffolk Words and Phrases*, a book which happens to have been printed in Woodbridge by Crabbe's friend Loder, 'grime' is included as a peculiarly Suffolk word, meaning 'Dirt – filthy'.[13] 'Peter Grimes' is a name loaded with nuances from Crabbe's own past.

The poem's opening lines are among the most familiar in Crabbe's work and, for that matter, in early nineteenth-century poetry, so it may not be easy to read them as if for the first time. But that is what has to be done:

> Old Peter Grimes made fishing his employ,
> His wife he cabin'd with him and his boy,
> And seem'd that life laborious to enjoy:
> To town came quiet Peter with his fish,
> And had of all a civil word and wish.
> He left his trade upon the sabbath-day,
> And took young Peter in his hand to pray:

But soon the stubborn boy from care broke loose,
At first refused, then added his abuse:
His father's love he scorn'd, his power defied,
But being drunk, wept sorely when he died. [XXII. 1–11]

For the first seven lines, Crabbe deliberately misleads the reader into supposing that the man he is describing, 'Old Peter Grimes', is the subject of his poem (I borrowed the same trick for the opening page of this book). He also, unusually though not uniquely, begins the poem with an emphatic rhyming triplet. Consequently, the benign character of old Peter Grimes the father, whose qualities echo those of Crabbe's grandfather, is at once firmly established as the yardstick by which the conduct of young Peter Grimes the son must be judged. And this conduct, though obviously far more extreme than that of Crabbe's father, seems motivated by the same sense of inadequacy and disappointment that drove the elder George Crabbe to violence and drunkenness. He becomes, ironically in the light of the Saltmaster's occupation, a poacher:

With greedy eye he look'd on all he saw,
He knew not justice, and he laugh'd at law;
On all he mark'd he stretch'd his ready hand;
He fish'd by water, and he filch'd by land:
Oft in the night has Peter dropp'd his oar,
Fled from his boat and sought for prey on shore;
Oft up the hedge-row glided, on his back
Bearing the orchard's produce in a sack,
Or farm-yard load, tugg'd fiercely from the stack;
And as these wrongs to greater numbers rose,
The more he look'd on all men as his foes. [XXII. 40–50]

There is a subtle disparity between content and tone here: we have met this before, when Jachin stole from the church collection. Though there is no doubt about Peter's criminality, the sprightly, engaged character of Crabbe's writing suggests a degree of sympathetic inwardness. This is to be expected, if Grimes is indeed modelled on the Saltmaster: even fathers and sons who fall out share an inviolable closeness. But it also suggests a further reason for comparing Grimes with a Shakespearean tragic hero: he is a figure who, like

Macbeth, will commit appalling crimes yet ultimately retain the reader's allegiance.

Crabbe does not spare us the details of Grimes's brutality; but he repeatedly draws back from them to record the blandly ineffectual responses of the townsfolk. His moral perspective becomes clear in these well-known yet extraordinary lines about the first of the apprentices:

> Some few in town observed in Peter's trap
> A boy, with jacket blue and woollen cap;
> But none inquired how Peter used the rope,
> Or what the bruise, that made the stripling stoop;
> None could the ridges on his back behold,
> None sought him shiv'ring in the winter's cold;
> None put the question – 'Peter, doest thou give
> The boy his food? – What, man! the lad must live:
> Consider, Peter, let the child have bread,
> He'll serve thee better if he's stroked and fed.'
> None reason'd thus – and some, on hearing cries,
> Said calmly, 'Grimes is at his exercise.' [XXII. 67–78]

The passage is a procession of damning negatives. Crabbe understands that Grimes's behaviour, like his own father's, is compulsive: he is possessed by forces which are both destructive and self-destructive, but he is in a crucial sense not to blame. On the other hand, the townspeople – 'A crowd of ordinary decent folk / Watched from without and neither moved nor spoke', as Auden chillingly puts it in 'The Shield of Achilles' – are entirely culpable: their normality both obliges them to act and prevents them from doing anything. Once again, there is the unmistakable note of a perception authenticated by autobiographical experience: did the Saltmaster's Aldeburgh neighbours complacently say to each other, 'Crabbe is at his exercise', when they heard children being beaten? It seems all too probable. Even when the arrival of the third apprentice, 'of manners soft and mild', eventually stirs the 'seamen's wives' to sentimental pity, this proves hopelessly ineffectual. Crabbe's summary of the consequence is unsparingly sarcastic: 'The pitying women raised a clamour round, / And weeping said, "Thou hast thy 'prentice drown'd."'

After this, Peter Grimes is prohibited from hiring further apprentices (even here, Crabbe's tone – 'The mayor himself with tone severe replied . . .' – is withering). He becomes reclusive and melancholic; but he also becomes extraordinarily like his creator. The most remarkable fact about the justly celebrated passage describing his desolate, solitary meanderings is that it is simultaneously a brilliant evocation of Crabbe's own *pleasures*. This is the botanist-poet who had written to Edmund Cartwright, '. . . give me a wild, wide fen, in a foggy day; with quaking boggy ground and trembling hillocks in a putrid soil', thoroughly enjoying himself:

> Thus by himself compell'd to live each day,
> To wait for certain hours the tide's delay;
> At the same times the same dull views to see,
> The bounding marsh-bank and the blighted tree;
> The water only, when the tides were high,
> When low, the mud half-cover'd and half-dry;
> The sun-burnt tar that blisters on the planks,
> And bank-side stakes in their uneven ranks;
> Heaps of entangled weeds that slowly float,
> As the tide rolls by the impeded boat.
> When tides were neap, and, in the sultry day,
> Through the tall bounding mud-banks made their way,
> Which on each side rose swelling, and below
> The dark warm flood ran silently and slow;
> There anchoring, Peter chose from man to hide,
> There hang his head, and view the lazy tide
> In its hot slimy channel slowly glide;
> Where the small eels that left the deeper way
> For the warm shore, within the shallows play;
> Where gaping muscles, left upon the mud,
> Slope their slow passage to the fallen flood; –
> Here dull and hopeless he'd lie down and trace
> How sidelong crabs had scrawl'd their crooked race;
> Or sadly listen to the tuneless cry
> Of fishing gull or clanging golden-eye;
> What time the sea-birds to the marsh would come,

> And the loud bittern, from the bull-rush home,
> Gave from the salt-ditch side the bellowing boom:
> He nursed the feelings these dull scenes produce,
> And loved to stop beside the opening sluice;
> Where the small stream, confined in narrow bound,
> Ran with a dull, unvaried, sadd'ning sound;
> Where all, presented to the eye or ear,
> Oppress'd the soil with misery, grief, and fear. [XXII. 171–204]

If these lines seem to comprise a vital part of the Crabbe jigsaw, that is because they lock exactly into place with several other important pieces: the child of 'Infancy – A Fragment'; the botanist with his specific interest in the East Anglian coast; the mild, sociable man with an inner craving for solitude; and the poet who here achieves his most astonishing fusion of Augustan form with Romantic sensibility. He is so intimately involved with this recollected scene and so intuitively close to his central character that he can effectively forget about Grimes and write as if the observing consciousness were his own (as, of course, it is): 'He nursed the feelings these dull scenes produce, / And loved to stop beside the opening sluice . . .' He humanises Grimes by permitting him to share his own consolations.

Crabbe further reinforces his and our sympathy for Grimes by cheekily resorting to a strategy available only to genuine coastal locals: poking fun at holiday-makers. After Grimes's winter exile, 'summer lodgers' start to appear, 'idly curious' and training their glasses on 'sea-port views, which landmen love to see'. One of them spies a solitary boatman on the river:

> Fisher he seem'd, yet used no net nor hook;
> Of sea-fowl swimming by no heed he took,
> But on the gliding waves still fix'd his lazy look;
> At certain stations he would view the stream,
> As if he stood bewilder'd in a dream,
> Or that some power had chain'd him for a time,
> To feel a curse or meditate on crime. [XXII. 240–46]

This provides the catalyst for what is really the pursuit of Grimes ('some curious, some in pity went'), his descent into madness, his confinement to

'a parish-bed' and his final description of nightmarish visions – a pheno-
menon with which Crabbe himself was becoming increasingly familiar. That
he is to be seen as a figure akin to Shakespeare's tragic villains is reaffirmed
by two glancing references to *Macbeth*. Grimes's concluding account is
described as 'A madman's tale, with gleams of waking sense', recalling
Macbeth's 'a tale / Told by an idiot, full of sound and fury, / Signifying
nothing' (V. 5. 25–7); while the image of his ghostly father who 'shook / His
hoary locks, and froze me by a look' is a clear echo of Macbeth's admonition
to Banquo's ghost, 'never shake / Thy gory locks at me' (III. 4. 49–50). There
is also, perhaps, a recollection of the witches' spectral parade of kings in
Grimes's vision of his father together with 'a thin pale boy in either hand'.
The devastating image, near the very end of the poem, in which the water
turns to a mixture of blood and fire which his father flings ('a red-hot liquor')
in his face, has a truly Shakespearian force. 'Grimes is a natural pheno-
menon, rather than a fallible, weak, or silly man,' writes Terence Bareham.
'There seems to be an original sin in Grimes which, for all his "strictness",
Crabbe seldom suggests that man is cursed with.'[14] In daring to reach more
deeply than ever before into his own and his father's psychology, and into the
landscape of his childhood, Crabbe had created one of the great tragic
characters of English literature.

6

'The opinion of the leading Reviews was again nearly unanimous,' writes
Crabbe's son, 'agreeing that *The Borough* had greater beauties and greater
defects than its predecessor, *The Parish Register*.' That is a cautious comment,
and so is his next remark: 'With such a decision an author may always be well
pleased; for he is sure to take his rank with posterity by his beauties; defects,
where there are great and real excellences, serve but to fill critical
dissertations.'[15] If only that were true. His vote of confidence is a curiously
guarded one, and he compounds this oddity by singling out for special praise
the felon's tale from Letter XXIII, 'Prisons', rather than the preceding poem,
'Peter Grimes', which he fails to mention. He seems nervous about *The
Borough*, which he discusses more briefly than some of his father's lesser
works, and we can only guess why this might be; but it is more than likely that
he was made uncomfortable by its emotional and social extremities. If he had

an inkling of the buried autobiographical sources of 'Peter Grimes', he must
have found it an even more shocking poem than Crabbe's other readers.

That his readers *were* shocked is beyond doubt; and none was more so
than one of his greatest admirers, Francis Jeffrey of the *Edinburgh Review*.
Jeffrey's notice of *The Borough* in that journal's April 1810 number is of
particular interest because its author seems to be struggling with himself.[16]
It is, incidentally, Jeffrey's opening observation – 'It has the same peculiarities, and the same faults and beauties; though a severe critic might perhaps
add, that its peculiarities are more obtrusive, its faults greater, and its
beauties less' – which Crabbe's son paraphrases in his summary of the
book's critical reception. While amiably disclaiming the title of 'a severe
critic', Jeffrey is plainly giving notice of his intention to be the next best thing
and, after a lengthy preamble, he arrives at his central quarrel with Crabbe:
'His chief fault, however, is his frequent lapse into disgusting representations; and this, we will confess, is an error for which we find it far more
difficult either to account or to apologise.' Jeffrey is perfectly aware, as he
insists, that 'powerful and pathetic poetry . . . abounds in images of distress',
because 'pain is a far stronger sensation than pleasure in human existence';
and on that matter, at any rate, he and Crabbe are in agreement. However:
'Every form of distress, whether it proceed from passion or from fortune, and
whether it fall upon vice or virtue, adds to the interest and the charm of
poetry – except only that which is connected with ideas of *disgust*, – the least
taint of which disenchants the whole scene, and puts an end both to delight
and sympathy.' Jeffrey realises that there is something tenuous about this,
for he rhetorically invites himself to explain 'the proper object of disgust' and
'the precise description of things which we think Mr Crabbe so inexcusable
for admitting'. His attempt to do so is a wonderful example of early
nineteenth-century muddle:

> It is needless, we suppose, to explain what are the objects of disgust
> in physical or external existences. These are sufficiently plain and
> unequivocal; and it is universally admitted, that all mention of them
> must be carefully excluded from every poetical description. With
> regard, again, to human character, action, and feeling, we should be
> inclined to term any thing disgusting, which represented misery,
> without making any appeal to our love or admiration. If the suffering

person be amiable, the delightful feeling of love and affection tempers the pain which the contemplation of suffering has a tendency to excite, and enhances it into the stronger, and therefore more attractive, sensation of pity. If there be great power or energy, however united to guilt or wretchedness, the mixture of administration exalts the emotion into something that is sublime and pleasing. Even in cases of mean and atrocious guilt, our sympathy with the victims upon which it is practised, and our active indignation and desire of vengeance, reconcile us to the humiliating display, and make a compound that, upon the whole, is productive of pleasure.

One can see Jeffrey's problem: he has to find a formula which will explain why he is offended by Crabbe's characters, without inadvertently condemning all sorts of figures in other, perfectly respectable works. As for the mysteriously undefined 'objects of disgust in physical or external existences', he has to fall back upon a non-existent rule book and a phrase ('it is universally admitted') of exactly the sort which Jane Austen invests with devastating irony in the opening sentence – already written although as yet unpublished – of *Pride and Prejudice*. His next paragraph defines the 'sufferers . . . upon whom we cannot bear to look' as 'the depraved, abject, diseased and neglected poor'. 'On the characters, the miseries, and the vices of such beings, we look with *disgust* merely,' he continues, though he concedes (in what may appear to us, and to Crabbe, as a more important point than Jeffrey recognises), that 'it may perhaps serve some *moral* purpose, occasionally to set before us this humiliating spectacle of human nature sunk to utter worthlessness and insignificance . . .' And so at last the generalities end and he returns to the author whose work he is reviewing:

They have no hold upon any of the feelings that lead us to take an interest in our fellow-creatures; – we turn away from them, therefore, with loathing and dispassionate aversion; – we feel our imaginations polluted by the intrusion of any images connected with them; and are offended and disgusted when we are forced to look closely upon those festering heaps of moral filth and corruption. It is with concern we add, that we know no writer who has sinned so deeply in this respect as Mr Crabbe, – who has so often presented us with spectacles which it is purely painful and degrading to contemplate, and bestowed such powers of conception and expression in giving us distinct ideas of what we must abhor to remember.

Jeffrey decorously vows to abstain from quotation to support his complaints, but adds that 'those who have perused the volume before us, will have already recollected the story of Frederic Thompson, of Abel Keene, of Blaney and Benbow, and a good part of those of Grimes and Ellen Orford, – besides many shorter passages'.

It is worth spending time on Jeffrey's pages, for they provide us with a startling reminder of how threateningly radical Crabbe could appear to the conservative taste of the period. The very characters to whom Jeffrey most violently objects are among those whom we are likely to find most memorable: they are, we may think, Crabbe's successes, and there is every reason to suppose that Crabbe thought so too. What Jeffrey regards as 'disgusting' – and the sceptical modern reader must surely feel that he protests too much – is precisely the clear-eyed social realism which for us authenticates the characters. There is nothing so 'disgusting' in Wordsworth's portraits of the poor, and they are the worse for it: the greater poet is also the less sharply observant one. Many contemporary readers wrinkled their noses at Crabbe's pungent view of humanity: even the otherwise well-disposed reviewer in the *British Critic* (March 1811) objected to 'such characters as those of Blaney and Peter Grimes, which having once read, we never wish to see again'.[17] Some, such as the anonymous writer in the *Monthly Mirror* of August 1810, attempted a charitable explanation: 'The fact is, that Mr Crabbe has lived a great deal in a smuggling neighbourhood, and has observed that the country there is a very different thing from what our Arcadian poets have represented it: he therefore very naturally falls into the other extreme, and sees nothing but vice in every village, and poverty in every cottage.'[18] This is subtly wrong on both counts. Aldeburgh was obviously 'a smuggling neighbourhood'; the inland Suffolk villages rather less so, although one recalls Crabbe's memorable altercation with Robert the bailiff at Parham. But the *Monthly Mirror's* reviewer forgets that Crabbe had also lived in very different places such as Belvoir Castle, Stathern and Muston; so the transference from life to work is based on a false premise as well as giving an inaccurate account of poems which are not exclusively concerned with 'vice . . . and poverty'. For the *Quarterly Review* (November 1810), Crabbe was 'the poet of reality, and of reality in low life'[19] who had deliberately set himself on a downward path: 'The impurities of a rural hamlet were sufficiently repulsive; – what then must be those of a maritime borough?' In this sense, *The Borough* was simply 'the legitimate successor of *The Village* and *The Parish Register*'.[20]

There were other, more persuasive complaints about *The Borough*: for instance, several reviewers greatly disliked Crabbe's Preface. It is not easy to quarrel with James Montgomery's estimate of it in his unsigned notice in the *Eclectic Review* of June 1810: 'This preface is a tissue of explanations and apologies to the extent of nearly *thirty pages*; and is altogether most singularly tiresome, unnecessary, and injudicious.'[21] The *Critical Review* of July 1810 described it as 'a long rambling preface, which is a mere of dull ill-written apologies',[22] while the *Monthly Mirror* took exception to Crabbe's appropriation of the reviewer's function: 'it looks more like a favourable *review*, than any thing else. We, as reviewers, must protest against this invasion of our province: we are put out of our bread, if every author is thus to become his own reviewer: the workman must not be his own overseer.'[23] Another problem, noticed by Jeffrey, is the wilful disunity of a sequence 'which consists altogether of a succession of unconnected descriptions, and is still more miscellaneous in reality, than would be conjectured from the titles of its twenty-four separate compartments'.[24] In the earliest notice of *The Borough* (*Monthly Review*, April 1810), Thomas Denman had put the point more strikingly: 'we have observed with surprise how little Mr Crabbe seems to be sensible of the value of a plot, or a leading subject. It is remarkable that, in the immense number of his characters, no two are represented as bearing any relation to or influencing the feelings of each other.'[25] Denman would surely have found this still more remarkable had he known, as we do, that Crabbe was an avid reader of fiction who had written at least three novels himself. In constructing *The Borough*, it simply seems not to have occurred to Crabbe, except in a limited way with the inhabitants of the almshouse, that its fabric might have been immeasurably enriched by allowing the central characters of one 'letter' to appear as background figures in others or by some form of linking narrative or plot.

Of course, all the early reviewers found passages to praise – sometimes choosing them inexplicably – and almost everyone had a list of grumbles about

Crabbe's rough-and-ready diction (some of his harmlessly amusing puns and quibbles caused special offence). But it is James Montgomery, in the *Eclectic Review*, who seems, for a while at least, to move beyond the critical constraints of his time: 'The master-piece of the volume, however, for energy of conception and effect, is the story of Peter Grimes, a ruffian from his very infancy, a ferocious tyrant and suspected murderer, who finally became a madman, tormented with the most gloomy visions, and self-convicted of the most atrocious crimes.' He goes on: 'We have been exceedingly struck with the peculiar and unrivalled skill, with which Mr Crabbe paints the horrors of a disordered imagination ...'[26] Although 'peculiar and unrivalled skill' may have been a more easily formulaic phrase for Montgomery than it is for us, it is surely the right one for Crabbe in 'Peter Grimes'.

Eight

Life's Common Cares

1811–1814

I

With the publication of *The Borough* and with the ordination of his two sons, Crabbe's financial difficulties were finally eradicated: he would be comfortably off for the rest of his life. Both sons became curates in the Vale of Belvoir and continued to live with their parents at the vicarage in Muston: 'all the domestic habits which I have described at Glemham were continued, with little exception,' says the biographer son.[1] There is something at least faintly disturbing about this: why (we might ask) waste time and expense on a Cambridge education in order to end up just where you began? But, of course, that is unfair. It fails to take into account the wretched poverty of most curates, the generally harmonious relationships within the family and, above all, the deteriorating condition of Mrs Crabbe, which cast a long shadow over what was otherwise an Indian summer of domestic contentment:

> My father having a larger and better garden than in Suffolk, passed much of his time amongst his choice weeds, and though (my mother growing infirm) we did not take a family walk as heretofore, yet in no other respect was that perfect domestication invaded. When the evening closed, winter or summer, my father read aloud from the store which Mr Colburn, out of his circulating library, sent and renewed, and nineteen in every twenty books of these were, as of old, novels; while, as regularly, my brother took up his pencil, and amused our unoccupied eyes by some design strikingly full of character; for he had an untaught talent in this way, which wanted only the mechanical portion of the art to give him a high name among the masters of the time. One winter he copied and coloured

some hundreds of insects for his father, from expensive plates sent for his inspection by the Vice-Master of Trinity; and this requiring no genius but pains only, I joined in the employment. 'Now, old fellows,' said my father, 'it is my duty to read to you.'[2]

It seems an enviably tranquil and civilised existence and yet, as the university-educated sons would have been inescapably aware, it is not much of a life: the gentle pace, the lack of socialising and the tightly restricted geographical orbit are all direct consequences of Sarah Crabbe's condition. However, Crabbe himself 'visited much more frequently than in Suffolk': his hosts included Sir Robert Heron, Sir William Welby and, in particular, Dr George Gordon, who was both Dean of Lincoln and rector of the neighbouring parishes of Sedgebrook with East Allington. Their hospitality, as they discreetly understood, could not often be returned: 'where the mistress is always in ill-health and the master a poet, there will seldom be found the nice tact to conduct these things just as they ought to be'. The biographer son may or may not have intended to suggest that poetry is a kind of infirmity; but there is in that conjunction a hint of impatience with his father which he is keen to dispel as rapidly as possible:

> My father was conscious of this; and it gave him an appearance of inhospitality quite foreign to his nature. If he neither shot nor danced, he appeared well pleased that we brought him a very considerable supply of game, and that we sometimes passed an evening at the assembly-room of our metropolis, Grantham. My mother's declining state becoming more evident, he was, if possible, more attentive than ever. He would take up her meals when in her own room, and sometimes cook her some little nicety for supper, when he thought it would otherwise be spoiled. 'What a father you have!' was a grateful exclamation often on her lips.[3]

Although Crabbe was certainly an extraordinarily attentive husband and father, he was less than exemplary in his role as Rector of Muston. The energy he devoted to his family and to working on his forthcoming *Tales* – to say nothing of those 'choice weeds' in his garden – made him, even by the standards of his time, a somewhat semi-detached clergyman. He had never overcome his dislike of the Muston flock, who had not only dragged him back from Suffolk but had punished him for his absence by enthusiastically turning to other sects; and they had never forgiven him for so peremptorily abandoning them in the first place. He would willingly attend the distressed and the sick, continuing to minister as a physician as well as a priest; he enjoyed rural customs such as beating the parish bounds, accompanied by children whom he would reward with oranges and nuts; but in other respects his engagement with his parishioners was minimal, his manner high-handed and his temper erratic. Largely unconcerned by theological debate within the Anglican church, he had become set in unstrenuous ways and he lacked any real incentive to challenge or question them: in a word, he had become dull. Alfred Ainger, after studying Crabbe's manuscript sermons, produced the damning instance of one 'preached first at Great Glemham in 1801, and afterwards at Little Glemham, Sweffling, Muston, and Allington; at Trowbridge in 1820, and again at Trowbridge in 1830'. Ainger's comment, though mildly phrased, is perfectly clear in its implication: 'The preacher probably held his discourses quite as profitable at one stage in the Church's development as at another. In this estimate of clerical responsibilities Crabbe seems to have remained stationary.'[4]

This is Crabbe's less admirable side and – in the context of the English church in the late eighteenth and early nineteenth centuries – it is not so very bad. Many country clergy were lazier and less scrupulous than Crabbe; most were far stupider. Our impression of them is coloured, in a generally favourable way, by the minority who wrote publishable poetry or (like William Jones and James Woodforde) kept memorable diaries. Terence Bareham has usefully pointed out that a traveller in early nineteenth-century England could have encountered 'as varied a collection of clerics as did Joseph Andrews' some sixty years earlier, although 'there would have been fewer Trullibers and fewer Thwackems'. He adds that if the traveller could have 'compassed time as well as space, within this same sixty years he could have met Gilbert White, Laurence Sterne, Crabbe, Sydney Smith, John Wesley, Malthus, and Cartwright, the inventor of the power loom'.[5] Of course, it was partly because the church's system of ordination and preferment was so chaotic and corrupt that splendidly eccentric figures managed to enter it and to flourish within it: Crabbe himself had been the beneficiary both of intensive lobbying and of dubious procedures such as the Lambeth degree. But they were exceptions, outnumbered not only by the mass of hard-working and impoverished curates but also by a great many self-interested idlers. 'It is really more remarkable,' writes Bareham, 'that the Georgian church did not collapse, than that it was marked by blemishes in its practice.'[6]

If Crabbe's relations with his parishioners were strained, they were no better with Belvoir Castle. The Duke had grudgingly accepted the dedication of *The Borough*, but he was a sporting young man uninterested in poetry: Crabbe's tenure of the ducal chaplaincy belonged to his childhood, and the botanising, poetical Rector of Muston would by now have struck him as a tedious relic. Crabbe understood this perfectly, of course: it was exactly the sort of personal alienation, brought about by the passage of time, which underlies many of his tales. Writing a little later to Walter Scott, he was to describe his status at the castle as 'one of the *old race*';[7] although this phrase had originally been used by a Belvoir hanger-on thirty years earlier, when the previous Duke (and he) had been young, its echo of *As You Like It* cannot have been lost on him. Now Crabbe found himself in his own equivalent of a greenwood exile from the ducal court, although in his case Duke senior was long dead. Perhaps this thought crossed his mind when he decided to dedicate his next book, *Tales*, to the Dowager Duchess.

2

The case for regarding the *Tales* of 1812 as Crabbe's masterpiece has been made in lively and compelling fashion by Howard Mills, in the Introduction to his edition of 1967. Mills approaches them from a different, less biographical direction, of course, and he is properly scathing about René Huchon, who (among other critical failings) tried to find unmediated autobiography everywhere he looked in Crabbe's poetry. But biography may have its more modest uses: far from endorsing Huchon's overliteral reading of the poems, what we already know about Crabbe will tend to make us wary about seeking a direct reflection of the life in the work. There *are* reflections, of course, but the mirror is a distorting one.

The *Tales* are not simply a development of *The Borough* in general and 'Peter Grimes' in particular: they are a consequence of that extraordinary poem. In it, Crabbe had at last discovered how to create a compelling, character-based narrative by using personal experience as a submerged force, a poetic undercurrent: the result, as we have seen, had disturbed and offended many of his readers. But Crabbe had listened to his critics and, in his Preface to *Tales*, he answered them. He acknowledged that 'reproof' might be helpful to a writer, 'since errors may be corrected when opportunity occurs'; whereas 'advice . . . may be of such nature, that it will be painful to reject, and yet impossible to follow it; and in this predicament I conceive myself to be placed'. His reason for not attempting the work suggested by Jeffrey, unified by theme and character – a sort of Epic Poem, he disingenuously calls it, though it need not have been like that at all – is, typically, both modest and cunning: 'In one continued and connected Poem, the reader is, in general highly gratified or severely disappointed; by many independent narratives, he has the renovation of hope, although he has been dissatisfied, and a prospect of reiterated pleasure should he find himself entertained.' In other words, there is a better chance of scoring a hit with these twenty-one skittles than with a single one: it is very nearly an admission that, in a work such as *Tales*, the author can slip in a few duds and get away with it.

Yet Crabbe is not quite so modest as he appears. In acknowledging that 'these compositions have no pretensions to be estimated with the more lofty and heroic kind of poems', he manages to hint – the lethal word is 'pretensions' – that it would take a fool to value such things. And there are fools enough, on both sides; in a single crafty sentence, he makes substantial claims for himself, between an opening swipe at foolish readers and a closing one at foolish poets: 'In vulgar estimation, indeed, all that is not prose passes for poetry; but I have not ambition of so humble a kind as to be satisfied with a concession which requires nothing in the poet, except his ability for counting syllables; and I trust something more of the poetic character will be allowed to the succeeding pages than what the heroes of the Dunciad might share with the author; nor was I aware that by describing, as faithfully as I could, men, manners, and things, I was forfeiting a just title to a name which has been freely granted to many whom to equal, and even to excel, is but very stinted commendation.' It is a spirited defence, underpinned by a quite engaging truculence, although one reviewer of *Tales* was to meet it head-on: 'To tell his story in parallel lines of ten syllables seems to be his sole ambition; and even the reader who admires the intimate knowledge of life and human nature, the accurate discrimination of character, and the ingenuity of invention that his effusions display, must be disposed to regret that he has not occasionally assumed a more lofty and animated tone . . .'[8]

But what of his shocking and 'disgusting' subject-matter? Here, Crabbe's self-justification may strike us as odd.

> . . . I must allow that the effect of poetry should be to lift the mind from the painful realities of actual existence, from its every-day concerns, and its perpetually occurring vexations, and to give it repose by substituting objects in their place which it may contemplate with some degree of interest and satisfaction; but what is there in all this, which may not be effected by a fair representation of existing character? nay, by a faithful delineation of those painful realities, those every-day concerns, and those perpetually-occurring vexations themselves, provided they be not (which is hardly to be supposed) the very concerns of the reader? for, when it is admitted that they have no particular relation to him, but are the troubles and anxieties of other men, they excite and interest his feelings as the imaginary exploits, adventures, and perils of romance; – they soothe his mind, and keep his curiosity pleasantly awake; they appear to have enough of reality to engage his sympathy, but possess not interest sufficient to create painful sensations.

This remarkable passage vividly illustrates the internal contradictions of Crabbe's literary aesthetic. In his engagement with 'painful realities', including both physical poverty and extreme psychological disturbance, he is amazingly modern; yet he sees the results of this engagement in anachronistically eighteenth-century terms – the representation of distress cannot distress *us*, because *we* have nothing in common with these low characters and their predicaments. On the contrary, our minds will be soothed and our curiosity kept pleasantly awake. It is a sharp reminder that the England of Crabbe's youth, which had fixed these ideas in his head, had almost no conception of 'high culture': art was there to provide a relaxing sort of pleasure, and that was all. But even if he failed to recognise that this notion of art was, by 1812, inadequate and out of date, Crabbe can hardly have been entirely unaware that for him the premise was, in any case, simply untrue: the low characters in his poems do have a great deal in common with him –

with his younger self, with his family, and with the world in which he grew
up – and that is the sense in which the poems are authenticated by
autobiography. He was doing something unallowed for by eighteenth-
century aesthetic convention, and it seems to have rattled him.

Interestingly, he concludes his Preface to *Tales* not with a summary of
what he hopes to have achieved in the book – for, honestly formulated, that
would have flatly contradicted his earlier assertions – but with an assurance
of its innocuousness. His final sentence is stuffed with negatives:

> Nothing will be found that militates against the rules of propriety
> and good manners, nothing that offends against the more
> important precepts of morality and religion; and with this negative
> kind of merit, I commit my book to the judgement and taste of the
> reader – not being willing to provoke his vigilance by professions of
> accuracy, nor to solicit his indulgence by apologies for mistakes.

So ends the piece which the late Professor Pollard described as 'Crabbe's
most important statement of his own view of his art'.[9] Compared, as it must
inescapably be, with Wordsworth's statement of *his* view of poetry, the
Preface to the *Lyrical Ballads*, it seems a tepid affair (though Wordsworth's
prose is no less lumpy than Crabbe's). He is so unambitious for his art, so
anxious to temporise on its behalf; and that is no doubt partly because he
wants to placate readers like Jeffrey and to sell his books to a cautious public.
But he could not unlearn the lessons which 'Peter Grimes' had taught him.

3

And the lessons of 'Peter Grimes' are repeatedly evident in *Tales*. One notable
instance of this which I mentioned much earlier on account of its demon-
strable biographical relevance, is 'The Lover's Journey'. On the surface, these
two poems have almost nothing in common; yet Crabbe's method in each case
is identical. Both the stories are fictional and the characters within them have
invented names; but they are founded on actual Suffolk landscapes which have
been re-created in exact, authenticating detail. Moreover, Crabbe boldly shares
with his central characters ways of looking at the world which can only be his
own: when Grimes contemplates the river and Orlando the road to Beccles,

they do so through their creator's eyes. As a result, both these stories possess a degree of depth and resonance which is usually absent when Crabbe attempts to create an entirely imaginary setting; indeed, when he strays from his home ground he sometimes seems not to have imagined a setting at all.

Two poems from *Tales*, 'The Parting Hour' and 'The Patron', will serve to illustrate in very different ways the heightened power which Crabbe achieves from this kind of transmuted biography. The first of these has at its core the story of his brother William, last seen by an Aldeburgh sailor on the coast of Honduras in 1803: Crabbe had probably heard this from the sailor himself, either while visiting his home town in the summer of 1805 or when he returned four years later with the draft version of *The Borough*. It would have made a good enough tale in itself, except for its open-endedness: it is not Crabbe's way to leave his characters unaccountably alive in distant countries. So he ingeniously provides a narrative frame, within which William's story becomes a tale within a tale:

> Beneath yon tree, observe an ancient pair –
> A sleeping man; a woman in her chair,
> Watching his looks with kind and pensive air;
> No wife, nor sister she, nor is the name
> Nor kindred of this friendly pair the same;
> Yet so allied are they, that few can feel
> Her constant, warm, unwearied, anxious zeal;
> Their years and woes, although they long have loved,
> Keep their good name and conduct unreproved;
> Thus life's small comforts they together share,
> And while life lingers for the grave prepare.
>   No other subjects on their spirits press,
> Nor gain such int'rest as the past distress;
> Grievous events that from the mem'ry drive
> Life's common cares, and those alone survive,
> Mix with each thought, in every action share,
> Darken each dream, and blend with every prayer. [II. 15–31]

These lines may seem out of character – or, at any rate, out of the character which Crabbe's reviewers had by now created for him. They provide a portrait of quiet goodness; and, almost magically, the couplets which elsewhere in the *Tales* are so often rough and ungainly here become gently unassertive. At this point in the tale we have no idea who these admirable old people may be, though we do know that for them, as for so many of Crabbe's characters, 'Life's common cares' are overshadowed by the memory of 'Grievous events'. After line 31, a chronological lurch hints at an explanation: the man, we may surmise, is Allen, the fourth son of David Booth (a typically sly biographical amendment: John, not William, was the Crabbes' fourth son, although since an elder son died in infancy William *was* in that sense the fourth). Allen and his childhood sweetheart Judith are both exemplary children, to the alarming extent that they are scarcely children at all: 'Thus early prudent and sedate they grew, / While lovers, thoughtful – and though children, true.' Their goodness will be its own reward, for happiness is to be denied them, as Crabbe suggests in a notably East Anglian version of the epic simile:

> So while the waters rise, the children tread
> On the broad estuary's sandy bed;
> But soon the channel fills, from side to side
> Comes danger rolling with the deep'ning tide;
> Yet none who saw the rapid current flow
> Could the first instant of that danger know. [II. 68–73]

The danger takes the rather vague form of a rich, distant, childless kinsman in search of 'some young Booth' to be his heir: this involves travelling to 'a Western Isle', though not a Scottish one. Allen, 'an enamour'd boy', is keen to seek his fortune, while 'faithful Judith his design approved'. This sets the scene for adventures, narrated in the second part of the tale, which are essentially William's: they include his prosperity, marriage and downfall on account of his suspect religion. All this Crabbe recounts effectively, although the scene is too far from Suffolk to engage his fullest interest. For that to happen, he must bring Allen home again; and he does so in a passage of Grimesian eloquence and intensity:

> No one was present; of its crew bereft,
> A single boat was in the billows left;
> Sent from some anchor'd vessel in the bay,

At the returning tide to sail away:
O'er the black stern the moonlight softly play'd.
The loosen'd foresail flapping in the shade;
All silent else on shore; but from the town
A drowsy peal of distant bells came down:
From the tall houses here and there, a light
Served some confused remembrance to excite:
'There,' he observed, and new emotions felt,
'Was my first home – and yonder Judith dwelt;
Dead! dead are all! I long – I fear to know,'
He said, and walk'd impatient, and yet slow. [II. 199–212]

The attentive reader of 'Peter Grimes' will see at once what is going on here. Just as in the great 'When tides were neap . . .' passage, Crabbe has fused his own memory into his character's, down to the smallest circumstantial detail: no one who has stood on Aldeburgh beach and heard the sound of bells from Church Hill will have the slightest doubt about the provenance of that image. And when Allen, feeling 'new emotions', reflects, 'There . . . Was my first home', he speaks for his author; the simple and exact paradox of 'walk'd impatient, and yet slow' is deeply rooted in Crabbe's ambivalent feelings about his own first home.

Counterpointing this is a quite different kind of allusiveness, for Allen is also Odysseus (in bringing him home from his sea voyage to the sound of celebratory bells, Crabbe may have had the Ancient Mariner in mind too). He wanders through his home town unrecognised, while others retell their versions of his tale:

'Yes,' said an elder, who had paused intent
On days long past, 'there was a sad event; –
One of these Booths – it was my mother's tale –
Here left his lass, I know not where to sail:
She saw their parting, and observed the pain;
But never came th'unhappy man again.'
'The ship was captured' – Allen meekly said,
'And what became of the forsaken maid?'
The woman answer'd: 'I remember now,

> She used to tell the lasses of her vow,
> And of her lover's loss, and I have seen
> The gayest hearts grow sad where she has been;
> Yet in her grief she married, and was made
> Slave to a wretch, whom meekly she obey'd
> And early buried – but I know no more.
> And hark! our friends are hast'ning to the shore.' [II. 237–52]

'The Parting Hour' thus contains within its outer framework not only Allen's account of his life, told to Judith in their companionable old age, but also these stories of his life and hers told to him: it is another of Crabbe's time-defying devices, at once Homeric and modern. Like 'Peter Grimes', the tale ends in a dream-world, as Allen remembers his lost wife and children, while Judith 'lays her knitting by, / These strong emotions in her friend to spy'. 'The Parting Hour' is not as extreme or as extraordinary a poem as 'Peter Grimes', but its combination of intensity and understatement is in its way almost more ambitious.

In 'The Patron' Crabbe uses his own experience to very different effect. This is the story of John, an ambitious young poet taken up by a wealthy patron, Lord Frederick Damer: both in outline and in specific details, this poetic progress has much in common with Crabbe's own, but that is a characteristic ruse. At the heart of the tale is a long letter from John's father, full of straightforward good sense to which the author evidently gives his full assent; the son, who takes no notice of it and eventually dies of hopeless love for his patron's sister, is clearly one of the silly young Romantics for whom Crabbe has little time. This ruse of attaching autobiographical qualities to a poet so unlike himself is notably effective in making an otherwise facile tale complex and interesting.

The teasing similarities between John and his author begin in child-hood: although, unlike Crabbe himself, he is a younger son, he is equally hopeless at practical matters and grows up captivated by popular poetry, 'all the hungry mind without a choice devours'. He takes up writing and is persuaded by a friend (a recollection perhaps of William Levett) to publish his work: 'In Magazines they claim'd their share of fame, / Though undistinguish'd by their author's name.' Once installed at Brandon Hall, John experiences the familiar problem of being neither a member of the family nor a servant: unwisely, and unlike his author, he aspires to the more elevated status, encouraged by his devotion to Emma. But when the family departs for London, John finds himself left behind and scorned by the servants, just as Crabbe had been when he was left behind at Belvoir. In the eyes of the departing ladies, he

> With anguish read – 'I pity but despise –
> Unhappy boy! presumptuous scribbler! – you
> To dream such dreams! – be sober, and adieu!'
> Then came the noble friend – 'And will my lord
> Vouchsafe no comfort? drop no soothing word?
> Yes, he must speak': he speaks, 'My good young friend,
> You know my views; upon my care depend;
> My hearty thanks to your good father pay,
> And be a student. – Harry, drive away.' [V. 455–63]

This prompts Crabbe to recall not his parting from Charles Manners, the fourth Duke of Rutland (which was an altogether friendlier affair), but his earlier fruitless pursuit of Lord North's patronage in 1780. John follows his patron in London, where he is coldly received by a 'well known servant': '"A while," said he, / "Be pleased to wait; my lord has company."' So John waits in a cold room, while 'Thrice upon his ear / Struck the loud clock, yet no relief was near'. Eventually he is told to 'attend / At twelve on Thursday'. The reader who knows of Crabbe's experience with North will be unsurprised by the outcome:

> Punctual again the modest rap declared
> The youth attended; then was all prepared:
> For the same servant, by his lord's command,
> A paper offer'd to his trembling hand:
> 'No more!' he cried; 'disdains he to afford
> One kind expression, one consoling word?' [V. 548–53]

At this point, however, the two poets, the author and his character, finally diverge. John returns to his father's house, where in due course he dies; Crabbe, by contrast, battled on and was eventually rewarded. Though he manages a decent sympathy for the deluded John, his own allegiance is beyond doubt; and this involves a distinction not only between two personalities – one resolute, the other feeble – but between two kinds of imagination. John fails because his view of the world is faulty: his capacity for self-delusion and his consequent lack of inner resilience are aspects of his inability to see clearly and steadily.

Crabbe knows this, and so does John's father who, in the central part of the poem, advises his son to cultivate 'virtues . . . of the sober kind' and to 'know the useful art of *acting dumb*'. Unlike his son, he understands precisely the amused contempt with which John will be viewed by his social betters:

> 'With pain I've seen, these wrangling wits among,
> Faith's weak defenders, passionate and young;
> Weak thou art not, yet not enough on guard,
> Where wit and humour keep their watch and ward:
> Men gay and noisy will o'erwhelm thy sense,
> Then loudly laugh at Truth's and thy expense;
> While the kind ladies will do all they can
> To check their mirth, and cry *"The good young man!"*' [V. 329–36]

Yet even here Crabbe's use of his own life is not quite straightforward. While we have no difficulty in identifying the middle-aged poet with the sensible father, his younger self had more in common with the son than he might have wished: that ironic cry of *'The good young man!'* must surely have been one overheard by the awkward young poetical chaplain at Belvoir. In 'The Patron', Crabbe drew on his own experience to support both sides of his argument, freeing the poem from the didactic aridity which marrs some of his other tales while actually increasing its force as a moral fable about how not to be a poet. Walter Scott, one of his most devoted readers, saw both sides too: he recalled how in his own youth he had so resembled 'your admirably painted 'young Lad', that I could hardly help saying, "That's me!" when I was reading the tale to my family';[10] yet he also wryly observed that if any of his sons had displayed poetic ambitions, 'I would make him get the tale of the patron by heart from beginning to end.'[11]

4

The moral universe of the *Tales* is circumscribed by Crabbe's own provincial life. This has both advantages and drawbacks: on the one hand, he is unusually well placed to enlighten blinkered metropolitan readers about the realities of rural existence; on the other, he displays astonishing ignorance and prejudice when he attempts to deal with matters which are beyond his scope. In 'The Widow's Tale', for example, Crabbe's rustic perspective works very clearly in his favour. Farmer Moss's daughter Nancy returns home from 'her school in town', fashionably well-educated but unable 'To pass a pig-sty, or to face a cow', and therefore ill-equipped to meet her destiny, which is to marry a young farmer called Harry Carr. Her true education – of the sort, familiar in Crabbe, in which wisdom is acquired through attending to an older character's narrative of experiences and sorrows   is gained from her friendship with a widow who challenges her facile notion of romantic love: 'I had once, like you / Such thoughts of love; no dream is more untrue . . .' When Nancy and Harry eventually marry, their respective talents – 'her neat taste' and his 'improving skill and vigorous arm' – will prove to be mutually beneficial. This is a moral equation which Crabbe, as a cultivated country-man himself, can carry off with perfect conviction. But the most vivid and memorable part of this poem comes near the beginning, where Nancy is confronted by her father's table manners:

> Her father's kitchen she could ill endure;
> Where by the steaming beef he hungry sat,
> And laid at once a pound upon his plate;
> Hot from the field, her eager brother seized
> An equal part, and hunger's rage appeased;
> The air, surcharged with moisture, flagg'd around,
> And the offended damsel sigh'd and frown'd;
> The swelling fat in lumps conglomerate laid,
> And fancy's sickness seized the loathing maid;
> But when the men beside their station took,
> The maidens with them, and with these the cook:
> When one huge wooden bowl before them stood,

Fill'd with huge balls of farinaceous food;
With bacon, mass saline, where never lean
Beneath the brown and bristly rind was seen;
When from a single horn the party drew
Their copious draughts of heavy ale and new;
When the coarse cloth she saw, with many a stain,
Soil'd by rude hands who cut and came again –
She could not breathe; but, with a heavy sigh,
Rein'd the fair neck, and shut th'offended eye;
She minced the sanguine flesh in frustrums fine,
And wonder'd much to see the creatures dine . . . [VII. 8–30]

It hardly needs to be said that this vigorously Hogarthian satire wonderfully conveys the gross manners of the farm kitchen and the daughter's understandable revulsion; but its energy comes, as we might by now expect, from more complex subterranean sources. Crabbe's position is by no means straightforward. There is the familiar note of relish – just as there was at Grimes's supposedly most desolate scenes – which suggests a degree of envious pleasure in this rough-and-ready life: Crabbe still has something about him of the excluded bookish child who would have liked to participate more fully in his brothers' boyish pleasures. And there is another, more recent echo here: the kitchen which the Crabbes had entered on their visit to Ducking Hall in 1790 – 'a set of manners and customs, of which there remains, perhaps, no counterpart in the present day', as the biographer son gently puts it – was more civilised than that of Farmer Moss, but not much. There too Crabbe's response had been ambiguous, his disapproval complicated by awareness that such a style of life was temperamentally beyond him. He knew that the kind of contentment attainable by a successful yeoman farmer would never be his.

'The Widow's Tale' snugly fits the more general moral template of Crabbe's *Tales*: characters who do not expect too much and who wait patiently for it – the defining features of his own courtship and marriage – are likely, with the exception of Rupert and Dinah in 'Procrastination', to be rewarded; those who are overambitious or precipitate and those who follow strange sects (or none) will probably be punished. The trouble, of course, is that such arrangements can appear arbitrary or perverse. Peter New, whose *George*

Crabbe's Poetry is the most detailed modern reading of the poems, writes that in the *Tales* Crabbe 'developed to its finest point his distinctive narrative form, in which both character and the more general insight that accompanies profound characterisation are embodied in a way nearer to the nineteenth-century novel than to the "portrait" of the major eighteenth-century satirists'. For New, the tales achieve 'a verbal texture closer than in all but the best work of the greatest novelists, and an economy of incident which, in comparison with the diffuseness of novels below the stature of the best, can also be seen as a strength'.[12] That ambitious-looking claim turns out to be rather tortuously hedged: New is not actually comparing Crabbe to the great novelists whom he sometimes resembles – to Austen or Eliot or Hardy – but to lesser writers and minor works. His point, nevertheless, is one which directs us towards the less arbitrary tales: those in which there seems to be at least the potential for things to turn out unexpectedly, as is usually the case with a novel.

'The Confidant' works in just this way. The admirable Anna, happily married to a yeoman called Stafford, has a guilty secret: in her youth she was seduced by a wicked Irish captain called Sedley – doubtless an oblique dig at the Restoration poet – by whom she had a child, now dead, in distant, sinful London. All this she unwisely confided to a viperish friend called Eliza, who subsequently reappears in the guise of a blackmailer, moving in with the couple and destroying their happiness. As a poem, 'The Confidant' is not especially distinguished, but as a tale it is one of Crabbe's best: partly because his moral sternness is relaxed so that Anna, despite her serious lapse, can be forgiven; and partly because, until quite near the end, the reader cannot be certain (any more than Anna or Eliza can) whether or not the marriage will be destroyed by Eliza's revelations. Similarly, 'The Wager' succeeds by admitting the possibility, albeit a slim one, that the wrong one of the two tradesmen, Counter and Clubb, will come to grief. (Clubbe, of course, was the name of the opium-prescribing doctor in Ipswich, who may have been a tactful invention: in adapting the name in 'The Wager', Crabbe is allowing himself another sly joke.)

Both in 'The Confidant' and in 'The Wager', there is a sense of good-humour, generosity and proportion. Anna and Stafford, Counter and Clubb inhabit Crabbe's home ground: they could have lived in *The Borough*. But difficulties arise when the moral and social contexts are less congenial, as they are in 'Edward Shore' and 'The Learned Boy'. 'Edward Shore' develops the least attractive aspect of 'The Patron': there, the father's robust common sense was saved from shading into philistinism by Crabbe's ability to anchor both sides of the argument in his own experience; here, the entire poem, from its sour opening line onwards ('Genius! thou gift of Heav'n! thou light divine!'), is infected with mean-spirited anti-intellectualism. The central premise – not such an unpromising one – is that the madness of clever people is more resilient than the madness of fools: 'Reason, through anguish, shall her throne forsake, / And strength of mind but stronger madness make.' Edward Shore is a dilettante and a doubter:

> Alas! though men who feel their eyes decay
> Take more than common pains to find their way,
> Yet, when for this they ask each other's aid,
> Their mutual purpose is the more delay'd:
> Of all their doubts, their reasoning clear'd not one,
> Still the same spots were present in the sun;
> Still the same scruples haunted Edward's mind,
> Who found no rest, nor took the means to find. [XI. 95–102]

Thus, he finds himself among the blind leading the blind. At moments like this, one can only wish that Crabbe the poet would loosen the dog collar of Crabbe the clergyman; for, in simply refusing to see that religious certainty may not always be available to restless minds, he denies himself the possibility of understanding or sympathising with his own character. It seems extraordinary that a writer who is as capable of surprisingly modern insights as Crabbe should be unable to find any empathy for Edward's intellectual predicament. For us, this unfocused spirit of enquiry – 'His mind reposed not, for he hated rest, / But all things made a query or a jest . . .' – will be no more than a symptom of youthful intelligence.

But for Crabbe in this mode, simplistic moral consequences must follow. When his closest friend and fellow sceptic is called away to visit a sick relative, Edward seduces the wife who is left behind; and nothing less, Crabbe implies, is to be expected of people with such unfixed morals. After this, a rapid decline follows, through drink – 'Wine is like anger; for it makes us strong, / Blind and impatient, and it leads us wrong' – to insanity:

Then as its wrath subsided, by degrees
The mind sank slowly to infantine ease;
To playful folly, and to causeless joy,
Speech without aim, and without end, employ;
He drew fantastic figures on the wall,
And gave some wild relation of them all;
With brutal shape he join'd the human face,
And idiot smiles approved the motley race. [XI. 424–31]

As usual, Crabbe's depiction of madness is brilliantly powerful; it is the mechanical, simplistic procession of cause and effect which is so dispiriting in 'Edward Shore'. Crabbe should have known better.

'The Learned Boy' is even more grotesque: it is the most disconcerting of all Crabbe's tales and perhaps the most vulnerably revealing one. On the surface, the story parallels Edward Shore's: Stephen Jones, a farmer's son, is indulged by his doting grandmother, sent off to school, gets ideas above his station and moves to London; there he falls in with the wrong intellectual company, becomes an atheist and eventually returns home to disgrace and punishment. It will be clear, even from this crude summary, that – the grandmother and the atheism apart – this progress also has a good deal in common with the young Crabbe's; indeed, one curiosity of the *Tales* is the regularity with which London appears as a place of unmitigated corruption, whereas it was (for all his difficulties) the starting-point for Crabbe's own success both as poet and as clergyman. That, however, is the least of the problems with 'The Learned Boy'. In the first part of the poem, the author's stance seems perfectly straightforward and the story has recognisably autobiographical elements: we learn that old Farmer Jones is something of a tyrant ('But still he govern'd with resistless hand, / And where he could not guide he would command') and that his son is soft but studious ('The father doubted – but to school was sent / The timid Stephen, weeping as he went'). In London, where he finds work as a clerk, he is painfully aware of his rustic manners: gradually, with the help of a fellow clerk, he acquires fashionable clothes, goes to the theatre, buys and reads books which challenge his provincial – and devout – ideas. These books he carefully arranges and displays; but it is this which provokes Crabbe to a strange, uncomfortable authorial intervention:

> The love of order, – I the thing receive
> From reverent men, and I in part believe, –
> Shows a clear mind and clean, and whoso needs
> This love, but seldom in the world succeeds;
> And yet with this some other love must be,
> Ere I can fully to the fact agree:
> Valour and study may by order gain,
> By order sovereigns hold more steady reign;
> Through all the tribes of nature order runs,
> And rules around in systems and in suns:
> Still has the love of order found a place,
> With all that's low, degrading, mean, and base,
> With all that merits scorn, and all that meets disgrace:
> In the old miser, of all change afraid,
> In pompous men in public seats obey'd;
> In humble placemen, heralds, solemn drones,
> Fanciers of flowers, and lads like Stephen Jones;
> Order to these is armour and defence,
> And love of method serves in lack of sense. [XXI. 309–27]

This certainly seems a disproportionate response to a young man ordering his books on their shelves. Partly, of course, it is very consciously a set piece, like Ulysses's great speech on order in *Troilus and Cressida*, to which it is clearly indebted. But this is hardly sufficient to explain an unmistakable buzz of bees in bonnets: it is the sound of Crabbe arguing with himself about his own love of order. He tries, with distinctly uncertain conviction, to justify this by asserting that it is underpinned by his faith ('some other love') while Stephen's is not. As with Edward Shore, he makes the mistake of assuming that a different set of ideas cannot count as ideas at all.

When Stephen returns home and attempts to explain his atheistic position – not, to be sure, with much tact – to his father, the consequences are terrible. Farmer Jones responds not with counter-argument but with a whip:

> 'Father, oh! father! throw the whip away;
> I was but jesting, on my knees I pray –
> There, hold his arm – oh! leave us not alone:

In pity cease, and I will yet atone
For all my sin –' In vain; stroke after stroke,
On side and shoulder, quick as mill-wheels broke;
Quick as the patient's pulse, who trembling cried,
And still the parent with a stroke replied;
Till all the medicine he prepared was dealt,
And every bone the precious influence felt;
Till all the panting flesh was red and raw,
And every thought was turn'd to fear and awe;
Till every doubt to due respect gave place –
Such cures are done when doctors know the case. [XXI. 505–18]

'This horrible passage,' says Howard Mills, 'is the only point where Crabbe shocks us – shocks us not with what he shows of others but of himself, his alien bigotry'. That is true, but it it is not the whole truth. Part of the problem is Crabbe's absurd moral arbitrariness, which has already forgiven Anna in 'The Widow's Tale' for her sexual transgression while punishing Edward Shore for his, largely because of the latter's independence of mind. Here, he compounds the offence by describing the father's brutally disproportionate action as 'medicine': he presumably intends thus to justify the treatment of a moral sickness with a physical remedy, but the result – especially in view of Crabbe's own medical expertise – is disastrous. As in the digression on order, he seems to be wrestling with demons of his own.

And that, of course, is the deeper problem here: we cannot read this passage without recalling 'Grimes is at his exercise' and wondering how to square Crabbe's attitudes to these two instances of physical assault. If both derive from his own father's violence, his apparent endorsement of Farmer Jones seems unaccountable; and the reader who returns to the text in the hope of discovering an ironic or satirical twist to reverse this endorsement is likely to be disappointed. In his review of *Tales*, Thomas Denman asserts that 'The Learned Boy' was 'borrowed from the 108th number of the *Tatler*, [which] relates how a foolish boy was horse-whipped by his father out of the errors of Atheism into the faith of a good Christian';[13] but this, if it affects our reading at all, merely adds to our difficulties. Why was Crabbe so attracted by this story that he felt compelled to versify it? Why, if indeed he had read it in the *Tatler*, could he not view it with adequate critical detachment? It is hard to avoid the feeling that he relishes Stephen Jones's punishment in a way which may throw retrospective light on his sympathy for Grimes and may also connect with the leathery apparitions of his dreams and the flagellant schoolmaster in *Tales of the Hall*. For whatever reason, Crabbe chooses to close his *Tales* on a note of appalling ignorance and prejudice.

5

Crabbe continued to trouble and confuse his reviewers. Jeffrey protested that an Epic was not what he had wanted at all; on the contrary, he was quite content with the length and variety of the *Tales*, though he would have liked 'more of the deep and tragical passions', 'less jocularity', 'rather more incidents' and 'rather fewer details'. Already it sounds as if he was not remotely satisfied. He then launched into one of those paragraphs, characteristic of early nineteenth-century reviewing, in which his professed admiration is so heavily qualified that there seems little left to admire. It is in fact a very shrewd analysis:

> The pieces before us . . . are mere supplementary chapters to *The Borough*, or *The Parish Register*. The same tone – the same subjects – the same style, measure, and versification; – the same finished and minute delineation of things quite ordinary and common, – generally very engaging when employed upon external objects, but often fatiguing when directed merely to insignificant characters and habits; – the same strange mixture too of feelings that tear the heart and darken the imagination, with starts of low humour and patches of ludicrous imagery; – the same kindly sympathy with the humble and innocent pleasures of the poor and inelegant, and the same indulgence for their venial offences, contrasted with a strong sense of their frequent depravity, and too constant a recollection of the sufferings it produces; – and, finally, the same honours paid to the delicate affections and ennobling passions of humble life, with the same generous testimony to their frequent existence, mixed up as before with a reprobation sufficiently rigid, and a ridicule sufficiently severe, of their excesses and affections.[14]

Jeffrey, like most of his contemporaries, underestimates the alterations in tone and texture which distinguish *Tales* from its predecessors, but in all other respects he provides a subtly shaded account of Crabbe's strengths and limitations. He goes on to recommend Crabbe's work 'to that great proportion of our readers which must necessarily belong to the middling or humbler classes of the community' because they are likelier than 'readers of any other description' to know what he is talking about: this seems a curious premise, until it becomes clear that what Jeffrey really has in mind is the strategic advantage of addressing such an audience – for there are, he says, at least two hundred thousand 'persons who read for amusement or instruction among the middling classes' as opposed to fewer than twenty thousand in the 'higher classes'. It is an important point: one of the reasons why Crabbe was so vastly more successful in the second decade of the nineteenth century than he had been in the ninth decade of the eighteenth century was that the constituency of readers he was addressing had expanded dramatically during the intervening thirty years. Jeffrey, again typically, proceeds to find fault with almost every individual tale before suddenly declaring Crabbe to be 'upon the whole, the most original writer who has ever come before us'.[15]

He was not alone in juggling self-contradictions: they were at the heart of Crabbe's reputation. The anonymous writer in the *Critical Review* for December 1812 remarked, in a tone of mildly amused exasperation, that it was 'not unusual at the present day to find one's self in a society of which one half is loud in extolling him as *a poet* in the truest sense of the word ... while the other is roused to indignation by the bare idea of what appears to them so exaggerated and almost blasphemous an elevation, and, running headlong to the contrary extreme, refuses him even the name of a poet ...' He added: 'The most remarkable feature in the present controversy is, that both parties are right ... we find ourselves also compelled to admit the justice of almost every censure and of almost every praise that he has received.'[16] Other reviewers complained about the uneven quality of the *Tales* – 'The Parting Hour', 'The Patron' and 'The Lover's Journey' were among those most widely admired, while no one had a good word for 'The Learned Boy' – or returned to the enduring problem of Crabbe's subject-matter: 'Mr C's grand fault,' grumbled the *Eclectic Review* (December 1812), 'lies in the choice of his subjects. It has all along been avowedly his aim to paint life, or rather the most loathsome and painful forms of life, in their true colours; to speak the truth, and nothing but the truth.'[17] The *Eclectic* reviewer was recalling Crabbe's early manifesto-statement from *The Village*, 'I paint the cot / As truth will paint it, and as bards will not', to which he remained unreconciled thirty years later despite Byron's eloquent endorsement of it in *English Bards and Scotch Reviewers*. The *British Review* of October 1812 took, very refreshingly, exactly the opposite line:

> . . . we really feel obliged to Mr Crabbe for giving us a little of truth instead of fiction in his poetry. We have been so long assailed by the wonderful and terrific in the poems and romances of the present day; our tranquility has been so long disturbed by knights and wizards, by Saracens and magicians, that it is some comfort to feel ourselves with Mr Crabbe in a whole skin among beings like ourselves, and without a hippogryph or dragon at our elbow.[18]

Nevertheless, the *British Review* found that 'in most of the tales simplicity exceeds its proper measure', while in 'one or two of them the main incident is too ordinary, and the moral too trite to be worth the rhymes in which they are conveyed'.

Several reviewers noted that Crabbe's style, with its somewhat mechanical approach to versification and its peculiar mannerisms, was (as the *Critical Review* put it) 'more apt to provoke the dangerous ridicule of parody than that of any poet of the present day'.[19] The most celebrated and successful contemporary parody, 'The Theatre', from *Rejected Addresses* by Horace and James Smith (1812), is for the most part an amiable affair on a topic dear to Crabbe's heart if hardly typical of his verse; but it becomes lethal when James Smith brilliantly catches Crabbe's habit of tediously elaborating the irrelevant interrelationships of several ludicrously named characters:

> John Richard William Alexander Dwyer
> Was footman to Justinian Stubbs, Esquire;
> But when John Dwyer listed in the Blues,
> Emanuel Jennings polish'd Stubbs's shoes.
> Emanuel Jennings brought his youngest boy
> Up as a corn-cutter, a safe employ;

In Holywell Street, St Pancras, he was bred
(At number twenty-seven, it is said),
Facing the pump, and near the Granby's Head:
He would have bound him to some shop in town,
But with a premium he could not come down;
Pat was the urchin's name, a red hair'd youth,
Fonder of purl and skittle-grounds than truth.

Crabbe himself took this in surprisingly good part: the *Rejected Addresses*
were 'excellent parodies . . . in their versification, they have done me
admirably'. They had indeed, although we might wonder whether the poet
who could open 'The Frank Courtship' with the couplet 'Grave Jonas
Kindred, Sybil Kindred's sire, / Was six feet high, and look'd six inches
higher' had much need of parodists. It is clear from one of Crabbe's letters
to Scott that he was flattered to find himself included among the Smiths'
targets, 'where you and I and Mr Southey and I know not who shine in the
eye of the public'.[20] When, some five years later, he met James Smith at
William Spencer's home near Richmond Park, he greeted him 'with a good-
humoured laugh' and the words, 'Ah, my old enemy, how do you do?'[21]

The Smiths, while accurately capturing Crabbe's style, made no attempt
to imitate his characteristic subject-matter; and his more conventional
reviewers, even when they disliked what he wrote about, very seldom noted
the most conspicuous omissions in *Tales*. Later readers may initially be
surprised that a book published in 1812 is so unconcerned with the great
issues of the day, especially the war with France; but in this Crabbe resembles
some of his great contemporaries (we do not, after all, look for an awareness
of European affairs, except as distant background, in the novels of Jane
Austen). What might more justly surprise us is the continuing absence in
Crabbe's imaginative world of *industry*. *The Borough*, we are to understand, is
set in an old-fashioned maritime community, without factories of any sort:

Of manufactures, trade, inventions rare,
Steam towers and looms, you'd know our Borough's share –
'Tis small: we boast not these rich subjects here,
Who hazard thrice ten thousand pounds a year;
We've no huge buildings, where incessant noise

Is made by springs and spindles, girls and boys;
Where, 'mid such thundering sounds, the maiden's song
Is 'Harmony in Uproar' all day long. [VIII. 1–8]

But the *Tales* do not share the earlier poem's geographical constraint. We
know that Crabbe was fascinated by his friend Cartwright's use of steam
power, and he can hardly have been unaware of the unrest this caused. By the
end of 1811, sporadic discontent had escalated into full-scale Luddite rebellion
and two thousand troops had been sent to Nottingham – some twenty miles
away from Muston – to quell it. Early in 1812, Byron made his maiden speech
in the House of Lords, in opposition to the Frame Work Bill (which increased
the penalty for frame-breaking from transportation to death): 'He had seen
with his own eyes, he declared, "the most unparalleled distress", and he
argued that only extreme poverty could have driven these hard-working
people into acts of violence.'[22] It is, at least on the face of things, extraordinary
that this subject – which not only concerned the poor but was a local issue in
the East Midlands – does not figure as a major theme in the *Tales*.

Part of the explanation seems to be that, as with the Gordon Riots in
1780, Crabbe simply found it impossible to see the individuals within the
mob and to isolate them imaginatively; in this, he is precisely unlike
Dickens. Although he recognises movements of opinion in moral and
theological terms, and shows their effect on individual characters, he has
almost no sense of the way in which political and industrial change affects
ordinary people: this aspect of his creative world remains rooted in the
eighteenth rather than in the nineteenth century.

6

Nevertheless, there was another reason why Crabbe's world in *Tales* was
largely a backward-looking and constricted one: the circumstances in which
the poems were written. Compared with his earlier work, they were
composed very rapidly. Partly because he was now well into middle age but
mainly because of Sarah's declining health, his life had become static: the
material for his poetry was now drawn from memory and imagination rather
than from fresh experience. Although tending to his wife's needs and
writing in his study were conveniently adjacent occupations, they were not

likely to extend his knowledge of the changing world outside. As he sat at his writing desk he could see Belvoir Castle in the distance, framed by its Gothic archway cut in the tall hedge of the rectory garden: it was a prospect which aptly symbolised his own isolation.

Crabbe had always been a poet who needed one friend – his intellectual equal or superior – with whom he could discuss the progress and the vexations of his life and work. Edmund Burke had been such a friend; as had, at different times, Charles Manners, Edmund Cartwright and Richard Turner. From 1812 onwards, this role was supplied by a younger writer whom he already admired, Sir Walter Scott, even though the two men would not meet until eight years later (incidentally, the dates of the Crabbe–Scott correspondence are hopelessly garbled by the biographer son who, for instance, has Scott writing in 1809 about Crabbe's 'The Patron', which was not published until 1812). Scott had ordered a copy of Crabbe's *Tales* from John Hatchard and, having received and read the book, wrote appreciatively to its publisher; Hatchard, combining common kindness with publisher's acumen, then hastened to forward this high-quality fan mail to his author. Crabbe's first letter to Scott, in October 1812, conveys in a single sentence both his need for literary friendship and his sense of enforced isolation at Muston: 'I have long entertained an hearty wish to be made known to a poet whose works are so universally read and so greatly admired, and I continued to hope that I might at some time find a common friend by whose intervention I might obtain that honour, but I am confined by duties near by home and my sickness in it.'[23]

A week later, Scott replied with the letter which I have already mentioned, in which he remembered identifying with the young poet in 'The Patron':

I am just honoured with your letter, which gives me the more sensible pleasure, since it has gratified a wish of more than twenty years' standing. It is, I think, fully that time since I was, for great part of a very snowy winter, the inhabitant of an old house in the country, in a course of poetical study, so very like that of your admirably painted 'Young Lad', that I could hardly help saying, 'That's me!' when I was reading the tale to my family. Among the very few books which fell under my hands was a volume or two of Dodsley's *Annual Register*, one of which contained copious extracts from 'The Village' and 'The Library', particularly the conclusion of book first of the former, and an extract from the latter, beginning with the description of the old Romancers. I committed them most faithfully to my memory, where your verses must have felt themselves very strangely lodged, in company with ghost stories, border riding ballads, scraps of old plays, and all the miscellaneous stuff which a strong appetite for reading, with neither means nor discrimination for selection, had assembled in the head of a lad of eighteen. New publications, at that time, were very rare in Edinburgh, and my means of procuring them very limited; so that, after a long search for the poems which contained these beautiful specimens, and which had afforded me so much delight, I was fain to rest content with the extracts from the *Register*, which I could repeat at this moment. You may, therefore, guess my sincere delight when I saw your poems in a later period assume the rank in the public consideration which they so well deserve.[24]

Quite apart from the generosity of Scott's praise, there is an almost telepathic affinity between the two writers. After all, it was Crabbe who had declared, on coming across *The Lay of the Last Minstrel*, 'A new and great poet has appeared!' and who, even before that, had found himself drawn towards exactly the 'miscellaneous stuff which a strong appetite for reading' had put into his head as well as into Scott's. And if Crabbe and Scott were unified by the kind of writers they were – storyteller-poets whose tastes had been shaped by wide but haphazard reading – they were similarly united by what they were not: they were not Wordsworth and Coleridge. The biographer son says that they shared 'manly and sensible views of literature and literary fame',[25] and in this he is surely right; modern readers inclined to baulk at 'manly' as a term of approbation will nevertheless see what he means. He is attributing to his father qualities of integrity and straightforwardness which are to be implicitly contrasted with the egotistical silliness of other writers. Moreover, while this distinguishes Crabbe from his great contemporaries among the first generation of Romantic poets (who were *sometimes* egotistical or silly), it separates him even more sharply from the second generation: they, in 1812, were hardly grown up, yet Crabbe was to outlive both Keats and Shelley by a decade.

Scott fully shared Crabbe's desire to forge links with sympathetic fellow writers: he intended to avail himself 'of the freemasonry of authorship' to send Crabbe 'a copy of a new poetical attempt, which I have now upon the anvil, and I esteem myself particularly obliged to Mr Hatchard, and to your goodness acting upon his information, for giving me the opportunity of paving the way for such a freedom'. This 'new poetical attempt' was *Rokeby*, published in January 1813, and Crabbe would write to thank Scott for sending him a copy on 5 March. Meanwhile, his next letter to Scott opened with a typical apology for his own inadequacies ('I am an idle man with few correspondents, you engaged more and with many'), before mentioning, rather dispiritedly, some of the odder characters who had written to him: 'a very angry writer' who had taken exception to the lines on Swedenborg in Letter IV of *The Borough* and a bumptious minor poet called Samuel Jackson Pratt. These miserable specimens made his newly launched correspondence with Scott all the more valuable to him: '. . . my want of communication with and even of knowledge of the men of genius in our days renders the opening of an intercourse with you highly pleasant and a motive for much self-gratulation, and I do accordingly gratulate myself and reflect on my acquisition with the spirit of a man growing rich: I have a new source of satisfaction'.[26] As is so often the case with Crabbe's prefaces and dedications, this courtly bowing and scraping masks an altogether more pragmatic purpose; for he is really anxious to make use of the authorial freemasonry which Scott had invoked.

What, he wants to know, has he done to deserve the recent hostility of a writer in the *Scottish Review*? 'Whatever he may think, I am a very middling, wellish-disposed kind of man, and not the profligate he would seem to hold forth . . . I know not how I have excited or deserved this anger,' he complains – a shade disingenuously, as it turns out, for he at once deduces an explanation which suggests that his knowledge of the literary world is shrewder than he cares to admit: '. . . possibly the civility of the older Edinburgh reviewer [Francis Jeffrey] (of whom I also am ignorant) may have caused a fit of spleen, for there is evidently among even the best of these critics a spirit of opposition as well as emulation . . .' Still, says Crabbe, 'I mean not to complain, to censure, to be discontented or to be thankful for whatsoever share I have had of their mel or their pel . . . I am perfectly satisfied to take the doses as they are dispensed and, though I may regard one doctor more than the other, yet the bitter-sweet considered as a whole will have beneficial effects . . .' Just as sometimes happens in his letters to Burke, once he has dispensed with his lengthy formalities, Crabbe becomes a completely different correspondent: the shy, stilted provincial poet has been transformed into a relaxed professional author, conceding (as authors must) that any review is better than no review and returning to his favourite image of the doctor and his medicine, in happier circumstances than when we last encountered it.

Turning from reviewers, he next wants to know about 'a gentleman in Edinborough' called Alexander Brunton, who has written to ask him to contribute to a proposed 'Book of Scotch Psalmody'. 'Let me first enquire, who is Mr Brunton? That is, in what situation? Should I give my time to a man who has no view to profit, who needs no assistance of that kind?' By this point, one imagines that Scott may have been wondering quite what he had taken on in initiating a correspondence with the Rector of Muston. In his next paragraph, however, Crabbe moves on to his own domestic matters, supplying among other things (surely to Scott's surprise) a curious and detailed account of his recurring medical condition:

> Mrs Crabbe is I trust in better health and, when not too much engaged, my head is tolerably free from giddiness and heat: I have this (I know not whether to call it) singularity in my complaint, that it comes on by rapid or more hasty composition, as writing recollections for a common-place or letters of information to one's family friends, on all such occasions, as thought quickly succeeds thought, an heat arises in the head and grows soon intense and serves as a warning for instant dismission of the business – slow composition, hammering out verses, dwelling on one idea, hurt me little, copying (which is mere copying) not at all, but writing a sermon, where the mind runs before the pen, is what I can seldom sit down to, the heat arises in five minutes – pardon this: I hope I have not a fellow sufferer in you, but you may have heard of suffering fellows in this, and I am interested in my hot-headed brethren.

The complaint – for which Crabbe the physician has no name, even though his excited prose implies that he may have been suffering from it at the moment of writing – is evidently one to which we would give the generic name of 'stress'. It may have involved high blood pressure or some form of a fairly common mental condition, such as depression or schizophrenia: it rather depends on how literally or figuratively Crabbe is using the word 'heat'. His distinctions between intellectual activities are interesting: most readers would have assumed that composing a poem is a more intense, and therefore stress-inducing, task than writing a sermon, but for Crabbe it is the other way round. And this tells us something both about his poetry (its characteristic orderliness is indeed a product of mostly low-intensity writing) and about his cyclical re-use of sermons which he now found almost impossible to write afresh. Furthermore, it is notable that he should choose to disclose such vulnerable information to an unmet fellow writer who, in distant Scotland, was for Crabbe scarcely less remote than the man in the moon.

Scott's reply was a model of helpful restraint: he dealt with the matters which seemed within his scope and ignored everything else. Crabbe was not to worry about the Scottish reviewers, whose opinions were 'really too contradictory to found anything upon them', while Brunton was 'a very respectable clergyman . . . you are quite safe with him'.[27] Scott was above all eager to reassure Crabbe that his *Tales* were 'universally admired here . . . the few judges whose opinions I have been accustomed to look up to, are unanimous'. 'Never be discouraged from the constant use of your charming talent,' he advised. With perfect intuition, he had assumed the encouraging, cajoling stance of Burke and Turner. Crabbe, in return, envied Scott's 'coolness and indifference to our monthly and quarterly critics' and confessed that he still read 'the more reputable and therefore more formidable of the clan' with both hope and fear: 'I know the weakness, and so does he who goes into a churchyard at midnight, but the hobgoblins have haunted his fancy and the reviewers mine, till in spite of our judgement we feel as if they were real dispensers of good and evil.'[28]

Such flimsy self-confidence, curious though it may seem in a successful writer approaching sixty, should come as no surprise in view of Crabbe's background and circumstances. More startling is his passing speculation, in the same letter, that the author of 'The Rime of the Ancient Mariner' might be 'Mr Lambe'. He thought it 'one story, if story it may be called, that shape or limb, beginning or end has none', and he wanted to bring it to Scott's attention because 'it does not describe madness by its effects but by imitation, as if a painter, to give a picture of lunacy, should make his canvas crazy, and fill it with wild unconnected limbs and distortions of features, and yet one or two of the limbs are pretty'. That sentence is all the more remarkable for reaching its central insight in the absence of two missing keys. One key is a chronological impossibility. Crabbe is trying to describe a kind of modernism which is almost a century ahead of him, for which he needs the language of Eliot or Pound, while the canvas he is imagining is, amazingly, to us a familiar one: it is Picasso's 'Guernica'. The other key might have been available to him if he had moved in different circles, for he would then have known that the other poet who was so obsessed by nightmares and madness was Samuel Taylor Coleridge and that he too was addicted to opium.

This sometimes perverse combination of insight and naïvety is, of course, one of Crabbe's most fascinating and maddening characteristics. From his brilliant comments on 'The Ancient Mariner' he veers swiftly back to more immediate but pedestrian matters. Should he allow a Mr Valpy to make payment in kind for his works? (No, Scott will tell him, he should have nothing to do with the 'precious impudent dog' who would try 'to barter the luminary of the Belvoir bard against the kitchen candlesticks and farthing candles'.)[29] He must now take his letter to the castle, so that it can be franked by Lord Robert Manners, the Duke's brother, and he looks forward to the ensuing conversation: 'You know Mr Scott?' and so forth. And he has written to his Suffolk friends about his new correspondent, while to Dr George Gordon, the Dean of Lincoln, he will conversationally remark, 'Mr Scott in his last letter . . .' He sounds charming, silly and puppyishly young. It seems not to occur to him that Scott, his junior by seventeen years, might be writing and saying the same sort of thing about him. Then, just as he is about to set off for Belvoir, another thought strikes him. In his last letter, Scott had described himself as 'fagging as a clerk' in the Supreme Court at Edinburgh. What on earth can he have meant by that? ' "Clerk" is a name for a learned person, I know, in our Church, but how the same hand which held the pen of *Marmion* and *The Lady of the Lake* holds that of a *clerk who fags*, unless, as I repeat, a clerk means something vastly more than I understand, is not to be comprehended: I wait for elucidation.'

To this, Scott has to explain, with the merest hint of affronted dignity, that he has gratefully exchanged his 'labour as a barrister for the honourable, lucrative and respectable situation of one of the clerks of our Supreme Court' and that in addition he holds 'in Commendam the Sheriffdom of Ettrick-forest (which is now no forest)'. This piece of amiable point scoring leads him to reflect that 'it is the most fortunate thing for bards like you and me to have an established profession and professional character', a sentiment very close to Crabbe's own beliefs. ('Accept my very sincere congratulations on your *Clerkship* and all things beside which you have had the goodness to inform me of,' writes Crabbe, a bit starchily, in his reply.)[30] Scott's only real tactical error is to assume that Crabbe is 'delightfully situated in the Vale of Belvoir', which he associates with Robin Hood.

But Crabbe, although he had been attached to it by a kind of ecclesiastical elastic for thirty years, had never liked anywhere less. In his letter of 29 June 1813, he provides a lively and candid account of his feelings about the place, together with a crisp *curriculum vitae*. It is partly a counterpart to the 'Bunbury Letter' of 1781, confirming the way in which Scott had taken over Burke's role, but it is also in its ironic dramatisation of Crabbe's relationship with Belvoir Castle an attractively vigorous piece of prose: if his novels had had these qualities, they would have been worth reading. For both these reasons, it deserves to be quoted at some length:

> With respect to my delightful situation in the Vale of Belvoir and under the very shade of the Castle, I will not say that your imagination has created its beauties, but I must confess that it has enlarged and adorned them. The Vale of Belvoir is flat and unwooded and save that an artificial straight-lined piece of water and one or two small streams intersect it, there is no other variety than is made by the different crops, wheat, barley, beans. The Castle, however, is a noble place and stands on one entire hill, taking up its whole surface, and has a fine appearance from the window of my parsonage, at which I now sit at about $1^1/_2$ mile distance. The Duke also is a Dukelike man and the Duchess a very excellent lady. They have great possessions and great patronage – but, you see this unlucky particle, in one or other of Horne Tooke's senses, will occur – 'But what?' – I will explain. I am one of the *old race*. 'And what then?'
>
> I will explain again. Thirty years since, I was taken to Belvoir by its late possessor as a Domestic Chaplain. I read the Service on a Sunday and fared sumptuously every day. At that time, the

Chancellor, Lord Thurlow, gave me a Rectory in Dorsetshire, small but a Living; this the Duke taught me to disregard as a provision and promised better things: while I lived with him on this pleasant footing, I observed many persons in the neighbourhood who came occasionally to dine and were civilly received. 'How do you, Dr Smith? How is Mrs Smith?' 'I thank your Grace, well.' And so they took their venison and claret. 'Who are these?' said I to a young friend of the Duke's. 'Men of the *old race*, sir: people whom the old Duke was in the habit of seeing and for some of them had done something and had he yet lived, all had their chance. They now make way for us but keep up a sort of connection.' The Duke and I were of an age to a week and, with the wisdom of a young man, I looked distantly on his death as my own. I went into Suffolk and married with decent views and prospects of views more enlarging somewhat further off; His Grace went into Ireland and died. Mrs Crabbe and I philosophised as well as we could and, after some three or four years, Lord Thurlow once more *at the request of the Duchess* (Dowager) gave me the Crown Livings I now hold, on my resignation of that in Dorsetshire. They were at that time worth about £70 or £80 a year more than that and now bring me about £400; but a long minority ensued. New connections were formed and when, some few years since, I came into this country (after a residence in Suffolk) and expressed a desire of inscribing my verses to the Duke, I obtained leave indeed, but I almost repented the attempt from the coolness of the reply. Yet recollecting that great men are beset with applicants of all kinds, I acquitted the Duke of injustice and determined to withdraw myself as one of the *old race* and give way to stronger candidates for notice; to this resolution I kept strictly and left it entirely to the family whether I should consider myself as a stranger who, having been disappointed in his expectation by unforeseen events, must take his chance and ought to take it patiently. For reasons I have no inclination to canvas, His Grace has obligingly invited me and I occasionally meet his friends at the Castle, without knowing whether I am to consider that notice as the promise of favour or as favour in itself. I have two sons, both in orders, partly from a promise given to Mrs Crabbe's family that I would bring them up precisely alike and partly because I did not know what else to do with them. They will share a family property that will keep them from pining upon a curacy and what more, I must not perplex myself with conjecturing. You find, sir, that you are much the greater man, for except what Mr Hatchard puts into my privy purse, I doubt whether £600 be not my total receipts, but he at present helps, and my boys being no longer at college, I can take my wine without absolutely repining at the enormity of the cost.

Thus Crabbe saw himself – or thus he presented himself to Scott – in the summer of 1813. He allows himself, deliberately or not, some liberties: he and Charles Manners were born within a year, not within a week, of each other; his long 'residence in Suffolk' shrinks into a parenthesis. His profoundly disgruntled relationship with Belvoir Castle is, however, both shrewdly and accurately conveyed. Strangely, he no longer mentions his wife's health.

7

Some time in 1812 or early 1813, Crabbe realised that it was possible not only to imagine but to anticipate another kind of life. This was partly Walter Scott's fault: the younger writer had prompted him to articulate his dissatisfactions with a clarity which made them unignorable, and the approach of old age reminded him that he had never really been young. There was also the now inescapable fact that Sarah's condition was rapidly deteriorating: Crabbe, with his medical experience and his unflinching realism, knew that she was unlikely to live very much longer. He had been the most devoted and considerate of husbands, and he had been deeply in love with his wife, but the urgency of love was by this time a distant memory. The memory was about to receive a number of unexpected jogs.

Writing to Scott in June 1813, Crabbe mentioned, as if it were a thing of small importance, that he had received 'a letter from a lady in Cornwall (St Columb) who obligingly offers me a pathetic Tale: unfortunately, I have done with Tales, but I was thankful'.[31] This is misleading on two counts: Crabbe had not 'done with Tales', as *Tales of the Hall* and *Posthumous Tales* were to demonstrate; and the Cornish lady and her Tale were not at all the kind of briskly closed matter which he means to imply. This lady, Charlotte Campion

Williams, was the daughter of a Cornish mine owner; born in 1782, she was almost exactly the same age as Jane Austen's friend Charlotte Williams, with whom she has sometimes been conflated.[32] She had written a story about a mine worker's troubled romantic life, in which love and constancy appear to have triumphed over adversity: this she sent to Crabbe in the spring of 1813, no doubt recognising in its combination of deprivation and morality a strong kinship with his own tales. It is indeed the sort of scheme which Jane Austen might have enjoyed, and it is certainly the sort of story which Crabbe might have put into verse, except that Cornish mines were as remote from his imagination as Nottingham factories. And there, no doubt with a civil reply from the rectory at Muston, the affair might have ended.

Instead, their correspondence blossomed over several months. Charlotte Williams, who was engaged to be married, apparently found nothing amiss with Crabbe's letters; but her fiancé – a recently ordained clergyman called Thomas Pascoe, whom she married on 31 October 1815 – declared them to be 'nothing less than love letters'. Charlotte Williams, believing Crabbe's wife to be alive, at first dismissed the idea, though she agreed to end the correspondence. Nevertheless, according to Sarah Hoare's friend Mrs John Farrar, 'The very next letter from the aged poet was a declaration of love, and a proposal to visit her . . . She was provoked with herself and the poet, and wished she had never sent him the story of the miner.'[33] We do not know the date of this 'very next letter': it is hardly likely to have preceded Mrs Crabbe's death, though it would be not much less extraordinary had it been written in the months immediately following. And one or other of these strange possibilities must have been the case, for early in 1814 Miss Williams asked her friend Charlotte Ridout to write on her behalf to Crabbe, informing him of the engagement; a garbled draft of Crabbe's highly emotional reply survives, dated 27 April 1814, and it is printed in the *Selected Letters and Journals.* That he was every bit as serious as the justly concerned Thomas Pascoe suspected is clear from the more considered – and notably candid – account of the affair he gave to Walter Scott a year or so later:

> I was, especially in the latter part of the correspondence *alone*; and a
> man alone, however aged, if he be in health and of certain com-
> plexion and has indulged in certain modes of thinking, he will let
> his   imagination   or   something   within   whisper   that,   his

correspondent being of different sex, she may be more to him than she now is. Yet this lady and I, whom even yet I never saw, laughed at the difference between 58 and 26, but it does not follow that they who laugh may not be in earnest: I grew, almost insensibly, fond of this writing in the dark; it became very interesting, so that my letters changed from their playful and masquerade character to downright earnest – and then it was time for my Goddess to own that she was bound by honour and promise to a sober youth, who was within call and waited for a falling rectory.[34]

There is, of course, an interesting parallel between Crabbe's relationship with Walter Scott and that with Charlotte Williams. In each case, he found it possible to be on the most intimate terms with someone he had never met; indeed, it seems altogether likely that this intimacy was possible for him precisely *because* he had never met them. Often awkward in his face-to-face encounters, he clearly found the process of 'writing in the dark' – in his own subtly evocative phrase – to these unseen friends, who lived towards the island's extremities, enormously liberating: if the term 'pen pal' had been invented, Crabbe would probably have disliked it, but he would have known exactly what it meant. What he could not have suspected at the time was that he was not the first author to have been approached by Charlotte Williams: Scott, he subsequently discovered, had also received 'a letter, letters, two, three perhaps more, with a ring or purse . . . from a lady in Cornwall, Miss C.C.W.' She seems to have made a habit of approaching writers with affectionate fan mail, until settling down with the Reverend Pascoe, who remained Vicar of St Hilary, Cornwall, for over fifty years. Of Charlotte Ridout, and indeed of Jane Austen, we shall hear more in due course.

That Crabbe was contemplating other romantic involvements before his wife's death is clear from two pieces of evidence closer to home. One is the curious poem called 'Storm and Calm', which he had written for the Duchess of Rutland's personal album in 1812. It is a conventional piece, in which the experience of early love is compared to a storm at sea; this is in due course succeeded by a calm apprehension of beauty; but, after a passage of years, the writer becomes weary of 'dull comforts' and longs for a return of the passionate, invigorating storm:

'Alas!' I cried, when years had flown –
Must no awakening joy be known?
'Must never Hope's inspiring breeze
Sweep off this dull and torpid ease –
Must never Love's all-cheering ray
Upon the frozen fancy play –
Unless they seize the passive soul,
And with resistless power control?
Then let me all their force sustain,
And bring me back the storm again!'

The poem evidently charts the successive stages in Crabbe's relationship with his wife, for he was to use almost identical terms in a letter to Elizabeth Charter: 'a life that for more than eighteen years was almost without incident, invariably cloudy and cheerlessly calm, without any storm to cause apprehension or any sunshine to dissipate the gloom'.[35] In the poem, however, he is careful to write about an abstract 'Love', which is not fixed to any individual. This has two consequences: on the one hand, it prevents the poem from being specifically hurtful to Sarah; on the other, it liberates the concluding wish for love's return from Mrs Crabbe and allows it to float, recklessly and hopefully, elsewhere. Among the places where it may have fleetingly landed was Sedgebrook, the home of Sir John Thynne, subsequently Lord Carteret, and his wife. After a visit to Sedgebrook in September 1812, Crabbe wrote to Dr Gordon: 'I know not in what manner to express my sense of the good humour and polite condescension of your friends. I am, as much as it is right and becoming, in love with Lady J. Thynne, and am greatly indebted for her obliging attention to a half-deaf village priest who several times gave her Ladyship the trouble of repeating what she was kindly observing to him . . .'[36] He is, of course, joking in his mock-courtly way; but the joke has its more serious, confessional edge, and from the courtly to the flirtatious is not such a huge step.

He was certainly on sufficiently intimate terms to joke with the Dean of Lincoln, for whom he often deputised at Sedgebrook and East Allington; George Gordon had become his closest confidant among the friends he could actually meet, and he was one of the few remaining social visitors at the Muston rectory. In a letter of April 1813 – written in some haste, before the arrival of 'our somewhat-quickened Mercury', who turns out to be an elderly messenger – Crabbe first reports to Gordon on various items of parish business before issuing a charming invitation:

> Will you dine with me on Sunday? I know among other good and happy properties, you can take the fare of the day as it happens, and we can give you the Sunday's joint and apple pie, in short you shall have a country rector's dinner and I am afraid no more, and now, on this condition, will you dine with me on Sunday? – Mrs Crabbe and her sons desire their respectful remembrances; we are in our usual state, rather I think improving than declining. – The old man appears and as I have nothing more to add than a return of your good and kind wishes, I will not detain you nor even Mercury himself . . .[37]

Tact is not a quality we always associate with Crabbe, but this is beautifully handled: Gordon would have understood precisely what was said and implied. Let us hope that he accepted the invitation and enjoyed the Sunday joint and apple pie.

Despite the invaluable assistance of his sons – especially George, who was now his father's curate at West Allington – 'Life's common cares' were pressing on Crabbe. In an attempt to alleviate them, he took his family to London during the summer of 1813: the biographer son says that his mother, 'though in a very declining state of health', had 'a strong inclination to see London once more',[38] but it sounds far more like his father's idea. They stayed at Osborne's Hotel, just off the Strand, for almost all the month of August; the expense was considerable and may have been borne at least partly by 'a friend in town' – the involvement of the Dowager Duchess is a distinct possibility – rather than by Crabbe himself. 'Went to London,' he noted in his diary. 'Arrived on the 2nd and returned on the 29th, lodged at the Adelphi, Osborne's Hotel. Bill £54. Carys. [carriages] £14. Expenses of many kinds about £70.' It was twenty-nine years since his last visit to the capital, but he seems to have been completely unfazed by it, visiting the botanic gardens, dining in coffee-houses and going to the theatre: at the Lyceum, he particularly enjoyed John Liston's farce *Sharp and Flat*, which had its first night on 4 August, and declared that Liston was 'a true genius in his way'.[39] Mrs Crabbe was usually too unwell to accompany her husband and sons; indeed, it is unclear what good the trip was supposed to do her, although she may have been seeking some treatment from a London specialist which the biographer son does not care to mention.

For Crabbe himself, the most satisfying aspect of the time was ushered in by the arrival one morning of a 'fine, tall, elderly man', John Bonnycastle. It was in 1807, after receiving Crabbe's *Poems*, that Bonnycastle had urged his old friend: . . . 'do not delay coming to see us any longer than you can possibly help'. They had 'not seen one another since their days of poverty, and trial, and drudgery; and now, after thirty-three years, when they met again, both were in comparative affluence, both had acquired a name and reputation, and both were in health'.[40] After this reunion at Osborne's Hotel, Crabbe did at last pay several visits to Bonnycastle's home in Woolwich; and he also met and dined with his earliest patron, Dudley North. In a poet of more Wordsworthian disposition, these encounters with friends unseen for so many years – to say nothing of the contrast between the penniless young man's and the eminent late-middle-aged poet's views of London – would have been the natural raw material for poetry; not for Crabbe.

Jane Austen, whose apparently whimsical though at least half-serious desire to be 'Mrs Crabbe' was a long-standing subject of amused comment within the Austen family, was also in London at this time, staying at her brother Henry's house in Henrietta Street, Covent Garden. In mid-September, she wrote to her sister Cassandra, 'I have not yet seen Mr Crabbe'; and, a little later in the same long letter: 'We had very good places in the box next the stage box – front and 2nd row, the three old ones behind of course. – I was particularly disappointed at seeing nothing of Mr Crabbe. I felt sure of him when I saw that the boxes were fitted up with crimson velvet.'[41] She is, of course, continuing the standing joke about her supposed infatuation, but it is notable that she was sufficiently well-informed to be aware both that Crabbe was visiting London and that he was fond of the theatre, while the association with crimson velvet probably derives from his description of Gwyn's home in 'The Gentleman Farmer': 'His taste was gorgeous, but it still was taste; / In full festoons the crimson curtains fell, / The sofas rose in bold elastic swell' (*Tales*, 1812). On her next visit to London, she coincidentally records seeing Crabbe's favourite comic actor, John Liston.[42]

Sarah's condition did not improve and at the end of August – just when Jane Austen was hoping to catch a glimpse of her hero – the Crabbes returned home. The trip may have been curtailed by the rapid deterioration in Mrs Crabbe's health, for at three o'clock in the morning of 21 September 1813 (not, as the biographer son says, 21 October), she died. She was buried at Muston, where her memorial, a simple marble slab, is to be found on the north wall of the chancel: 'Sarah, Wife of the Rev. George Crabbe, late Rector of this Parish.' · A few days after her death, Crabbe himself became so ill that he requested that his wife's grave should not be closed while his own life was in danger: the 'disease', says his son, 'bore a considerable resemblance to acute cholera without sickness';[43] he deduces that this 'alarming illness' was brought on by 'anxiety and sorrow', as, of course, it may have been. Later biographers have been content to agree with him, although the more prosaic and probable explanation is that the Crabbes brought a virus back from London which proved fatal to the weakened Sarah though not to her more robust husband. The son adds that his father was eventually cured by emetics which, even in 1813, would have been a curious remedy for 'anxiety and sorrow'.

This is not to suggest that Crabbe was hard-hearted: on the contrary, his grief was quite as devastating as his son implies, though subtly different in kind. The task of sustaining a happy marriage had long ago become an impossible one, but that would not have prevented him from experiencing guilt at his failure. Perhaps he had tried too hard: 'Never was there a better husband, except that he was too indulgent,' said Sarah's sister, Mary Elmy. On one of his wife's letters, Crabbe had written: 'Nothing can be more sincere than this, nothing more reasonable and affectionate; and yet happiness was denied.'[44] There is something self-conscious about that calm eloquence, as if it were his message for posterity. If so, it is a generous one: we can only guess at the troubled reality of his and Sarah's later years together. But we should not treat with outraged astonishment (as Huchon and Blackburne both do) Samuel Rogers's later remark: 'Crabbe was nearly ruined by grief and vexation at the conduct of his wife for about seven years, at the end of which time she proved to be insane.'[45] Rogers's friendship with Crabbe began in 1815, so it covers the very years in which he would have felt able to speak frankly about his late wife. There is also Southey's more temperate but essentially corroborative testimony, in a letter of 1808: 'It was not long before his wife became deranged, and when all this was told me by one who knew him well, five years ago, he was still almost confined in his own house, anxiously waiting upon this wife in her long and hopeless malady. A sad history! It is no wonder that he gives so melancholy a picture of human life.'[46]

One letter of condolence came from Alethea Lewis who, as William Levett's fiancée Alethea Brereton forty years earlier, had been responsible for Crabbe's first meeting with her friend Sarah Elmy at Ducking Hall. If there was anyone alive to whom he could open his heart so soon after his wife's death, it was to her. 'She has been dying these ten years,' he wrote. 'She is gone. I cannot weigh sorrows in a balance or make comparisons between different kinds of affliction, nor do I judge whether I should have suffered most to have parted with my poor Sally, as I did part . . . or to have seen her pass away with all her faculties, feelings, senses acute and awake as my own.' At last he could be specific about her decline, describing it in terms which suggest that Rogers's account was anything but exaggerated: 'The will sometimes made an effort, but nature forbad: the mind was clouded, and by degrees lost. Then too were the affections wrecked . . .' Their summer visit to London had been 'a trying and anxious time'; he had 'hoped something from novelty', but in fact Sarah's 'debility' had become worse while they were there. 'Medical men could do nothing: my poor Mrs Crabbe only lived to the present; we could not speak of the past. We could not hope together for the future . . .' He only rallies a little when he comes to speak, with Larkinesque self-deprecation, of his own condition:

> I never was a stout fellow, but Oh! my poor shrunken limbs and
> hollow features: you would smile, for I will not allow you to laugh. I
> looked in the glass this morning and do say, it is a very respectable
> old-looking sick face, chop-fallen to be sure, but as handsome as
> ever it was – but it is time to leave this and thank you once again for
> your letter . . .[47]

With his head full of Shakespeare, as the epigraphs to his poems show, Crabbe would have meant the comparison he so wryly implied in 'chop-fallen': 'Quite chop-fallen?' is Hamlet's rhetorical question to the skull of Yorick, the dead jester.

In these circumstances it is perhaps not surprising that when Crabbe recovered – as he did by the end of October – he began to rediscover a lightness of tone which had been largely absent since the days of his botanising letters to young Edmund Cartwright. On 1 November, he wrote to George Gordon:

> I am almost ashamed to send so small a basket of those yellow apples which appeared to me upon the tree as a much larger quantity, nor will I undertake to prove, as I was not the operator, that all which were gathered were deposited in my receptacle . . . I proposed this fine morning to have been at Sedgebrook, but my sons persuade me that the balloon to be launched from Nottingham this day will with the present wind come near the Vale of Belvoir: I think not much of a thing which twenty other things may prevent, but yet I wait.[48]

William Cowper, Jane Austen's other favourite poet, had also been inordinately fond of balloons. Meanwhile, at Edward Austen Knight's home, Godmersham Park in Kent, Jane Austen herself had learnt from Cassandra of Mrs Crabbe's death:

> No, I have never seen the death of Mrs Crabbe. I have only just been making out from one of his prefaces that he probably was married. It is almost ridiculous. Poor woman! I will comfort *him* as well as I can, but I do not undertake to be good to her children. She had better not leave any.[49]

8

While Crabbe had been emotionally unsettled by the protracted illness and eventual death of Sarah, he was about to be unsettled in a more literal sense. In November 1813, he was asked by the Duke of Rutland to relinquish the parish of Muston in exchange for the vacant living, which was also in the Duke's gift, of Trowbridge in Wiltshire: Muston was required for the Reverend Henry Byron – a cousin of Lord Byron and a distant relative of the Dean of Lincoln – who was then Rector of Granby, a small and unprofitable parish. Hardly anyone has a good word to say for the Duke, who is usually accused of insensitivity in springing these proposals on Crabbe so soon after Sarah's death. However, on this occasion he seems to have behaved decently enough: he had tactfully avoided any suggestion that Crabbe, for whom he had no great fondness, should move while there was an invalid wife to be cared for, and he seems to have guessed (correctly, as it turned out) that the Rector of Muston might now welcome a change of scene. Certainly, Crabbe had no objection to the idea of moving from a place he disliked; and, as winter drew on, he felt increasingly disgruntled in the rectory which, although it had seemed tolerable while there had been the needs of his wife to preoccupy him, was now, he realised, 'patched and pieced', neither 'comfortable nor completely secure'.[50] On the other hand, he was attracted to the South-West, which he remembered with pleasure and which had suddenly become plentifully supplied with romantic young ladies called Charlotte. What bothered him was money.

'Muston is, I confess, my Lord, not the place it has been to me, nor should I be sorry to leave it,' he wrote to the Duke on 17 November.[51] He understood the 'advantages and difficulties' of the proposal: 'the great population of Trowbridge will demand exertions unusual in this place, and duties I am seldom called to perform, and the mixture of inhabitants will require care and caution, which no one here would look for or could appreciate'. Although this looks – and is intended to look – both candid and sensible, it is in fact rather subtle: Crabbe manages to imply both an adaptability to new circumstances which he would not notably exhibit and a quiet disdain for the unobservant and unappreciative people of Muston. He cunningly sets out both his credentials for his new post and his reasons for leaving his old one; then, having prepared his ground, he turns to the financial difficulty. Simply, he suspects that the living of Trowbridge will be worth less than Muston and West Allington; he knows that, because of the increased post-enclosure value of West Allington, he would not be permitted to hold this in addition to Trowbridge; and, as a solution, he proposes to resign West Allington to his son, George, who has been acting as his curate there. His own income would be reduced; however, George's independence would also reduce his outgoings.

A week later, he had received financial estimates of Trowbridge from its recently departed incumbent, Gilbert Beresford: 'I doubt not his correctness,' Crabbe told the Duke, before going on to express considerable and well-founded doubt about his figures. He now saw clearly that to give up Muston for Trowbridge alone would involve 'hazarding difficulties and lessening my income'; even so, his own calculations, which he made before the end of the year (he jotted them down at the end of his 1813 diary), were by no means discouraging:

Value of Trowbridge living	
Tithe of 1778 acres of land	460. – –
Glebe 50 acres	174. – –
House etc.	50. – –
Offerings, fees and payments for evening lessons	81. 7. –
Staverton payment	17. – –
	—————
	782. 7. –

With every day that passed, the prospect of moving to a busier place became more enticing; for in Muston he had become, as he memorably put it, 'a solitary with a social mind, a hermit without an hermit's resignation'. And so, abandoning his earlier and subtler approach, he now launched an emotional appeal to the Duke's sense of natural justice, bolstered by one of his periodic résumés of his own career:

> Thirty years have passed since I had the honour of being received at Belvoir Castle: Lord Thurlow, the then Chancellor, had given me two small parishes in Dorsetshire, but his Grace forbad my residence, saying he would provide better for me; and, after this, the Duchess was pleased to offer me these rectories and to ask Lord Thurlow to exchange those formerly given, for them, and he did so: these were nearly £100 the more valuable, but being held by a Lambeth degree and dispensation both costly. It was some years before I could clear myself of this small incumbrance, but neither at that time nor since have I presumed to ask for anything, and now when your Grace in the latter part of my life offers me such prospect, it mortifies, it distresses me that I dare not accede: for in truth, my Lord, I dare not unless you would condescend to enlarge my view or to lighten my expenditure by this provision for my son. Nor can it be difficult, I think, my Lord: the Chancellor is the patron of both Muston and West Allington. It is not like asking for a vacant benefice, which he might wish to present to another . . . [52]

The style is extraordinary, a throwback to the overornate, unpleasantly grovelling letters of his earliest appeals to prospective patrons: it goes some way to making Crabbe's sincerity sound disingenuous. But the fifth Duke was not a particularly subtle man, so it worked.

No sooner had the Duke decided to let Crabbe have his way than the scheme began to unravel. Up popped Sir William Welby, formerly MP for Grantham and now Lord of the Manor at West Allington, who wanted his son John to have the living. So the Duke suggested Croxton in its stead for Crabbe's son – 'on enquiry,' Crabbe noted with satisfaction, 'I find it is equal in value to West Allington at this time or rather better'[53] – but, by the end of December, this tentative offer seemed to have been withdrawn, for Crabbe had learnt 'that Croxton, upon which we so much depended, is disposed of' while 'West Allington is beyond doubt secured to one of the Mr Welbys'. Since he had decided that it would be impossible for him to accept Trowbridge on its own, he once more glumly contemplated ending his days at Muston, but what he most disliked was the uncertainty: 'I cannot direct my man to buy a pig, nor my maid to make a purchase at Grantham, without the question occurring, "How long am I to be in this place?" and, though I now think the answer might be "As long as I live", yet till that be made more certain, all other things seem to be equally indeterminate.'[54] The whole business was becoming impossibly muddled; and in any case the Duke had other things on his mind.

The Duke's son and heir, Lord George John Frederick Manners, who had been born on 20 August 1813, was baptised at Belvoir Castle on 4 January 1814, the Duke's own thirty-sixth birthday, by the Duke's cousin, Dr Charles Manners-Sutton, Archbishop of Canterbury. It was a grand occasion. The Prince Regent and his brother, the Duke of York, were both present, as were numerous aristocratic connections of the Manners family, including John Fane, Earl of Westmorland and William Lowther, Earl of Lonsdale and son of the notorious 'bad earl'. John Thoroton, the son of Crabbe's friend Robert Thoroton, now the Duke's domestic chaplain and Rector of Bottesford, received a knighthood from the Prince. With so many sons featuring in the proceedings, it was indeed a day for Crabbe to feel that he was 'one of the *old race*': he seems to have found the whole affair mildly ridiculous when he reported on it satirically to his friend the Dean of Lincoln – noting, for example, how Lady Welby and the Prince Regent 'renewed their

acquaintance, by youthful manoeuvres almost too violent for her ladyship'.[55]
Uncertain of his own role – part Poet Laureate, part court jester: it was hard
to shake off the mask of Yorick – he produced a curious celebratory poem of
150 lines. In places he seems to be recycling the vocabulary and the rhymes
of Wordsworth's 'Immortality Ode':

> Accept the Homage grateful Numbers pay,
> Exulting all in this triumphant Day;
>> When all in one event rejoice,
>> And mine is as the public Voice –
>> An Echo to the general Joy
> That thanks thee for the noble Boy!
> All join in Wishes for the generous Race,
>> That through revolving Ages it may run –
> Blest each lov'd Daughter with the Mother's Grace
>> And with the Father's Virtue every Son;
> Whilst you, the happy Parents, look around,
> With Love rewarded and with Honour crown'd.

But his straggling benediction for the 'happy infant' was in vain: the child
died before he was a year old, on 15 June 1814.

When the Duke returned to the troublesome business of clergymen and
their livings, he may have thought that Henry Byron had a claim to West
Allington, for he decided that Welby's son must have Croxton. To Crabbe he
wrote: 'Let me ask you whether the vicarage of Granby would suit the ideas
of your son.'[56] Granby was, of course, the very parish from which Byron
wished to escape because its income was too small to live on; so Crabbe had
no trouble in deciding whether it 'would suit the ideas' of his son. The next
day, he wrote to George Gordon:

> Now, my dear Sir, if my *translation* depend upon my son's taking
> Granby or my taking it, it will never be accomplished, and this I can
> but conceive his Grace must, if he deigned to think, have thought
> for himself; he must surely know of a village so very near to him,
> that it is the poorest benefice in his gift; that it long stood at £80, but
> may be now at £100, that the house is an hovel no decent labourer

would live in, and in short that if my son resided he must live in misery for this wretched subsistence, and if he did not (and to that, nothing would tempt him I believe) the curacy would, and justly, take all the income.[57]

He informed the Duke that Trowbridge plus Croxton – whether in his son's name or his – was the only one of the available options which would induce him to move. The Duke's reply, dated 21 February 1814, suggests either that he had discovered the use of irony or, a no less attractive alternative, that his chief concern all along had been to engineer a beneficial change for Crabbe:

As I have only had your interest and welfare in view during the whole of our late correspondence upon the subject of Trowbridge, it is impossible that I can feel disposed to arraign any decision which you make upon the propositions submitted to you. It rejoices me to have pleasant tidings to communicate. I had offered Croxton to Sir W. Welby for his son John, but both Sir William and his son have in the handsomest manner waived all right to that living in your favour, and I can assure you there is no longer any objection to your receiving Trowbridge and Croxton, upon resigning Muston and Allington. If this arrangement should be satisfactory to you, be so good as to write a letter to the Chancellor resigning the preferment which you now hold under the Crown, and send me a presentation to Trowbridge, and to Croxton, which I shall be ready at the earliest opportunity to sign.[58]

Somewhat to his own surprise, Crabbe had got almost exactly what he wanted (as did John Welby, who succeeded him at West Allington after all). On 23 February, he wrote to the Duke's solicitor, Thomas Hill Mortimer, requesting that he should draw up the presentations to Trowbridge and Croxton Kerrial; three days later, visiting his friend the Dean of Lincoln, he realised that the lapsed rectorship of Trowbridge might pose a problem, and he dashed off a panicky supplementary letter to Mortimer: 'I scarcely know whether I be correct in my opinion that it become right for me to trouble you with another letter, having consulted the Dean at whose house I am on a visit, I learn no more than this, that lapsed livings are presented either by the Patron or the Bishop, as the latter may or may not recede from this claim, because though he may adopt the Patron's views with respect to the incumbent he may nevertheless choose to present the Benefice himself.'[59] He wanted to make absolutely sure that Trowbridge would be his before resigning Muston, and in a postscript he added a request which looks improbable, given that Trowbridge and Croxton were in different – and distant – dioceses: 'I should be glad if it be possible to have one journey suffice for both Benefices.' But, once again, he got what he wanted.

On 15 March, he travelled to Buckden Palace in Huntingdonshire, where the next day he was instituted as vicar of Croxton Kerrial by the Bishop of Lincoln; and from there he went on to London, where the Bishop of Salisbury instituted him as Rector of Trowbridge. He noted in his diary for 18 March: 'Instituted to Trowbridge. At night to see Kean in Shylock.' Two evenings later, he was 'at Drury Lane. Kean in *Hamlet*';[60] the following day, he called on his erstwhile landlord, Mr Vickery. For a man in his sixtieth year who only a few months earlier had been dangerously ill, this was a notably busy week: the effortless transition from ecclesiastical preferment to a night at the theatre is especially pleasing and wholly in character. He has the air of someone calmly picking up the threads of a life which had been interrupted many years earlier. He travelled to Trowbridge on 22 March: there he met Mr Fletcher, the curate who had been in charge of the parish since Gilbert Beresford's departure, and inspected the church and rectory: 'I like the country around Trowbridge extremely and Trowbridge itself very well,' he told George Gordon.[61] By 25 March he was back in London; and on 18 April he inducted his successor, Henry Byron, at Muston.

All seemed to be going rapidly to plan when, much to Byron's annoyance, two typically Crabbeish matters intervened to delay the changeover. Crabbe had been appalled at what he found when he visited his new rectory at Trowbridge. Beresford, the previous incumbent, had contrived to borrow – from the fund established by Queen Anne for the renovation of clergy houses – the enormous sum of £1,490, or approximately three times the clear annual income from the living: with this, he had instituted grandiose improvements, including the addition of two new rooms 'of unusual magnitude', which had been left incomplete at his departure. Consequently, Crabbe had 'discovered rooms yet unfinished, and in the larger, the floor not laid, nor is the work complete without; in fact, there appeared to be, what indeed was the case, a sudden stop put to the design'.[62] This would have been sufficient to alarm anyone, but for Crabbe, who had become particular about houses (Muston rectory was 'patched and pieced' and the vicarage at Granby 'an hovel'), it was intolerable: he wished 'to have the house made for me, as my sons would be obliged to make it in case of my decease'. There was also a real possibility that the new incumbent would find himself liable to repay the loan, together with the interest neglected by Beresford, and to complete the works at his own expense. Furthermore, there was a potential difficulty with tithes. Crabbe had been made wary by his past experience – he knew, for instance, that moving to a living in September could deprive him of this income until October of the following year – and he rightly suspected that the complications of the Trowbridge transfer might deprive him of residual tithe income due to him since Beresford left in the preceding June. Crabbe was thus, as Thomas C. Faulkner has (with admirable lucidity) explained, 'faced with the prospect of paying over £100 to complete the house, payment of £120 interest and principal on the loan, payment of taxes and rates of all kinds, and not receiving any tithe income until October of 1814'.[63]

Beresford, perfectly aware of all this, invited Crabbe to meet him on the neutral ground of a friend's house, 'as more convenient for me, he believed, than his own'; possibly he thought he could explain the problems away to a bumpkin from Suffolk. But Crabbe, too canny to fall for that, declined the invitation, pleading 'my want of time and some indisposition from my late journey', although the real reason, as he told Mortimer, was that he 'considered that I had no experience in such matters and . . . they should come under the consideration of one more able to determine respecting them'. Here he did himself an injustice – he was capable of arguing about money with a tenacity which would have startled Beresford – even though his tactics were sound. He mistrusted his own temper. 'I should be very sorry,' he wrote, 'to meet Mr Beresford on any terms than those of perfect amity'; and there was precious little hope of that. In fact, he had taken a justifiable dislike to everything about Beresford, including his slippery letters, which were full of insistences that the matters between them 'require *nicety* and are of *peculiar sort*'. 'Information was what I sought of Mr Beresford when I wrote to him a few weeks since,' he grumbled, 'and his letter contained the invitation before mentioned and the above expressions of the *nicety* etc required'.[64] These negotiations were destined to drag on for most of his first year at Trowbridge.

Crabbe had intended to leave Muston in early May – on 12 April he told Mortimer he would be in Trowbridge 'after three weeks' – but, detained by these legal difficulties, he decided to make good use of the delay. On 2 May he visited his sisters-in-law Eleanor and Mary Elmy in Beccles before going on to Aldeburgh, where he stayed with his sister Mary Sparkes until 10 May. It was a brief parting tour of East Anglian places which he might never see again. He devoted one day 'to a solitary ramble among the scenery of bygone years – Parham and the woods of Glemham, then in the first blossom of May,' says the biographer son.[65] He 'did not return until night' and recorded 'this mournful visit' in a brief elegiac poem:

> Yes, I behold again the place,
>   The seat of joy, the source of pain;
> It brings in view the form and face
>   That I must never see again.
>
> The night-bird's song that sweetly floats
>   On this soft gloom – this balmy air,
> Brings to the mind her sweeter notes
>   That I again must never hear.
>
> Lo! yonder shines that window's light,
>   My guide, my token, heretofore;
> And now again it shines as bright,
>   When those dear eyes can shine no more.
>
> Then hurry from this place away!
>   It gives not now the bliss it gave:
> For Death has made its charm his prey,
>   And joy is buried in her grave.

Abundantly clear though they may be to us, the reasons for this Suffolk excursion were lost on Henry Byron, who only saw the departing Rector of Muston taking a gratuitous holiday while he was kept waiting: 'Mr Byron has reproved me (I had almost said reproached) for my delay . . . as he cannot judge of the motives for my late journey into Suffolk,' wrote Crabbe a fortnight later, adding that he was 'only seven days beyond his own time'.[66] By this time, he and his sons were in lodgings in Grantham, having finally left Muston on 19 May. Some of his more hostile parishioners, says the biographer son, 'carried this unkind feeling so far as to ring the bells for his successor, before he himself had left the residence',[67] but Huchon plausibly suggests that it was the aggrieved and impatient Byron who started the peal, ringing out his predecessor by ringing himself in.[68]

Though uncertainties would come soon enough, for the moment Crabbe could look forward cheerfully to the future:

I must hasten to Trowbridge, where, while this hurrying, yet not ill-natured successor of mine is urging me to be speedy in my exit, the patient and good-natured minister of that place [Fletcher], who is engaged and much wanted in a new situation, kindly and patiently waits for me, and even presses me to do all my business before I release him. It is a happiness when we find one man thus compensating by his virtues for the inconsideration of another.[69]

He hastened at his own pace, however, for on 27 May he was once again in London where he saw 'Kemble in *Macbeth*'. Then, at last, he set off for Wiltshire, and on 1 June 1814 he arrived in Trowbridge.

Nine

Writing in the Dark

1814–1819

I

Crabbe had spent a good deal of his life confounding expectations, and he was about to do so again. Mr Fletcher, the curate who had deputised at Trowbridge for almost exactly a year, was a popular and enthusiastic preacher: some of the parishioners had unsuccessfully petitioned the Duke of Rutland in an attempt to secure the living for him. Whatever his virtues, Crabbe, with his recycled sermons read from yellowing sheets of paper, was less than inspiring in the pulpit; so on that score he was bound to be a disappointment. Many of his new flock resented the fact that this elderly rustic poet, whose East Anglian accent was as impenetrable to them as their Wiltshire dialect was to him, had been foisted on them by the Duke. Some, who had not read his work, expected him to be a wild Byronic figure; others, who had, were certain that he would be a dull moraliser. In the event, both groups were confounded, while Crabbe himself was 'healthfully excited' by the warmth of his reception 'among the most cultivated families of Trowbridge and its vicinity' and particularly 'by the attractive attentions of the young and gay among them . . . who, finding the old satirist in many things very different from what they had looked for, hastened to show a manifest partiality for his manners, as well as admiration for his talents'.[1] That is the biographer son, of course, overegging the compliments and telling, as we shall discover, rather less than half the truth. Yet even the grouchy James Bodman, when he published his *A Concise History of Trowbridge* later in 1814, commented: 'Mr Crabb seems to be a very moderate and very peaceable clergyman.' It was misspelt praise, but it was praise none the less.

Crabbe landed on his feet, wobbled for a few days, then carried on with renewed confidence. On the day of his arrival, he dined with John Waldron, owner of the Bridge Woollen Mills, and his family at Westcroft House: they may well have been connected with Miss Waldron of Normanston – who was a native not of Suffolk but of Tamworth in the West Midlands – but, even if they were not, the coincidence must have struck Crabbe as a benign omen; Waldron was, of course, the middle name of his younger son, who would in due course become his curate at Trowbridge. Two days later, he was inducted by the retiring curate, and at that point his resolve seems temporarily to have failed him. He was on his own among strangers, further than ever before from his East Anglian roots, living with unresolved financial problems in his barely habitable, half-finished rectory. He faced the inevitable crisis of wondering what on earth he was doing there. Then, on 5 June, he preached his first sermon, a generous and conciliatory one 'on the mutual tolerance which Christian sects should practise towards one another, in the interest of their common task'.[2] From then on, his spirits began to recover. On 8 June, he noted in his diary: 'Evening, – solitary walk – night – change of opinion – easier, better, happier.'

One reason for his returning confidence was his discovery that Trowbridge was not, after all, quite so unfamiliar a kind of place as he might have at first supposed. It was a textile-making market town of some eight thousand inhabitants, skirted by a river and with the remains of a medieval castle: in many respects, a larger version of Bungay. In the years immediately preceding Crabbe's arrival, the production of woollen cloth had been revolutionised by developments in which his friend Edmund Cartwright had been a pioneering force. Water power was introduced in the 1790s – the borough's largest water-driven factory was at Staverton, on the River Avon, rather than on Trowbridge's humbler tributary the Biss – and from 1805 onwards, when the town became linked by canal to the Somerset coalfield, steam power. The castle grounds were sold for industrial development in 1814: 'The earliest years of Crabbe's incumbency at Trowbridge saw factories and dyehouses built on the site, and by the time of his death the town contained some twenty factories and several large dyehouses.'[3] This sort of pattern was familiar to him from other newly industrialised towns, such as Doncaster and Nottingham; while the presence of numerous dissenters, whom he now at last sought to placate (those who had read Letter IV of *The Borough* needed some placating), was uncomfortably reminiscent of Muston. Kenneth Rogers quotes two lines of nineteenth-century descriptive doggerel – 'Trowbridge steeple, long and little, / Narrow streets and shabby people'[4] –

which make it sound, for better or for worse, very much Crabbe's sort of town.

Even his problematic rectory had the curious virtue of engaging him on familiar territory: he had been quarrelling about houses ever since Ducking Hall. With its combination of structural failings and legal snags, the rectory of St John's, Trowbridge, provided ample scope for him to exercise this talent. He took up these matters with Thomas Timbrell – a lawyer who was also a partner in the banking house of Ludlow, Barton and Timbrell, and, since 1809, Lord of the Manor of Trowbridge – to whom he also addressed his further vexation about an unfinished footpath: 'Whether you or Mr Beresford complete this footway is a matter I have nothing to do with,' he wrote, 'but it certainly must be done by somebody and I am so far from apologising to the magistrates, that I should require it, if they did not as part of the engagements entered into by my predecessor and relating to the Rectory.'[5] The forthright candour is characteristic, while in urging Timbrell to make haste in 'finishing the affair and getting all *settled legally and securely*', he reached for the two words which precisely describe his approach to finance and property. A few months later, he complained to his friend the Dean of Lincoln:

> I have obtained nothing of my predecessor in this rectory except an honest confession of embarrassments, and it is evident that I must live in unfinished and even unfloored rooms or be at expense myself, for I am informed that the sum borrowed was exhausted, and this is not the sole misfortune; I have indeed by many efforts and some threatening obtained a promise from the late sequestrators, that a part of the sums so inconsiderately paid to Mr Beresford and his solicitor shall be accounted to me, but I must wait long and lose a considerable part of my dues even then . . .[6]

But at the same time as he was grumbling about his Trowbridge predecessor, his successor at West Allington, John Welby, was grumbling about him: for there, the parsonage, unoccupied during the period of his son's curacy, had fallen into serious disrepair and Crabbe, as the outgoing rector, was liable for the dilapidations. Yet this was a relatively trifling matter in comparison with the irritations at Trowbridge, compounded as they were by his loneliness in a large house. 'Of all places, this parsonage is the worst,' he sighed, perhaps with a degree of glum relish. '"Never less at Home than when at Home" is the burthern of the song of the Rector of Trowbridge.'[7]

We may suspect that, especially when courting sympathy from his female correspondents, he overdid this gloom. For, despite the problems it at first caused him, the sixteenth-century rectory, twin-gabled and built of grey stone, was the handsomest and grandest of all Crabbe's church houses: 'the original mullioned windows on the two principal floors had been replaced by eighteenth-century sashes, but survived in the attics, and the central doorway was entered through an eighteenth-century doorcase. Gilbert Beresford's unfinished addition was in a plain Italian style.'[8] The elegant glass-fronted bookcases which Crabbe had fitted in his study remained until the rectory was demolished a hundred and fifty years later. There were some six acres of grounds, 'studded with fine old trees, the most notable of which may be regarded as Crabbe's mulberry'.[9] Photographs of the rectory exterior, of the study and of the mulberry tree were fortunately included in Broadley and Jerrold's *The Romance of an Elderly Poet*.

Socially, Trowbridge fulfilled his expectations in one respect but fell short of them in another. Although he was, as his son says, warmly received by prosperous townsfolk such as the Waldrons – a social class, non-existent in rural Leicestershire, with whom he found he could mix easily – he was soon aware that these agreeable, cultivated people were unlikely to provide him with much in the way of literary or intellectual stimulus: 'though I have a fixed habitation,' he wrote, 'and am tied to a place by contracts and duties, yet my mind does not love to abide there, nor among eight thousand minds can meet with one that makes this the favourite home'.[10] But he had only to travel ten miles to arrive at Bath: there were daily coaches from Trowbridge, and Crabbe made frequent use of them. His base in the city, the Castle and Ball Inn in Northgate Street, was conveniently placed for forays into a sophisticated cultural and social life of which he had been almost entirely deprived since his youthful spell as a member of Burke's circle. On 25 August 1814 he recorded that he had been 'elected of the Reading Society and News Room'; and he had probably also joined the Bath Harmonic Society, where his fellow members included Richard Warner, the Rector of Great Chalfield and Curate of St James's in the city, who was 'one of the chief literary ornaments of Bath' – a versatile and enormously prolific author whose *History of Bath* (1801) 'has not been superseded', according to the *DNB*. At last he could spend regular evenings at the theatre: many of his favourite actors appeared at Bath in 1814–15, including Edmund Kean, John Kemble and, following her retirement from the London stage in 1814, Mrs Dorothea Jordan.

It had never occurred to Crabbe that there was any conflict between his religious office and his enjoyment of plays – by this time he had, in any case, an understandable sense that his advanced years and considerable literary reputation gave him the freedom to do pretty much as he liked – but when a group of actors visited Trowbridge itself in August 1815, he received an unpleasant shock:

> There are a company of comedians with us and I went with parties twice and once looked in for half an hour, and here is one of my parishioners – anonymous! – who has written to me, oh! you cannot think with what solemn and enthusiastic severity: telling me that I am partaker and encourager of their sins in an high degree and, though I once should have smiled at both the abuse and the opinion, my want of health and spirit renders me subservient to this man's dulness and pride, for pride I suppose must in part dictate such sentiments. The poor players he stigmatises as wretches most pernicious and tells me I am as bad for encouraging them.[11]

As is so often the case with Crabbe's dejections, the timely utterance contains its own remedy: no sooner has he complained that he lacks spirit than he most spiritedly attacks his correspondent's 'dulness and pride'. He was shaken, nevertheless, and he was also dismayed to discover that 'the duties of a residing rector in a populous town' actually involved a good deal of work. Having told the Duke of Rutland, in November 1813, that 'the great population of Trowbridge will demand exertions unusual in this place', he ought not to have been surprised, but his theoretical acceptance of such exertions had not prepared him for the bothersome reality. Two years later, he was bitterly complaining about the 'unpleasant and necessary occupations': 'I begin, no not begin, I continue to regret the loss of my former leisure and to perceive the rector of a populous town loses much more in comfort than he gains in consequence'.[12] And by Boxing Day 1815, he had worked himself into a state of exasperation not only with his parishioners but with Christmas itself:

... it is true certainly that people are not born, neither do they die, at any particular part of the year, but they marry and baptise, and moreover the Priest is thought to be a very churlish Priest if he be not particularly attentive and sociable at certain seasons. A merry Christmas! call they it? No indeed, it is a very troublesome, fatiguing Christmas and I long for the repose of the New Year when the twelfth day tells the superstitious that holidays are over.[13]

The tone is ambiguous: this sardonic grumbling brings its own sort of pleasure. He sounds exactly like Philip Larkin during an enjoyably irksome spell at the library.

2

When Crabbe's two sons paid their first visit to Trowbridge, they were warmly greeted by their father; he had walked out of the town to meet them and was keen to point out the various houses in which he had been kindly received. Later that day, however, Crabbe's mood altered and deepened:

The evening of our arrival, seeing us conversing cheerfully as we walked together in the garden before his window, it seemed to have brought back to his memory the times when he was not alone: for happening to look up, I saw him regarding us very earnestly, and he appeared deeply affected. That connection had been broken, which no other relationship can supply.[14]

The biographer son attributes his father's melancholy to his mother's death, and of course he is right to do so. He is too discreet, or perhaps too disingenuous, to suggest more complex motives; for by then Crabbe's intense sense of loneliness had less to do with lingering bereavement than with unfulfilled love. When he comes to this matter, the son tries for a relaxed tone but ends up sounding awkward and coy: his father, he says, 'was peculiarly fond of the society and correspondence of females . . . and I believe no better proof could be given of the delicacy and purity of his mind and character';[15] the 'various incidents in his own later history that might afford his friends fair matter for a little innocent jesting' were a 'pardonable sort of weakness'. According to the son, 'though *love* might be out of the question, I believe he inspired feelings of no ordinary regard in more than one of the fair objects of his vain devotion'; none of this, however, 'for a moment disturbed the tranquillity of his family'.[16]

It was not quite like that. The process of emotional liberation – which Charlotte Williams had begun during Mrs Crabbe's lifetime – had, since Sarah's death and Crabbe's move to Wiltshire, developed into something approaching an addiction. The biographer son is nearer the mark when he writes, a little later on, 'I am persuaded that but few men have, even in early life, tasted either of the happiness or the pain which attend the most exquisite of passions, in such extremes as my father experienced at this period of his life.'[17] During his early years at Trowbridge, Crabbe was romantically involved with a number of younger women including Charlotte Ridout, Elizabeth Charter, Maria Waldron, Florentina Long and Sarah Hoare; there were also other 'favourites' among his Trowbridge flock, a former parishioner from Muston called 'Fanny' and further acquaintances met on visits to Bath and London. Of course, his manners towards young ladies were expansive in the style of a slightly earlier period and his florid compliments were sometimes mistaken for unintended intimacy. One country gentleman complained that 'the first time Crabbe dined at my house he made love to my sister'; while an unimpressed recipient of his attentions, described by the biographer son as 'the writer of some of the happiest *jeux d'esprit* of our day', declared that 'the cake is no doubt very good, but there is too much sugar to cut through in getting at it'.[18] Yet seriousness and silliness are by no means incompatible: one may easily prompt the other. Despite an experience of life which was unusually wide in terms of social mobility, Crabbe remained emotionally inexperienced: because he had found his first love early and had remained so steadfastly loyal to her, he was now inclined to behave 'exactly as a man of five-and-twenty would have done under the same circumstances'.[19] The very thought of being in love was enough to make him dizzy.

For Crabbe, 'writing in the dark', the transition from Charlotte Williams to Charlotte Ridout was barely perceptible. He had taken a fancy to the name, and there was no reason for him to imagine the two young women as other than interchangeable: 'the letters of the second Charlotte, for Charlottes they were both, were pleasant and flattering to me and a calm kind of affection began to take place in my mind . . .'[20] But, whereas her predecessor had been swiftly steered into a suitable marriage with a man of her own age, Charlotte Ridout 'rejected the proposal of a youth eligible in every respect, except a certain degree of weakness in his intellects'[21] and in July 1814 offered to engage herself to the vicar of Trowbridge, on whom she had not yet set eyes. Crabbe replied to this surprising offer on 2 August, with a degree of bashful confusion, and agreed to meet her the following month: this encounter took place at the Devon coastal resort of Sidmouth – home of Charlotte's aunt, Lady Floyd, the second wife of General Sir John Floyd – where the Ridout family were on holiday. There, 'the pair walked at least twice in one day on Sidmouth terrace'.[22] Crabbe had set off from Trowbridge on 22 September and stayed overnight in Taunton; he reached Sidmouth the next day, meeting Charlotte's parents, John and Caroline Ridout of Baughurst in Hampshire, for the first time. On 26 September, he noted in his diary, using the cipher he reserved for matters of personal importance, 'Declaration – Acceptance'. It was a year to the week since Sarah's death.

Crabbe's alacrity in embracing this arrangement – especially when we recall his reaction to his father's remarriage – is no less astonishing than the Ridout family's grudging acceptance of it. Though he found an ally in Charlotte's mother, he was less enamoured of 'a vixen A[unt, i.e. Lady Floyd] who was angry and obstinate and a foolish passionate Brother, a Fa[ther] who cared for nothing and a Sister who wrote of carriages and follies of that nature'.[23] He seems to have imported two of these undesirable relations – the aunt and the brother – into an otherwise non-autobiographical poem about a deceived and unhappy lover which is cagily quoted by the biographer son: 'It is even possible that I may be wrong in suspecting any allusion to his personal feelings.'[24] Charlotte's own motives, though they puzzled her family and may strike us as somewhat naïve, are by no means incomprehensible. She was attracted (as, after all, Jane Austen had been) by the idea of becoming 'Mrs Crabbe': the prospect of being mistress of Trowbridge rectory evidently appealed to her and, according to Mrs Farrar, she 'was very proud of her engagement to so celebrated a poet'. Such literary hero-worship is rather touching and wholly understandable in one who had declined another proposal on account of the suitor's weak intellect. Like Dorothea Brooke, she imagined herself as the devoted amanuensis of a literary clergyman in his declining years, while on a more practical level she may have shared the common misapprehension that successful authors are invariably well-off. If there was a touch of Dorothea's intellectual idealism in Charlotte Ridout, there was also a good deal of common sense.

Her prospective husband, despite his years, was the less clear-headed of the pair. On returning to Trowbridge at the end of September, he wrote a curious poem 'To a Lady, on Leaving Her at Sidmouth': the first and last stanzas are at once conventional and passionate – precisely what the occasion demands, in fact – but they are separated by a disproportionately long digression, in which he jealously imagines a younger rival, and an odd lurch into the 'night and death' world of his nightmares. In a poet of Keats's and Shelley's generation this clash of registers might appear to be an unsurprising symptom of the 'romantic agony'; in Crabbe, it seems unintentionally to transform a sad but hopeful occasion into an ominous one:

> Yes! I must go – it is a part
>   That cruel Fortune has assign'd me –
> Must go, and leave, with aching heart,
>   What most that heart adores, behind me.
>
> Still I shall see thee on the sand
>   Till o'er the space the water rises;
> Still shall in thought behind thee stand,
>   And watch the look affection prizes.
>
> But ah! what youth attends thy side,
>   With eyes that speak his soul's devotion –
> To thee as constant as the tide
>   That gives the restless wave its motion?
>
> Still in thy train must he appear,
>   For ever gazing, smiling, talking?
> Ah! would that he were sighing here,
>   And I were there beside thee walking!
>
> Wilt thou to him that arm resign,
>   Who is to that dear heart a stranger,

And with those matchless looks of thine
   The peace of this poor youth endanger?

Away this fear that fancy makes,
   When night and death's dull image hide thee!
In sleep, to thee my mind awakes;
   Awake, it sleeps to all beside thee.

Who could in absence bear the pain
   Of all this fierce and jealous feeling,
But for the hope to meet again,
   And see those smiles all sorrow healing!

Then shall we meet, and, heart to heart,
   Lament that fate such friends should sever;
And I shall say – 'We must not part';
   And thou wilt answer – 'Never, never!'

The tone is almost elegiac, as if the poem's complex emotion is already becoming recessed into the past: it disconcertingly resembles the tone we hear in Hardy, writing about the same coast in the poems which memorialise his first wife.

When Charlotte's father visited Trowbridge in November – the cause of much interested tongue-wagging in the town – it became clear that there was little money on either side: Charlotte would bring no dowry to speak of, while Crabbe's inherited property was held in trust for his sons (the peak of his authorial prosperity was yet to come). Suddenly apprehending Charlotte's likely future predicament as an impoverished young widow after his death – 'I would not hazard the distress she must feel as my widow, for I could not look forward to saving much for her, though we might have lived decently enough for a few years perhaps'[25] – Crabbe broke off the engagement. Or so, at any rate, he persuaded himself: it seems much likelier, and not especially disgraceful, that during the autumn of 1814 he realised that a man who could so easily capture the affection of one young lady could do the same for others. Why should he sacrifice his new-found freedom to the constraints of marriage from which he had so lately been released? For, however much he might grumble about his parish chores, in his external life he had never felt more energetic; as he had absolutely no intention of turning into a dried-up old clergyman like Casaubon, he had no need of a Dorothea to attend – still less to inhibit – his every move.

Crabbe recorded the stages of this disengagement, rather obliquely, in his diary:

Nov. 5   Mr Ridout. Letter from Miss Wylliams.
Nov. 8   Mr Ridout went.
Nov. 14   To Mr Ridout.
Nov. 15   Recd from Charlotte perse.
Dec. 14   Charlotte's picture.

The chronology of negotiations with Charlotte's father followed by (presumably) the return of Charlotte's portrait is relatively clear; but the coincidental arrival of a letter from Charlotte Williams on the same day as Mr Ridout and the reference to the 'perse' are both tantalising. Did Charlotte Williams attempt, successfully as it turns out, to dissuade Crabbe from marrying her friend? Was the purse a returned gift of Crabbe's? Still more intriguing is the delay of almost a month before Crabbe returned Charlotte's portrait: for by mid-December he may well have met Elizabeth Charter.

3

Crabbe had quickly established a network of acquaintances in and around Bath. One important catalyst was Colonel John Houlton, of Farleigh Castle, three miles west of Trowbridge; this family were not members of the landed gentry but beneficiaries of eighteenth-century social mobility, having prospered in the town and bought their stately home with the proceeds. The Colonel was a friend of George Gordon, Dean of Lincoln, and of William Lisle Bowles, the poet and vicar of Bremhill, whom Crabbe met when dining at Farleigh Castle in February 1815. Somewhat overdoing his feelings of isolation and insecurity, as was so often his habit, Crabbe expressed his appreciation in extravagant terms: 'Never,' he wrote to them, 'did any kind beings in your situation of life and surrounded by friends of your own class show such repeated and unwearied attention to a man situated as I am and almost standing alone in society.'[26] Colonel Houlton had also introduced him to Mr and Mrs John Norris, of Hawley in Hampshire (and subsequently of Hughenden Manor, Buckinghamshire, which Norris inherited in 1816), who when in Bath stayed at 103 Sydney Place; and through them, in turn, Crabbe met General William Peachey, whose Bath residence was at 11 Pulteney Street.

William Peachey's first wife, Emma, née Charter – the youngest daughter of Thomas Charter (1741–1810) and his wife Elizabeth (1749–1804), of Lynchfield House, Lydeard, near Taunton – had died in 1809. Mrs Charter's father, the Reverend Alexander Malet, had been Rector of Combe Florey, Somerset, and Maiden Newton, Dorset. Her brother was Charles Malet, of Wilbury Park, near Salisbury: he enjoyed a distinguished career with the East India Company as resident minister at Poona and acting governor of Bombay, became a Fellow of the Royal Society and was created baronet in 1791; he died in 1815. The Charters' son, Thomas Malet Charter (1781–1836) was Lord of the Manor of Seaton, on the coast between Lyme Regis in Dorset and Sidmouth in Devon: he was credited with transforming 'an obscure hamlet into the rank of a fashionable watering-place' and his wife was famous for her collection of polished beach pebbles. Elizabeth Charter, born in 1782, was a year younger than her brother Thomas and a year older than her late sister Emma. She lived with her elder sister Louise at Norton Fitzwarren, near Taunton, but the relatively recent deaths of her parents and her younger sister – together, no doubt, with a fondness for Bath – had cast her in the role of companion, confidant and adviser to her brother-in-law, General Peachey; and it was at 11 Pulteney Street, some time in the winter if 1814–15, that she encountered George Crabbe.

Elizabeth Charter was then in her early thirties, older than Charlotte Ridout and very much wiser. If Crabbe had not yet returned Charlotte's portrait, meeting Elizabeth would have decided him; if, as is perhaps likelier, he had already done so, he must have congratulated himself on his lucky escape. Of course, unlike either of the Charlottes, Elizabeth had the advantage of existing for him from the start as a physical presence rather than as an imagined correspondent; she was also, from her experience with her brother-in-law, accustomed to a close, confidential relationship with an older man. She was arguably the second great love of Crabbe's life and, although she was never to marry him (nor anyone else), for over a decade she would be closer to his inner self even than his sons. His teasingly candid letters to her, which in 1913 were collected by A. M. Broadley and Walter Jerrold in *The Romance of an Elderly Poet*, are the liveliest he ever wrote. Yet she is unmentioned in the biographer son's *Life*: at the time he was writing it, Elizabeth Charter was still alive (she died in 1860) and he was a West Country curate; so both tact and decorum prevented him from describing the most enduring relationship of his father's later years.

This relationship, despite its uncharacteristically face-to-face beginning, was soon to assume the epistolary nature of Crabbe's intimacies with Walter Scott and Charlotte Williams. There was a perfectly practical reason for this: in the spring of 1815, General Peachey remarried and Elizabeth ceased to be a regular visitor to Bath. In his letters, Crabbe continually begs her to return to the city – 'the prospect you held out to me of making Bath the place of your residence gave me hope of seeing you';[27] 'I am vexed that you do not go to Bath, and cannot help it'[28] – and even urges her to 'burn that house that keeps you there, in what is the county?, Somerset?, but for that I might on my visit to Bath next week see you'.[29] Or, failing that:

> I am sorry for your cottage as you term it and wish I could puff it
> away with all my heart: I am sure I will try, but we have no persons
> in Trowbridge who are not connected with factories and business in
> the place: sure it cannot be that you will be altogether determined in
> your measures by the disposal of or retaining this house! I do not
> love such dependant resolutions: No, dear Miss Charter, go to Bath
> for you said you would – at or near Taunton how shall I see you?[30]

Nevertheless, the ludicrous sequence of meetings proposed and deferred, stretching over a period of years, tells a rather different story. Crabbe's excuses for not keeping his engagements with Elizabeth Charter include both weddings – he is '. . . detained, I mean, by this unexpected partiality of this young lady for a Rector's Blessing, a kind of flattery I am by no means reconciled to and yet she is, in a certain degree, a Favourite'[31] – and funerals – 'Poor Mrs Bythesea required the last attentions a friend and minister could pay, and her funeral also made my attendance necessary'[32] – as well as various other kinds of parish business. At one point, he invites Elizabeth to stay 'for a month or two' at his rectory, accompanied by her sister Louise as chaperone: 'It would be great charity, and I suppose that great blockhead the public would not growl, would it? Our gravity considered? I do not know your sister, do I? Nor she me?'[33] But he must surely have realised that conventional propriety ruled this out of the question, and in his next letter he seems to concede as much: 'Yes, indeed, I know the growling of the public: the virtuous monster, so delicate in its apprehensions, so severe in its judgement and so depraved in its indulgences.'[34] (Evidently he had not forgiven them for disapproving of his theatrical tastes.) He proposes instead to visit her at Norton Fitzwarren: 'You do then admit men-visitors, who are not relatives!'[35] But a little later, returning from a trip to Dawlish in the impeccably respectable company of the Long family, he practically passes her door, yet still cannot bring himself to call on her:

> It was my purpose, it was indeed my earnest wish to stop at Taunton in my way from Dawlish to this place where I am now endeavouring to resign myself to my usual occupations, but the family I was domesticated with had determined on our continuing together until we should reach our homes, and the carriage which we possessed went with too much rapidity to allow even a few minutes' delay. I was mortified, but the advantage to me of my younger friends and their attentions which I knew not how to relinquish, made me accede to their proposal . . .[36]

So it goes on. While Crabbe was no doubt entirely sincere in his belief that he wanted someone with whom to share his lonely rectory ('. . . could I see other creatures walking in the garden, and looking at these shrubs, I should find some beauty in them myself'),[37] we may suspect that his deeper and more complex need was for an intimate correspondent, to whom he could continue 'writing in the dark'. Separation, not proximity, enabled him to reveal himself.

His letters to Elizabeth Charter are both craftily and involuntarily revealing. He has the knack of simultaneously confessing his weaknesses and trading on them: 'I had no idea that a man of my age could feel these schoolboy sensations,' he writes, 'but I do and there is a want of intimacy of local association that I suppose is not to be overcome.'[38] The feeling is authentic enough, but he makes it slyly disingenuous by attaching it to a retrospective fondness for Leicestershire. It is the lack of *belonging* which torments him. 'I do envy you for belonging to so many people,' he says in the same letter; and, a little later, 'I cannot bear to belong to nobody.'[39] His sense of deracination 'is increased when I walk through this populous town, and then I cannot avoid thinking there is not one being among these who either loves or hates, or has an hope or a fear that centres in, me'.[40] Nevertheless, his self-pity is tempered by his wry acknowledgement that his 'foolish complaints and half-voluntary diseases'[41] may indeed be self-induced.

Crabbe recounts his friendships with other women – not only those who preceded Elizabeth Charter but also, though with one important exception, those whom he had newly met – in terms which have an appearance of unusual frankness. Charlotte Williams is described, in a genuinely revealing phrase, as 'my invisible girl', yet there is something curiously cloying about this confessional mode:

> Something of impropriety was hinted by her as we proceeded, and I then might have convinced myself as I did the lady that I was in my 58th year and this with my profession, and I cannot tell what more, put an end to all scruples of the kind; so we wrote on and shall I say the very truth? I must! Let me whisper then, that I soon began to dream dreams of unseasonable happiness. I fancied this Nymph unlike her Sister Nymphs, one who would forget my Time of Life . . .[42]

It is those nymphs who cause most trouble for the modern reader. They reappear when, in a subsequent letter, he turns to Charlotte Ridout:

> The fancied, the visionary love of a man at that period of Life for a Nymph whom he had not seen, as well as the prepossession of another Nymph for this romantic admirer of her Friend, known to her by letters only, and these directed and addressed to another woman, all this forms a tale for an Arabian Night, and is too crazy for sober belief, and yet it had very nearly determined the colour of the years which it may please Heaven to allot me.[43]

The tone inescapably suggests something of John Betjeman's or Philip Larkin's predilection for schoolgirls in gymslips; and Crabbe, for better as well as for worse, has much in common with Betjeman and Larkin. Yet even more striking, in this talk of nymphs and Arabian nights, is a hint of

Romanticism's more exotic side, which we do not always associate with Crabbe: it is indeed 'too crazy for sober belief'.

That phrase is not used idly. Crabbe himself seems to have been uncertain about precisely what had happened with Charlotte Ridout, how the affair had ended and (above all) what she had done next. For in July 1815 he wrote to Elizabeth Charter: 'Did I tell you Miss R is married? married in January last! Now that is a little surprising, not that she should marry or that she should not marry me, but that – it should be in January . . .'[44] It is more than a little surprising: it is frankly impossible. He had only returned her portrait in mid-December, and he can scarcely have imagined that she would have either gone back to her former simple-minded suitor or married after an entirely new engagement of just three or four weeks. He was anxious to convince himself, however; early in 1816, he repeated the improbability – 'I believe Miss Ridout is married?' – with the addition of some convoluted and repetitive self-justification:

> I have no motive but an earnest wish to know that she lives in comfort, whom I permitted myself, in the balancing my own mind, to keep in suspense. Strange! that it could be: but so it was. Perhaps I have observed before in writing to you on this subject – the only person to whom I could seriously write of it – that Miss Rxx in a correspondence of considerable length with her friend and herself, both then unknown personally and her friend to this day: and these letters being half poetical, half in earnest, her young mind began to build a fairy-structure upon such slight foundation and that work of building was so pleasant that neither the age of her correspondent while his person was kept out of sight, nor afterwards the person could overthrow that strong edifice that Fancy and Hope had built. It was my duty to have done that as soon as I perceived it, but I was in some degree caught myself and I need not say, flattered. I am very glad now; to have left a young widow without provision had been dreadful to me and now if I have said all this before, laugh at and forgive me.[45]

Unconsciously perhaps, but nevertheless crucially, Crabbe has shifted the balance of responsibility. Whereas in his earlier accounts, the 'dreams' and 'visionary love' were follies of his own, now it is Charlotte's 'young mind' which creates 'a fairy-structure' founded on 'Fancy and Hope'. He is desperate to convince himself – and Elizabeth Charter – that he has done the right thing. But Charlotte Ridout had not married in 1815, nor did she every marry; and the 'vixen' Aunt Floyd, who had initially opposed Crabbe's engagement to her niece, would afterwards never forgive him for breaking it off. Three years later, he would ruefully report to Mrs Houlton that 'a certain young lady, whom I once saw at Sidmouth and had some hope that I might see at Trowbridge, is still with her Aunt Floyd and I hope as happy as an aunt can make her'.[46]

For her part, Elizabeth Charter, who had vowed to avoid emotional entanglements of her own, encouraged Crabbe in his amorous pursuits: 'you would have me hunt Charlottes,' he complained, 'but you will not seek Charles's, nor be sought, so far as you can help it, and I can perceive no fair reasoning in all this'.[47] He hardly needed encouraging. He appraised a Miss Bellair, whom he met at General Peachey's, before briskly deciding: 'No, Miss B is not the lady I want, even if by some favour of fortune we were placed together.' Nevertheless, he went on: 'Shall I confess to you that I have been trying to train up a lady or two for these good offices of friendship, but hitherto I must not boast of my success.' He is more than half-serious – Maria Waldron and Florentina Long are the obvious candidates – but he is also angling his way towards a teasing compliment, for he knows 'a young lady who appears to possess [the requisite qualifications], but I cannot for an instant indulge the vanity that insinuates she has the affection and thus I must try and reconcile myself to my solitude'.[48] His attempt 'to train up a lady or two' may seem less grotesquely patronising if we accept that Florentina (or Flora) Long was only seventeen years old at the time, as Broadley and Jerrold say:[49] this seems plausible enough, given the dates of her siblings – two older brothers and three sisters – although Crabbe in a later letter seems to imply that she was twenty-six (Charlotte Ridout's age and thus perhaps a slip of the pen). Her parents were Richard Godolphin Long (1761–1835), the MP for Wiltshire, and his wife Florentina. Crabbe was a frequent guest at their home, Rood Ashton, two miles south-east of Trowbridge: 'It is one of my houses of call and there is something domestic in a visit there that agrees with my kind of pensive and childish longing for such alliances and associations.'[50] Together with the Waldrons, the Longs were the family with whom he had the easiest social relationship in his immediate vicinity.

His relationship with Flora Long was an innocently avuncular one which acquired its teasing overtones largely for Elizabeth Charter's amusement. 'Here is a Miss Long,' he brightly informs her, though without troubling to mention that she is a child rather than a rival, 'Flora Long, and she is not unlike a Flora . . . I thank her for appearing to feel some interest in the solitary Rector of an adjoining Parish, not her own, and therefore I am doubly grateful, and yet there is something whimsical in the wood-and-grove walks of so unequal a pair . . .'[51] In another letter she becomes, with possibly mischievous intent, the 'elder' of 'the Miss Longs' – as indeed she is, though only because her eldest sister, Ellen, married in 1812 – and receives from Crabbe something less like a lover's testimonial than a school report, in which she is praised for her 'good sense, her application, her reasonable piety, her unaffected and simple manners (manners easy and almost rural, for rustic I will not say), and a kind of temperate and cheerful gravity'. He adds: 'This Flora has called me Friend for a considerable time past and I believe has all that regard which arises from a confidence that I shall not so act as to disgrace her for her bad choice nor cause in her repentance for the partiality.' He mentions other friends too – Miss Waldron and her cousin Miss Everett – but ends with a postscript which shows how well he understands the playful ambiguity of the word 'friend':

> When we say my Friend Mr A or Mrs B or Miss C, or my Friend the Lord Chancellor! or that good Friend of mine Sir John – with some variation of the phrase and mode of using the word, many other expressions might be used – in all which the word FRIEND might mean very, very differently. Even so dear Miss C, so I and you and all use it. Our affections have more variety than our language. [52]

There was never any question, beyond a wistful parenthesis ('Still if I had been twenty years younger and she ten older, no'),[53] of an attachment to Flora Long nor to Maria Waldron, although his partiality to both was sufficiently conspicuous to provoke gossip among his parishioners and joshing from Mrs Norris.

One would very much like to introduce Crabbe to another younger woman at this point, and that of course is Jane Austen. Since his move to Trowbridge, they had shared a virtually identical map of their social connections –

including Hampshire, Wiltshire and Somerset, with a focal meeting point at Bath – and they almost certainly had acquaintances in common. Moreover, there is that beguiling web of coincidences centred on *Mansfield Park*, whose heroine Fanny Price is named after a character in *The Parish Register*: it has a patient clergyman called Edmund (Burke, Cartwright, Crabbe's deceased son) as hero; a nautical sub-plot in which the domestic details for Portsmouth might have been based on Crabbe's Aldeburgh or his *Borough*; and a meddlesome aunt called Mrs Norris, who could quite easily have been a mutual friend (Jane Austen was not averse to borrowing real people's names). It is all so tempting and all so impossible; for *Mansfield Park* was begun in 1811 and published in 1814, just too early for these neat symmetries to click into place. And although Jane Austen's letters are famously incomplete, if Crabbe had met this admirer who so wished to be 'Mrs Crabbe', he would certainly have told, and teased, Elizabeth Charter about it.

At least, we may assume he would have done so. Early in 1816, Richard Warner, that notable clergyman and 'literary ornament' of Bath, was asked by Hannah Hoare, the second wife of the banker Samuel Hoare, for an introduction to Crabbe. The Hoares' principal home at Hampstead, then just outside London, was a magnet for the political and cultural élite, and they also had a family house at Cromer in Norfolk; they were visiting Bath with Sarah, Samuel Hoare's daughter by his first marriage. Crabbe rather sniffily described Hoare as 'a banker of whom most monied people have heard', but he was as usual enchanted by the ladies. Mrs Hoare was 'very obliging and entertaining' and, as for her stepdaughter, 'Miss Hoare is very lively, frank, and mistress of some pleasant – what shall I say? – accomplishments'.[54] In no time at all, he found himself accepting invitations to visit them at Hampstead and perhaps even at Cromer. All this he would eventually tell Elizabeth Charter; but for the moment he breathed not a word about Sarah Hoare.

4

Towards the end of 1814, Crabbe had gladly welcomed his two ordained sons into his rectory for an indefinite period as his companions and assistants. Though they were fond of him, there is every sign that they found the arrangement tiresome; nor was this altogether surprising, with their father alternately grumbling about his flock and falling ridiculously in love with

women of their own age. There is anecdotal evidence to suggest that they
persuaded him to break off his engagement with Charlotte Ridout,[55] and
there is certainly an acerbic edge to some of his passing comments about
them: detained in Trowbridge by a wedding, he notes that 'he has two sons
in orders and both at this time *well* enough to witness those Vows and
pronounce that Blessing'.[56] They stayed until the following spring when,
says the biographer son, 'my brother and I, thinking it probable that we
might soon settle, for life, each in some village parsonage, and that this was
the only opportunity of seeing something of our native country – leaving my
father in sound health and among attached friends, absorbed by his duties,
his new connections and amusements – quitted Trowbridge about the same
time, and continued absent from it, sometimes in London together, sometimes apart in distant places in the kingdom, for nearly two years'.[57] He
means well, but his account typically smoothes over the rough edges: his
father's health was variable – he would increasingly complain of that 'heat'
in his head which had troubled him much earlier – and he had a decidedly
mixed opinion of his new acquaintances. Crabbe, also typically, tried not to
begrudge his sons' desertion, and failed:

> During the last winter I had my sons both companions and
> assistants, and they have left me to a solitude which I am not
> accustomed to and to servants who better suit men with stronger
> spirits: yet I must not blame these young men, nor do I, they have
> no connections here and their friends and little property lie in a
> different county: at my decease if connections were formed at least
> of common kind, they would be painful whether preserved or
> broken off and it may be wisdom to form none. I have some here
> who pay all the exterior respect and even attention I could
> reasonably desire, but (with the exception of one family) I must not
> look in Trowbridge for substitutes for my sons.[58]

The extent to which he missed them was brought home to him by a small but
absurd incident that autumn. Returning from a holiday in Exmouth with his
friends the Longs, he stayed overnight in Exeter: 'In coming home, my son,
whom I had not seen, and I past each other as both slept at Exeter and took
places in different coaches in the same office.' It is exactly the sort of

mischance which might have occurred in the work of his favourite novelist, Henry Fielding, and he still sounds like Parson Adams. But to his trusted correspondent Elizabeth Charter he touchingly adds: 'I may venture to tell you, but I dare not say to many, how this affected me: I knew that rationally thinking I am not the less likely to see him hereafter, for that accidental missing him, but the Father and the Fool did not feel so and that I am both at times is but too true even to myself.'[59]

Feeling isolated and introspective during the winter months, he revisited his childhood in a most uncharacteristic, purely autobiographical poem, which he completed in April 1816: 'Infancy – A Fragment'. On it he noted in his cipher: 'My Own Life'. That his own life was now in a flux of seesawing emotions usually more associated with youth than with age was evident both to him and to his friends, some of whom, such as the irrepressible and over-energetic Mrs Norris, tried to divert him into cheerfulness. She invited him to Hawley House, where he found himself surrounded by 'the clergy, tutors to the young men of the neighbouring Military College [Sandhurst] . . . men of cultivated minds united to women of agreeable manners'. If he sounds unenthusiastic, this was because such routine socialising allowed him 'no time for my peculiar engagements'; having endured 'introductions to some persons pleasant and to some of whom pleasantry is not the characteristic', he was left with a sort of befuddled admiration for 'the domestic virtues of my friend, her Sunday efforts and benevolent exertions'[60] though without any sense of having enjoyed himself. Writing from Hawley to Colonel and Mrs Houlton, he provided a franker account of Mrs Norris's 'Sunday efforts', which he had been obliged to share: 'She took me three miles this morning to her parish church, the wind cold as October and the preacher dullest of the dull, and yet there she goes rather than to the College Chapel because Duty bids her.'[61]

The indefatigable Norrises wanted him to travel with them to Wales, but he was in fact on his way to London – where he looked forward to combining the business of seeing his publisher John Hatchard with the pleasure of visiting the Hoares – and thence to Suffolk. With Hatchard he discussed the work-in-progress which was eventually to become *Tales of the Hall* and he may have voiced some authorial disappointment about the sales of his earlier books: the recent publication by Henry Colburn of a 'Biographical Account of the Rev. George Crabbe, LL.B.' in *The New Monthly Magazine and*

Universal Register – Crabbe disparagingly called it 'Colburn's Monthly Magazine Museum, or some such title'[62] – had reminded him that other publishers might take an interest in him, but he had no serious thought of deserting Hatchard, whom he now regarded as an old friend. It was at Hatchard's bookshop in Piccadilly that, quite by chance, the biographer son found Crabbe one day in August 1816, in the inner room: 'there stood my father, reading intently, as his manner was – with his knees somewhat bent, insensible to all around him. How homelike was the sight of that venerable white head among a world of strangers!'[63] This was the unplanned prelude to an altogether more significant family reunion, for father and son were to meet again a week or two later at Beccles, the home of Crabbe's sisters-in-law, the Misses Elmy; and there, John Waldron Crabbe was to announce his engagement to Anna Maria, daughter of Dr William Crowfoot of Beccles. His father was unaffectedly delighted by the match, though even here there is a hint that he and his hot-tempered younger son had not always enjoyed the most placid of relationships:

> . . . never, so far as I can now judge, saw I two young people more affectionately bound to each other: indeed knowing the young man's warmth of temper and tenderness of heart, his strength of affection and ardency of feeling I am alarmed lest an impediment should arise, though it appeared as if my presence and consent were alone wanted. Of that they might be pretty well assured: nothing but defect of character and evidence of impropriety and immorality on either part would make me a divider of two youthful and affectionate spirits and of these evils I saw none. They will I believe marry and I hope – for a while – reside with me.[64]

No impediment did arise: John Crabbe married Anna Crowfoot at Beccles on 2 December 1816. Shortly afterwards they moved to the rectory at Trowbridge, where John served as his father's curate for the following sixteen years. His elder brother, the biographer son, married Caroline Matilda, the daughter of Thomas Timbrell, on 3 April 1817, and became curate of Pucklechurch (with Wick and Abson), some twenty miles from Trowbridge.

Before returning to Wiltshire, Crabbe travelled on to Aldeburgh, to visit his sister Mary Sparkes and her family: he had both to pass on the cheerful news of his son's engagement and to mourn the recent death of one of the Sparkes's children. If there is in this sequence of events a feeling of Crabbe's past life hammering on the door of the present, it was to be confirmed by two unrelated occurrences during the autumn of 1816. On 26 October, Belvoir Castle, which was in the process of being extensively refashioned under the direction of James Wyatt, was substantially destroyed by a fire in its west wing: this may have been started by the accidental ignition of 'flammables in a carpenters' and painters' work-room',[65] although a far from implausible account in the *Gentleman's Magazine* of November 1816 found evidence of unlocked gates and arson and declared that 'opinion is, that it has been done by *Luddites*'. Crabbe had not much sympathy to waste on the Duke of Rutland – 'He will I doubt not bear the loss, like one of his family' – but he was much grieved by the destruction of eleven paintings by Sir Joshua Reynolds: 'A painter so eminent, a man so agreeable and friendly; happily he escaped a misfortune that he would severely have felt.'[66] Reynolds had died in 1792. The subsequent, much grander rebuilding of Belvoir was designed by the Reverend Sir John Thoroton, the chaplain-architect and son of Crabbe's friend Robert Thoroton, who curiously combined his twin vocations by modelling the new ballroom on parts of Lincoln Cathedral.[67]

The other, equally unexpected reminder of the past arrived in the shape of a letter from a woman in Ireland, Mary Leadbeater, who appeared to be a perfect stranger. But she was, as she hastened to explain to him, nothing of the sort; for, as Mary Shackleton, she had been present with her father, Richard Shackleton, at Edmund Burke's house in Charles Street on that memorable occasion in June 1784 at which George Crabbe had introduced his new wife Sarah to his friend and patron. 'My dear father,' she now reminded him, 'told thee, that "Goldsmith's would now be the *deserted* village". Perhaps thou dost not remember this compliment; but I remembered the ingenuous modesty which disclaimed it.'[68] Besides being a valuable addition to Crabbe's roster of long-distance correspondents, Mary Leadbeater would prove to be unusually subtle in drawing out information about his work, all of which she had read: 'Thy characters, however singular some of them may be, are never unnatural; and thy sentiments, so true to domestic and social feelings, as well as to those of a higher nature, have the convincing power of reality over the mind; and *I* maintain that all thy pictures *are drawn from life*. To inquire whether this be the case, is the excuse which I make to myself for writing this letter.'

Crabbe's reaction was interesting and greatly to his credit. Mrs Leadbeater, as her prose style hints, was a Quaker, and even before he begins his reply Crabbe pays her the gentle compliment of dating his letter, in the Quaker style, 'Trowbridge, 1st of 12th month, 1816.' He then summons up all his most winning charm:

> Mary Leadbeater! – Yes, indeed, I do well remember you! Not Leadbeater then, but a pretty demure lass, standing a timid auditor while her own verses were read by a kind friend, but a keen judge. And I have in my memory your father's person and countenance, and you may be sure that my vanity retained the compliment which he paid me in the moment when he permitted his judgement to slip behind his good humour and desire of giving pleasure – Yes, I remember all who were present; and, of all, are not you and I the only survivors? It was the day – was it not? – when I introduced my wife to my friend. And now both are gone! and your father, and Richard Burke, who was present (yet again I must ask – was he not?) – and Mrs Burke! All departed – and so, by and by, they will speak of us. But, in the mean time, it was good of you to write. Oh very – very good.[69]

Mary Leadbeater's letter had been addressed to 'George Crabbe, at Belvoir Castle', and its recipient gives a good-natured account of how he comes to be, not in a stately home in Leicestershire, but 'in the parsonage of a busy, populous, clothing town, sent thither by ambition, and the Duke of Rutland'. Banter and pleasantry give way, however, to a remarkably candid reply to Mrs Leadbeater's enquiry – firm evidence, if such be needed, that Crabbe knew an intelligent letter when he saw one:

> Yes, I will tell you readily about my creatures, whom I endeavoured to paint as nearly as I could and dared; for, in some cases, I dared not. This you will readily admit: besides, charity bade me be cautious. Thus far you are correct: there is not one of whom I had not in my mind the original; but I was obliged, in some cases, to take them from their real situations, in one or two instances to change even the sex, and, in many, the circumstances. The nearest to real life was the proud, ostentatious man in the 'Borough' [Sir Denys

Brand in Letter XIII, 'The Alms-House and Trustees'], who disguises an ordinary mind by doing great things; but the others approach to reality at greater or less distances. Indeed, I do not know that I could paint merely from my own fancy; and there is no cause why we should. Is there not diversity sufficient in society? and who can go, even but a little, into the assemblies of our fellow-wanderers from the way of perfect rectitude, and not find characters so varied and so pointed, that he need not call upon his imagination?

This wonderful passage is as revealing about his poetry as any Crabbe ever wrote; and it must seem to us ironic that it should occur in a private letter rather than in any of his often stodgy and convoluted prefaces. Yet it is true to the man: that he should take the care to write so truthfully and so gracefully to an almost-stranger is one of the quietly admirable things about him.

5

William Lisle Bowles, the 'brother versifier' whom he had met at Farleigh Castle, was to be the unlikely agent of Crabbe's re-entry into literary society. Bowles's parish of Bremhill, three miles north-west of Calne, was close to Bowood House, the home of his patron the Marquis of Lansdowne, where he was a regular visitor and where in due course Crabbe was invited. With the sort of irony which occurs repeatedly in Crabbe's later life, confirming his self-perception as a member of the 'old race', the third Marquis was the son of that Lord Shelburne to whom he had so floridly and fruitlessly appealed for patronage in 1780. Although Bowles, who was eight years younger than Crabbe, had gathered a large and various literary acquaintance, he was chiefly regarded as an amiable eccentric in the tradition of Parson Adams. His vicarage garden was a monument to the picturesque, with a grotto and a hermitage, complete with crucifix and missal, and the sheep which roamed his glebe had bells tuned in thirds and fifths. When Madame de Staël visited Bowood in 1813, Bowles fell from his horse and injured his shoulder in his eagerness to get there. After Lansdowne had explained his clerical visitor's courageous and no doubt somewhat battered state, Madame de Staël began a long, complimentary speech, only to be interrupted by Bowles's modestly intended disclaimer: 'O ma'm, say no more, for I would have done a great deal more to see so great a curiosity.' She is said to have remarked to Lansdowne, 'I see he is only a plain country clergyman without any tact, although a great poet.'[70] But he was not a great poet: his importance had already become historical, based as it was on his *Fourteen Sonnets, Elegiac and Descriptive, Written during a Tour* (1789), which had revived the form and influenced Coleridge and Southey; in Richard Warner's satirical book *Bath Characters* (1808), published under the pseudonym Peter Paul Pallet, Bowles appears thinly disguised as 'Bill Sonnet'. Crabbe (who had rather hoped to pass on to him the unwelcome commission of composing an inscription for the tomb of Sir Charles Malet, Elizabeth Charter's uncle) certainly had his measure: 'He is a good and pleasant man and his verses are like him – not so good verses as I conceive he is a man though.'[71] However, this charming character, who felt 'like a daisy in a hothouse' in London, introduced Crabbe to Thomas Moore and Samuel Rogers and was thus largely responsible for his reappearance in metropolitan literary life.

During 1815 and 1816, Crabbe frequently complained about his lack of assistance at Trowbridge – 'My sons are not with me,' he told Bowles, 'and I have no unengaged neighbours among the clergy, though the curate of Hilperton might perhaps baptise an infant or marry a couple for me'[72] – although in the circumstances he seems to have travelled about with remarkable freedom. But once John Crabbe had been installed as curate at the beginning of 1817, his father was able to plan his expeditions with more confidence. In the spring he stayed with the Hoares at Hampstead and in mid-June he set off for London once more, this time at the invitation of Samuel Rogers, on a more extended visit: he travelled with his friend William Waldron and arrived on 19 June, going first to Hampstead, before moving to a lodging at 37 Bury Street in the West End. He spent just over a month in the capital and for all but the first few days he kept a journal, which survives in the reasonably full but nevertheless edited (and probably censored) version printed by his son in the *Life*. It is a very different affair from that other London journal, the one he kept in the spring of 1780: it is less thoughtful and more fragmentary, simply because his days are so much more crowded, and it is also a view from inside the rooms whose doors were once slammed in his face. In fact, the two journals stand as prologue and epilogue to a great central portion of life which was lived almost entirely elsewhere.

At first, he found it hard to adjust to his transformed status. Writing to Samuel Rogers on 22 June, three days after his arrival, he instinctively lurches towards the exaggerated, self-effacing politeness of much earlier days. It does not occur to him that he is at least as eminent a person as Rogers:

> I will breakfast with you in the morning, or on Tuesday, or *on both*: one principal purpose of my coming to town again was the pleasure you held up to me when I was so kindly received by you: you told me that I should see Lord Holland, and you made your own house all that was pleasant and engaging. What, dear Sir, can I say? Do not, however, permit me to intrude too much on your time, for I well know how you are consulted and engaged, but, speaking for myself alone, I would say, dear Sir, dispose of me as it seems best to you. I will dine with you when you can take me into your company, and I will wait on Lord Holland when it shall appear to you that his Lordship will be disposed to receive me. In fact, I will commit myself to you in that way which, to a mind like yours, I may safely do with propriety. You will be a guide to me, and I shall do what is proper and becoming; neither presuming on the kindness which is shown to me, nor coldly withdrawing myself from the honour which I know how to estimate. My few engagements and my small business in town I reckon as nothing – the society to which you introduce me is all! I can put nothing – of my concerns here – in comparison with it.[73]

But this guarded formality quickly softened: by 25 June, he was noting in his diary, with easy familiarity, 'Mr Rogers and the usual company at breakfast', as if he had been breakfasting with Rogers all his life. It was probably on one of these occasions that Crabbe described to Rogers the miserable nature of his later married years.

The 1817 London Journal consists of two layers. The top layer, the easier to understand and the more immediately striking, is his account of the astonishing number of eminent persons he managed to meet in a relatively short time. On the first Monday of his total immersion in London life, 23 June (the dates of the early entries, as printed in the *Life*, are retrospective: they deal with the previous day's events), he met, as well as Rogers and his family, Mr and Mrs Thomas Moore and 'the Italian gentleman' Ugo Foscolo. The Moores were shortly to be numbered among Crabbe's Wiltshire neighbours when they moved to Sloperton Cottage, just south of Bowood, at the suggestion of Lord Lansdowne. With Foscolo, Crabbe seems reluctantly to have discussed Dante. In the evening he went to John Kemble's final performance, in *Coriolanus* at Covent Garden, at the end of which Kemble delivered an emotional speech: he bade his audience 'a long and unwilling farewell' and the stage was strewn with wreaths of laurel.

Two days later, Crabbe found himself summoned to Holland House and was once again struck by the way in which he was now a generation adrift: although Henry Vassall Fox, Lord Holland, was the dedicatee of *Poems* (1807), it was of course his late uncle, Charles James Fox, who had been among Crabbe's supporters and admirers. Among the guests there whom Crabbe met for the first time was Thomas Campbell who, in a grateful letter later the same day, wrote: 'That time, and that spot, in the library of Holland House, I shall never forget, when you shook me a second time by the hand.'[74] And Campbell was as good as his word, for in 1834 he provided the biographer son with a vivid and perceptive account of that momentous occasion seventeen years earlier:

The first time I met Crabbe was at Holland House, where he and Tom Moore and myself lounged the better part of a morning about the park and library; and I can answer for one of the party at least being very much pleased with it. Our conversation, I remember, was about novelists. Your father was a strong Fieldingite, and I as sturdy a Smolletite. His mildness in literary argument struck me with surprise in so stern a poet of nature, and I could not but contrast the unassumingness of his manners with the originality of his powers . . .

The part of the morning which I spent at Holland House with him and Tom Moore, was one, to me at least, of memorable agreeableness. He was very frank, and even confidential, in speaking of his own feelings. Though in a serene tone of spirits, he confessed to me that since the death of his wife he had scarcely known positive happiness. I told him that in that respect, viz. the calculation of our own happiness, we are apt to deceive ourselves. The man whose manners are mild and tranquil, and whose conversation is amusing, cannot be positively unhappy.

When Moore left us we were joined by Foscolo; and I remember as distinctly as if it had been yesterday, the contrasted light in which Crabbe and Foscolo struck me. It is not an invidious contrast – at least my feelings towards Ugo's memory intend it not to be so – yet, it was to me morally instructive, and, I need hardly say, greatly in favour of your father. They were both men of genius, and both simple. But what a different sort of simplicity! I felt myself between them as if I had been standing between a roaring cataract and a placid stream. Ugo raged and foamed in argument, to my amusement, but not at all to your father's liking. He could not abide him. What we talked about I do not recollect; but only that Ugo's impetuosity was a foil to the amenity of the elder bard.[75]

Evidently the graceful surroundings and distinguished company kept Crabbe on his best behaviour. Campbell's account rings true, even though it sharply conflicts with the biographer son's recollection of his father at this stage of his life: 'Argument he sustained with great impatience: he neither kept close to his point, nor preserved his temper.' Perhaps, like many irascible people, Crabbe enjoyed the unusual luxury of listening quietly to someone who was even more hot-tempered than himself.

Later that day, he met Charles James Fox's widow ('All the remains of a fine person; affectionate manners and informed mind') and his sister: 'I remember meeting her thirty years since; but did not tell her so, and yet could not help appearing to know her; and she questions me much on the subject. Parry it pretty well.' This is the kind of tact which Crabbe could usually produce for women but seldom for men, and the sentiment strikingly resembles that of another elderly poet surrounded by the images of his youth – Yeats in 'The Municipal Gallery Revisited' ('I met her all but fifty years ago / For twenty minutes in some studio'). The company also included the Duchess of Bedford, Countess Bessborough – 'a frank and affectionate character, mother of Lady Caroline Lamb' – and Henry Brougham (afterwards Lord Brougham and Vaux, Lord Chancellor). Crabbe was wonderfully unfazed by this milieu, a fact which must have made him all the more impressive to those whose first impression was of a rather old-fashioned country parson; but of course the Duke of Rutland's former chaplain had long ago lost any exaggerated regard for the aristocracy. He saw them very clearly, and that clarity is conveyed by occasional laconic asides in his journal. Five words sum up this day: 'The confidence of high fashion.'

They certainly valued his company, as the events of the next two days – which are confusingly conflated in the *Life* – were to prove. At breakfast on 26 June with Henry Brougham and Lady Holland, it emerged that Crabbe had no ticket for the next day's party in honour of Kemble, to be held at the Freemasons' Tavern in Great Queen Street, at which Lord Holland was to speak and Thomas Campbell to read a celebratory ode. All attempts to procure a ticket for an understandably booked-out occasion had failed: 'This represented to Lady Holland, who makes no reply.' After a morning at Holland House, Crabbe spent the evening with Rogers and Moore. The next morning he received 'a paper containing the admission ticket, procured by Lady Holland's means: whether request or command I know not.' When he and Rogers reached the Freemasons' Tavern, they at first took their places among the 'common seats' until Campbell and James Perry, the editor of the *Morning Chronicle*, found them and they were 'invited into the committee-room'; at dinner, Crabbe sat next to Lord Erskine and close to 'a son of Boswell' (presumably the younger, James). After Holland's speech, the recited ode and further speeches by Campbell, Kemble and the French tragedian François Joseph Talma, Crabbe and Rogers left to 'go to Vauxhall to meet Miss Rogers and her party. Stay late.' He seems to have taken a predictable fancy to Rogers's sister Sarah.

Many of Crabbe's London days are rather like this, testifying to extra-ordinary stamina in a sixty-two-year-old man unaccustomed to city life. On 30 June a new time-consuming complication occurred when he visited John Murray, whose 'handsome drawing room' contained, as he shrewdly noticed (though the phrase was tactfully omitted from the first edition of the *Life*), 'Books of all, but especially of expensive, kinds'[76] as well as portraits of celebrated authors; and to this gallery Murray proposed to add Crabbe. 'Mr Murray wishes me to sit. Advise with Mr Rogers. He recommends.' In the event, he sat for two portraits, by Thomas Phillips and H. W. Pickersgill: he makes this sound a tedious chore – 'Agree to go to Mr Phillips, and sit two hours and a half' (7 July); 'Mr Phillips. Sit again' (8 July) – but it provided a useful respite from relentless socialising and enabled him to compose in his head the thirty lines of verse he set himself to write each day. For Murray, adding Crabbe to his drawing-room wall was the natural prelude to adding him to his publisher's list.

'I foresee a long train of engagements,' wrote Crabbe on 1 July, more or less summing up the entire expedition. The following day, after meeting the Duke of Rutland and learning the full details of the paintings destroyed in the Belvoir Castle fire, he dined at Sydenham with the Campbells, Thomas Moore and Samuel Rogers. Once again, Campbell was full of praise for him: 'Crabbe is absolutely delightful,' he told his sister, 'simple as a child, but shrewd, and often good-naturedly reminding you of the best parts of his poetry. He took his wine cheerfully – far from excess; but his heart really seemed to expand, and he was full of anecdote and social feeling.'[77] Crabbe concluded that day's journal entry with the two words 'Poets' Club', which would have been self-explanatory to him and which Campbell subsequently elucidated in his letter to the biographer son:

One day – and how can it fail to be memorable when Moore has commemorated it? – your father, and Rogers, and Moore, came down to Sydenham pretty early in the forenoon, and stopped to dine with me. We talked of founding a Poets' Club, and even set about electing the members, not by ballot, but *viva voce*. This scheme failed, I scarcely know how; but this I know, that a week or so afterwards, I met with Perry, of the *Morning Chronicle*, who asked me how our Poets' Club was going on. I said, 'I don't know – we have some difficulty of giving it a name, – we thought of calling ourselves *the Bees*.' 'Ah,' said Perry, 'that's a little different from the common report, for they say you are to be called *the Wasps*.' I was so stung with this waspish report, that I thought no more of the Poets' Club.[78]

To the modern reader, Campbell, Moore and Rogers will probably be figures of minor importance, with only Crabbe seeming to be a poet of any consequence. But this was not how they appeared to themselves. In a letter to Elizabeth Charter written after his return to Trowbridge (incorrectly dated 12 July by Broadley and Jerrold), Crabbe clearly indicates his perspective: 'Now no more of Poetry: I had enough in Town, where I daily met all our principal rhymers except Lord Biron [sic] who is not in England and the Poets of the

Lakes who form a Society by themselves, and at once exclude and are excluded by our pride and theirs.'[79] There is nothing especially boastful about 'all our principal rhymers': it is simply a statement of the position as Crabbe perceived it. He would have been glad to meet Byron, who had praised him as 'Nature's sternest painter, yet the best' in *English Bards and Scotch Reviewers* and who would shortly write to John Murray: 'Crabbe's the man, but he has a coarse and impracticable subject.'[80] However, the dismissal of the Lake Poets as a kind of provincial splinter group by a poet who had barely set foot in the capital for thirty-five years has an irony which he presumably did not intend.

On 3 July he was in a brisk mood, having heard from his deputising son: 'Letter from Trowbridge. I pity you, my dear John, but I must plague you.' John must have been finding the full load of his father's duties irksome, but Crabbe had no intention of cutting short his stay. He then met Robert Bloomfield. A different sort of writer would have recorded his kinship with a fellow East Anglian poet of humble background, but not Crabbe:

> Robert Bloomfield. He had better rested as a shoemaker, or even a farmer's boy; for he would have been a farmer perhaps in time, and now he is an unfortunate poet. By the way, indiscretion did much. It might be virtuous and affectionate in him to help his thoughtless relations; but his more liberal friends do not love to have their favours so disposed of. He is, however, to be pitied and assisted.

One can see here exactly what Campbell meant when he found Crabbe both 'simple' and 'shrewd' – there is no false sentiment or humbug in his lucid assessment of Bloomfield's plight – just as one can see why less well-disposed observers may have detected in him a rather chilly hauteur. The rest of the day was spent with Earl and Countess Spencer at Wimbledon: 'The grounds more beautiful than any I have yet seen; more extensive, various, rich.' Rogers, Richard Heber and James Stanhope were also present; the following morning this company was joined by Lady Holland, while in the evening Crabbe dined at Lansdowne House with Sir James Mackintosh and Thomas Grenville among the other guests. He recalled 'My visit to Lord Lansdowne's father in this house, thirty-seven years since!'

On 5 July, however, the 'long train of engagements' seems to have been temporarily interrupted and Crabbe had a day to himself. He wrote his thirty lines – 'done; but not well, I fear' – and dined at George's Coffee-House in the Strand. He was, of course, a much keener observer of urban life than the provincial contexts of his poetry suggest: 'Stay late in Holborn,' he wrote. 'The kind of shops open at so late an hour. Purchase in one of them. Do not think they deceive any person in particular.' The nuance in that final sentence is surely one which would have pleased Dickens.

Then it was back into society, and into the sort of difficulty which was bound to occur sooner or later: on 7 July he found himself double-booked. The Hoares expected him at Hampstead, but he had agreed to dine with Rogers at Sydenham; as this was the more specific engagement he kept it, writing apologetically to Samuel Hoare. The day's journal vividly illustrates the hectic pace of Crabbe's London life, which was unsurprisingly beginning to affect his health. Apart from dining with Rogers, he had a long sitting with Phillips, while the performance at Covent Garden that evening was a double bill, consisting of *Othello* and *Katherine and Petruchio* (based on *The Taming of the Shrew*) in which Eliza O'Neill played the parts of Desdemona and Katherine:

> Abide by the promise, and take all possible care to send my letter; so that Mr Hoare may receive it before dinner. Set out for Holborn Bridge to obtain assistance. In the way find the Hampstead stage, and obtain a promise of delivery in time. Prepare to meet our friends at Mr Rogers's. Agree to go to Mr Phillips, and sit two hours and a half. Mrs Phillips a very agreeable and beautiful woman. Promise to breakfast next morning. Go to Holborn. Letter from Mr Frere. Invited to meet Mr Canning, &c. Letter from Mr Wilbraham. Dinner at Mr Rogers's with Mr Moore and Mr Campbell, Lord Strangford, and Mr Spencer. Leave them, and go by engagement to see Miss O'Neil, in Lady Spencer's box. Meet there Lady Besborough, with whom I became acquainted at Holland House, and her married daughter. Lady B. the same frank character: Mr Grenville the same gentle and polite one: Miss O'Neil natural, and I think excellent; and even her 'Catherine', especially in the act of yielding the superiority to her husband, well done and touching. Lady Besborough obligingly offers to set me down at twelve o'clock. Agreed to visit the Hon. W. Spencer at his house at Petersham, and there to dine next day with Mr Wilbraham.

The Hoares felt badly let down – an indication, although Crabbe seems not to have appreciated this, of how highly they valued his company – and a rift developed which would take several months to heal. This cast a shadow over his remaining time in London and brought on his recurrent stress-related illness, as he explained to Elizabeth Charter. In retrospect, he could grudgingly admit that he should have gone to Hampstead to apologise in person, instead of waiting – in that dangerous state of combined shyness and arrogance – for them to write forgivingly to him:

> A peevish and now regretted misunderstanding took place between me and my friends at Hampstead: I am afraid I was captious because they were rich, and being the greater people in the World's estimation, I was, perhaps, unnecessarily proud. They did not forgive an apparent neglect which I could not prevent and for which I made every possible apology and fatigued myself, even to illness, in seeking to prevent their expectation and inconvenience, but I did not afterwards go over to them as I now think I ought to have done, depending upon their yielding and sending to me. How it will terminate I know not, but these little interruptions of friendship are very painful; yet Mrs Hoare is in such situation, and so knew of mine that I think she should have done something towards meeting, – but I will only judge myself.[81]

The attempt to have it both ways is utterly characteristic. Even in his sixties, Crabbe would cling to his belief that other – wealthier and more fortunate – people ought to know how to behave properly when he, the Saltmaster's son from Aldeburgh, was unsure of himself. But his distress is characteristic too, and entirely genuine.

Roger Wilbraham, the bibliophile and horticulturist, was an old friend of Crabbe: they had first met at Little Glemham in the autumn of 1794. 'I hear that you are received by every one as you ought to be, which I always told you would be the case,' he wrote.[82] Crabbe dined with him at Twickenham on 10 July and enjoyed an excursion which included Hampton Court and Pope's house; at Richmond Hill he was reminded that Sir Joshua Reynolds had lived nearby. His journey to Twickenham was, however, complicated by an incident in which he once more appears in his comical and benevolent guise:

Ask what is the name of every place except one, and that one is Twickenham, and so go at least a mile beyond. Walk back to Twickenham. Meet a man carrying a child. He passed me, but with hesitation; and there was, as I believed, both distress and honesty. As he watched my manner, he stopped, and I was unwilling to disappoint him. The most accomplished actor could not counterfeit the joy and surprise at first, and then the joy without the surprise afterwards. The man was simple, and had no roguish shrewdness.

The following day, he fulfilled his other promise in the same vicinity when he dined at Petersham: William Spencer, 'grandson to the Duke of Marlborough', 'married, at nineteen, a very beautiful and most accomplished woman, in the court of the Duke of Weimar. She was sixteen. His manner is fascinating, and his temper all complacency and kindness.' Spencer was a minor poet and a translator. 'I am informed Mrs S. has very extraordinary talents,' Crabbe adds, but unfortunately he omits to say what these talents were. Sir Henry Englefield, the Catholic writer and antiquary who had recently published his *Description of the Principal Picturesque Beauties, Antiquities, and Geological Phenomena of the Isle of Wight*, was also present – on 19 July Mrs Spencer and Sir Henry are described as 'two favourite characters' – and altogether it was a 'very delightful morning'. In the evening the party was joined by the Duke and Duchess of Cumberland: he was George III's fifth son, subsequently King Ernest I of Hanover, while she was 'Daughter of the Duke of Weimar and sister to the Queen of Prussia'. Impressive though Crabbe found this, his summary of these two days has nothing to do with aristocratic connections and strikes a far more subtle note: 'All this period pleasant, easy, gay, with a tincture of melancholy that makes it delicious. A drawback on mirth, but not on happiness, when our affection has a mixture of regret and pity.'

There is a gap of two days in the journal at this point – a tantalising lacuna, given the note of heightened and complex emotion on which that entry for 11 July ends – and when the entries resume, Crabbe's mood remains complicated. On 14 July he received a 'welcome letter' from Elizabeth Charter, which had in fact been quite unnecessarily delayed by his own instruction that she should 'Direct, if you please, (that is I mean if you will be good and write to me) Mr Hatchard's, Bookseller, Piccadilly, London'[83] at a time when

Hatchard was visiting Brighton. 'This makes the day more cheerful. Suppose it were so. Well! 'tis not!' It is a rare instance of Crabbe admitting to *himself* – rather than in his letters to her, which have always an element of teasing fancifulness – the seriousness of his emotional attachment to Elizabeth Charter. His friends Moore and Rogers were leaving for Calais on the following morning and he resolved to see them off; but he was too late and went to church at St James's instead. 'Write some lines in the solitude of Somerset House, not fifty yards from the Thames on one side, and the Strand on the other; but as quiet as the sands of Arabia.' Although it sounds like an interlude of welcome repose and tranquillity, it was no such thing: 'I am not quite in good humour with this day; but, happily, I cannot say why.'

Crabbe's time in London was drawing towards its close. Phillips's portrait was finished (or so he thought) on 16 July, 'which allows me more time'; he dined with the Spencers in Curzon Street and re-encountered Lady Bessborough together with a young lady, unintroduced, who turned out to be Lady Caroline Lamb. His relations with his son in Trowbridge, to whom he wrote on 17 July, were becoming increasingly strained: 'They are correct in their opinion: yet I love London; and who does not, if not confined to it?' It had taken him exactly forty years to come round to Dr Johnson's point of view, and 'They' (his son and daughter-in-law) evidently suspected that he was finding it impossible to leave the place. Sir Henry Englefield, whose friendship was the warmest among the men he had met during his stay, either called or was visited almost every day. He dined with his future publisher, John Murray, at Albermarle Street on 18 July, a civilised day – 'The dinner in every respect as in a nobleman's house' – which was somewhat disrupted late in the evening: 'At eleven o'clock enters Lady Caroline Lamb. She offers to take me on a visit to her company at twelve o'clock. I hesitated, for I had curiosity; but finally declined.' He had read *Glenarvon* and in a letter to Colonel John Houlton[84] rather archly disapproved of the book; now he found himself having to sidestep its author's eccentric invitations. The next day, she wrote to him imploring him to 'drink tea alone with me *tonight* or *tomorrow* at 9 – or Monday – only let me know'.[85] But it was too late: he was fully engaged for his remaining days.

On 19 July, he had to sit while Phillips retouched his portrait. Then, the 'ridiculous' Foscolo reappeared and dragged him off to visit 'Lady Flint, and sister, and nieces'; but he was 'paid for compliance', for he found them 'delightful women'. After visiting Mrs Spencer (and finding Sir Henry there), he dined at Lord Binning's, where the very distinguished company included George Canning, William Huskisson, Frederick Robinson (later Earl of Ripon) and Charles Manners-Sutton. The following morning Crabbe awoke 'ill' and 'nervous', so that he 'was half inclined to make apologies, and not join the pleasantest of all parties'. But, as usual, he persuaded himself into sociability and was once again rewarded. Once again, the key to his happiness was Sir Henry Englefield:

> At seven go to Sir Harry Englefield. A large house that overlooks the Park and Serpentine River. Disappointed of Mr Spencer; but Mrs Spencer, and Miss Churchill, and Miss Spencer dine with us. Mr Murray and Mr Standish. Nothing particularly worthy of remark at dinner; but after dinner, one of the best conversations since I came to town. Mr Spencer and Miss Churchill chiefly; on the effect of high polish on minds; chiefly female; Sir Harry sometimes joining, and Miss Spencer. A very delightful evening. Sir Harry's present of Ariosto's inkstand. Of double value, as a gift, and from the giver. Mr Standish and Mr Murray leave us. Part painfully at one o'clock. Yes, there are at Trowbridge two or three; and it is well there are. Promise (if I live) to return in the winter.

Clearly, the evening was not without that 'tincture of melancholy' which for Crabbe distinguished true happiness from mere mirth. He slept badly, dreamed vividly, and prepared himself as best he could for his last full day in London. He had a meeting in Holborn with his financial adviser John Palin, many social calls to make, and a dinner engagement with Canning at Gloucester Lodge (where he especially relished the 'Ministerial claret'). It was a 'lively day'. 'And here,' he added, 'I may close my journal, of certainly the most active, and, with very little exception, – that is, the exception of one or two persons – the most agreeable of all excursions – except – '

In fact, he did not quite close his journal on this pleasingly enigmatic note. He travelled on 22 July to visit the Norrises at Hughenden: he doubtless told Mrs Norris, of whom he was fond, much about his adventures in London and perhaps something of his misadventures too. His next journal entry shows very clearly the gloom which had settled upon him after leaving the city as well as reaffirming his peculiar dislike of music:

A vile engagement to an oratorio at church, by I know not how many noisy people; women as well as men. Luckily, I sat where I could write unobserved, and wrote forty lines, only interrupted by a song of Mrs Brand – a hymn, I believe. It was less doleful than the rest. Party at dinner. Music after dinner, much more cheerful and enlivening than at church. Solitary evening walk. Things soon become familiarised, when the persons are well known. Thought of Sunday next, and wrote about half a sermon upon confirmation.

Two days later, he was on his reluctant way back to Trowbridge. 'The visit to London,' he wrote on 25 July, 'has, indeed, been a rich one. I had new things to see, and was, perhaps, something of a novelty myself.'[86]

6

Beneath the surface of Crabbe's London Journal for 1817 lies a second layer, a shadow-journal which the biographer son must have partly obliterated. It starts on the day when Crabbe moved to his lodgings in Bury Street, and it emerges into a dim partial light if we focus on those puzzling observations which apparently have nothing to do with his movements in polite society. On 28 June he writes: 'Seek lodgings. 37 Bury Street. Females only visible . . . My new lodgings a little mysterious.' And the next day, after a visit to Kensington Gardens: 'Return to my new lodgings. Enquire for the master. There is one, I understand, in the country. Am at a loss whether my damsel is extremely simple, or too knowing.' Apart from the day on which he wandered late in Holborn, noticing the shops, the entries are then straight-forward enough until 8 July, when the enigmatic point about 'simplicity' reappears: 'I even still doubt whether it be pure simplicity, a little romantic, or – a great deal simplified. Yet I may, and it is likely do, mistake.' On 9 July he suffered 'A day of indisposition unlike the former' and in the evening went to a 'not very enlivening' play, *The Magpie, or the Maid?* by Isaac Pocock, without specifying any company: a minor omission, except that the following day's entry begins 'Apology for last night.' As we have already seen, Crabbe's emotional state seems to have become more excited from 11 July onwards: there are those two perplexingly missing days, while on 15 July he was 'not quite in good humour . . . but, happily, I cannot say why'. By 20 July (after his curious nocturnal encounter with Lady Caroline Lamb) he was sleeping badly and feeling unwell on waking; having described the leave-taking on that 'delightful evening' he adds: 'The impression rather nervous, and they will smile at—, I am afraid; but I shall still feel.' Then, on 21 July, the day before his departure from town, he records another troubled night's sleep, this time accompanied by alarming dreams:

> I would not appear to myself superstitious. I returned late last night, and my reflections were as cheerful as such company could make them, and not, I am afraid, of the most humiliating kind; yet, for the time time these many nights, I was incommoded by dreams, such as would cure vanity for a time in any mind where they could gain admission. Some of Baxter's mortifying spirits whispered very singular combinations. None, indeed, that actually did happen in the very worst of times, but still with a formidable resemblance. It is doubtless very proper to have the mind thus brought to a sense of its real and possible alliances, and the evils it has encountered, or might have had; but why these images should be given at a time when the thoughts, the waking thoughts, were of so opposite a nature, I cannot account. So it was. Awake, I had been with the high, the apparently happy: we were very pleasantly engaged, and my last thoughts were cheerful. Asleep, all was misery and degradation, not my own only, but of those who had been. – That horrible image of servility and baseness – that mercenary and commercial manner! It is the work of imagination, I suppose; but it is very strange.

This journal entry is clearly the starting-point for 'The World of Dreams', which was also written in 1817. Finally, there is that trailing 'except' in the passage, already quoted, with which this entry ends: the editors of the *Selected Letters and Journals* take it to refer to another 'excursion' (they suggest the visit to Sidmouth in 1815), but the exception might just as easily be an individual with whom his experience had been less than 'agreeable'.

These assorted hints may add up to something or nothing. It is possible that he felt he had foolishly betrayed undue affection for one member of his circle (perhaps Sarah Rogers) and that this is what others would 'smile at' and he would 'still feel'; it is also clear that he was disconcerted by the behaviour of Lady Caroline Lamb, which unsettled his last few days. But, taken as a whole, these shadowy asides point to an involvement of a different sort. The 'mysterious' lodgings in Bury Street ('Females only visible'), the 'extremely simple, or too knowing' damsel, the worry about 'simplicity' becoming 'a little romantic', the unexplained apology, and the appearance in his dream of something very like a brothel all suggest that Crabbe had become entangled with a prostitute. Alethea Hayter, as we have already seen, thought that this incident, as it appears in 'The World of Dreams', referred back to 1780; and that may well be the case. But at the age of twenty-five, Crabbe had been shy, inexperienced and impoverished; at the age of sixty-two, he was once again single, far more confident and reasonably prosperous. His reawakened passion had been thwarted by the breaking-off of his engagement to Charlotte Ridout and the reluctance of Elizabeth Charter to revisit Bath; moreover, he was safe in the relative anonymity of a capital city, well out of range of gossiping parishioners. It is not at all impossible that he should have sought a sexual encounter with a prostitute, nor that he should have been subsequently disgusted by the 'horrible image of servility and baseness – that mercenary and commercial manner'. We cannot, of course, be certain; but, far from diminishing Crabbe, the suggestion may help to round out his humanity.

Lilian Haddakin is right to say that ' "The World of Dreams" is clearly neither a "dreamt poem" like "Kubla Khan" nor a record of one particular dream just as it occurred, but an account of a representative dream'.[87] Surprisingly, this contributes to its powerful effect: the re-sorting of dream elements becomes almost a re-dreaming, and the images which jostled in the logic of night are all the more disturbing when re-examined by the glare of daylight. Stanzas V to VIII are evidently based on London:

> Where am I now? and what to meet?
>   Where I have been entrapt before:
> The wicked city's vilest street –
>   I know that I must now explore.
> The dark-brow'd throng, more near and more,
>   With murderous looks are on me thrust;
> And lo! they ope the accursed door,
>   And I must go – I know I must!

That female fiend! – What is she there?
  Alas, I know her. – Oh, begone!
Why is that tainted bosom bare?
  Why fix'd on me that eye of stone?
Why have they left me thus alone?
  I saw the deed – why then appear?
Thou art not form'd of blood and bone!
  Come not, dread being, come not near!

So! all is quiet, calm, serene;
  I walk a noble mansion round –
From room to room, from scene to scene,
  I breathless pass, in gloom profound;
No human shape, no mortal sound –
  I feel an awe, I own a dread,
And still proceed – nor stop nor bound –
  And all is silent, all is dead.

Now I'm hurried, borne along,
  All is business! all alive!
Heavens! how mighty is the throng,
  Voices humming like a hive!
Through the swelling crowd I strive,
  Bustling forth, my way to trace;
Never fated to arrive
  At the still-expected place.

Although we should not assume that there is any literal or logical proximity between the scenes in the poem – this is, after all, the world of dreams – it is interesting that the two stanzas about the brothel are immediately followed by one about a great house, now ominously deserted, and another about a throng of business people which may have its origin in Crabbe's visits to his financial adviser in Holborn.

Thereafter, the poem's scope widens considerably. He dreams (in Stanza X) about his dead seafaring brother and (in Stanzas XVI to XX) about his late wife; he falls from 'the loftiest tower', yet lands safely on the ground and rests on the sea; he is confronted in 'a large and Gothic hall' by an assembly of kings, 'Majestic, frozen, solemn, still', surely a memory of *Macbeth*; this in turn dissolves into a fragrant garden, but this too vanishes in further images of squalor. In the end, the dreamer wakes to a 'freedom' perversely compromised by the fact that writing the poem will compel him to revisit his dreams.

7

Crabbe greatly disliked writing new sermons and mercilessly recycled old ones: 'vamping a few old sermons' was his own jaunty phrase for this process in a letter to Elizabeth Charter.[88] Broadley and Jerrold mildly remark that he was not 'over-arduous in the matter of sermon-writing', before noting his habit of repeating them at approximately two-yearly intervals in the same church: they found one which had been delivered at Trowbridge on 24 December 1815, 9 February 1817, 4 April 1819 and 4 February 1821 (as well as at Pucklechurch on 26 October 1817), while another had seen service on 10 December 1815, 23 February 1817, 21 March 1819, 4 February 1821 and 5 May 1831.[89] His enemies – such as the anonymous parishioner who described him as 'an Ass and a fool and A Laughin Stock for decenters'[90] – might have said that, since Crabbe was so ineffective a preacher, the content of his sermons went largely unnoticed in any case. However, the sermon 'upon confirmation' which he began at Hughenden on 23 July and completed the following day, before returning to Trowbridge, was one of special importance: it was to be preached in Devizes on 15 August, at the triennial visitation of the Bishop of Sarum, Dr John Fisher, for the confirmation of 1,370 young people. The *Bath Chronicle* of 21 August provided a 'pompous account'[91] of the occasion:

> The [sermon] was preached by the Rev. and justly celebrated Geo. Crabbe, rector of Trowbridge, on 1 Cor.x.6.; and as a prose composition subtracted nothing from the fame which he has acquired as an original English bard. Commencing with a slight but masterly analysis of the nature of man, as a creature prone to oscillate in his opinions, and then to push them to extremes; it exemplified the truth of this representation in a rapid, but luminous

sketch of the events of ecclesiastical history, from the promulgation of the Gospel to the present moment; and inferred the necessity of preventing that prevailing tendency to religious sentiment, which is, happily, so remarkable in these days, from vibrating into the wildness of fanaticism, or the darkness of superstition.[92]

Pompous it may have been, but Crabbe was quietly pleased to receive a good press for a sermon. The *Bath Chronicle* added that 'at the special request of the Bishop, universally seconded by the Clergy present, the Sermon of the Preacher for the day is speedily to be published': not speedily enough for Crabbe, however, who on 11 September was 'a little vexed that my Sermon cannot be printed before I go'[93] on holiday with the Waldrons to the coast of Devon.

He was, in his usual self-cancelling way, anxious to persuade Elizabeth Charter to join him at places which she was most unlikely to visit: '. . .what say you dear Miss Charter to a *sea-port* or some village on the coast? I found Dawlish very pleasant and I am sure, almost sure, you would like the walk which is left by the falling tide below the rocks; but I will engage to find beauties in any part of the country which you may choose.'[94] But the Waldrons, ignorant or forgetful of any painful associations their choice might have for him, settled on Sidmouth and he glumly assented. 'I am nearly indifferent, though two years since I said "No more Sidmouth" but that is over and out of remembrance.' On his return, having 'spent one month not unpleasantly' – 'The sea was a most interesting object and the walks on the other side of the town in all their autumn glory'[95] – he found that Trowbridge rumour had once again married him off to Maria Waldron and that even Elizabeth Charter had heard about it:

I know not how the report originated. Miss W. and I were together at Sidmouth, so were we at Dawlish the year before and so possibly if we live (and she unmarried) we may be at some other place in the next autumn. Her father is one of my best friends here and she joins in making my hours, many of them, comfortable. Few persons more interest me and though I should grieve to lose her, I should be glad to see her placed in a comfortable state of wifehood. You will not now pay much regard to reports of my marrying, at least with this lady.[96]

His holiday had involved one lucky escape whose significance he was keen to play down: 'At Sidmouth were the family of Ridout but I knew not.'[97] Yet, shortly afterwards, this naggingly recurrent aspect of Crabbe's life took a grimly farcical turn: for, following her father's death in November, Charlotte Ridout moved to Bath. All his old anxieties were reawakened: 'I am afraid the females of the family are left by the father much abridged of their comforts, but they have a relation at Sidmouth and a married brother in good circumstances . . .'[98] He must have tried hard to forget that he had once described these two useful relations as, respectively, 'a vixen A[unt] . . . angry and obstinate and a foolish passionate Brother . . .'; but even if he succeeded in this, he cannot have failed to be struck by the appalling irony that the woman whom he had failed to marry because he might leave her as a penniless widow had instead been left, very much sooner, as a penniless spinster. Neither can Elizabeth Charter, who rather unkindly wondered whether in these circumstances Crabbe might not resume his relationship with Charlotte Ridout. His affronted response to this suggestion shows just how guilty he felt about the whole affair:

> I think my dear Madam that my unguarded and brief connection with Miss Rxx cannot be *fully* known to you, though I dare believe that the indiscreet part of it has long since reached you, but if you had known *how* it terminated you would have concluded that a renewal was all but impossible. It has caused me pain and I hope it was not altogether selfish. I did not see or try to see Miss Rxx either at Sidmouth or Bath, but I was desirous of knowing something of her views and her situation which however I could not learn.[99]

In that last sentence, he sounds less like a poet or a clergyman than a provincial solicitor. It was his final word on the matter.

During the spring of 1818, gossip in Trowbridge about the rector's supposed marriage was supplanted by gossip about his political allegiance. Although Crabbe had little interest in the greater political issues of his time – Thomas Moore noted his 'indifference to most of the general topics, whether of learning or politics, which diversify the conversation of men of the world'[100] – he had so far remained loyal in his support of the Whig cause. The General Election of June 1818 was a fiercely contested one: as early as February, he was unsettled by 'this horrid election-business',[101] and in April he wrote that he was 'troubled by our Wiltshire candidates and I have the misfortune to have three votes for different places all contested, and one I believe which will not be'.[102] In Wiltshire, he supported the Whig candidate, John Benett, 'to whom the manufacturing interest, the prevalent one in his parish, was extremely hostile', against the ultimately victorious Tory, William Long Wellesley, who was the Duke of Wellington's nephew. The biographer son makes the persuasive point that Crabbe's parishioners, even though they disliked his political opinions, nevertheless admired his 'boldness and uncompromising perseverance in the midst of opposition and reproach':

> During the violence of that contested election, while the few friends of Mr Benett were almost in danger of their lives, he was twice assailed by a mob of his parishioners, with hisses and the most virulent abuse. He replied to their formidable menaces by 'rating them soundly'; and though he was induced to retire by the advice of some friends, who hastened to his succour, yet this made no change in his vote, habits, or conduct. He continued to support Mr Benett; he walked in the streets always alone, and just as frequently as before; and spoke as fearlessly.[103]

In fact, Crabbe seems not to have voted in Wiltshire after all:

> I was first called to Cambridge to vote for two gentlemen who had claims upon my services and on my return I stayed in London to avoid if I could voting at our Wiltshire Election and yet if I had been wanted in one part I held myself in readiness to set off, so that I was engaged to the place, and depended upon my friends in town for keeping me out of idleness: I was in Covent Garden during most part of the content, but was perfectly quiet and walked through the great collection of people as calmly and undisturbed as if they had known how insignificant and indifferent I was . . .[104]

8

It had been Crabbe's intention to complete *Remembrances* – the sequence of linked narrative poems which became *Tales of the Hall* – before the end of

1817: 'I found in London sufficient encouragement to go on with my book and I talked of Christmas as a probable season when I might have it ready.'[105] This 'encouragement' must have come from friends such as Campbell, Moore and Rogers, for so far he had made no firm plans for the book's publication, although it is entirely possible that John Murray had already expressed an interest in having the poetry as well as the poet's portrait. But Christmas came and went, the complexities of emotional life and the vexations of politics distracted him, and Crabbe often felt unwell, 'a poor giddy-headed creature' burdened by 'the small cross accidents in life'.[106] By the summer of 1818, he was working hard to finish the book by *that* Christmas: 'I am every day, if not fulfilling a duty at least performing a task, and I rise two hours earlier that I may be ready with my verses at the time I have promised.'[107] Again, the idea of a promised delivery date is slightly mysterious: any such promise must have been made to himself and to his friends, for he had as yet neither committed the book to Hatchard nor negotiated with Murray.

The collection was substantially complete by the time he set off in the autumn on one of his increasingly ambitious tours: 'My verses are not yet entirely ready, but do not want much that I can give them,' he told Mary Leadbeater early in September. 'Some time in the passing year I believe some publisher will advertise them.' Elizabeth Charter had gone to Christchurch, so he wrote in his customary terms of wishing that he could be there with her, rather than in the various places he was actually going to be: 'We should have some pleasant walks within view of the sea, that first great object of my admiration and indeed the first of my notice.' But this was not going to happen. On 14 September he was at Bath,

in my way to London and from thence without stopping one night, to Cromer in Norfolk, there by appointment of long standing to pass two weeks with my friends Mr Hoare and his family – from thence I go to my sister at Aldborough and stay a few days. Then I mean to cross the country to Belvoir Castle, the Seat of the Duke of Rutland, where I am invited and shall stay a few days. Beyond this I have no immediate appointment, and if it were possible to go to Town and so to Christchurch I do think I should venture to join your party, but you will be gone! and I must not indulge the thought! – No! Dear Miss Charter, pleasant as it would be I dare not.[108]

In the event, he was to be detained beyond his expectations at almost every stage of his journey and did not return to Trowbridge until mid-December. He stayed longer than he had originally intended with the Hoares, with whom he had now repaired his friendship; in his letters to Elizabeth Charter, he continued to be reticent about them, mentioning them always as a family and avoiding specific references to Sarah, the daughter. Then he 'went to Norwich and passed two days with Mrs Opie, who has written some pleasant books, particularly the *Father and Daughter*'.[109] Amelia Opie, widow of the painter John Opie, now lived with her father, James Alderson, a Norwich doctor; among her novels were *Father and Daughter* (1801), which Crabbe perhaps remembered from his voracious fiction-reading days at Great Glemham, *Adeline Mowbray* (1802), *Simple Tales* (1806) and – then quite recently – *Valentine's Eve* (1816). She gave up writing novels a few years later on her conversion to Quakerism, to which Crabbe, as we have seen, was by no means unsympathetic.

From Norwich he proceeded as planned to Aldeburgh, where he spent some days with his sister, Mary Sparkes, but he did not go on to Belvoir and was probably glad enough to forego his visit: he would have mourned the destroyed paintings and had no residual affection for the refashioned castle. Instead, he visited his brother, Robert Crabbe, in Southwold for the first time in many years and from there went on to Beccles, which was now the home both of his sister-in-law, Mary Elmy, and John Crabbe's father-in-law, William Crowfoot. He stayed at least a week, for he preached at Beccles on both Sunday 18 October and Sunday 25 October; at this point, however, he found himself 'beset by insurmountable obstacles'. Mary Elmy had some unspecified business in London on which Crabbe agreed to accompany her; even in 1818, this does not sound a complicated excursion, but he contrived to turn it into one and to extend it for the best part of a month:

> I have in Beccles a sister – sister to Mrs Crabbe – with whom I have been in habits of friendliness, but not intimacy, till on a visit to that place, where also reside the family of my son's wife, we became associated and she having to go to Town on business, accompanied me and we dwelt together in Maddox Street a longer time than either of us expected; so that a month was thus added to the one spent in visits to my friends and on business of any importance,

none indeed but the usual kind of filing and polishing rough and harsh lines. With this lady, politeness would have demanded my return to Beccles if affection had not and there, by that kind of gentle compulsion which your sex knows so well how to apply, I was induced to stay one other week.[110]

This 'one other week' was the last in November, for Crabbe accompanied Mary Elmy back to Beccles on Monday 23 November and again preached there both on the Wednesday and on the following Sunday. He had now been away from home for two and a half months without achieving the practical objective of his journey, which was to sell his new book to a publisher. The reasons for this delay are plain enough from his letter of 31 October to Elizabeth Charter: '. . . I have verses to sell and have too much diffidence to set a large price upon my own work and yet too much pride to take a small one . . . If I ask £2000 and they will bid me only half the sum what will my vanity do? – Go home I believe with my goods and wait the rise of the market.'[111] He knew this could hardly be a sensible option: before going back to Beccles with Mary Elmy, he had written both to Samuel Rogers – 'I must immediately return and, if I do any business, it must be done without delay'[112] – and, on the day of his departure, to John Murray. This letter called for some delicacy – he was dissatisfied with Hatchard ('Mr Hxx') but wished to remain on terms of civility with him – which Crabbe manages with considerable skill:

My not waiting upon you for some time past makes an apology necessary, if I would not appear unmindful of your obliging attentions. The truth is that I have been considerably indisposed and even painfully so for some days. I was likewise in some degree restrained by not feeling myself perfectly disengaged from all those expectations which Mr Hxx might have in consequence of our former engagements: these are now entirely done away and he is satisfied that I mean no more to proceed in the manner we have done. Mr Hxx in our conversation, urged the integrity of his dealings by me and the success of our publications, neither of which I disputed, but argued that the integrity wanted knowledge and the success was much less than by a judicious mode of conducting our business it would have been. Being now freed from any claims or expectations of this nature, I am at liberty to address you freely on the subject, but I am under the necessity of going into the country where I purpose to remain a few days only and when I return to Town, I hope for the pleasure of seeing you again.[113]

The implication that Hatchard's 'integrity' and 'success' were simultaneously beyond reproach and seriously deficient is masterfully handled; Crabbe even manages to turn his imminent absence in Suffolk into a kind of courtesy, as this will give Murray a time for leisurely reflection. Next, he invokes the opinion of Sir Henry Englefield (that the collection will be 'too long for the fastidiousness of modern readers'), only to take issue with it and to add that, naturally, Murray's judgement will be superior to either Sir Henry's or his own. He also, with the modest insistence that 'this is a secondary consideration', remarks that after 'four years' labour and of late almost incessant, I confess that I should love to have my books presented to the public in an advantageous and respectable manner . . .' His primary consideration, he added frankly, was to make money.

Murray's response, in the first week of December, was to offer Crabbe £3,000 for the new work together with the copyright of his previous books: it was a handsome proposal, and Crabbe was inclined to accept it. Thomas Moore, when told about it on 6 December, agreed; but Rogers, who evidently fancied himself in the role of a literary agent conducting what we should now call a rights auction, thought that this sum could be obtained for the new work on its own and proposed a counter-approach to Longmans. On 7 December, Rogers met Owen Rees, a partner in Longmans, who told him that he could not possibly afford to offer anything like the £3,000 recently paid to Moore for his successful *Lalla Rookh: An Oriental Romance* (1817); the most Longmans would pay for the whole of Crabbe's work was £1,000. In thus contriving to flatter Moore, the third member of this triumvirate, in the same moment as he dampened Crabbe's expectations, Rees played a skilful hand and showed sound commercial judgement. It now seemed all too possible that, should he hear of Longmans' figure, Murray would reconsider his own offer: Crabbe, in some alarm, at once wrote to his prospective publisher but received no immediate reply. Accordingly, the next day, Moore and Rogers set off to visit Murray with the intention of casually mentioning his offer to Crabbe, as Moore himself recalled in a letter to Murray much later:

> In this crisis it was that Mr Rogers and myself, anxious to relieve our poor friend from his suspense, called upon you, as you must well remember, in Albermarle Street; and seldom have I watched a countenance with more solicitude, or heard words that gave me more pleasure, than when, on the subject being mentioned, you said, 'Oh yes – I have heard from Mr Crabbe, and look upon the matter as all settled.' I was rather pressed, I recollect, for time that morning, having an appointment on some business of my own; but Mr Rogers insisted that I should accompany him to Crabbe's lodgings, and enjoy the pleasure of seeing him relieved from his suspense. We found him sitting in his room, alone, and expecting the worst; but soon dissipated all his fears by the agreeable intelligence which we brought.[114]

Moore tactfully underplays the fact that Crabbe's 'suspense' and 'fears' were wholly the result of Rogers's meddlesome intervention, in which he had colluded. As soon as the position with Murray was clarified, Crabbe wrote in civil but businesslike fashion to Hatchard: 'I fully acknowledge the integrity of your dealings with me . . . though I differ in judgement,' he said; however, 'you must allow me to add that I must claim for myself my rights and exercise them as I deem most beneficial to my interests.' These rights, he continued, included a share of unsold copies as well as the copyright of his entire work: 'that is, the right to proceed in future with you or any other person in the sale or publication of them in the manner most agreeable or convenient to myself'.[115] A man who could write in these terms had no need of his amateur literary agents; indeed, having dealt with Hatchard, Crabbe seems, rather understandably, to have become wary of his other London friends and their clever ways. Moore mistakes this caution for mere quaintness:

> When he received the bills for £3000, we earnestly advised that he should, without delay, deposit them in some safe hands; but no – he must 'take them with him to Trowbridge, and show them to his son John. They would hardly believe in his good luck, at home, if they did not see the bills.' On his way down to Trowbridge, a friend at

Salisbury, at whose house he rested (Mr Everett, the banker), seeing that he carried these bills in his waistcoat pocket, requested to be allowed to take charge of them for him, but with equal ill-success. 'There was no fear,' he said, 'of his losing them, and must show them to his son John.'[116]

He reached Trowbridge in mid-December; and what his son, the hard-working curate, actually thought when his father returned, after three months' gallivanting and with £3,000 in his pocket, is unhappily not recorded.[117]

By 23 December, Crabbe was able to give Elizabeth Charter some account of his negotiations (admitting that he had rejected £1,000 but coyly declining to specify the sum he had accepted) and to tell her that he now had 'the first printed sheet' of proofs. But the book, still called *Remembrances*, had yet to receive its final title. On 28 December – these dates give the distinct impression that John shouldered most of the clerical burdens of Christmas – he wrote to Murray, having almost completed his corrections and additions to the first sheet, with his muddled thoughts on this matter. Clearly, Moore and his £3,000 for *Lalla Rookh* were still niggling him:

> *Remembrances* I do not like though I am not able to assign any very good reason for disapproving it: *Tales of the Hall* would I think be more inviting, but a title has occurred to me which I prefer to either, though I would not adopt it without your approbation, and I am aware that it may convey no very appropriate meaning; it must indeed have a second or explanatory title, though even of that I am not certain. What will you think of *Forty Days, or A Series of Tales Told at Binning Hall*? I grant it has no great meaning, but I can make the visit of one brother just of that duration and I do not conceive the obscurity of a title to be any objection to the book. Not one person in fifty knew what *Lallah Rookh* meant and what little of association there is in the mind with such title as 'Forty Days' is in its favour. It implies narrative but as I said before I leave it to your consideration so far as you may think it worth any.[118]

Over the next few months, Crabbe proved to be a nightmarish author for Murray to deal with. He was revising and sending in instalments the latter part of *Tales of the Hall* at the same time as he was correcting (and further revising) proofs of the earlier sections. He punctuated these revisions with *faux-naïf* protestations of the sort which drive publishers into blind fury – 'I have . . . added about sixty lines and of course have done mischief to the letterpress but I hope this is of no material consequence';[119] 'I use the terms Royal 8vo etc without much knowledge of them but I borrow them of Mr Hatchard'[120] – and sententious apologies for his delays: 'My son is an obliging assistant to me in my parochial duties, but a population of more than 8000 inhabitants often compel me to give personal attention.'[121] He continued to dither about the title, and it was Murray who settled on *Tales of the Hall* towards the end of January. To make matters worse, Henry Colburn, who three years earlier had published the 'Biographical Account' of Crabbe in his *New Monthly Magazine*, decided that *he* had been given some sort of undertaking that he would be the publisher of *Tales of the Hall*, even though (as Crabbe sturdily pointed out) 'Mr Colburn never saw a line of this poem in his life, nor ever offered any terms nor was ever asked.'[122] He was rattled, nevertheless, and was evidently relieved to report at the start of February that Colburn, in his librarian's guise, had 'sent my young people his box of circulating ware as usual'. Crabbe therefore concluded that 'his mind is softened and made up to his disappointment if it really was one. Of course I require no more. I have no love of warfare.'[123] Some of those with whom he had quarrelled might have had their doubts about that.

9

Tales of the Hall was published in June 1819 and entered at the Stationers' Register on 3 July: 'The new work had, at least, as general approbation as any that had gone before it; and was not the less liked for its opening views of a higher class of society than he had hitherto dealt much in.'[124] If the critical response was largely favourable, this was because most reviewers were now inclined to emphasise Crabbe's mellowing strengths. 'He delights to look over society with a keen, scrutinising, and somewhat stern eye, as if resolved that the human heart should not be suffered to conceal one single secret from his inquisitorial authority,' said *Blackwood's Edinburgh Magazine*. 'Of all men of this age, he is the best portrait-painter.'[125] In the *Edinburgh Review*, Francis Jeffrey listed some of the characteristics of 'this great writer': apart from being 'the greatest *mannerist*, perhaps, of all living poets', Crabbe had 'an unrivalled and an almost magical power of observation', 'an anatomy of character and feeling not less exquisite and searching', 'an occasional touch of matchless tenderness' and 'a deep and dreadful pathetic', as well as 'the sure and profound sagacity of the remarks with which he every now and then startles us'.[126] Jeffrey was, of course, something of a veteran in Crabbe reviewing – this, he remarked, was 'our *fourth* article on Mr Crabbe's productions' – and he observed, more truthfully than he could possibly have known, that 'Mr C. seems to become more amorous as he grows older, – the interest of almost all the stories in this collection turning on the tender passion – and many of them on its most romantic varieties'.[127] The *Christian Observer* also noticed 'the remarkable preponderance, in these volumes, of love stories; and the various feelings, bad and good (not always the latter), detailed in connexion with the passion of love'.[128]

The *New Monthly Magazine* made a virtue of Crabbe's unfashionability: 'We have been amused, soothed, delighted, instructed and bettered, by the perusal of these volumes; and we are inclined to think, that, when the works of some of his *brilliant* contemporaries are consigned to forgetfulness, *The Tales of the Hall* will be read with applause, and the name of Crabbe be pronounced with increasing esteem and regard by posterity.'[129] But the *Eclectic Review* was more cautious in its praise: 'Compared with Mr Crabbe's former volumes, the *Tales of the Hall*, exhibit, we think, no marks of decay or exhaustion of faculty, and they are, upon the whole, less obnoxious to criticism than some of his productions.'[130] The most sustained attack on *Tales of the Hall* – and the review, it must be admitted, most likely to find echoes in the minds of later readers – came from the *British Critic*: 'We think that he has never yet written so unequally; and we fear we may add never with so great a preponderance of his peculiar faults.'[131] In Crabbe, 'not a wart, a wrinkle, or a freckle, escapes faithful notice; nay, sometimes, we are convinced, that he reddens the rubicundity of a nose, and distorts the obliquity of an eye'; as for his versification, 'it is the most untunable in our language, the merest scrannel scraping that ever grated on mortal ear'.[132] The writer concluded: 'If [Crabbe] would permit us to make a *corps d'élite* of his lines, we would promise to burn all our obnoxious criticism, and in so doing we should perform a duty not a little grateful to ourselves, and which, indeed, Mr Crabbe might justly demand at our hands.'[133]

The *British Critic*'s view was apparently shared by 'that great blockhead the public'; according to Samuel Smiles, *Tales of the Hall* failed even to sell out its first edition, much of which was remaindered at a third of its cost, and the magnanimous John Murray lost around £2,500 on his deal.[134] The collection is certainly uneven: too much of it is obviously the product of Crabbe's mechanical habit of writing thirty lines a day, and it was probably not improved by his chopping and changing while the work was being typeset. Although a certain conversational flatness may be justifiable in the long passages of spoken storytelling, the authorial narrative is often just as lazy:

> The morning shone in cloudless beauty bright;
> Richard his letters read with much delight;
> George from his pillow rose in happy tone,
> His bosom's lord sat lightly on his throne.
> They read the morning news – they saw the sky
> Inviting call'd them, and the earth was dry. [VIII. 1–6]

These lines would have been of little use to the authors of *Rejected Addresses*: they are beyond parody. Elsewhere, in a memorable quatrain from 'The Elder Brother', a tale added in late January 1819,[135] Crabbe achieves a degree of self-parody – with both an unscannable line *and* a ludicrously bathetic rhyme – which must have made the Smiths gasp with admiration:

> 'Something one day occurr'd about a bill
> That was not drawn with true mercantile skill,
> And I was ask'd and authorised to go
> To seek the firm of Clutterbuck and Co. . . .' [VI. 469–72]

But there is a still more fundamental flaw to *Tales of the Hall*. Ironically, in providing what Jeffrey and others had so long demanded, a collection of stories united by an overall narrative framework, Crabbe sacrificed much of the earlier tales' enlivening directness. The problem is glancingly suggested in the course of some admiring remarks by F. R. Leavis:

> Actually, it is in the later work, the Tales of the various collections,
> that [Crabbe] is (or ought to be – for who reads him?) a living classic,

because it is in this work that he develops to the full his peculiarly eighteenth-century strength. His strength is that of a novelist and of an eighteenth-century poet who is positively in sympathy with the Augustan tradition, and it is one strength. The Augustan form, as he adapts it, is perfectly suited to his matter and to his outlook – matter and outlook that have close affinities with Jane Austen's, though he has a range and a generous masculine strength that bring out by contrast her spinsterly limitations (we remember D. H. Lawrence's excessively unsympathetic allusions to her).[136]

Although Leavis's forthrightness deserves a cheer, and his argument serves *Tales* (1812) well, his comments inadvertently suggest why *Tales of the Hall* is less successful than the earlier collection. Crabbe's, as he says, is a 'peculiarly eighteenth-century strength'; thus, insofar as this strength 'is that of a novelist', it belongs to a kind of specifically eighteenth-century novelist who was almost extinct by 1819. It is worth recalling Crabbe's conversation with Thomas Campbell, in which he avowed himself a 'Fieldingite' rather than a 'Smolletite', and the particular view of narrative method that this implies; for many of the stories within *Tales of the Hall* resemble those tales-within-a-tale which characteristically occur in Fielding's fiction (and which impatient readers skim over). Their insistence on *telling* rather than *showing* is what may make them less than engrossing to us: it is hardly Crabbe's fault that he lived before Henry James, but it explains why his subsequent readers, even more than his contemporaries, tend to find *Tales of the Hall* heavy going.

The collection is held together by the reunion of two long-lost half-brothers, George and Richard, who recount their experiences and (together with Jacques, the rector) tell a number of stories: they are Crabbe's yin and yang, his Apollonius and Dionysus, the complementary opposites which make up his own contradictory being. 'Crabbe's personal tenets are apportioned between the two characters,' as Terence Bareham says. 'They show the best side of latitudinarianism – its tolerance, its liberality, and its general eclectic sanity.'[137] And, as we shall discover, the rector too is a man of decidedly Crabbe-like qualities. George, the prosperous though unfulfilled bachelor squire who now lives in the house he could once only admire, is a subtle portrait of a man comfortably at ease with everything except himself:

Ease leads to habit, as success to ease,
He lives by rule who lives himself to please;
For change is trouble, and a man of wealth
Consults his quiet as he guards his health;
And habit now on George had sovereign power,
His actions all had their accustom'd hour:
At the fix'd time he slept, he walk'd, he read,
Or sought his grounds, his gruel, and his bed;
For every season he with caution dress'd,
And morn and eve had the appropriate vest;
He talk'd of early mists, and night's cold air,
And in one spot was fix'd his worship's chair. [II. 51–62]

There is a story by Saki called 'The Unrest-Cure': that is exactly what George needs and what Richard, his more widely travelled and liberal-minded brother, will provide. 'The world he travelled was the book he read', we are told; in the course of this self-education, Richard has acquired a wife called Matilda and children, but he lacks the bachelor George's wealth and security. Interestingly, Crabbe's own boyhood memories and love of nature are given to Richard, perhaps suggesting a wistful envy of his own seafaring younger brothers. Just as in 'The Parish Clerk', 'Peter Grimes' and 'Infancy – A Fragment', once Crabbe taps into this autobiographical source, his writing acquires the glow of authenticity:

'I loved to walk where none had walk'd before,
About the rocks that ran along the shore;
Or far beyond the sight of men to stray,
And take my pleasure when I lost my way;
For then 'twas mine to trace the hilly heath,
And all the mossy moor that lies beneath:
Here had I favourite stations, where I stood
And heard the murmurs of the ocean-flood,
With not a sound beside, except when flew
Aloft the lapwing, or the gray curlew,
Who with wild notes my fancied power defied,
And mock'd the dreams of solitary pride.

'I loved to stop at every creek and bay
Made by the river in its winding way,
And call to memory – not by marks they bare,
But by the thoughts that were created there.
    'Pleasant it was to view the sea-gulls strive
Against the storm, or in the ocean dive,
With eager scream, or when they dropping gave
Their closing wings to sail upon the wave:
Then, as the winds and waters raged around,
And breaking billows mix'd their deafening sound,
They on the rolling deep securely hung,
And calmly rode the restless waves among.
Nor pleased it less around me to behold,
Far up the beach, the yesty sea-foam roll'd;
Or, from the shore upborn, to see on high
Its frothy flakes in wild confusion fly;
While the salt spray that clashing billows form,
Gave to the taste a feeling of the storm.' [IV. 447–76]

It is the exactness of recollected detail that brings a welcome tang of reality
to these lines: Crabbe *knows* 'the gray curlew' and 'the yesty sea-foam', and
the delight in solitude, even to 'take my pleasure when I lost my way', is
deeply rooted in his psyche. And yet in other ways the passage may strike us
as tired and predictable, and not only because it revisits a scene familiar from
earlier poems: that weary procession of alliterative epithets – 'hilly heath',
'mossy moor', 'winding way', 'breaking billows' – is one clear symptom of a
diction which is beginning to lose its sharpness.

    The device of the two half-brothers enables Crabbe to conduct a series of
dialogues with himself, giving to each opinions which he finds perfectly
reasonable if not obviously compatible. For instance, he contrasts their
responses to the rural world around them. Richard sees, and genuinely
appreciates, the unspoilt pastoral:

There is delicious quiet in this scene,
At once so rich, so varied, so serene;
Sounds too delight us – each discordant tone

Thus mingled please, that fails to please alone:
This hollow wind, this rustling of the brook,
The farm-yard noise, the woodman at yon oak –
See, the axe falls! – now listen to the stroke!' [IV. 69–75]

George, on the other hand, has no time for the country's 'charms' and
instead draws Richard's attention to his 'model for all farms':

'Look at that land – you find not there a weed,
We grub the roots, and suffer none to seed.
To land like this no botanist will come,
To seek the precious ware he hides at home;
Pressing the leaves and flowers with effort nice,
As if they came from herbs in Paradise;
Let them their favourites with my neighbours see,
They have no – what? – no *habitat* with me.' [IV. 80–87]

Obviously the botanical Crabbe ought to side with Richard; in the event,
his evenhandedness is little short of miraculous. He brilliantly enters into
George's rational and necessary point of view, giving him an absolutely
plausible voice: the final line, in which he can hardly bring himself to
splutter out the word 'habitat', is a triumph. At one level, the argument is
grounded deep in Crabbe's past, in the distinction between his own
coastal (and botanising) childhood and the inland farming country to
which he was transplanted as an apprentice; at another, it recasts the
debate between the romantic view of nature and the 'improvers'. Above
all, it illustrates Crabbe's remarkable ability to hold simultaneously in his
head opposing – at their simplest, traditional and modern – views of the
world.

Crabbe treats this so much as a matter of course that his audacity may
pass unnoticed. Lilian Haddakin[138] shrewdly draws our attention to an
extraordinary moment, near the beginning of 'Delay Has Danger', where his
interest in fossils leads him to a matter-of-fact observation which might,
were it not for this duality, have astounded his conventional clerical self. The
movement from pastoral (for this is Richard exploring the landscape) to
science is seamless:

He rode to Ripley through that river gay,
Where in the shallow stream the loaches play,
And stony fragments stay the winding stream,
And gilded pebbles at the bottom gleam,
Giving their yellow surface to the sun,
And making proud the waters as they run.
It is a lovely place, and at the side
Rises a mountain-rock in rugged pride;
And in that rock are shapes of shells, and forms
Of creatures in old worlds, of nameless worms,
Whose generations lived and died ere man,
A worm of other class, to crawl began. [XIII. 4–15]

Crabbe is wonderfully unflustered – it is simply what he has observed and what he knows – by what he implies here about the impossibility of Genesis, the age of the planet and the worm-like origins of man.

The tales themselves are on the whole more conventional and less interesting than the framing narrative of *Tales of the Hall*: they vary from the inordinately long to the merely anecdotal. Crabbe's approach to what he should put into his framework had been notably cavalier: having 'pledged myself (idiot as I am) to compose another book' in the spring of 1816, he asked Elizabeth Charter for 'some versifyable anecdotes',[139] while other letters suggest that he envisaged the collection as consisting wholly or mostly of ghost stories. He may also have been unsure about the complicating role of the rector Jacques, who inescapably becomes another sort of self-portrait. In 'The Natural Death of Love', he makes Jacques the recipient of the criticisms he had received from some of his Trowbridge flock and, of course, offers a sturdy defence:

'Heathens,' they said, 'can tell us right from wrong,
But to a Christian higher points belong.'
Yet Jacques proceeded, void of fear and shame,
In his old method, and obtain'd the name
Of *Moral Preacher* – yet they all agreed,
Whatever error had defiled his creed,
His life was pure, and him they could commend,

Not as their guide, indeed, but as their friend;
Truth, justice, pity, and a love of peace,
Were his – but here must approbation cease . . . [XIV. 23–32]

At the start of 'Sir Owen Dale', which is narrated by the rector, the brothers – speaking strangely in unison – tease him in terms which closely mirror Crabbe's own grumbles about his parochial duties:

'What has detained thee? some parochial case?
Some man's desertion, or some maid's disgrace?
Or wert thou call'd, as parish priest, to give
Name to some new-born thing that would not live,
That its weak glance upon the world had thrown,
And shrank in terror from the prospect shown?
Or hast thou heard some dying wretch deplore,
That of his pleasures he could taste no more,
Who wish'd thy aid his spirits to sustain,
And drive away the fears that gave him pain?' [XII. 5–14]

This is a typically inward sort of joke, since only Crabbe and a few intimate friends would have known how much he privately complained about duties which in public he performed with conscientious good humour. Like 'The Preceptor Husband' and 'Delay Has Danger', 'Sir Owen Dale' is a story very much in the tradition of Crabbe's earlier tales. His proposal to a much younger woman having been rejected, Sir Owen persuades his nephew to court her with the express intention of breaking her heart in revenge (this couple, unhappily for modern British readers, are called Charles and Camilla); however, after observing the admirable behaviour of a tenant disappointed in love, Sir Owen repents and forgives. It is a moral tale in which folly is transformed by experience to wisdom, and it glances at Crabbe's disappointment with Charlotte Ridout just as 'The Old Bachelor' owes something to his postal affair with Charlotte Williams. This kind of matter suits the balanced distinctions and antitheses of the heroic couplet: 'It was his wish in peace with all to live; / And he could pardon, but could not forgive' [XII. 90–91]; 'He felt dismay'd, as he perceived success / Has inverse ratio, more obtaining less' [XII. 229–30];

But then that mind unaided ran to waste:
He had some learning, but he wanted taste;
Placid, not pleased – contented, not employ'd –
He neither time improved, nor life enjoy'd. [XII. 106–9]

Effective and apparently effortless, this is a style which Crabbe must have been able to compose in his sleep by this time; and that ease, of course, is both a strength and a weakness.

In the final section of *Tales of the Hall*, 'The Visit Concluded', Crabbe does something extraordinary. As the end of Richard's stay at Binning Hall approaches, he is alarmed by an uncharacteristic absence of letters from Matilda; nevertheless, he pays his farewell visits, in the course of which he is surprised and troubled by the rector's apparent indifference to his departure. George, meanwhile, enthuses about a nearby property he has bought and which he insists that Richard should visit before he leaves. When it seems impossible to persuade Richard to prolong his visit, George spells out the ways in which his younger brother has enriched his life:

'Richard,' said George, 'I see it is in vain
By love or prayer my Brother to retain;
And, truth to tell, it was a foolish thing
A man like thee from thy repose to bring
Ours to disturb – Say, how am I to live
Without the comforts thou art wont to give?
How will the heavy hours my mind afflict –
No one t'agree, no one to contradict;
None to awake, excite me, or prevent;
To hear a tale, or hold an argument;
To help my worship in a case of doubt,
And bring me in my blunders fairly out.' [XXII. 233–44]

Conversely, as he leads up to an as yet unexplained strategy for retaining his younger brother's company, George indicates ways in which he might enrich Richard's life:

'We part no more, dear Richard! thou wilt need
Thy Brother's help to teach thy boys to read;
And I should love to hear Matilda's psalm,
To keep my spirit in a morning calm,
And feel the soft devotion that prepares
The soul to rise above its earthly cares.
Then thou and I, an independent two,
May have our parties, and defend them too;
Thy liberal notions, and my loyal fears,
Will give us subjects for our future years;
We will for truth alone contend and read,
And our good Jacques shall oversee our creed.' [XXII. 406–17]

What is happening here? Though Richard obligingly remains 'puzzled', the reader will have guessed. The newly purchased house, with its grounds which recall Jonson and Marvell ('There too the garden walk, the elms design'd / To guard the peaches from the eastern wind'), is to be Richard's as a gift; indeed, Matilda and the children, thanks to the arrangements of the collusive Jacques (whose earlier untroubled response to Richard's supposed departure is thus explained), are already installed there. It is a perfect fairy-tale ending, and if it leaves us feeling a little queasy that is partly because we may not believe in fairy-tales but mainly because we doubt the morality of manipulating others' lives, however benignly, in quite this way: it is precisely the unease we feel at the end of *Bleak House*, when John Jarndyce presents his ward Esther and her husband, Allan Woodcourt, with a house and similarly idealised garden – a scene in which Dickens may well have been remembering the conclusion of *Tales of the Hall*. For Crabbe, though, this resolution has a deep personal significance. In uniting the two brothers who represent two aspects of his own personality, and even contriving to involve the rector Jacques in his closing equation, Crabbe has symbolically healed his divided self. It is as if Humpty Dumpty had put himself together again after all.

10

Crabbe was unflustered by fame and unsurprised by its fickleness. That spring he had travelled into London in the company of a lady whose husband was 'a reading and studying farmer' and who knew 'what is read and talked of':

> She spoke of most of those of whom other people talk, and among other things, asked me if I knew Crabbe? I did not act generously, for I evaded the question; and then she told me that she was invited to meet him at dinner at Mr West's, the painter. I thought it proper to put the lady right; which, however, was a matter of no importance: she went on in the same way; but I, of necessity, withdrew a part of my attention.[140]

He arrived in town in time for the 'singular and grand' dinner at Somerset House on 1 May which preceded the Royal Academy's summer exhibition: though he could by now airily remark that it 'was like all very large dinners', he was nevertheless impressed by the 'imposing air of dignity' and pleased to meet several of his friends (unfortunately, 'Lord Holland was prevented by a fit of the gout'). His portrait by Phillips was exhibited; venturing no opinion of it himself, he was happy to believe it good because others said so and because Lord Holland was 'to have it copied, and placed with those in his library' at Holland House. A few days later, having been elected a member of the Literary Society, he was to dine at the Thatched House Tavern in St James's Street: 'When I have seen my brethren, and paid my subscription, I shall better judge whether the honour makes amends for the costs.'

He stayed in London for the publication of *Tales of the Hall* and in early July returned to a Trowbridge once more gripped by electoral ferment. One of the two Wiltshire MPs, Paul Methuen, had resigned through ill health (in fact, he would live until 1849, serving again as MP for North Wiltshire in the 1830s before being created Lord Methuen in 1838). In the resulting by-election, John Benett, who had been the unsuccessful Whig candidate in the 1818 election, was opposed by one of his own former supporters, John Dugdale Astley, much to Crabbe's disgust: 'Mr Astley is come to eat venison and give away beer, and the people drew his carriage and prostrate themselves to their temporary idol.'[141] To John Murray, he wrote 'in the midst of confusion, noise and contention', fearing that this election would 'have all the virulence and enmity of the last'.[142] His anxieties were amply confirmed: on 22 July, the *Devizes and Wiltshire Gazette* reported that

Trowbridge magistrates had asked for military assistance and a 'troop of the 16th Lancers was dispatched from Bristol'.[143] In the event, Benett won the seat by a majority of 166 votes.

Disliking his market town more than ever during these turbulent days, Crabbe was as usual wishing he could be with 'my dear Miss Charter', with whom 'a walk by the sea-sand or indeed on any quiet earth would be great comfort'. 'I do wish to be at the sea,' he repeated. 'These excursions on and near the sea . . . so dwell in the memory, on the heart I should say; some feel the pleasure in retrospection.' The coast, his earliest source of comfort and of inspiration, was always with him in his imagination; but instead of visiting it, with or without Elizabeth Charter, he had to content himself with a letter in which, evidently at her prompting, he summarised his own and others' reactions to *Tales of the Hall*:

> And did you feel anxiety about my *Tales*? Kind Miss Charter. I scarcely know what parts are favourites with me, because an author generally has motives which his readers have not: the most elaborate and favourable criticism at present is that of the Edinborough Magazine, *Blackwoods*: it is indeed most friendly but whose I know not: it mentions the Tale of 'Ellen' and of C. a compounded kind of relation, founded on revenge, a story of a Farmer Ellis. Some friends of mine at Hampstead, Mrs Hoare, wife of Mr Hoare the banker, a lady of excellent judgement if I may be allowed to say so, likes the story of the Brothers, called 'Smugglers and Poachers'. A lady much younger indeed prefers the too-long story of Lucy and Jane and the first ghost-story of Lady Barbara is the favourite of certain friends in Town. I have now told you Dear almost all I know: my own partiality is with the relation of the Brothers, Richard's Education if I may so call it, but pray judge for yourself.

Kind Miss Charter would have had to buy her own copy, however; for, careful as ever with money, Crabbe had decided he could not afford to send the book to his friends. This sounds parsimonious enough as it is, and he made matters worse by admitting that copies *had* been sent to the Duchess of Rutland, Lord Holland, Walter Scott and Samuel Rogers ('who had all sent their books to me'), and that he had thought about ordering 'forty or fifty copies for my friends secretly, but the expense and not knowing even then where to stop deterred me'; Elizabeth Charter, though by now accustomed to being one among several intimate friends of Crabbe, cannot have much liked this relegation to one among fifty. 'I believe a copy was sent to Lord Byron but not by me,' he added, 'yet Mr Murray sends me all his works and I have rec'd *Don Juan*: a singularly careless, immoral work! Whether immortal I cannot say.'[144]

That *Don Juan* should not have been much to Crabbe's taste – or, at any rate, the taste he chose to reveal to Elizabeth Charter – is unsurprising. Byron, of course, greatly admired Crabbe and in the suppressed dedication to *Don Juan* had praised him in terms which echoed his letter to John Murray of 15 September 1817, warning the Lake Poets that 'Scott, Rogers, Campbell, Moore, and Crabbe will try / 'Gainst you the question with posterity'; and Crabbe's interest was sufficiently engaged by *Don Juan* for him to parody the poem and satirise its author in 'Sir Denys Banger':

> Sir Denys fled, pursued by hate and curses,
>   To Greece, where soft voluptuous ease man blesses:
> But of this leisure nought the Muse rehearses,
>   Save that he sought young maids with jetty tresses,
> With eyes that cannot be described by verses,
>   With elegance in all their steps and dresses –
> Of these he purchased a sufficient number,
> To make the will, but not the conscience, slumber.[145]

At least Sir Denys seems to have confined his attentions to the maids. Crabbe was, however, bothered in a more general way about the state of poetry and especially of *poets*. Although he continued to compose and to seek out stories which he might versify, some of which would eventually appear as *Posthumous Tales*, he clearly recognised that *Tales of the Hall* was likely to be his last book; he worried about his friends and contemporaries, and about his own place among them. He was reasonably well off himself and living in a rare period when poetry might earn a decent living, but his main concern was with money:

> Poetry does pretty well in these times, but not poets. I hear that Mr Anacreon Moore is obliged to go abroad on acct. of the decision which

calls on him for £6000, a debt contracted without a fault on his part and almost without a possibility of avoiding it. Lord Byron is also self-banished. Bowles and I are priests struggling with the clamour and infidelity of the times. Campbell is poor with a family and Scott alone is said to be wealthy. Well! I do not grieve nor do I hope my Brethren, these are better days than those of greater men. I have my shilling for the poor and none of us is without bread for himself.[146]

Crabbe's Wiltshire neighbour Thomas Moore, who held the sinecure of Admiralty Registrar for Bermuda, had been forced into temporary exile (hence 'Anacreon') in France, because of a debt incurred by his deputy; he was able to return when his liability was reduced to £1,000, in the repayment of which he was assisted by a loan from Lord Lansdowne. How much Crabbe was aware of Byron's personal circumstances is unclear: despite the ease with which he now moved in metropolitan circles, he remained capable of extraordinary naïvety. However, the image of himself 'struggling with the clamour and infidelity of the times' is somewhat compromised by the large proportion of his life he was presently spending away from his clerical duties. A week or so later, he returned to the subject in a letter to Mary Leadbeater, in similar terms though with an interesting addition:

Money and versification have not of late that utter dissociation and repugnancy they had of old. Scott is wealthy. Lord Byron might be. Moore is indigent only by accident. Rogers is rich and bountiful. The Lake Poets, if they have not money, say they want none, and I, who do not say so, have as much as does me good.[147]

By this time, both Wordsworth and Coleridge were approaching fifty, yet Crabbe makes them sound like a pair of idealistic young hippies. Of Keats and Shelley, who might have better fitted this description, he has nothing at all to say: he had barely heard of them. At moments like this, he indeed reveals himself as one of the 'old race'.

In the late summer of 1819, he repeated the East Anglian expedition which had so pleasurably delayed him the previous year, staying first with the Hoares at Cromer and then visiting Amelia Opie and her father in Norwich. From there he travelled on to Newmarket, entirely forgetting (in a reversion to his Parson Adams self) that his arrival would coincide with the first October race meeting, 'and the consequence was that at 12 o'clock at night I found myself in the street without a prospect of a bed or even a room to sleep'. No longer the young man to curl up in a haystack with a book, his worldly-wise older self fortunately took command of the situation:

> I sought the Rutland Arms, the principal inn and was assured by the waiter that there was not a vacant bed in the house or the town. I sought then the widow – mistress of the house – and by a little art and management that is, by making use of the name of the Duke of Rutland, who was then at his seat of Cheveley adjoining Newmarket, I obtained first an hearing and afterwards a bed. To give me credit – for I almost doubted whether I obtained full belief – the Duke was kind enough to call on me next day and then of course I was a great man with both the lady of the inn and every waiter in her dominion: I stayed a few days with his Grace and then returned to my parsonage where I found my daughter and her little one in pretty good health and preparing to leave me for a visit to another grandpapa in Suffolk.[148]

It was, of course, not the first time Crabbe had set foot inside Cheveley. He had stayed there when, as chaplain, he accompanied the Duke's father and his family on their visits for the racing at Newmarket. Long before that, he had been the fourteen-year-old errand boy from Mr Smith, the apothecary of Wickhambrook.

Ten

A Lusty Winter

1820–1832

I

When the Regency ended and the third decade of the nineteenth century began, Crabbe was in his mid-sixties. His health was beginning to decline – the 'heat' in his head, of which he had so long complained, was now supplemented by recurrent *tic douloureux* or chronic neuralgia – and he often found himself depressed or irritated by parochial duties and by politics; yet, despite these vexations, things had turned out better than he could possibly have imagined in the miserable days following Sarah's death or in the uncertain early months at Trowbridge. His final collection of tales had been a critical if not a commercial success and he was recognised everywhere as one of the great literary figures of his time. His elder son George and wife Caroline, happily installed at Pucklechurch, were raising a rapidly expanding family: their daughter Caroline, born in 1818, was followed in 1819 by a son, George, the fourth in succeeding generations to bear the name; there would be two more daughters, Katharine and Sophia, and another son, Thomas. Although John and Anna's first child died within six months, they would have two daughters, Georgiana and Emily, who would eventually marry her cousin George. Crabbe was never to fulfil his wistful dream of a second marriage – a possibility which in truth had vanished with Charlotte Ridout – but in every other respect the familial vacancies were amply filled; while his dynastic instinct was gratified by the grandson who shared his name, he doted on the granddaughters in whom he at last found some consolation for his own lost daughter, Sarah Susannah.

Caroline – properly, Carolina Matilda; familiarly, Carry – was his favourite. Shortly before her grandfather's sixty-eighth birthday in 1822, she sent him 'an intelligible scrawl' which prompted this delighted, and delightful, reply:

> My dear Carry, – Your very pretty letter gave me a great deal of
> pleasure; and I choose this, which is my birthday, that in it I may
> return you my best thanks for your kind remembrance of me; and I
> will keep your letter laid up in my new Bible, where I shall often see it;
> and then I shall say, 'This is from my dear little girl at Pucklechurch.'
> My face is not so painful as it was when I wrote to papa; and I
> would set out immediately, to see you all, with great pleasure, but I
> am forced, against my will, to remain at home this week by duty; and
> that, you know, I must attend to: and then, there is an engagement
> to a family in this place, Waldron by name, who have friends in
> Salisbury, and among them a gentleman, who, though he is young,
> will have grandpapa's company, and grandpapa, being a very old
> man, takes this for a compliment, and has given his promise,
> though he is vexed about it, that he will be in Trowbridge at that time
> . . . And so, my dear, you will say to papa and mamma, 'You must
> forgive poor grandpapa, because he is so puzzled that he does not
> know what he can do, and so vexed beside, that he cannot do as his
> wishes and his affection would lead him; and you know, dear papa
> and mamma, that he grows to be a very old man, and does not know
> how to get out of these difficulties, but I am sure that he loves to
> come to us, and will be here as soon as ever he can.' . . .
> I have written a very long letter to my Carry; and I think we suit
> each other, and shall make fit correspondents: that is, writers of
> letters, Caroline to grandpapa, and grandpapa to Caroline. God
> bless my dear little girl. I desire earnestly to see you, and am your
> very affectionate Grandpapa[1]

Caroline, who was four years old, must have treasured this stately and
gracious letter; her grandfather, meanwhile, clearly relished the acquisition
of yet another young female correspondent. She was probably not much
older when she undertook the ambitious task of tidying up Crabbe's library:

> Would the reader like to follow my father into his library? – a scene
> of unparalleled confusion – windows rattling, paint in great request,

books in every direction but the right – the table – but no, I cannot find terms to describe it, though the counterpart might be seen, perhaps, not one hundred miles from the study of the justly-famed and beautiful rectory of Bremhill. Once, when we were staying at Trowbridge, in his absence for a few days at Bath, my eldest girl thought she should surprise and please him by putting every book in perfect order, making the best bound the most prominent; but, on his return, thanking her for her good intention, he replaced every volume in its former state; 'for,' said he, 'my dear, grandpapa understands his own confusion better than your order and neatness.'[2]

The habit of bookishness was one which Caroline was keen to acquire and Crabbe to encourage. 'You and I both love reading,' he wrote to her some years later,

and it is well for me that I do; but at your time reading is but one employment, whereas with me it is almost all. And yet I often ask myself, at the end of my volumes, – Well! what am I the wiser, what the better, for this? Reading for amusement only, and, as it is said, merely to kill time, is not the satisfaction of a reasonable being. At your age, my dear Caroline, I read every book which I could procure. Now, I should wish to procure only such as are worth reading; but I confess I am frequently disappointed.[3]

Another Caroline inspired more complicated feelings in Crabbe. He had met King George IV when he was Prince of Wales, at Drury Lane as long ago as 1783; and again, when he was Prince Regent, at Belvoir Castle in 1814. Crabbe as a clergyman could hardly fail to have strong moral misgivings about the new king, yet as a poet he had done rather well out of the Regency which had, moreover, created the London cultural and social ambience he had come so much to enjoy: the paradox of 'Prinny', as Terence Bareham says, was that 'his catastrophic irresponsibility, his open flouting of moral conventions and his brash opportunism gave a savour to the spirit of the age'.[4] George IV's difficulties with his estranged and intransigent wife, Caroline of Brunswick, fiercely divided loyalties in the country: the people of Trowbridge, who seemed to have acquired a taste for annual displays of civic disorder, were strong in her support following the abandonment of the Bill of Pains and Penalties against her in 1820. 'The town was illuminated on her acquittal,' writes Kenneth Rogers, 'and a week later a copy of the *Courier* newspaper was publicly burnt in the market-place before 4,000 spectators because of the way in which the illuminations had been misreported.'[5] Crabbe, wearied by the disturbances of two elections, was greatly distressed by this renewed threat to his comfort and security: when he wrote to Thomas Phillips on 21 November, it was 'amid the roar of cannon and that of a tumultuous populace assembled to show their joy and to demand shows of the same kind from those who reside among them'. Being disinclined to participate in this spectacle, he feared for his own safety: he was unsure 'of having a room to retire to on the morrow, with a whole window in it' since 'there is no setting bounds to the exertions of a crowd, in a place like this, when once they entertain the idea, be it right or wrong, that you are not of their opinion'.[6] Although both he and his windows escaped unscathed, he thought it prudent to write to the Duke of Rutland, dissociating himself from 'the sentiments of and conduct of a noisy multitude': 'Your Grace will I trust pardon me this avowal of my opinions, as it would much distress me to be supposed an advocate for this popular frenzy or neutral in a cause of such moral as well as political importance.'[7] It was a sensible, politic letter; but he was perhaps rather more 'neutral', or at least divided, in his feelings that he could easily admit to his patron.

2

The biographer son[8] says that his father was fond of quoting old Adam's words from *As You Like It*:

> Though I look old, yet I am strong and lusty;
> For in my youth I never did apply
> Hot and rebellious liquors in my blood,
> Nor did not with unbashful forehead woo
> The means of weakness and debility.
> Therefore my age is like a lusty winter,
> Frosty but kindly. [II.iii.47–53]

For most of the 1820s, he was as good as his resolve, continuing to travel whenever his long-suffering son and curate could spare him. In March 1820, he was in London, to meet for the first time in person a long-standing and newly knighted friend: 'I went to Town for eight days, almost my sole business being to meet Mr – or as we now write Sir Walter Scott,' he told Elizabeth Charter. 'I had heard so much of him and accurately that he was the very man whom I expected to see, plain, very friendly and very agreeable.'9 This encounter had taken place at John Murray's in Albermarle Street, and Crabbe could not resist adding that he had found convenient lodgings within two minutes' walk, in Brewer Street, where 'they have four little pretty girls for me to play with when I am childish, which occurs very frequently'. Scott invited him to visit Edinburgh, a trip Crabbe would have cheerfully undertaken almost immediately; but John and Anna, following the death of their first child, were taking an extended holiday away from Trowbridge, and his own health was troublesome. The next summer, he was once more unwell – 'my face is yet at times painful and every kind of exertion soon wearies me' – and in any case he found himself detained in Trowbridge by the preparations for George IV's Coronation: 'in collecting money, planning modes of rejoicing, in ordering processions and in writing a sermon, this latter falls to me exclusively and I have made my head ache'.10 Consequently, it was the summer of 1822 before he could make his grand excursion to Scotland and thus leave England for the first time in his life.

In June he set off for London, where he stayed at his favourite lodgings in Brewer Street: he visited the exhibitions at the British Institution and the Royal Academy; breakfasted with Francis Chantrey (who was sketching him for a bust) and Samuel Rogers (at whose house he met Washington Irving); dined with John Murray, with whom he discussed 'four or five little stories' on which he was working; and was 'much at Hampstead' with the Hoares. He was as yet undecided whether he should go on to Suffolk or to Scotland: he resolved to write to Sir Walter Scott and 'prepare for a journey northward for that it will be in both cases'.11 This he did on 10 July, assuring his potential host that he intended to be 'modest in my expectations': 'Let me see you, if so it may be, for one day in any place to which I can be conveyed and I will content myself with gazing on your wonders and works at Edinborough and return a greater man by all the information I can retain; and perhaps an happier by all the pleasures I have enjoyed.'12 Writing a formal letter could still bring on a fit of this archaic overelaboration in Crabbe, and Scott's cautious reply suggests that he wondered whether the old man was sinking into his dotage. He would be delighted to welcome Crabbe to Abbotsford – indeed, he had hoped to do so two years earlier – although he would have to be in Edinburgh for the King's proposed visit, on or around 12 August; 'but I fancy you will avoid that period of tumult and bustle, though if your health permitted it would be a curious sight to see.' He was 'anxious about your travelling so far alone' and wished Crabbe would bring one of his sons with him. And he had a clear recommendation to offer about the most comfortable way for his elderly guest to travel:

> If you do not fear the sea the steamboat brings you close in to Edin. in sixty hours certain with as much ease as if you were in an easy chair. At Edin. you are about 35 miles from Abbotsford with all convenience of public coaches – one called the Blucher starts at eight and lands you within a mile of us at three where when we hear of your motions the carriage will meet you. If on the contrary you come by land you will do best to take us on your road to Edinbrough coming down the western great Carlisle road and turning off at Selkirk which is four miles to the west of us.[13]

Crabbe, of course, took none of this advice. He arranged his schedule exactly to coincide with the King's. He did not bring one of his sons, but instead engaged a former servant of Samuel Hoare's to accompany him, 'though not without some question whether a man who has served a banker in Lombard Street will consider a maker of sermons or teller of tales, a priest or an author worthy his services'. This servant he sent to enquire 'for the coach that goes to Edinborough by the great Carlisle Road'; the Hoares, meanwhile, advised him to rest at Grantham or Newark, but he had taken a fancy to York, after which he would 'rest no more till I arrive at the house of my friend'.[14] He was as obstinate and as independent as ever.

But Crabbe was never to see Abbotsford. By the time he reached Scotland, on 5 August, Sir Walter and his family were already in residence at Castle Street, Edinburgh, in readiness for the royal visit, and Crabbe found himself plunged into that 'tumult and bustle' to which his host (who, of course, had not read the London journal of 1817) wrongly thought him unaccustomed. Nevertheless, he did not entirely warm to Edinburgh: 'singular' is the cautious word that recurs in his descriptions of it, and he evidently found the Scots strange, noting 'the singularity of appearance and manners – the peculiarities of men, all gentlemen, but remote from our society – leaders of clans – joyous company'.[15] Partly as a matter of strategy, he seems to have decided to affect naïvety whenever it suited him, but John Gibson Lockhart – Scott's son-in-law, who left the most attractive account of the visit – had his measure when he wrote of 'his *apparent* simplicity of look and manners'. Lockhart's version of Crabbe's first encounter with Scottish culture was probably embellished for the biographer son's benefit, but it is certainly true to his father's spirit:

> Mr Crabbe had, I presume, read very little about Scotland before that excursion. It appeared to me that he confounded the Inchcolm of the Firth of Forth with the Icolmkill of the Hebrides; but John Kemble, I have heard, did the same. I believe, he really never had known, until then, that a language radically distinct from the English, was still actually spoken within the island. And this recalls a scene of high merriment which occurred the very morning after his arrival. When he came down into the breakfast parlour, Sir Walter had not yet appeared there; and Mr Crabbe had before him two or three portly personages all in the full Highland garb. These gentlemen, arrayed in a costume so novel, were talking in a language which he did not understand; so he never doubted that they were foreigners. The Celts, on their part, conceived Mr Crabbe, dressed as he was in rather an old-fashioned style of clerical propriety, with buckles in his shoes, for instance, to be some learned abbé, who had come on a pilgrimage to the shrine of Waverley; and the result was, that when, a little afterwards, Sir Walter and his family entered the room, they found your father and these worthy lairds hammering away, with pain and labour, to make themselves mutually understood in most execrable French. Great was the relief, and potent the laughter, when the host interrupted their colloquy with his plain English 'Good-morning.'[16]

While Crabbe evidently found his mask of innocent surprise excellent cover for his favourite occupation of quiet observation, it also made it difficult for others to know whether he was actually enjoying himself. 'All is, as you may suppose, bustle and a continual accession of strangers,' he wrote to his younger son on 9 August. 'The Highland Chieftain and his Officers and followers make a respectable but singular appearance.'[17] A week later, he professed to be no less amazed: 'The Highland Chiefs come hither and some of their followers who speak no language except Galic exhibited yesterday specimens of the custom and manner of the Highlands.'[18] It was a good ruse. 'He is such a sly hound,' wrote Scott, 'that I never could find out whether he was pleased or no but astonished he certainly was.'[19]

Crabbe found much to interest him but, as Lockhart discovered, he was far from being a typical tourist. When Lockhart took him to Salisbury Craigs, to admire the view, 'he appeared to be more interested with the stratification of the rocks about us'; unimpressed by Edinburgh's New Town, he instead liked to ramble 'after nightfall by himself, among some of the obscurest wynds and closes', to the alarm of his host, who had him discreetly followed by a caddie; and 'when the old dame who showed us Darnley's armour and boots complained of the impudence, as she called it, of a preceding visitor, who had discovered these articles to be relics of a much later age, your father warmly entered into her feelings; and said, as we came away, "this pedantic puppyism was *inhumane*"'.[20] At such moments, imaginative truth interested him more than historical verity. In the journal which he kept for the amusement of Sarah Hoare, and which has therefore a very different tone from the journal he kept for his own record in London, exactly the same note appears:

> I went to the palace of Holyrood House, and was much interested; –
> the rooms, indeed, did not affect me, – the old tapestry was such as
> I had seen before, and I did not much care about the leather chairs,
> with three legs each, nor the furniture, except in one room – that
> where Queen Mary slept. The bed has a canopy very rich, but time-
> stained. We went into the little room where the Queen and Rizzio
> sat, when his murderers broke in and cut him down as he struggled
> to escape: they show certain stains on the floor; and I see no reason
> why you should not believe them made by his blood, if you can.[21]

For Sarah Hoare, he obligingly listed some of the Scots nobility he had met, respectfully giving them their correct form with the same care he had shown in using the Quaker form of dates to Mary Leadbeater: 'There were, also, Lord Errol, and the Macleod, and the Frazer, and the Gordon, and the Ferguson; and I conversed at dinner with Lady Glengarry, and did almost believe myself a harper, or bard, rather – for harp I cannot strike – and Sir Walter was the life and soul of the whole.'[22] When he had first contemplated this expedition, he had asked Scott 'whether a journey into Scotland would be of benefit to me in a disease which then oppressed me', and it sounds very much as if he had been prescribed the national medicine: he must have been as unfamiliar with malt whisky as with every other aspect of Scottish culture. Evidently it did the trick: 'It was a splendid festivity, and I felt I know not how much younger.' When the King arrived on 15 August, Crabbe was presented to him and astounded to find himself instantly remembered; to mark the occasion he composed a forty-line poem, 'Lines on His Majesty's Visit to Scotland', which is conventionally respectful though hardly inspired:

> O give me to breathe, while this scene I describe:
>   A Monarch in Scotland I see,
> When she pours from her Highlands and Lowlands each tribe,
>   Who are loyal, and happy, and free.

However, he would have liked to mix with Scottish literary society, in a leisurely way, and for this he had chosen precisely the wrong moment. He met Francis Jeffrey, the editor of the *Edinburgh Review* and his most supportive critic over the years, and William Blackwood, whose eponymous *Edinburgh Magazine* had also been kind to him. A dinner at Lockhart's with 'three of the supposed writers or symposiasts of the inimitable *Noctes Ambrosianae*; viz. his host himself, the far-famed Professor [John] Wilson [Christopher North], whom he termed "that extraordinary man" and the honest Shepherd of Ettrick [James Hogg]' was thought by the biographer son to have been 'an evening cheaply purchased by a journey from Trowbridge',[23] but his father might not have gone quite so far. For him, 'the pleasure of half an hour's confidential conversation with Sir Walter' towards the end of an evening was the greatest reward of his journey to Edinburgh. On retiring to bed, he would insist on having a lamp and writing materials at his bedside: 'Dear Lady,' he told Lady Scott, 'I should have lost many a good hit, had I not set down, at once, things that occurred to me in my dreams.'[24] He was working both on relatively straightforward tales for Murray's projected further volume of tales and on a different, more difficult long poem which he provisionally called 'Misery'.

But he was homesick in a way that he never had been in England. 'Do pray consider my distance and let me hear from you once at least before I leave Edinborough,' he implored his negligent younger son, who was hopeless at writing letters. 'Do consider where I am.'[25] He looked forward to being on his way home: 'though I am not desperately weary, I begin to think of a resting place which however Beccles may be.'[26] Beccles it was. 'From Scotland,' he later told Elizabeth Charter, 'I returned by way of Berwick and reached the house of a sister [in law] in Suffolk about two months after my departure from home and three before my return to the quiet and solitary room in which I reign sovereign and where I am now giving this account to my friend in Taunton.'[27] His friend in Taunton had been feeling neglected, and with some justification; for his most intimate confidante was now in Hampstead.

3

The poem which Crabbe called 'Misery' or his 'Misery verses', and which was to become 'The Voluntary Insane', is in every respect a curiosity. He seems to have begun it, as Felix Pryor[28] has argued, before March 1822 and to have completed it by 25 November, when he wrote to Mary Leadbeater that among the 'three or four pieces of versification' which he considered publishing was 'one more essay at the description of a kind of insanity or hallucination'.[29] But he did not publish it: instead, he copied it into a notebook for Sarah Hoare, which is where it remained until her great-great-great-great-nephew Felix Pryor stumbled upon it in December 1989. The poem is, at just over 1,200 lines, longer than most of Crabbe's tales; its eight-line tetrametric stanzas are rhymed ababcdcd and partly indented (though at lines 2, 4, 5 and 7, rather than alternately), so it has a formal kinship with poems such as 'Hester', 'Sir Eustace Grey' and 'The World of Dreams'. This sets it apart from the body of Crabbe's tales, which are, as Tennyson pointed out, characterised by 'a tramp, tramp, tramp, a merciless sledge-hammer thud'.[30] 'The Voluntary Insane' is certainly merciless, but the sledgehammer is largely spared.

The subject is a young woman, Matilda, who is left in charge of her uncle's illegitimate and sickly infant son; partly to spare the child further suffering though mainly to protect her own inheritance, she suffocates the boy. Rushing 'maddened from the scene', she meets the father and at once realises what she must do:

> My part was taken. I must seem
>   To be as one whose troubled breast,
> Like those who labour in a dream,
>   Is by insane sad thoughts possessed:
>   I will not answer – I am pressed
> By grief too heavy – so I took
>   His hand and held it, and he guessed
> The evil that my action spoke! [1057–64]

That, however, is precisely what he has failed to guess, believing Matilda to be distraught because she was alone with the child when he died: 'Ah! my poor girl, wert thou alone / When Death this sudden visit paid?' To her astonishment no one, neither the neighbours nor 'the law', for a moment suspects her of foul play: 'So have I acted; from that hour, / Appearing never to regain / My former self . . .' But this strategy, as Hamlet discovered, is fraught with danger. To be compelled to act madness may be even worse than being mad; it may, in fact, be simply another form of insanity. It is a question which Crabbe lobs back at the reader: 'Now judge you; is she or not insane?' Matilda is capable of acting sanely enough in most contexts – she is 'in just one thought astray, / Erring in just that single way' – but she is tormented by guilt which only can find its release in her deathbed confession of the truth to a priest.

The shape of this tale – the crime, the guilt, the insanity and the deathbed release – is very like that of 'Peter Grimes'. Indeed, there are moments when Matilda sounds exactly like Grimes's spiritual twin:

> She has her places where she goes
>   To set her struggling sorrows free –
> They seem congenial to her woes:
>   She there beholds the restless sea,
>   The marshy ditch, the one bare tree
> With bending boughs, the bleak broad fen –

> And these with her sad mind agree,
> And soothe her when she flies from men. [145–52]

Nevertheless, to be Grimes's spiritual twin at a moment like that is also to be Crabbe's. We may be reasonably confident that this exemplary man never murdered an infant, yet he carries through his life and work an extraordinarily inward understanding of guilt: obviously, the deaths of his wife and of so many of his children had affected him, but it seems more deeply rooted than that – perhaps that passage about the declining day in 'Infancy – A Fragment' is the key to Crabbe after all. Nor should we be too gloomy on his behalf about this: it made him the man he was. Philip Larkin once said that negation was to him as daffodils were to Wordsworth; and, we might add, as inner guilt was to Crabbe.

'The Voluntary Insane' is not, as Felix Pryor claims, Crabbe's masterpiece, but it is a fine poem nevertheless. Why, then, did it not appear either in his lifetime or in the *Posthumous Tales*? The obvious reason is that the conjunction of infant mortality and subsequent insanity was too close to his own experience; there remains the strong possibility that Sarah felt herself responsible for the death of at least one of her children, and that this triggered her mental decline. There was also, of course, a straightforward commercial explanation for the non-appearance of this or any other further poems in book form before Crabbe's death: had *Tales of the Hall* proved financially successful, Murray might have coaxed his author into compiling a further volume along the lines of *Poems* (1807) – the kind of collection which, by including some pieces which were not tales in heroic couplets, could have rekindled and extended Crabbe's reputation. But that was not to be. Two more recent domestic considerations may also have played a part in Crabbe's suppression of 'The Voluntary Insane': John and Anna had suffered the loss of their first child and the name he had rather surprisingly used in the poem, Matilda, was also the middle name of Caroline, his favourite grandchild. 'The Voluntary Insane' was a poem he needed to write and had to hide.

He was, in fact, writing as prolifically as ever during the early 1820s. Drafts of 'The Deserted Family' and of 'The Farewell and Return' from *Posthumous Tales* are dated 'Highgate 16 June 1822' and 'Hampstead July 24 1822' respectively, while 'Joseph and Jesse', first published in *New Poems by George*

Crabbe, is to be found in the same notebook.[31] The notebook containing 'The Voluntary Insane', which Crabbe 'Copied for Miss Hoare 1824', also includes 'Sir Denys Banger', 'The Irish Lovers' and 'The Madman's Dream', as well as 'a dozen or so dried plants pressed between its leaves, including several grasses (of which the son remarks: "In botany, grasses, the most useful, but the least ornamental, were his favourites")'.[32] A further notebook, inscribed 'Flowers, &c. FOR M. HOARE', where 'M.' evidently stands for 'Miss', includes 'The Flowers' and two incomplete poems, 'Where am I now?' and 'In a neat cottage', the latter dated 'Bath, Feb. 1822'.[33] This poem is interesting, as Arthur Pollard remarks, as 'the only example of Crabbe's blank verse that I know', although 'fragmentary and lacking in finish'.[34] Howard Mills liked it well enough to include it, with some editorial tidying, in his selection of 1967, from which I quote the opening lines:

> In a neat cottage hid from public view,
> Within a valley bounded by a wood,
> Near to the coast, but distant from a town,
> With the kind sister of a mother dead
> Dwelt a fair damsel named Elizabeth.

We might leap to identify a 'damsel named Elizabeth' who shared a cottage near Taunton with her sister, but Crabbe is up to his old trick of using an actual name and situation to introduce an unrelated tale. The poem is strangely unfocused, although when we reach the storm in which 'the river and the ocean met' and meet 'a rude amphibious crew' (near relatives, surely, of the 'wild amphibious race' in *The Village*) we seem to lurch back forty years. The versification is, even by Crabbe's standards, so rough that he may have been experimenting with a blank verse first draft which he intended later to rewrite in rhyming couplets.

4

On his return to Trowbridge from Edinburgh, via Beccles and London, Crabbe found a letter from the Duke of Rutland inviting him to Belvoir. This was a journey which might have been sensibly combined with the excursion he had just completed but now, as winter drew on and Christmas approached, it was the last thing he wanted. Once more, he declined, pleading illness and exhaustion, 'pain and the dread of cold'. He was feeling his age, after an eventful summer and autumn, and suffering badly from his *tic douloureux,* which he had come (perhaps disingenuously) to associate especially with the exertions of his parish duties when his son was absent, as he was in the early months of 1823. 'Long experience has made me in a great measure acquainted with the nature of my disorder and the methods of relief: one of the most efficacious would be an absence from these perpetual calls upon my attention,' he told Elizabeth Charter,[35] who had sent him, as people will, a bad poem by a friend of hers to read and may have detected a tart ambiguity in his grumble about the calls on his attention. Later that year, however, he managed his annual visit to the Hoares at Cromer, followed by familial calls in Suffolk; at Aldeburgh in October, he felt that the time had come for some valedictory lines on a place he might never see again. It had, as White's 1844 *Suffolk* makes clear, 'been totally changed' in the early years of the nineteenth century: the sandy lanes of Crabbe's childhood had been replaced by 'excellent turnpike roads', and 'instead of the clay-built cottages, which gave the place a mean and squalid appearance, are now seen neat and comfortable dwellings, and several large and handsome mansions, which are the occasional retreat of persons of rank and fortune'.[36] Crabbe gives these developments his wry blessing:

> Thus once again, my native place, I come
> Thee to salute – my earliest, latest home:
> Much are we alter'd both, but I behold
> In thee a youth renew'd – whilst I am old.
> The works of man from dying we may save,
> But man himself moves onward to the grave.

He is remembering Sir Walter Ralegh's 'What is our Life?': 'Thus march we playing to our latest rest – / Only we die in earnest, that's no jest.'

Such intimations of mortality were not wholly without reason. Going on to visit his sister-in-law, he 'was ill at Beccles and was in pain daily: I took medicine and had relief but no cure.' After this, at Hampstead, he was in such severe pain that the Hoares insisted that he should consult the leading specialist, 'famed for his success in this disease', Robert Kerrison of

Burlington Street; Lord Carlisle had endured *tic douloureux* for twenty-one years before Kerrison cured him, although Crabbe conceded that 'a Lord's cure is no more than another man's'. Back at home at Trowbridge, he sent the biographer son a typical patient's account of his treatment, one which promises to spare all the details and then provides them nevertheless:

> I liked my physician, not because he would take no fees, but because he was interested, at least he appeared so: he saw me three times and was very particular. He prescribed and I am and have been for these 28 days under his care. He directs my diet. I will not weary you with particulars. I take no wine, but he allows me a little brandy and as much water as I can desire. He orders chicken which I like well or boiled mutton which I like indifferently and he permits some fish occasionally. Once in four days I take a draught that confines me to my room and the other three, are given large doses of bark, strong and bitter. Such is the way I proceed in. I am better certainly but such quantity of bark keeps one in a state of disorder and I am mortified to feel that I can yet take no duty upon me.[37]

He was variously, and sometimes simultaneously, prescribed 'bark', or quinine, 'extract of hemlock' and 'blue pills' of steel, all of which he tried with a degree of amused scepticism appropriate to one who had himself been a physician of sorts. 'Steel applied in one way will no doubt cure any pain,' he told Francis Chantrey, 'and I am not without hope that it will be efficacious when taken in my way.'[38] With his diet, he behaved with his usual agreeable obstinacy. At first, he was inclined to make much of his heroic abstinence: 'I tried many things, but not till I saw Dr Kerrison did I attend to my diet; by his advice I left off wine and eat very sparingly of meat, in fact abstinence is I verily believe a relief in all complaints and a cure in many.'[39] But in the end, while persuading himself that he was abiding faithfully by his diet, he contrived to modify it out of existence: 'Mutton and chicken . . . are the prescribed meats, yet we take the liberty of substituting veal and game when we get them and that is not unfrequently.'[40] He seems cheerfully oblivious to the fact that taking liberties was exactly what he was not meant to do.

Most of his expeditions were now either confined to places within easy reach of Trowbridge – to the Marquis of Bath's at Longleat (where he dined in August 1824), to Bath itself, to Bowles's rectory at Bremhill and, of course, to his son's parsonage at Pucklechurch – or focused on the Hoares at Hampstead and his family connections in Suffolk. 'I rhyme at Hampstead with a great deal of facility,' he wrote in June 1825, 'for nothing interrupts me but kind calls to something pleasant.'[41] Although Samuel Hoare died a month later, Sarah and her stepmother – sisterly companions who both lived until 1856 – continued the Heath House tradition of hospitality to writers, artists and intellectuals, and Crabbe's son wryly remarks that 'the death of the head of that family . . . rather increased than diminished his attachment for its other members'.[42] He now liked to regard his visits to the Hoares as primarily domestic in character and took far less pleasure in the socialising which he had once so much enjoyed, as a letter to his son at Pucklechurch in the summer of 1828 makes clear:

> I have seen many things and many people: have met Mr Southey and Mr Wordsworth; have been some days with Mr Rogers and at last have been at the Athenaeum, but not at the Royal Institution, which however I purpose to visit: I have my home with my friends here and exchange it with reluctance for any other. If I add that I have gone up the Thames in a steam-boat to Richmond and seen the picture galleries and some other exhibitions, I have related all my gratifications of this kind: not only is my chief pleasure here, but in other places I am not satisfied . . .[43]

Wordsworth later told the biographer son, 'my opportunities of seeing your excellent father were rare, and I was never in correspondence with him. Some three or four times I have met him at Mr Hoare's on Hampstead Heath, and once or twice at Mr Rogers's, but upon none of these occasions was I fortunate enough to have any private or particular conversation with him.'[44] The starchy reserve of that letter is partly explained by its occasion – it was written in 1834, after Crabbe's death – yet it seems likely that neither poet would have much enjoyed 'private or particular conversation' with the other: they were both too similar and too awkwardly different to have got on. Nor, unfortunately, is there any evidence that Crabbe met Coleridge, who was based relatively nearby in Highgate, during his visits to the Hoares.

Both enjoyable and melancholic duties took him to Aldeburgh. He agreed to sponsor his old friend John Wilson Croker – co-founder of the *Quarterly Review* and of the Athenaeum, of which Crabbe became an early member – as Tory candidate in the election of 1826, in an apparently effortless instance of personal regard taking precedence over party allegiance. Compared with the excitements of elections in Trowbridge, it was a tranquil affair: 'Some witty gentleman pasted up a paper "The Election: a Farce by Lord Hertford &c" but the sailors did not understand it and nobody seemed to give it notice. It is not the place for squibs.'[45] But he had also been drawn there by the death of his brother-in-law Thomas Sparkes, and he was much depressed by the resulting familial turmoil: 'There will be trouble at Aldborough if everyone does not give up their own wills and fancies in some degree for the general comfort.' When he eventually returned home, he felt 'like a man arrived in port and faring richly after a voyage of trouble'. His sister, Mary Sparkes, died the following year.

The somewhat accident-prone propensity of Crabbe's youth resurfaced in his old age. In September 1824, a pleasant expedition to Swansea with the Waldrons had a most unfortunate conclusion, as he explained with stoical good humour to the biographer son:

> I went on Thursday the 9th inst. with J. Waldron and his sister to Clifton and the next day in the steam boat to Swansea, where we stayed till Wednesday last: I wished to return by the same way that I went, but was too easily persuaded to sail over to Ilfracomb in a little dancing packet; the wind unfavourable and the sea rough. We were nine hours sailing 24 miles (or 28?) and I was grievously affected, so that I do not believe I have yet recovered from the painful sensation of that frequent and ineffectual sickness, for when I was sick at first, I found no great evil in that effect, but when I became exhausted and yet sick, it was so severe that I do not mean to try it again; or the motive must be strong indeed.[46]

It is a nautical version of the kind of reckless adventure that Cobbett allows himself to be talked into in *Rural Rides*: the two men share a spirit of undefeated resilience, even when old enough to know better. Even six years later, in September 1830, he was still able to deal lightly with 'a rather alarming incident' which occurred on a visit to Hastings:

I had been out of the coach a very short time, while other passengers were leaving it on their arrival at their places; and, on getting into the coach again, and close beside it, a gig, with two men in it, came on as fast as it could drive, which I neither saw nor heard, till I felt the shaft against my side. I fell, of course, and the wheel went over one foot and one arm. Twenty people were ready to assist a stranger, who in a few minutes was sensible that the alarm was all the injury. Benjamin was ready, and my friends took care that I should have all the indulgence that even a man frightened could require. Happily I found them well, and we are all this morning going to one of the churches, where I hope I shall remember that many persons, under like circumstances, have never survived to relate their adventure.[47]

Perhaps understandably, he reported a week later that his impression of Hastings was 'not very favourable': 'I prefer Lyme, I prefer Cromer, I prefer Sidmouth and Dawlish.'[48] Nevertheless, he added next day that he had done 'injustice to Hastings: there was sand this morning, wet and wavering in ridges indeed, but still sand at low water, far as I could throw a stone'.[49] His recovery to stone-throwing fitness so soon after his foot and arm (presumably his *other* arm) had been run over is as remarkable as it is characteristic. 'The beach at Hastings', he conceded, was 'not unlike that at Aldborough'. It was his last visit to the sea.

5

Crabbe contemplated his own old age in a spirit of calm and grateful acceptance: 'I feel the pleasant cloud of oblivion, weakness and alienation from the things around me gradually – I would not wish it to be rapidly – increasing: it is not disgust nor dislike to the world we live in, nor by any means is it indifference, but assuredly there comes on in age an abstraction of self from those about us.'[50] He found his thoughts turning 'to the past or to the future' rather than to 'things immediately present'. Enquiring about the apple blossom in the garden at Pucklechurch, after a late frost in May 1826, he abruptly adds: 'I cease to feel an interest of the kind.'[51] Sometimes his memory let him down. At the foundation banquet for the Literary Institution in January 1825, he halted in mid-speech and simply confessed that he had quite forgotten what he had intended to say. Bowles, who was sitting next to him, recalled: 'He was received with universal acclamation and the simplicity and candour of his manner felt by every one in the room.'[52] Although he enjoyed visiting his friends, he found the arrangements and disarrangements of travel increasingly irksome: 'I do not love the preparation for going away: the collecting of articles wanted, the brushing up of portmanteaus, the saying good-bye to one's neighbours, and taking leave of the folk westwards [the Waldrons].'[53] Moreover, these articles and portmanteaus could all too easily be forgotten at the end of a visit. 'You will not wonder that I forgot something,' he wrote to Sarah Hoare, having just left Hampstead; 'my wonder is that I remember anything.'[54] To his elder son, he ruefully confessed: 'I am rather surprised and hurt at my loss of memory.'[55]

In fact, his engagement with the world around him – and, for that matter, his memory – remained unusually sharp. In 1825, when he was seventy-one, he was appointed a magistrate at Trowbridge, an office he discharged both diligently and critically, and he continued to officiate as rector until a fortnight before his death. Even his final holiday, when he joined the Hoares at Clifton in October 1831, turned into an unexpected and curiously appropriate adventure. Among the most outspoken opponents of the Reform Bill, which was passed by the Commons on 21 September but defeated in the Lords on 7 October, were Sir Charles Wetherell, who led the opposition in the Commons, and Robert Gray, Bishop of Bristol, who voted against the bill in the Lords. 'Sir Charles Wetherell, to be sure, is not popular, nor is the Bishop,' wrote Crabbe; 'but I trust that both will be safe from violence – abuse they will not mind.'[56] However, when Wetherell, despite warnings of civil disorder, insisted upon visiting the city as Recorder to open the assizes on Monday 31 October, 'riots broke out which resulted in nearly a hundred dead, the destruction of the Mansion-house, Bishop's Palace, Customs House, Bridewell, New Gaol, Gloucester County Prison, and the Excise Office'.[57] Crabbe, who had been looking forward to a restful time with his friends, staying in 'one of the most beautiful as well as comfortable rooms you could desire' with a view of 'the Avon and its wooded and rocky bounds', suddenly found himself once again at the scene of a riot and its aftermath, as he told the biographer son:

Bristol, I suppose, never, in the most turbulent times of old, witnessed such outrage. Queen's Square is but half standing; half is smoking ruin. As you may be apprehensive for my safety, it is right to let you know that my friends and I are undisturbed, except by our fears for the progress of this mob-government, which is already somewhat broken into parties, who wander stupidly about, or sleep wherever they fall wearied with their work and their indulgence. The military are now in considerable force, and many men are sworn in as constables: many volunteers are met in Clifton church-yard, with white round one arm, to distinguish them; some with guns, and the rest with bludgeons. The Mayor's house has been destroyed, – the Bishop's palace plundered, but whether burnt or not I do not know. This morning, a party of soldiers attacked the crowd in the Square; some lives were lost, and the mob dispersed, whether to meet again is doubtful. It has been a dreadful time, but we may reasonably hope it is now over. People are frightened certainly – and no wonder, for it is evident these poor wretches would plunder to the extent of their power. Attempts were made to burn the cathedral, but failed. Many lives were lost. To attempt any other subject now would be fruitless. We can think, speak, and write only of our fears, hopes, or troubles. I would have gone to Bristol today, but Mrs Hoare was unwilling that I should. She thought, and perhaps rightly, that clergymen were marked objects. I therefore only went about half way, and of course could learn but little. All now is quiet and well.[58]

Crabbe's inquisitive fearlessness, which had so often guided him – from his cheeky exploration of Newgate after the Gordon Riots in 1780 to his nocturnal wanderings among the alleys of Edinburgh in 1822 – remained undiminished, and only Mrs Hoare's prudent restraint prevented him from behaving exactly as he had over fifty years earlier.

Buoyed up rather than exhausted by all this excitement, he left the Hoares in early November to go to Pucklechurch; the following Sunday, he preached in a 'firm and loud' voice at both of his son's churches. 'I will venture a good sum that you will be assisting me ten years hence,' said the son cheerfully. 'Ten weeks' was Crabbe's prescient reply.[59] He returned to Trowbridge in good health before the end of November, and at the start of the new year was suffering from nothing worse than 'lassitude and stupidity'. 'I am a poor old man and foolish; but happily I have no daughter who vexes me,' he wrote.[60] He knew he was fortunate in his sons, even though he liked to complain about the hot-tempered and unbookish John, who was 'one of the vilest of correspondents'; nevertheless, he assured George, 'he is a *right good fellow and never father more* rejoiced in his sons than your truly affectionate Geo Crabbe'.[61]

On 29 January 1832, the biographer son 'received a letter from my brother, stating that [their father] had caught a sharp cold, accompanied with oppression in the chest and pain in the forehead, for which he had been bled.' He expected to receive some account of the patient's improvement the following day, but instead 'a chaise drove to the door, which my brother had sent me to save time. In fact, all hope of recovery was already over.'[62] Crabbe became feverish and delirious, in his lucid moments acutely aware, in his gruffly self-deprecating way, of the nuisance he was causing: 'What a trouble I am to them all!' he said, when told of the endless stream of enquiries and presents from his friends, and he instructed his sons to 'make an entertainment' to thank them all. During the long night of 2 February, the brothers took turns at their father's bedside: George, his elder son and future biographer, heard him distinctly say, 'All is well at last!' His younger son, John, was with him when George Crabbe died at seven o'clock on the morning of 3 February 1832.

Epilogue:
The River and the Sea

I

It was Hazlitt, of course, who started the trouble: his attack on Crabbe in *The Spirit of the Age*, published anonymously in 1825, is as brilliant as it is misguided. But his target was characteristically unflustered:

> I am told that I or my verses, or perhaps both, have abuse in a book of Mr Colburn's publishing, called 'The Spirit of the Times'. I believe I felt something indignant: but my engraved seal dropped out of the socket and was lost, and I perceived this vexed me much more than the 'spirit' of Mr Hazlitt.[1]

Hazlitt's account of Crabbe is wrong on both counts, the critical and the biographical. For his description of 'a repulsive writer' and 'a sickly, a querulous, a uniformly dissatisfied poet' simply will not tally with the words on the page; while his notion of 'a country clergyman . . . in a small curacy', excluded from the 'learned colleges and halls, where he passed his youth' is comically at odds with the facts of Crabbe's actual life.[2] Nevertheless, Hazlitt articulated something more powerful than accuracy or truth: for, long before his death, Crabbe had become not merely unfashionable but inimical to the spirit of his age.

Over a century later, F. R. Leavis surprisingly repeated the same judgement. Crabbe, he wrote, 'was hardly at the fine point of consciousness in his time. His sensibility belongs to an order that those who were most alive to the age – who had the most sensitive antennae – had ceased to find sympathetic.'[3] That, we might retort on Crabbe's behalf, all depends on where you are standing: his concerns may not have always coincided with those of the metropolitan intelligentsia, but there was nothing wrong with his antennae when it came to the world in which he actually lived. In any case, the idea that a poet must be 'alive to the age' is a highly questionable one: mightn't it be arguable that the most interesting writers are likely to go against the grain of their times, to be awkward individuals rather than subscribers to cultural fashion? Crabbe's reputation has perversely suffered from the fact that he was the wrong kind of rebel. The image he presented to the early twentieth century is perfectly caught by Somerset Maugham in *The Moon and Sixpence*:

> Who now, for example, thinks of George Crabbe? He was a famous poet in his day, and the world recognised his genius with a unanimity which the greater complexity of modern life has rendered infrequent. He had learnt his craft at the school of Alexander Pope, and he wrote moral stories in rhymed couplets. Then came the French Revolution and the Napoleonic Wars, and the poets sang new songs. Mr Crabbe continued to write moral stories in rhymed couplets. I think he must have read the verse of these young men who were making so great a stir in the world, and I fancy he found it poor stuff. Of course, much of it was. But the odes of Keats and of Wordsworth, a poem or two by Coleridge, a few more by Shelley, discovered vast realms of spirit that none had explored before. Mr Crabbe was dead as mutton, but Mr Crabbe continued to write moral stories in rhymed couplets.[4]

Dead as mutton; and then there was that name, so unnecessarily extended from 'the sour fruit' or 'the crusty fish': 'Professional writers,' said T. H. White in *The Age of Scandal*, 'by some strange fatality, had even begun to have ridiculous names, like Crabbe, Hogg, etc.'[5] If only he had been called something more resonant: Samuel Taylor Coleridge, for example.

Yet Crabbe's influence has been immense and enduring where it matters most, in the work of subsequent writers. Clear echoes of his social realism – his interest in the unfashionable and the impoverished, his attention to local detail – are to be found in the novels of Charles Dickens, George Eliot and Thomas Hardy; while poets such as Hardy (again), Roy Fuller and Philip Larkin followed his example in forging a creative identity from an unpromising provincial background and in viewing their worlds with a dour, dryly humorous relish which careless readers may mistake for pessimism. In these rather important senses, Crabbe is at the centre rather than the margin of the English literary tradition.

2

After their father's death, Crabbe's two sons returned to Suffolk. The *Life*, on which George had begun work several years earlier, was completed before he left Pucklechurch; after extensive revision and editing by J. G. Lockhart, it appeared as part of the eight-volume collected edition published by John Murray in 1834. In the following year, George was appointed to the living of Bredfield and Pettistree, near Woodbridge, where he remained until his death in 1857; apart from the *Life*, he was the author of *An Outline of a System of Natural Theology* (1840) and *Short Conclusions from the Light of Nature* (1849). His younger brother, John, was presented to the livings of Great and Little Glemham by the widow of his father's benefactor, Dudley North; he died in Beccles in 1840. George, the younger son of George and Caroline Crabbe, married his first cousin, Emily, the younger daughter of John and Anna Crabbe, in 1851; he became Rector of Merton in Norfolk, where he died in 1883.

The poet's younger brother and last surviving sibling, Robert Crabbe, the retired glazier of Southwold, died in 1835. Charlotte Ridout died, two months before Crabbe, in 1831; but Elizabeth Charter and Maria Waldron both long outlived their intimate friend, dying in 1860 and 1872 respectively. Neither they nor Sarah Hoare ever married.

3

He seems to fade into the sea-mist and disappear before our eyes. His Trowbridge parishioners commissioned a memorial, completed in August 1833: Byron's well-known compliment is, with an inevitability which would surely have prompted a weary smile from its subject, not merely quoted but misquoted. 'As a writer, he is well described by a great contemporary as "Nature's sternest painter, yet her best."' In any case, while Byron correctly identified nature and sternness as vital ingredients, by eliding them he somehow missed the point: Crabbe, more subtle and elusive than that, escapes once again.

Although there are Crabbes to be found on just-decipherable tombstones in many an East Anglian churchyard, the physical presence of George Crabbe's houses has largely vanished too. His father's home at Slaughden was claimed by the sea; Ducking Hall was pulled down; his parsonages were demolished; the Belvoir Castle he knew was destroyed by fire. These disappearances are mostly in the nature of things and perhaps not to be mourned; but the destruction of the rectory at Trowbridge, which had remained essentially as Crabbe had left it, as recently as 1964, was an unforgivable act of vandalism in an age which should have known better. Lady Whincup's at Rendham remains, and has a blue plaque recording Crabbe's residence there, although neither a courteous knock at the door nor an equally polite letter has elicited any response from its owner: it would have been good to stand, if only for a moment or two, in a house inhabited by Crabbe.

But if Crabbe has a ghost, he smiles at the destruction of the buildings in which he once lived. 'Give me a wild, wide fen, in a foggy day,' he says; and he is almost right. Better still, as a place to meet Crabbe, is the landscape of 'Peter Grimes' and 'Infancy – A Fragment', which his father before him had surveyed, in a steely midwinter light: the bleak shingle spur that leads from Slaughden Quay to Orford Ness, between the river and the sea.

Acknowledgements

During the years in which *George Crabbe: An English Life* has undergone its slow metamorphosis from outline to first draft to second draft to finished book, I have received invaluable help from many people, some of whom (at library information desks or on the other end of phone lines) have inevitably remained anonymous. But I want to record my most grateful thanks to the following for their advice and encouragement: Nick Ash, Anthony Bardsley, Jonathan Barker, David Evans, Guy Gladwell, Claire Harman, Selina Hastings, Stephen Morgan, Peter Morrow, Rosalind Porter, Lorna Quorn, Nick Scarr, Michael Schmidt, Peter Scupham, Margaret Steward, Will Sulkin, Jenny Uglow, Robert Wells. Everyone who writes about Crabbe is indebted to the late Professor Arthur Pollard, who died while I was working on this book. My mother heroically read through a first draft which contained even more errors and omissions than the final one.

Kate Pool at The Society of Authors was impeccably helpful and efficient in dealing with contractual matters. I am once again grateful to the Authors' Foundation for financial assistance towards the research and travel expenses incurred in writing this book.

Some sections of *George Crabbe: An English Life* have previously appeared, in slightly different versions, in *PN Review* and *The Times Literary Supplement*.

Quotations from Crabbe's poems are generally based on the three volume *Poems of George Crabbe*, edited by A. W. Ward (Cambridge, 1905–7), *New Poems by George Crabbe*, edited by Arthur Pollard (Liverpool, 1960), and *The Voluntary Insane*, edited by Felix Pryor (London, 1995). In many cases, I have also consulted other editions listed in the Bibliography. Typographical conventions have been adjusted to modern usage: for example, passages of speech are indicated by quotation marks at the beginning and end rather than at the opening of every line.

Crabbe's own prefaces are usually quoted from the earliest editions: printer's errors and dropped characters have been silently corrected. Crabbe's letters and journals are sometimes haphazard in spelling and oddly punctuated; since my quotations are drawn from a wide variety of edited and unedited sources, I have regularised both spelling and punctuation where necessary, while preserving eccentricities which seem essential to Crabbe's tone. In many cases, the unmodernised texts may be found in *Selected Letters and Journals of George Crabbe*, edited by Thomas C. Faulkner with Rhonda L. Blair (Oxford, 1985). Quotations from *The Life of George Crabbe by his Son* are from the edition introduced by Edmund Blunden (London, 1947).

A word needs to be added about the three previous full-length biographies of Crabbe, all of which have been at my side during the writing of this one. The son's *Life* is, of course, the most important of the three: in places, it is incomparably evocative and (since it is out of print at the time of writing) I haven't hesitated to quote it where my own version would merely have been a dim paraphrase. But it is full of inaccuracies and, because of its date (1834), deeply reticent about the friends of Crabbe's later years. Huchon's *George Crabbe and his Times* (1907) is crammed with far more detail than I have included here; although he corrects many of the son's errors, Huchon has little feeling for the poems. He glances only retrospectively at Crabbe's correspondence with Sir Walter Scott and says nothing at all about Elizabeth Charter, thus ignoring two of the most interesting relationships in Crabbe's life. Howard Mills's description of the book as 'one of the first modern mindless card-index biography doctorates' is, alas, not unfair. Neville Blackburne's *The Restless Ocean* (1972) leans very heavily both on the son's life, which is perfectly excusable, and on Huchon's, which is not. It is an amiable book and might easily have been a useful one, except that Blackburne continually paraphrases when he should have quoted and provides no sources: the result is that, while *The Restless Ocean* is full of interesting material, one can seldom be sure about who said what or whose words are actually being used. Although I am enormously indebted to all three of these books, their peculiar shortcomings may suggest why I have felt it worthwhile to offer a fourth.

Bibliography

This brief and selective bibliography lists 1) some important editions of Crabbe's work, 2) books on Crabbe which I have consulted and/or quoted in the text, and 3) other works cited in the text. I have not included either in this bibliography or in the notes standard works – such as the novels of Jane Austen or the poems of Wordsworth – which are available in so many different editions that references to any one are unlikely to be of use.

1. Works by Crabbe

(a) First editions

Inebriety: A Poem in Three Parts (Ipswich: C. Punchard, 1775)

The Candidate: A Poetical Epistle to the Authors of the Monthly Review (London: H. Payne, 1780)

The Library (London: Dodsley, 1781)

The Village (London: Dodsley, 1783)

The Newspaper (London: Dodsley, 1785)

Poems (London: Hatchard, 1807)

The Borough (London: Hatchard, 1810)

Tales in Verse (London: Hatchard, 1812)

Tales of the Hall (London: John Murray, 1819)

The Works of the Rev. Geo. Crabbe, with the Life by his Son (8 volumes, London: John Murray, 1834)

(b) Selected modern editions

Poems by George Crabbe, edited by A. W. Ward (3 volumes, Cambridge: Cambridge University Press, 1905–7)

The Poetical Works of George Crabbe, edited by A. J. and R. M. Carlyle (London: Oxford University Press, 1914)

New Poems by George Crabbe, edited by Arthur Pollard (Liverpool: Liverpool

University Press, 1960)

Tales, 1812, and other selected poems, edited by Howard Mills (Cambridge: Cambridge University Press, 1967)

Selected Letters and Journals of George Crabbe, edited by Thomas C. Faulkner with Rhonda L. Blair (Oxford: Clarendon Press, 1985)

The Complete Poetical Works, edited by Norma Dalrymple-Champneys and Arthur Pollard (3 volumes, Oxford: Clarendon Press, 1988)

The Voluntary Insane, edited by Felix Pryor (London: Richard Cohen, 1995)

2. Books about Crabbe

The Life of George Crabbe by his Son, 1834. With an Introduction by Edmund Blunden (London: Cresset Press, 1947)

Ainger, Alfred, *Crabbe* (London: Macmillan, 1903)

Bareham, Terence, *George Crabbe* (London: Vision, 1977)

Blackburne, Neville, *The Restless Ocean* (Lavenham: Terence Dalton, 1972)

Broadley, A. M. and Walter Jerrold, *The Romance of an Elderly Poet* (London: Stanley Paul, 1913)

Evans, J. H., *The Poems of George Crabbe: A Literary and Historical Study* (London: Sheldon Press, 1933)

Haddakin, Lilian, *The Poetry of Crabbe* (London: Chatto & Windus, 1955)

Huchon, René, *George Crabbe and his Times 1754–1832* (London: John Murray, 1907)

New, Peter, *George Crabbe's Poetry* (London: Macmillan, 1976)

Pollard, Arthur (editor), *Crabbe: The Critical Heritage* (London: Routledge & Kegan Paul, 1962)

Whitehead, Frank, *George Crabbe: A Reappraisal* (Selinsgrove: Susquehanna University Press, 1995)

3. Other works cited in the text

Ackroyd, Peter, *London: The Biography* (London: Chatto & Windus, 2000)

Arnott, W. G., *Alde Estuary* (Ipswich: Norman Adlard, 1952)

Blythe, Ronald, *Talking about John Clare* (Nottingham: Trent Books, 1999)

Boswell, James, *The Life of Samuel Johnson* (1791; London: Everyman, 1992)

Brewer, John, *The Pleasures of the Imagination* (London: HarperCollins, 1997)

Carpenter, Humphrey, *Benjamin Britten* (London: Faber, 1992)

Connolly, Cyril, *Enemies of Promise* (1938; Harmondsworth: Penguin, 1961)

Cowper, William, *Poetical Works* (London: Oxford University Press, 1934)

—, *The Centenary Letters* (Manchester: Carcanet, 2000)

Croft, P. J., *Autograph Poetry in the English Language* (London: Cassell, 1973)

Forster, E. M., *Howards End* (1910; Harmondsworth: Penguin, 1941)

—, *The Prince's Tale and other uncollected writings* (London: André Deutsch, 1998

—, *Two Cheers for Democracy* (1951; Harmondsworth: Penguin, 1965)

Fuller, John, *Collected Poems* (London: Chatto & Windus, 1996)

Gittings, Robert, *Young Thomas Hardy* (1975; Harmondsworth: Penguin, 1978)

Goodwyn, E. A., *Elegance and Poverty in Bungay* (Bungay: Morrow, 1989)

—, *George Crabbe and Beccles* (n.d.)

Grosskurth, Phyllis, *Byron: The Flawed Angel* (London: Hodder & Stoughton, 1997)

Hardy, Thomas, *The Return of the Native* (1878; London: Macmillan, 1974)

Harman, Claire, *Fanny Burney* (London: HarperCollins, 2000)

Hayter, Alethea, *Opium and the Romantic Imagination* (London: Faber, 1968)

Hazlitt, William, *Lectures on the English Poets* and *The Spirit of the Age* (1818/1825; London: Everyman, 1910)

Hicks, Penny, *Historic Houses* (London: AA Publishing, 1994)

Holmes, Richard, *Coleridge: Early Visions* (London: Hodder & Stoughton, 1989)

Johnston, Kenneth R., *The Hidden Wordsworth* (London: Pimlico, 2000)

Le Faye, Deidre (editor), *Jane Austen's Letters* (Oxford: Oxford University Press, 1996)

Leavis, F. R., *Revaluation* (London: Chatto & Windus, 1936)

Levin, Bernard, *Conducted Tour* (London: Jonathan Cape, 1981)

Lonsdale, Roger (ed.), *The New Oxford Book of Eighteenth-Century Verse* (Oxford: Oxford University Press, 1984)

Martin, W. Keble, *The Concise British Flora* (London: Michael Joseph, 1965)

Maugham, Somerset, *The Moon and Sixpence* (1919; Harmondsworth: Penguin, 1944)

Moor, Edward, *Suffolk Words and Phrases* (London: R. Hunter, 1823)

Parker, Rowland, *Men of Dunwich* (London: Collins, 1978)

Pevsner, Nikolaus and John Newman, *The Buildings of England: Dorset* (Harmondsworth; Penguin, 1972)

— and Enid Radcliffe, *The Buildings of England: Suffolk* (Harmondsworth: Penguin, 1974)

Plumb, J.H., *England in the Eighteenth Century* (Harmondsworth: Pelican, 1950)

Pottle, Frederick A. (ed.), *Boswell's London Journal* (London: Heinemann, 1950)

Seymour, John, *The Companion Guide to East Anglia* (London: Collins, 1970)

White, T. H., *The Age of Scandal* (1950; Harmondsworth: Penguin, 1962)

White, William, *History, Gazetteer, and Directory of Suffolk* (Sheffield: R. Leader, 1844)

Notes

One: *The Sea and the River*

1. Rowland Parker, *Men of Dunwich*, p. 264.
2. René Huchon, *George Crabbe and his Times*, p. 7.
3. i.e. George Crabbe III; but since this sounds more like a Hollywood actor or a country and western singer than a nineteenth-century English clergyman, I generally refer to him as 'the biographer son' or, where the context permits, 'the son'.
4. *The Life of George Crabbe by his Son*. With an Introduction by Edmund Blunden, p. 4.
5. Neville Blackburne, *The Restless Ocean*.
6. *Life*, p. 4.
7. *Life*, p. 4.
8. *Life*, p. 12. But the sceptical reader will note that since John was thirteen years younger than George, this remark must either date from the latter's return to Aldeburgh after his apprenticeship or have been colourfully improved by the biographer son.
9. *Life*, p. 14.
10. E. A. Goodwyn, *Elegance and Poverty*, p. 36.
11. E. A. Goodwyn, *George Crabbe and Beccles*, p. 6.
12. *Life*, p. 14.
13. *Life*, p. 15.
14. Goodwyn, *George Crabbe and Beccles*, p. 5.
15. *Life*, p. 14.
16. Thomas C. Faulkner with Rhonda L. Blair, *Selected Letters and Journals of George Crabbe*, pp. 409–10.
17. GC to Edmund Burke, 26 June 1781.
18. Huchon, p. 30.
19. Blackburne, p. 29.
20. *Life*, p. 15.
21. See, for instance, P. J. Croft, *Autograph Poetry in the English Language*, I, pp. 90–91.

Two: *The Surgeon's Apprentice*

1. Kenneth R. Johnston, *The Hidden Wordsworth*, p. 43.
2. GC to Burke, 26 June 1781.
3. *Life*, p. 100.
4. GC to Burke, 26 June 1781.
5. *Life*, pp. 17–18.
6. *Life*, p. 17.
7. Ronald Blythe, *Talking about John Clare*, p. 20.
8. GC to Burke, 26 June 1781.
9. *Life*, p. 18.
10. Robert Gittings, *Young Thomas Hardy*, p. 55.
11. *Life*, p. 32.
12. *Life*, pp. 18–19.
13. *Life*, p. 33.
14. *Life*, p. 26.
15. E. M. Forster, *Howards End*, p. 23.
16. John Brewer, *The Pleasures of the Imagination*, p. 224.
17. In his entry on Crabbe in the *Dictionary of National Biography*, p. 1353.
18. *Life*, p. 19.
19. GC to Burke, 26 June 1781.
20. *Life*, p. 20.
21. Terence Bareham, *George Crabbe*, p. 139.
22. *Life*, p. 27.
23. Huchon, p. 19.
24. Brewer, p. 463.
25. GC to Burke, 26 June 1781.
26. Blackburne, p. 51.
27. *Life*, p. 28.
28. 'The *Custom-House* is a small building, at the south end of the town, near the *Slaughden Quay*, on the river Alde, where vessels as large as 200 tons receive and discharge their cargoes, and where there is also a yard in which ships are built.' William White, *History, Gazetteer, and Directory of Suffolk*, p. 156.
29. Huchon, p. 29.
30. Blackburne, p. 50.
31. *Life*, p. 29.
32. GC to Burke, 26 June 1781.
33. Aldeburgh Vestry Book, 12 December 1770.
34. *Life*, p. 28.
35. GC to Burke, 26 June 1781.

36. *Life*, p. 29.
37. GC to Burke, 26 June 1781.
38. *Life*, p. 29.
39. Peter Ackroyd, *London: The Biography*, pp. 676–7.
40. *Life*, p. 29.
41. *Life*, p. 34.
42. *Life*, p. 36.
43. *Life*, p. 31.
44. *Life*, p. 32.
45. *Life*, pp. 34–5.
46. *Life*, p. 37.
47. Huchon, p. 79.
48. *Life*, pp. 37–8.
49. *Life*, p. 39.

Three: *A Stranger in the City*

1. Frederick A. Pottle (ed.), *Boswell's London Journal*, p. 44.
2. *Life*, p. 44.
3. *Life*, p. 50.
4. *Life*, pp. 43–4
5. Alethea Hayter, *Opium and the Romantic Imagination*, p. 178.
6. *Life*, p. 44.
7. *Life*, pp. 52–3.
8. *Life*, p. 53.
9. *Life*, pp. 53–4.
10. Roger Lonsdale (ed.), *The New Oxford Book of Eighteenth-Century Verse*, p. 200.
11. *Life*, p. 54.
12. *Life*, p. 56.
13. *Life*, pp. 57–8.
14. *Life*, p. 44.
15. *Life*, pp. 46–7.
16. *Life*, pp. 58–9.
17. *Life*, pp. 65, 74.
18. Brewer, p. 94.
19. *The New Oxford Book of Eighteenth-Century Verse*, p. 201.
20. GC to Burke, 26 June 1781.
21. *Boswell's London Journal*, p. 59.
22. J.H. Plumb, *England in the Eighteenth Century*, p. 137.
23. *Life*, pp. 71–2.
24. Ackroyd, p. 488.
25. *Life*, pp. 72–4.
26. James Boswell, *The Life of Samuel Johnson*, p. 926.
27. Quoted by Ackroyd, p. 486.
28. *Life*, pp. 67–71.
29. *Life*, p. 49.
30. *Monthly Review*, lxiii, September 1780; Arthur Pollard (ed.), *Crabbe: The Critical Heritage* (hereafter *CH*), p. 34.
31. *Critical Review*, l, September 1780; *CH*, p. 35.

32. *Gentleman's Magazine*, l, October 1780; *CH*, p. 36.
33. GC to Burke, ? February 1781.
34. GC to Burke, 27 March 1781.
35. 'Autobiographical Sketch', quoted in *Life*, p. 85.
36. *Life*, p. 86.
37. *Life*, p. 87.
38. *Monthly Review*, lxv, December 1781; *CH*, p. 39.
39. *Life*, p. 89.
40. *Critical Review*, lii, August 1781; *CH*, p. 37.
41. *Life*, pp. 89–90.
42. *Life*, p. 86.
43. *Boswell's London Journal*, pp. 91–2.
44. Huchon, p. 128.
45. Burke to Sir Charles Bunbury, 4 October 1781.
46. GC to Burke, 9 October 1781.
47. GC to John Nichols, 6 August 1781.
48. *Life*, p. 88.
49. Huchon, p. 129.
50. Blackburne, p. 84.

Four: *The Duke's Chaplain*

1. Bareham, p. 23.
2. Huchon, p. 134.
3. *Life*, p. 95.
4. Blackburne, p. 85.
5. *Life*, p. 96.
6. Huchon, p. 16.
7. J.H. Evans, *The Poems of George Crabbe*, p. 22.
8. Thurlow to GC, 29 May 1782.
9. *Life*, p. 99.
10. *Life*, p. 98.
11. *Life*, p. 99.
12. *Life*, pp. 99–100.
13. *Life*, p. 101.
14. *Life*, p. 100.
15. Huchon, p. 141.
16. *Life*, p. 107.
17. Richard Holmes, *Coleridge: Early Visions*, p. 3.
18. Alfred Ainger, *Crabbe*, p. 48.
19. GC to Burke, 26 August 1782.
20. Huchon, p. 145.
21. Boswell, *The Life of Samuel Johnson*, p. 1173.
22. Huchon, pp. 145–6.
23. Boswell, pp. 952, 957.
24. John Seymour, *The Companion Guide to East Anglia*, p. 39.
25. *Monthly Review*, lxix, November 1783; *CH*, p. 43.
26. William Cowper, *Poetical Works*, p. 147.
27. William Cowper, *The Centenary Letters*, p. 65.

28. *Life*, p. 108.
29. *Life*, p. 109.
30. Beccles Parish Register.
31. Huchon, p. 174.
32. *Life*, p. 114.
33. Huchon, p. 175.
34. *Life*, p. 111.
35. Evans, p. 26.
36. Ainger, p. 62.
37. GC to Burke, 9 March 1785.
38. *Life*, p. 101.
39. *Critical Review*, lix, April 1785; *CH*, p. 45.
40. *Monthly Review*, lxxiii, November 1785; *CH*, pp. 46–7.
41. Evans, p. 32.
42. *Life*, p. 112.
43. Ainger, p. 61.
44. *Life*, p. 112.
45. *Life*, p. 121.
46. GC to Charles Manners, fourth Duke of Rutland, 29 September 1785.
47. GC to James Dodsley, 17 January 1788.
48. *Life*, p. 119.
49. *Life*, p. 107.
50. Huchon, pp. 190–91.

Five: *The Botanical Gardener*

1. *Life*, p. 119.
2. Huchon, p. 189.
3. *Life*, pp. 117–18.
4. GC to Edmund Cartwright, 23 August 1789.
5. GC to Edmund Cartwright, 24 October 1789.
6. GC to Edmund Cartwright [son], 29 February 1790.
7. GC to John Nichols, 22 August 1789.
8. *Life*, p. 117.
9. *Life*, p. 122.
10. *Life*, pp. 123–4.
11. *Life*, pp. 125–6.
12. *Life*, p. 126.
13. *Life*, p. 127.
14. *Life*, p. 128.
15. *Life*, pp. 138–9.
16. *The New Oxford Book of Eighteenth-Century Verse*, p. 113.
17. Hayter, pp. 49–50.
18. Hayter, p. 188.
19. Hayter, p. 183.
20. *Life*, p. 116.
21. Hayter, p. 31.
22. GC to John Nichols, 7 September 1790.
23. GC to Edmund Cartwright [son], 5 September 1792.
24. GC to Edmund Cartwright [son], 15 September 1792.

25. GC to Edmund Cartwright [son], 1 October 1792.
26. *Life*, p. 129.
27. White, *History, Gazetteer, and Directory of Suffolk*, p. 169.
28. Sarah Crabbe to GC, 22 October 1792.
29. *Life*, pp. 129–30.
30. *Life*, p. 130. Another daughter, Sarah, born on 10 February 1791, had lived less than a week.
31. GC to Edmund Cartwright [son], 4 September 1793.
32. *Life*, p. 131.
33. *Life*, p. 133.
34. *Life*, p. 145.
35. *Life*, p. 133.
36. GC to Edmund Cartwright [son], 22 July 1794.
37. GC to Edmund Cartwright [son], 22 July 1794.
38. John Fuller, *Collected Poems*, p. 419.
39. W. Keble Martin, *The Concise British Flora*, p. 152.
40. *Life*, p. 141.
41. *Life*, p. 142.
42. GC to Edmund Cartwright [son], 3 February 1795.
43. *Life*, p. 116.
44. GC to Edmund Cartwright [son], 7 July 1796.
45. *Life*, p. 134.
46. Huchon, p. 195.
47. *Life*, p. 140.
48. T. H. White, *The Age of Scandal*, p. 71.
49. GC to Edmund Cartwright [son], 7 July 1796.
50. *Life*, p. 134.

Six: *Telling Tales*

1. *Life*, p. 134.
2. *Life*, pp. 135, 136.
3. *Life*, p. 140.
4. *Life*, p. 143.
5. *Life*, p. 228.
6. GC to John Nichols, 21 August 1798.
7. GC to John Nichols, 19 February 1799.
8. *Life*, p. 144.
9. Huchon, pp. 197–8.
10. Thomas Hardy, *The Return of the Native*, p. 197.
11. *Life*, p. 145.
12. Huchon, p. 198.
13. *Life*, p. 148.
14. Peter New, *George Crabbe's Poetry*, p. 49.
15. Blackburne, p. 124.
16. *New Poems*, p. 1.
17. *Life*, p. 147.

18. *New Poems*, pp. 10–15.
19. *Life*, p. 146.
20. *Life*, p. 147.
21. *Life*, p. 167.
22. Huchon, p. 198, quotes a letter from Thomas Twining, dated 13 October 1803: 'I suppose you will not ask me why I leave Colchester, I leave it because I am afraid to stay in it. Many have left, more are preparing to leave it; though I think there is very little danger, yet I should be very uneasy to stay here and run the risk. And if I stay till the moment of alarm upon the coast, I may not be able to get away at all unless I walk away with a knapsack on my back.'
23. *Life*, p. 153.
24. GC to James Wenn, 1 August 1805.
25. Bareham, p. 91.
26. *Life*, p. 155.
27. *Life*, p. 156.
28. Huchon, p. 221.
29. Huchon, p. 222.
30. Huchon, p. 222n.
31. *Life*, p. 141.
32. GC to John Hatchard, 20 May 1807.
33. GC to Sir Charles Bunbury, 8 October 1807
34. Lord Holland to GC, n.d.
35. GC to John Nichols, 5 December 1807.
36. *Oxford Review*, iii, January 1808; *CH*, p. 54.
37. *Life*, p. 158.
38. *Edinburgh Review*, xii, April 1808; *CH*, pp. 56–7.
39. *Life*, pp. 157–8.
40. Huchon, p. 251.
41. John Bonnycastle to GC, 24 October 1807.
42. Jane Burke to GC, 30 November 1807.
43. William Mansel to GC, 29 October 1807.
44. *Selected Letters and Journals*, p. 84n.
45. GC to John Nichols, 20 January 1809.
46. GC to John Nichols, 17 March 1809.

Seven: *In Search of Peter Grimes*

1. *Life*, p. 168.
2. GC to Elizabeth Charter, 9 November 1824.
3. GC to Mary Leadbeater, 1 December 1816.
4. *The Listener*, 29 May 1941; E. M. Forster, *The Prince's Tale and other uncollected writings*, pp. 127–32.
5. E. M. Forster, *Two Cheers for Democracy*, pp. 176–92.
6. Humphrey Carpenter, *Benjamin Britten*, p. 156.
7. Forster, *The Prince's Tale*, pp. 127–8.
8. Forster, *The Prince's Tale*, p. 129.
9. Bernard Levin, *Conducted Tour*, p. 69.
10. Carpenter, p. 224.
11. Frank Whitehead, *George Crabbe*, p. 83.
12. GC to Francis Chantrey, 11 December 1822.
13. Edward Moor, *Suffolk Words and Phrases*, p. 155.
14. Bareham, p. 40.
15. *Life*, p. 169.
16. *Edinburgh Review*, xvi, April 1810; *CH*, pp. 84–99.
17. *British Critic*, xxxvii, March 1811; *CH*, p. 135.
18. *Monthly Mirror*, viii, August 1810; *CH*, p. 114.
19. *Quarterly Review*, iv, November 1810; *CH*, p. 117.
20. *Quarterly Review*, iv, November 1810; *CH*, p. 127.
21. *Eclectic Review*, vi, June 1810; *CH*, p. 100.
22. *Critical Review*, xx, July 1810; *CH*, p. 107.
23. *Monthly Mirror*, viii, August 1810; *CH*, p. 112.
24. *Edinburgh Review*, xvi, April 1810; *CH*, p. 93.
25. *Monthly Review*, lxi, April 1810; *CH*, p. 83.
26. *Eclectic Review*, vi, June 1810; *CH*, p. 105.

Eight: *Life's Common Cares*

1. *Life*, p. 171.
2. *Life*, pp. 171–2.
3. *Life*, p. 173.
4. Ainger, pp. 67–8.
5. Bareham, pp. 34–5.
6. Bareham, p. 32.
7. GC to Walter Scott, 29 June 1813.
8. *Scourge*, October 1812; *CH*, p. 162.
9. *CH*, p. 147; cf. New, pp. 4–6.
10. Walter Scott to GC, 21 October 1812.
11. Walter Scott to GC, 1 June 1813.
12. New, p. 101.
13. *Monthly Review*, lxix, December 1812; *CH*, p. 174.
14. *Edinburgh Review*, xx, November 1812; *CH*, p. 164.
15. *Edinburgh Review*, xx, November 1812; *CH*, p. 170.
16. *Critical Review*, ii, December 1812; *CH*, pp. 175–6.
17. *Eclectic Review*, viii, December 1812; *CH*, p. 185.
18. *British Review*, iv, October 1812; *CH*, p. 157.
19. *Critical Review*, ii, December 1812; *CH*, p. 184.
20. GC to Walter Scott, 5 March 1813.
21. *Life*, p. 254.
22. Phyllis Grosskurth, *Byron*, p. 149.
23. GC to Walter Scott, 13 October 1812.
24. Walter Scott to GC, 21 October 1812.

25. *Life*, p. 166.
26. GC to Walter Scott, 21 December 1812.
27. Walter Scott to GC, January 1813.
28. GC to Walter Scott, 5 March 1813.
29. Walter Scott to GC, 1 June 1813.
30. GC to Walter Scott, 29 June 1813.
31. GC to Walter Scott, 29 June 1813.
32. e.g. by Blackburne, p. 156.
33. Mrs John Farrar, quoted in *Selected Letters and Journals*, p. 140n.
34. GC to Walter Scott, 25 June 1815.
35. GC to Elizabeth Charter, 14 March 1815.
36. GC to George Gordon, 10 September 1812.
37. GC to George Gordon, 15 April 1813.
38. *Life*, p. 178.
39. *Life*, p. 179.
40. *Life*, p. 179.
41. Jane Austen to Cassandra Austen, 15–16 September 1813.
42. Jane Austen to Cassandra Austen, 9 March 1814.
43. *Life*, p. 182.
44. *Life*, p. 182.
45. Samuel Rogers to Ticknor; quoted by Huchon, p. 196; Blackburne, p. 145.
46. Robert Southey to Neville White, 30 September 1808; quoted by Ainger, p. 74.
47. GC to Alethea Lewis, 25 October 1813.
48. GC to George Gordon, 1 November 1813.
49. Jane Austen to Cassandra Austen, 21 October 1813.
50. GC to George Gordon, 9 December 1813.
51. GC to John Henry Manners, fifth Duke of Rutland, 17 November 1813.
52. GC to John Henry Manners, fifth Duke of Rutland, 23 November 1813.
53. GC to George Gordon, 9 December 1813.
54. GC to George Gordon, 31 December 1813.
55. GC to George Gordon, 14 January 1814.
56. John Henry Manners, fifth Duke of Rutland, to GC, 15 February 1814.
57. GC to George Gordon, 16 February 1814.
58. John Henry Manners, fifth Duke of Rutland, to GC, 21 February 1814.
59. GC to Thomas Hill Mortimer, 26 February 1814.
60. A. M. Broadley and Walter Jerrold, *The Romance of an Elderly Poet*, p. 15.
61. GC to George Gordon, 5 April 1814.
62. GC to Thomas Hill Mortimer, 12 April 1814.
63. *Selected Letters and Journals*, p. 138.
64. GC to Thomas Hill Mortimer, 19 April 1814.
65. *Life*, p. 184.
66. GC to George Gordon, 21 May 1814.
67. *Life*, p. 183.
68. Huchon, p. 382.
69. GC to George Gordon, 21 May 1814.

Nine: *Writing in the Dark*

1. *Life*, pp. 186–7.
2. Huchon, p. 384.
3. Kenneth H. Rogers, 'Trowbridge in George Crabbe's Time', in *Selected Letters and Journals*, pp. 147–8.
4. Rogers, in *Selected Letters and Journals*, p. 161.
5. GC to Thomas Timbrell, ? September 1814.
6. GC to George Gordon, 11 February 1815.
7. GC to Elizabeth Charter, 23 August 1815.
8. Rogers, *Selected Letters and Journals*, p. 151.
9. Broadley and Jerrold, p. 20.
10. GC to Elizabeth Charter, 14 March 1815.
11. GC to Elizabeth Charter, 23 August 1815.
12. GC to Elizabeth Charter, 11 November 1815.
13. GC to Elizabeth Charter, 26 December 1815.
14. *Life*, p. 185.
15. *Life*, p. 192.
16. *Life*, p. 193.
17. *Life*, p. 195.
18. *Life*, p. 234.
19. *Life*, p. 195.
20. GC to Elizabeth Charter, 3 May 1815.
21. GC to George Gordon, 11 February 1815.
22. Blackburne, p. 155.
23. GC to Elizabeth Charter, 5 May 1815.
24. *Life*, p. 193.
25. GC to Elizabeth Charter, 5 May 1815.
26. Broadley and Jerrold, pp. 86–7.
27. GC to Elizabeth Charter, 26 July 1815.
28. GC to Elizabeth Charter, 11 November 1815.
29. GC to Elizabeth Charter, 26 December 1815.
30. GC to Elizabeth Charter, 28 August 1815.
31. GC to Elizabeth Charter, 14 March 1815.
32. GC to Elizabeth Charter, 18 July 1816.
33. GC to Elizabeth Charter, ? April 1816.
34. GC to Elizabeth Charter, 1 May 1816.
35. GC to Elizabeth Charter, 18 July 1816.
36. GC to Elizabeth Charter, 12 October 1816.
37. GC to Elizabeth Charter, 5 May 1815.
38. GC to Elizabeth Charter, 2 July 1815.
39. GC to Elizabeth Charter, 23 August 1815.
40. GC to Elizabeth Charter, 26 July 1815.
41. GC to Elizabeth Charter, 11 September 1815.
42. GC to Elizabeth Charter, 5 May 1815.
43. GC to Elizabeth Charter, 6 June 1815.
44. GC to Elizabeth Charter, 26 July 1815.
45. GC to Elizabeth Charter, 2 January 1816.
46. GC to Mary-Anne Houlton, 3 March 1819.
47. GC to Elizabeth Charter, 2 July 1815.

48. GC to Elizabeth Charter, 6 June 1815.
49. Broadley and Jerrold, p. 122.
50. GC to Elizabeth Charter, 18 June 1815.
51. GC to Elizabeth Charter, 3 July 1815.
52. GC to Elizabeth Charter, 11 September 1815.
53. GC to Elizabeth Charter, 2 January 1816.
54. GC to Elizabeth Charter, 11 February 1817.
55. *Selected Letters and Journals*, p. 406.
56. GC to Elizabeth Charter, 14 March 1815.
57. *Life*, p. 191.
58. GC to Elizabeth Charter, 25 November 1815.
59. GC to Elizabeth Charter, 11 November 1815.
60. GC to Elizabeth Charter, September 1816.
61. GC to Colonel John Houlton, 11 August 1816.
62. GC to Elizabeth Charter, 26 February 1816.
63. *Life*, p. 191.
64. GC to Elizabeth Charter, September 1816.
65. *Selected Letters and Journals*, p. 198n.
66. GC to Elizabeth Charter, 18 November 1816.
67. Penny Hicks, *Historic Houses*, p. 101.
68. Mary Leadbeater to GC, 7 November 1816.
69. GC to Mary Leadbeater, 1 December 1816.
70. Huchon, p. 391.
71. GC to Elizabeth Charter, 25 November 1815.
72. GC to William Lisle Bowles, 24 July 1815.
73. GC to Samuel Rogers, 22 June 1817.
74. *Life*, p. 208.
75. *Life*, pp. 211–12.
76. *Selected Letters and Journals*, p. 211.
77. Huchon, p. 397.
78. *Life*, p. 212.
79. GC to Elizabeth Charter, 7 August 1817.
80. Byron to John Murray, 15 September 1817.
81. GC to Elizabeth Charter, 7 August 1817.
82. Roger Wilbraham to GC, 7 July 1817.
83. GC to Elizabeth Charter, 20 June 1817.
84. GC to Colonel John Houlton, 11 August 1816.
85. Lady Caroline Lamb to GC, 19 July 1817.
86. *Life*, p. 222.
87. Lilian Haddakin, *The Poetry of Crabbe*, p. 31.
88. GC to Elizabeth Charter, 8 June 1815.
89. Broadley and Jerrold, pp. 121–2.
90. Huchon, p. 384.
91. GC to Elizabeth Charter, 22 August 1817.
92. Broadley and Jerrold, p. 183.
93. GC to Elizabeth Charter, 11 September 1817.
94. GC to Elizabeth Charter, 20 August 1817.
95. GC to Elizabeth Charter, 29 October 1817.
96. GC to Elizabeth Charter, 1 December 1817.
97. GC to Elizabeth Charter, 29 October 1817.

98. GC to Elizabeth Charter, 5 February 1818.
99. GC to Elizabeth Charter, ? February 1818.
100. *Life*, p. 235.
101. GC to Elizabeth Charter, February 1818.
102. GC to Elizabeth Charter, 15 April 1818.
103. *Life*, p. 189.
104. GC to Elizabeth Charter, July 1818.
105. GC to Elizabeth Charter, 7 August 1817.
106. GC to Elizabeth Charter, 15 April 1818.
107. GC to Elizabeth Charter, July 1818.
108. GC to Elizabeth Charter, 14 September 1818.
109. GC to Elizabeth Charter, 31 October 1818.
110. GC to Elizabeth Charter, 23 December 1818.
111. GC to Elizabeth Charter, 31 October 1818.
112. GC to Samuel Rogers, November 1818.
113. GC to John Murray, 23 November 1818.
114. *Life*, p. 232.
115. GC to John Hatchard, 8 December 1818.
116. *Life*, pp. 232–3.
117. According to Blackburne (p. 183), Crabbe did not receive this payment until the following June, when *Tales of the Hall* was published; but, since the £3,000 was in the form of '3 notes for £1000 each at 6 months date', to be paid on publication he would have been given the notes in December 1818, as Moore's account implies.
118. GC to John Murray, 28 December 1818.
119. GC to John Murray, 3 January 1819.
120. GC to John Murray, 9 March 1819.
121. GC to John Murray, 28 January 1819.
122. GC to John Murray, 10 January 1819.
123. GC to John Murray, 1 February 1819.
124. *Life*, pp. 230–31.
125. *Blackwood's Edinburgh Magazine*, v, July 1819; *CH*, p. 222.
126. *Edinburgh Review*, xxxii, July 1819; *CH*, pp. 227–8.
127. *Edinburgh Review*, xxxii, July 1819; *CH*, p. 235.
128. *Christian Observer*, xviii, October 1819; *CH*, p. 268.
129. *New Monthly Magazine*, xii, September 1819; *CH*, pp. 254–5.
130. *Eclectic Review*, new series xiii, February 1820; *CH*, p. 289.
131. *British Critic*, new series xii, September 1819; *CH*, p. 239.
132. *British Critic*, new series xii, September 1819; *CH*, pp. 242–3.
133. *British Critic*, new series xii, September 1819; *CH*, p. 246.
134. Huchon, p. 429; Blackburne, p. 185.
135. GC to John Murray, 22 January 1819.

136. F. R. Leavis, *Revaluation*, p. 125.
137. Bareham, p. 98.
138. Haddakin, pp. 33–4.
139. GC to Elizabeth Charter, April 1816.
140. GC to Maria Waldron, 7 May 1819.
141. GC to Elizabeth Charter, 25 August 1819.
142. GC to John Murray, 20 July 1819.
143. *Selected Letters and Journals*, p. 272n.
144. GC to Elizabeth Charter, 25 August 1819.
145. *The Voluntary Insane*, p. 101.
146. GC to Elizabeth Charter, October 1819.
147. GC to Mary Leadbeater, 5 November 1819.
148. GC to Elizabeth Charter, October 1819.

Ten: *A Lusty Winter*

1. GC to Caroline Crabbe, 24 December 1822.
2. *Life*, pp. 228–9.
3. GC to Caroline Crabbe, 24 January 1830.
4. Bareham, p. 127.
5. Rogers, *Selected Letters and Journals*, pp. 159–60.
6. GC to Thomas Phillips, 21 November 1820.
7. GC to John Henry Manners, fifth Duke of Rutland, 30 November 1820.
8. *Life*, p. 192.
9. GC to Elizabeth Charter, 7 April 1820.
10. GC to Elizabeth Charter, 16 July 1821.
11. GC to George Crabbe [son], July 1822.
12. GC to Sir Walter Scott, 10 July 1822.
13. Sir Walter Scott to GC, 16 July 1822.
14. GC to Sir Walter Scott, 23 July 1822.
15. *Life*, p. 239.
16. *Life*, p. 243.
17. GC to John Waldron Crabbe, 9 August 1822.
18. GC to John Waldron Crabbe, 15 August 1822.
19. *Selected Letters and Journals*, p. 291n.
20. *Life*, p. 244.
21. *Life*, pp. 239–40.
22. *Life*, p. 239.
23. *Life*, p. 241.
24. *Life*, p. 246.
25. GC to John Waldron Crabbe, 9 August 1822.
26. GC to John Waldron Crabbe, 15 August 1822.
27. GC to Elizabeth Charter, 27 January 1823.
28. *The Voluntary Insane*, pp. 34–7.
29. GC to Mary Leadbeater, 25 November 1822.
30. *CH*, p. 368.
31. *New Poems*, pp. 5–6.

32. *The Voluntary Insane*, p. 31.
33. *New Poems*, pp. 4–5.
34. *New Poems*, p. 12.
35. GC to Elizabeth Charter, 27 March 1823.
36. White, pp. 156–7.
37. GC to George Crabbe [son], 30 January 1824.
38. GC to Francis Chantrey, 15 December 1822.
39. GC to Elizabeth Charter, 8 July 1824.
40. GC to George Crabbe [son], 6 November 1825.
41. *Life*, p. 255.
42. *Life*, p. 250.
43. GC to George Crabbe [son], 5 July 1828.
44. Broadley and Jerrold, p. 297.
45. GC to George Crabbe [son], 28 June 1826.
46. GC to George Crabbe [son], 24 September 1824.
47. GC to John Waldron Crabbe, 28 September 1830.
48. GC to John Waldron Crabbe, 6 October 1830.
49. GC to John Waldron Crabbe, 7 October 1830.
50. GC to Elizabeth Charter, 9 November 1824.
51. GC to George Crabbe [son], 4 May 1826.
52. Huchon, p. 468.
53. GC to George Crabbe [son], 17 September 1825.
54. GC to Sarah Hoare, 28 July 1828.
55. GC to George Crabbe [son], 14 January 1830.
56. GC to George Crabbe [son], 26 October 1831.
57. *Selected Letters and Journals*, p. 378n.
58. *Life*, pp. 276–7.
59. *Life*, p. 278.
60. GC to George Crabbe [son], 7 January 1832.
61. GC to George Crabbe [son], 9 September 1830.
62. *Life*, p. 279.

Epilogue: *The River and the Sea*

1. *Life*, p. 256.
2. William Hazlitt, *Lectures on the English Poets* and *The Spirit of the Age*, pp. 331–3.
3. Leavis, p. 128.
4. Somerset Maugham, *The Moon and Sixpence*, p. 12.
5. White, p. 15.

Index

Speculation necessary
because of easy, conversational
idiom.

botanist